The Behavioral Revolution
and Communist Studies

Applications of

Behaviorally Oriented

Political Research

on the

Soviet Union

and Eastern Europe

Fp

The
Behavioral
Revolution
and
Communist
Studies

EDITED BY

ROGER E. KANET

THE FREE PRESS, NEW YORK
COLLIER-MACMILLAN LIMITED, LONDON

The Free Press
A Division of The Macmillan Company
866 Third Avenue, New York, New York 10022

Collier-Macmillan Canada Ltd., Toronto, Ontario

Library of Congress Catalog Card Number: 73–116810

printing number
1 2 3 4 5 6 7 8 9 10

For Joan, Suzanne, and Laurie

Contents

Preface

In February 1968, Mr. John Stuckey, then an M.A. candidate at the University of Kansas, indicated an interest in taking a directed readings course from me using behavioral studies of Soviet and East European politics. My initial reaction was that it would be impossible to find enough of such studies to justify a readings course. On second thought, I suggested that we might supplement the published material with unpublished manuscripts that I had acquired during the year or so prior to that time. Eventually the idea of having some of these manuscripts reworked and published crossed my mind—the end result is the present volume. In the meantime, a number of the articles printed below have appeared in journals, but the majority are being published for the first time. I wish to thank the authors for their promptness in revising their initial manuscripts.

Obviously a word is in order about the title of this volume. "The Behavioral Revolution" does not indicate a violent overthrow of all that has gone before in the field of political science—although some of my colleagues may think otherwise. Nor does it refer to a change in the physical or moral behavior of political scientists and Communist specialists. It is merely a term popularly used to refer to the increased focus in political science on observable political actions of individuals and groups, as opposed to a concentration on constitutional and legal questions. The second part of the title also needs a word of explanation. "Communist Studies," as used here, refers to studies on the Soviet Union and Eastern Europe. Obviously a strict definition also includes China, Cuba, North Korea, Mongolia, and North Vietnam; however, the need for a relatively descriptive title and the awkwardness of such possibilities as "The Behavioral Revolution and Studies on the Soviet Union and Eastern Europe" brought me back to the less accurate, but more succinct, one chosen. The purist might also point out that Tsarist Russia, which is examined in one article, was not Communist and, therefore, does not fit under the present title. I agree, but once again fall back to the defense of the succinctness of the title.

The present volume attempts to make available, to both political scientists and specialists on Communist studies, analyses which bring together techniques from both fields. It is hoped that these studies will help to bridge the communications gap that has developed between the two groups of scholars and that both will begin to recognize the value of one another's work.

I wish to thank Charles Gati for his helpful comments on the organization of this volume, the Graduate School of the University of Kansas for financial assistance that facilitated the preparation of the manuscript, and Miss Blythe Huston who typed much of it. I wish, also, to extend my appreciation to those, named by a number of the authors, who commented on earlier drafts of some of the selections.

R. E. K.

Contributors

CARL BECK is Professor of Political Science and Sociology and Director of the University Center for International Studies, University of Pittsburgh. He received his Ph.D. from Duke University in 1959 and is the author of *Contempt of Congress* (1959), *Political Elites: A Computerized and Select Bibliography* (1968), as well as articles on bureaucracy, political elites, and the analysis of aggregate data in *Journal of Politics, American Behavioral Scientist, Social Science Information, Comparative Political Studies*, and other journals.

FREDERIC J. FLERON, JR. is Associate Professor of Political Science, State University of New York at Buffalo, and received his Ph.D. from Indiana University in 1968. He is editor of *Communist Studies and the Social Sciences: Essays on Methodology and Empirical Theory* (Chicago: Rand, 1969). He is also author of a number of articles that have appeared in *Polity, Soviet Studies, Canadian Slavic Studies*, and *Comparative Politics*.

CHARLES GATI is Associate Professor of Political Science, Union College, and received his Ph.D. from Indiana University in 1965. He is the author of articles on American and Soviet Foreign Policy that have appeared in *World Politics*, and *Canadian Slavic Studies*, as well as other journals. He is presently completing a book-length study of Soviet foreign policy which is scheduled to be published by Pegasus.

MICHAEL P. GEHLEN is Professor and Chairman of Political Science, University of New Mexico, and received his Ph.D. from the University of Texas in 1963. He is the author of *The Politics of Co-existence: Soviet Methods and Motives* (Bloomington: Indiana U.P., 1967) and *The Communist Party of the Soviet Union: A Functional Analysis*, as well as articles on recruitment patterns and the party apparatus that have appeared in *American Political Science Review, Journal of Politics, American Behavioral Scientist, Western Political Quarterly*, and other journals.

DANIEL C. HELDMAN is Assistant Professor of Political Science at Marshall University and a Ph.D. candidate in the Political Science Department at the University of Texas. He is the author of an article on controls in Soviet science and ideology in *Problems of Communism*, XVI, 1 (1967) and is presently doing doctoral research on Soviet policy toward developing countries.

ERIK P. HOFFMANN is Assistant Professor of Political Science at the State University of New York at Albany and received his Ph.D. from Indiana University in 1967. He is a contributor to *Communist Studies and the Social Sciences* (Chicago: Rand, 1969), edited by Frederic J. Fleron, Jr. and author of an article on communications theory that has been published in *Canadian Slavic Studies*. At present he is working on a study of ideological administration in the Soviet Union.

P. TERRENCE HOPMANN is Assistant Professor of Political Science at the University of Minnesota and received his Ph.D. from Stanford University in 1969. Mr. Hopmann is the author of "International Conflict and Cohesion in the Communist System," *International Studies Quarterly*, XI (1967), 212–36. At present he is working in conjunction with Ole R. Holsti and John D. Sullivan on a book to be entitled *International Alliances: Unity and Disintegration*, which will be published by Dorsey.

GERARD A. JOHNSON is an NDEA Fellow and Ph.D. candidate in the Department of Political Science at the University of Pittsburgh. He is also a research assistant in the Archive on Political Elites in Eastern Europe at the University of Pittsburgh. His doctoral research is on political socialization and leadership in Poland.

ROGER E. KANET is Associate Professor of Political Science at the University of Kansas and received his Ph.D. from Princeton University in 1966. He is the author of a number of articles on Soviet foreign policy that have appeared in *Canadian Slavic Studies*, *Russian Review*, *Viertaljahresberichte* der Friedrich-Ebert-Stiftung, and *Soviet Studies*. At present he is working on a book-length study of Soviet policy toward developing countries.

WILLIAM R. KEECH is Associate Professor of Political Science at the University of North Carolina, Chapel Hill, and received his Ph.D. from the University of Wisconsin in 1966. He is the author of *The Impact of Negro Voting* (Chicago: Rand, 1968), as well as articles that have appeared in *American Political Science Review* and *Journal of Politics*.

RITA MAE KELLY is Research Scientist at the Center for Research in Social Systems, the American University, and received her Ph.D. from Indiana University in 1967. She is the former editor of *Sputnik Studenta* published at the University of Minnesota and the author of articles that have appeared in *Marab: A Review* and *Soviet Studies*.

MILTON G. LODGE is Assistant Professor of Political Science at the University of Iowa and received his Ph.D. from the University of Michigan in 1966. He is the author of *Soviet Elite Attitudes Since Stalin* (Columbus: Merrill, 1969) and of articles on the Soviet elite in *American Political Science Review*,

Midwest Journal of Political Science, and coeditor of *Comparative Communist Political Leadership* (Pittsburgh: U. of Pittsburgh P., forthcoming).

MICHAEL J. MCBRIDE is Assistant Professor of Political Science at Whittier College and received his Ph.D. from Purdue University in 1969. His doctoral dissertation was a study of political elites in five East European countries. He is also the coauthor of an article on Soviet elites that appeared in *American Political Science Review*.

J. THOMAS MCKECHNIE is an instructor in Political Science at Chatham College and a Mellor Fellow and Ph.D. candidate in Political Science at the University of Pittsburgh. His doctoral research is on political recruitment and change in the Czechoslovak Communist Party.

DON CARL ROWNEY is Associate Professor of History at Bowling Green State University and received his Ph.D. from Indiana University. He is coeditor of *Quantitative History: Selected Readings in the Quantitative Analysis of Historical Data* (Homewood: Dorsey, 1969).

JOEL J. SCHWARTZ is Assistant Professor of Political Science at the University of North Carolina, Chapel Hill, and received his Ph.D. from Indiana University in 1965. He is the author of *Soviet Fathers versus Soviet Sons: Is There A Generational Conflict?* (Pittsburgh: U. of Pittsburgh P., Monograph Academic Disciplines, 1966) and *Soviet Politics and Government* (New York Harper, 1969), as well as an article in *American Political Science Review*.

ROBERT S. SHARLET is Assistant Professor of Political Science at Union College, and received his Ph.D. from Indiana University in 1968. He is the coauthor of *Legal Aspects of Verification in the Soviet Union* (Washington: U.S. Arms Control and Disarmament Agency, 1967) and the author of the forthcoming *Soviet Modernization: An Interpretation of Communist Political Development*, as well as articles in *Journal of Developing Areas, Canadian Slavic Studies*, and *Soviet Union and Eastern Europe*.

PAUL SHOUP is Associate Professor of Government and foreign affairs and director, Center for Russian and Communist Studies, University of Virginia, and received his Ph.D. from Columbia University in 1960. He is the author of *Communism and the Yugoslav National Question* and has published articles in *American Political Science Review* and *Slavic Review*.

The Behavioral Revolution
and Communist Studies

INTRODUCTION

The Behavioral Revolution
and Communist Studies

ROGER E. KANET

I

During the past two decades political science as an academic discipline
has undergone a number of significant changes. First of all, the concerns
of political scientists have been expanded beyond the traditional geographic limits of the United States and Western Europe to include non-
Western political systems. This new interest has forced political scientists

Notes to the selection begin on page 8.

to reconsider their former preoccupation with formal, specialized governmental institutions, since many of the Asian and African systems lacked such formal political structures. Gabriel Almond and James Coleman, for example, argued that to analyze the political systems of developing areas it is necessary to concentrate on the functions performed by the system rather than on governmental institutions.[1] This new focus required the redefinition of many concepts that had been used to explain political behavior in the European-American world, as well as the introduction of new concepts. The growing interest in non-Western political systems also helped produce the present emphasis on the importance of social and economic variables for an understanding of politics.[2]

A second major development in political science has been a greatly increased emphasis on rigor and precision. Already in the pre-World War II period a concern for more precise methods of analysis was evident among some political scientists, but it was not until the 1950s that this became a major concern.[3] This new emphasis on scientific rigor, along with the growing interest in non-Western societies, led many political scientists to examine the studies of sociologists and anthropologists, where they found analyses of social stratification and the relationship of social and economic factors to politics. As Harry Eckstein points out, these two developments tended to reinforce one another, for it was easier "to develop theories subject to rigorous testing by taking certain social and economic categories and relating them to politics . . . than by taking the often unmeasurable 'pure' phenomena of politics as such. . . ."[4]

This entire development in political science is often referred to rather loosely as the behavioral revolution, by which is meant a concentration on both the observable political actions of individuals and groups and the psychological processes which influence these actions—e.g., perceptions, motives, and attitudes. The expected end result will be the identification of uniformities in political behavior that can be expressed in generalizations or theories with explanatory or predictive power.[5] In order to accomplish this, rigorous research techniques should be employed in the collection of data; generalizations must be stated in such a way that they can be tested against empirical data; and, as far as possible, quantifiable data should be employed.[6]

Not only has the approach to the study of politics shifted, but the topics examined and the questions asked are far different from the traditional concerns of political science, such as the nature of the state, the historical development of constitutions, etc. Political scientists have increasingly devoted their attention to such topics as elite recruitment, the processes of political socialization (the methods by which political values, attitudes, and knowledge are transmitted), voting behavior, the importance of groups in the political process, etc. They are concerned with the importance of socioeconomic and psychological factors in influencing political decisions and the processes of policy implementation.

A general assessment of two decades of behavioral influence in political science is beyond the scope of this introduction; however, a brief comment on the results to date is in order. Political scientists have not achieved the ultimate goal of creating a truly scientific discipline of political science. In fact, some of the work of the past two decades has apparently run into "deadends." Practitioners who have attempted to develop a more rigorous discipline of political science fall into two categories. First, there are those who have emphasized the development of grand theoretical designs aimed at explaining the entire political universe. Most of these theories, although excellent examples of deductive reasoning, have had little relationship to empirical reality. As Heinz Eulau has correctly pointed out, it is almost impossible to derive testable propositions about politics from many of these works.[7] Second, there are those who have gone to the other extreme—what Roy Macridis has called "inputism"[8]—of collecting data without really assessing its relevance to a political question, or without even having formulated the question. This can lead to an emphasis on trivia or to the elimination of the "political" in supposedly political analysis.

Most recent political research, however, fits neither of these extreme categories. Increasingly scholars are focusing on empirical analyses of parts of political systems and are generating hypotheses based on empirical data rather than deductive reasoning. They are providing the kinds of data on political systems that some day may be used to develop a general theory of politics. In the meantime they are creating a political vocabulary of terms that are generally—though by no means universally—understood and accepted by their colleagues. They are also finding new ways to use quantifiable data for the purpose of better explaining political behavior.

The prospects for the future development of behavioral research are mixed. On the one hand, there is the considerable progress made to date in permitting the political scientist to make predictions about future political behavior based on statistical generalizations. This is especially true in such areas as the study of voting behavior and public opinion. On the other hand, there is the presently almost insuperable problem in many research areas of finding reliable, quantifiable data. This is especially true when survey research methods cannot be employed, either because of prohibitive costs or because of uncooperative governments, as in most Communist political systems.

In most areas of political research, however, significant progress has been made since the 1940s. Twenty years ago little was known about the process of political development, but in the ensuing decades a virtual flood of studies, both detailed descriptive studies and more general comparative studies, have greatly increased our knowledge and understanding of processes of political development, as well as the social, economic, and psychological factors that affect this development.[9] Although we are still not able to give a precise answer to the question, "What is political development and how does it occur?" we have a conceptual framework and much more information that better enable us to give an answer.

II

During the same period that political science was undergoing the major changes outlined above, the study of the Soviet Union and other Communist systems emerged as a major academic concern. Both private and public funds were provided to establish centers and institutes for the study of Communist systems because, although the Soviet Union had become a major participant in international affairs, there were very few individuals in the West, including members of the academic community, who had any familiarity with the Communist countries. Most of the books and articles written during the twenties and thirties were extremely naive—for example, one American scholar saw the purges of the thirties as a necessary stage on the Soviet Union's road to constitutional government. Until the postwar period and the publication of studies by Julian Towster, Samuel N. Harper, Barrington Moore, Jr., and, in particular, Merle Fainsod, there existed no mature, systematic account of the Soviet political system.

As a result of the research of area specialists during the past twenty years, we now have a much clearer understanding of the Soviet Union and the East European countries. These scholars have provided us with detailed studies of the organizational structure of the Communist Party and the power struggles that have occurred within it. They have examined the methods employed by the party to achieve and maintain control over the rest of the population. They have provided us with information about social change caused by revolution and about the gradual maturing of a revolutionary sociopolitical system.

Without the work of area specialists, our knowledge of the political and social processes at work in the Communist states would be as abysmal as it was twenty years ago. Unfortunately, for a long time most students of Communist political systems ignored the methodological changes being made by political scientists, and a wide gulf was created between the two groups. Not only were they unmindful of one another's work, they became almost incapable of communicating with one another. The area specialists tended to focus primarily on the description and explanation of specific events, while their colleagues in political science emphasized comparative empirical research and generalizations. Because of this the political scientists have ignored most of the work on Communist political systems and have viewed the area specialists as marginal to the discipline.[10] On the other hand, many Communist area specialists have observed with alarm what Adam Ulam has referred to as "the rise of a new and militant faith called behavioralism [whose] content is vague, but [whose] ritual is rather precise [and] requires the solemn objurgation of history."[11] Many students of Eastern Europe and the Soviet Union have emphasized the uniqueness of the Communist system and have produced primarily descriptive studies. On the whole, they have not attempted to relate them to studies of comparable phenomena in other political systems produced by political scientists. As Walter Laqueur has pointed out, "the contribution to the field of Soviet studies of the more modern trends in sociology and political science has been on the whole negligible."[12] This fact is a result of the communications gap that has developed between the two groups of scholars.

The question that arises is "Why?" What is there about the study of the Soviet Union and Eastern Europe that makes it so different from studies of the United States, Western Europe, and Africa? Is the access to data so limited that behavioral research has been impeded, or are the Communist systems really so unique that it is impossible to employ the methodological tools of political analysis that have been developed elsewhere?[13] One of the important factors impeding the development of behavioral research techniques in Communist studies has been the difficulty of obtaining such relatively simple data as income and trade statistics and the "facts" of politics in the Communist states. Until such data had been obtained, it was meaningless to begin speaking of model-building. A second important consideration stems from the historical development of Communist or Soviet studies. Many of the early students were emigrees whose interests focused almost exclusively on the Soviet Union and/or Eastern Europe, and their training was not in political science, but in history or law. In addition, much of their work was primarily policy-oriented, and the authors were interested in obtaining additional information about Communist systems rather than in methodological questions or in similarities between Communist and other political systems. Unfortunately, many of their successors also did not keep up with methodological developments in political science. In addition, the emphasis on the uniqueness of the Communist system made comparison with other political systems almost impossible. This orientation tended to stress the control features of the system, while ignoring the policy-making processes. The underlying assumption was that the political process, as it operates in non-Communist systems, did not exist in the Soviet Union or Eastern Europe.

What are the advantages to be gained by students of the Soviet Union and Eastern Europe in obtaining a familiarity with, and employing in their own research, techniques developed in systematic political science? Or, expressed differently, what are the shortcomings in the area approach to the study of Communist society that political science techniques might help overcome?

As already noted, although the country or area approach to the study of politics, as employed by most specialists on Communism, permits the scholar to amass huge amounts of data about the history, culture, economy, and political system itself, it also tends to ignore the outside world and to overemphasize the uniqueness of the Communist system. Communist systems have been viewed as manifestations of a social sickness and, as such, not comparable with other political systems.[14] Related to this weakness of the area approach is the failure to ask important questions about the Communist systems themselves. By focusing on the uniqueness of the Communist party-state, some scholars have tended to ignore questions concerning decision-making procedures and methods of policy implementation. They have dealt little with the influence of socioeconomic or educational background on the attitudes of leaders and the policies that groups of leaders support or oppose. In other words, the split between political science and Communist studies has denied the latter the potential stimulation in asking questions about the processes of politics that could be derived from their political science colleagues. How effective are socialization processes in the Communist systems? Are the hypotheses developed by Karl Deutsch and Amitai Etzioni about political unification applicable to a study of Comecon?[15] How relevant are the studies of non-Communist bureaucracies to the study of the party or the state bureaucracy in the Soviet Union?

III

In the past few years, increasing numbers of scholars—primarily younger men who have been trained both as area specialists and as political scientists—have begun to apply to the study of Communist systems some of the approaches and hypotheses that have been generated in systematic political science.[16] They have become interested in the formation and competition of groups within the Communist Party— a subject that few besides Boris Nicolaevsky had studied in the past.[17] However, rather than basing their analyses on Kremlinological techniques of reading between the lines of official party or governmental publications, they have examined the career patterns of members of the political elite or have conducted detailed content analyses of published statements in order to discover similarities or divergencies in the policy orientation of various occupational specialists in the Soviet Union and Eastern Europe.[18] Others have attempted to view the Communist system as a means of achieving rapid modernization and have employed some of the insights developed in the literature on political and economic modernization.[19]

The following pages attempt to incorporate methods and findings of political science research into analyses of various aspects of political behavior in the Soviet Union and Eastern Europe. With one exception, the articles all deal with imperial Russia and the Soviet Union, yet the approaches employed here should be, with necessary modifications, applicable to the study of political behavior in other Communist systems as well. The first group of studies deals with the characteristics of the political elites in the Soviet Union and Eastern Europe, including their socioeconomic and educational backgrounds, their motivations and attitudes toward policy, the means by which they reach leadership positions, and the ways in which lower elites can influence policy. The second group of articles concerns various aspects of policy implementation in tsarist Russia and the Soviet Union. The final section covers a number of aspects of Soviet behavior in international politics. Obviously this volume makes no attempt to present a complete and integrated analysis of Communist political systems, nor even of the Soviet system. However, these contributions will, hopefully, help to convince both political scientists and area specialists of the value of closer attention to one another's work. For the student of Communist political systems, these selections will provide a deeper insight into the actual workings of Soviet politics. For the student of comparative or international politics they will provide new data against which general propositions can be tested.

Notes

1. See Gabriel Almond and James Coleman, *The Politics of Developing Areas* (Princeton: Princeton U. P., 1960), esp. "Introduction" and "Conclusion."

2. See Harry Eckstein, "A Perspective on Comparative Politics. Past and Present," in Harry Eckstein and David E. Apter (eds.), *Comparative Politics: A Reader* (New York: Free Press, 1963), p. 25. Eckstein's essay is still the best brief history of the development of the subdiscipline of comparative politics.

3. See, for example, David E. Apter, "Theory and the Study of Politics," *American Political Science Review*, LI (1957), 747–62, where he calls for the application of theoretically pertinent research based on specialized unambiguous concepts.

4. Eckstein, *op. cit.*, p. 25.

5. See David Easton, "The Current Meaning of 'Behavioralism,' " in James C. Charlesworth (ed.), *Contemporary Political Analysis* (New York: Free Press, 1967), p. 16. Among the early forerunners of the behavioral approach in political science were Charles E. Merriam, *New Aspects of Politics* (Chicago: U. of Chicago P., 1925); Harold D. Lasswell, *Psychopathology and Politics* (Chicago: U. of Chicago P., 1930); and Herbert A. Simon, *Administrative Behavior* (New York: Macmillan, 1947). For an interesting discussion of the origins of the behavioral movement see Don R. Bowen, *Political Behavior of the American People* (Columbus: Merrill, 1968), Chap. 1.

6. For a brief list of the assumptions and objectives of the behavioral approach see *Ibid.*, pp. 16–17. See also Albert Somit and Joseph Tanenhaus, *The Development of Political Science: From Burgess to Behavioralism* (Boston: Allyn, 1967), pp. 178–79.

7. Heinz Eulau in James C. Charlesworth (ed.), *A Design for Political Science: Scope, Objectives and Methods*, Monograph 6 (Philadelphia: American Academy of Political and Social Science, 1966), pp. 202–3. See also Sidney Verba, "Some Dilemmas in Comparative Research," *World Politics*, XX (1967), 112.

8. Roy C. Macridis, "Comparative Politics and the Study of Government: The Search for Focus," *Comparative Politics*, I (1968), 84–5.

9. See, for example, the excellent study of Robert T. Holt and John E. Turner, *The Political Basis of Economic Development: An Exploration in Comparative Political Analysis* (Princeton: Van Nostrand, 1966), in which the authors examine the political factors relevant to economic development in Great Britain, France, China, and Japan. Other examples of research on development include Daniel Lerner, *The Passing of Traditional Society: Modernizing the Middle East* (New York: Free Press, 1958); David E. Apter, *The Politics of Modernization* (Chicago: U. of Chicago P., 1965); and Lucian W. Pye, *Politics, Personality, and Nation Building: Burma's Search for Identity* (New Haven: Yale U. P., 1962).

10. For a brief examination of this point see Robert Sharlet, "Concept Formation in Political Science and Communist Studies," *Canadian Slavic Studies*, I (1967), 640–2. Dankwart A. Rustow has gone so far as to state: "But beyond [training social scientists in difficult languages and providing them with central collections of rare library materials] as a source for insights in the social sciences, area study is almost obsolete." See his "Modernization and Comparative Politics: Prospects in Research and Theory," *Comparative Politics*, I (1968), 45.

11. Adam Ulam, "USA: Some Critical Comments," *Survey*, 50 (1964), 57. This issue is entitled "The State of Soviet Studies." For a discussion of the dichotomy between the social sciences and Communist studies see Frederic J. Fleron, Jr., "Soviet Area Studies and the Social Sciences: Some Methodological Problems in Communist Studies," *Soviet Studies* XIX (1968), 313–39. For a survey of much of the work published before 1968 see Paul Shoup, "Comparing Communist Nations: Prospects for an Empirical Approach," *American Political Science Review*, LXII (1968), 185–204, reprinted as Chap. 1 below.

12. Walter Laqueur, "In Search of Russia," *Survey* 50, (1964), 49. Daniel Bell presents an interesting discussion of various approaches to the study of Soviet politics in "Ten Theories in Search of Reality: The Prediction of Soviet Behavior in the Social Sciences," *World Politics*, X (1958), 327–65. Ivan Volgyes points to some of the problems involved in the use of an area approach in "The Relevance of an Area Study Approach to the Politics of Eastern Europe," *The Rocky Mountain Social Science Journal*, V, 2 (1968), 127–32.

13. Robert C. Tucker attempted to incorporate the study of Communist systems into an overall model of authoritarian political systems in an article entitled "Towards a Comparative Politics of Movement-Regimes," *American Political Science Review*, LV (1961), 281–9. See, also, his more recent article, "On the Comparative Study of Communism," *World Politics*, XIX (1967), 242–57. In a symposium published in the *Slavic Review*, XXVI (1967), 1–28, a number of scholars discussed the need to integrate the study of Communist systems with the study of comparative politics.

14. This position has been taken by Hannah Arendt in *The Origins of Totalitarianism* (New York: Harcourt, 1951), esp. Chaps. 11–12.

15. Karl W. Deutsch *et al.*, *Political Community and the North Atlantic Area* (Princeton: Princeton U. P., 1957) and Amitai Etzioni, *Political Unification: A Comparative Study of Leaders and Forces* (New York: Holt, 1965).

16. Obviously not all of those who are applying the "newer" techniques to the study of the Soviet Union and Eastern Europe can be classified as "younger scholars." Some of the most interesting work has been done by such men as John A. Armstrong, Vernon Aspaturian, Alex Inkeles, John H. Kautsky, Alfred G. Meyer, H. Gordon Skilling, Jan F. Triska, Robert C. Tucker, and others.

17. See, for example, Boris Nicolaevsky, "Battle in the Kremlin," series of six articles in *The New Leader*, XL, 30–35 (July 29–Sept. 2, 1957). Also, Franz Borkenau, *World Communism: A History of the Communist International* (Ann Arbor: U. of Michigan P. 1962, reprint), Ch. 9; Carl Linden, *Khrushchev and the Soviet Leadership, 1957–1964* (Baltimore: Johns Hopkins, 1966); Robert Conquest, *Power and Policy*

in the USSR (New York: St. Martin's, 1961); and Sidney Ploss, *Conflict and Decision-Making in Soviet Russia* (Princeton: Princeton U. P., 1965).

18. See, for example, Milton Lodge, "Soviet Elite Participatory Attitudes in the Post-Stalin Period," *American Political Science Review*, LXII (1968), 827–39, reprinted below; Milton Lodge, " 'Groupism' in the Post-Stalin Period," *Midwest Journal of Political Science*, XII (1968), 330–51; and Carl Beck, "Bureaucratic Conservatism and Innovation in Eastern Europe," *Comparative Political Studies*, I (1968), 275–94.

19. See John H. Kautsky, "An Essay in the Politics of Development," in Kautsky (ed.), *Political Change in Underdeveloped Countries: Nationalism and Communism* (New York: Wiley, 1962) and Charles Gati, "Modernization and Communist Power in Hungary," to appear in *East European Quarterly* (1971).

PART 1

A Survey of Empirically Oriented Literature on Communist Polities

In this section an excellent summary of the development of comparative Communist studies by Paul Shoup is reprinted from the *American Political Science Review*. Besides providing a very useful bibliography of current research, the author discusses many of the theoretical problems facing the student of comparative Communism—for example, problems of classification of different types of Communist political systems, the conceptualization and testing of models that can be applied to these systems, and the collection and evaluation of comparative data.

Shoup also points out that most of the work done to date represents an attempt to develop middle-range theory in such areas as elite behavior, social stratification, and the development

12

of interest groups. He refers to work being done not only by Western scholars, but also by East European and Soviet social scientists.

1

Comparing Communist Nations: Prospects for an Empirical Approach

PAUL SHOUP

The past decade has witnessed a rapid, but uneven, growth in comparative studies. While certain types of political systems have received the lion's share of attention, others have remained backwaters of comparative research, experiencing little or no development in the application of comparative techniques. The comparative study of communist states, until recently, fell into the latter category—relatively neglected

Reprinted with permission from *American Political Science Review*, LXII (1968) 185–204. Notes appear as in the original, at the end of the selection on page 36.

and certainly not enjoying the reputation and prestige of work with newly emerging nations or Western political systems.

Now this state of affairs is undergoing a change, or at least the promise of one. In the past several years, the possibility of developing comparative techniques in the study of communist political systems has become the object of growing interest and has provoked not a little discussion and debate.[1] The opportunities and the problems that face this field—especially in developing empirically oriented comparative analysis—are the subject of the present article.

I. THE RECENT STUDIES OF COMMUNIST SYSTEMS

The comparative study of communist systems, although only recently attracting interest as a source for generating new insights into the nature of communist systems, has roots in a long and productive tradition of cross-national research on the Soviet Union and Eastern Europe. Descriptive comparisons of the political systems of the communist bloc have appeared with regularity since World War II,[2] and have recently been utilized in the study of the communist nations of Asia.[3] For well over a decade, experts on communist countries have been making contributions to comparative works on political parties, interest groups, public administration and other specialized fields of study amenable to cross-national analysis.[4] The study of ideological and political developments in the communist world has been conducted largely within a comparative framework,[5] while an extensive literature has developed on the comparative study of communist legal systems[6] and differences and similarities in the process of modernization in China and the Soviet Union.[7] In sheer volume, this material undoubtedly equals and perhaps exceeds comparative studies dealing with Western political systems, or under-developed countries.

It is nevertheless true that this considerable body of literature has not produced a method of studying communist states which could be called distinctively comparative. The use of comparative data has been limited; typologies of communist systems have not developed to any great degree, and there has been conspicuously lacking, in the study of communist systems, a conceptual framework, such as the notion of pluralism or the process of modernization, which could unify and orient empirical studies of communist states along comparative lines.[8]

There are many reasons why this has been so. The need to develop a familiarity with a wide variety of cultures and languages, the paucity of empirical information on communist systems, and the difficulties and dangers involved in carrying out on-the-spot research have in the past discouraged persons from attempting comparative work with communist countries. In the realm of comparative theory, the fact that existing methodology has been derived largely from experience with Western political systems has created special problems for comparative work with communist states.

Perhaps the single most important factor discouraging comparative research with communist systems in the past was the monolithic uniformity of communist states. Once having analyzed the communist political system as it existed in the Soviet Union, there was usually little to be gained, it seemed, from broadening the scope of the analysis to include a number of communist nations. Even when variations in political forms did exist (such as the presence of a pseudo multi-party system in certain communist countries), the obvious artificiality of the differences in question militated against utilizing the comparative approach.

For a number of reasons the barriers to comparative work just enumerated no longer appear so formidable. Communist political systems are more and more characterized by institutional differences and contrasting economic and social policies. Perhaps even more important is the fact that the evolution taking place in the communist world is for the most part in a "Western" direction. Rightly or wrongly, the consequence of this has been that tested methods of comparative analysis, such as the study of interest groups, now appear applicable to communist political systems for the first time.

The evolution of communist political systems in a direction which encourages the utilization of comparative techniques is not universal, nor is there agreement on its importance. It is still felt by many that communist states, because they are organized from above with little regard for popular feelings or social pressures, are not amenable to most forms of comparative analysis even when they differ one from another. In its extreme form this attitude finds expression in the assertion that only the ideologies and policies of the directing organs of the parties concerned are the determining, and therefore comparable, elements of communist political systems.[9]

Without becoming too deeply involved in the implications of this view of totalitarian political systems, it can be suggested that there has often in the past been manifest an unjustifiably rigid attitude toward the scope of comparative analysis and its applicability to communist nations. In point of fact it is impossible to state categorically that comparative analysis will always produce better results with one type of political system than another. Inevitably, a great number of variables influence the outcome of comparative work; as a consequence, the research techniques employed, or the aims of the particular study, may be as important in determining the practicality of employing the comparative method as the identity of the group of nations chosen for the purposes of comparison. This, in fact, has always been true, even when communism was confined largely to the Stalinist totalitarian model.

Several examples may be given to illustrate this point. While some counting techniques apply better to non-communist than to communist systems, there are cases, such as in the comparative analysis of elites, in which mathematical correlations have been more extensively used in comparative work with communist countries than with non-communist ones.[10] There are many types of functional problems, such as are apparent in the manipulation of mass communications to enhance the authority of a regime, which can be studied by comparative methods in communist states when such an approach might prove impractical, or less rewarding, when applied to other types of systems. Systems analysis was first employed in comparative work with communist states,[11] and the first proposal to develop a "working model" of an advanced contemporary society was made in conjunction with the Harvard study of the Soviet Union.

In the search for subjects amenable to comparative study, it must be borne in mind that one's concept of the limits of the comparative method necessarily plays an important role. Comparisons of national units, while they constitute an obvious starting point for measuring the utility of comparative research, are not the only way in which work in the field is conducted.

Replicative studies, for example, may make valuable contributions to comparative work and never compare nations as such. There is also a place in the comparative approach for the study of different periods in one nation's development (so-called vertical comparisons) and the analysis of regional differences within one country if they have, as part of their purpose, the study of similarities and differences among political systems. One or another of these methods may, at any given time, prove more useful or have greater potential than another when dealing with a specific type of political system, and it is a sign of maturity in comparative analysis that the application of one of these methods is not thought to exclude or pre-empt the use of others.

One might sum up the argument so far by suggesting that while the comparative method has not in the past produced distinctive insights or techniques in connection with the analysis of communist political systems, a wide array of comparative approaches is available for use in the study of these systems, and there is no *a priori* reason why many cannot be applied with equal success to both communist and non-communist nations alike.

The task of applying the comparative method to communist systems nevertheless involves difficult problems of method and theory, if only because the emergence of a new field of comparative research has usually been tied to the development of concepts which form "take-off points" for comparison. It is a perplexing and even sensitive point how such a theory is to emerge in the field of comparative communist studies, or even whether it should be sought for at all. No discussion of the prospects for comparative work with communist systems can avoid the difficulties encountered in the search for a secure foundation on which to build this new field, however, and it is with this fundamental problem that the next part of the discussion is concerned.

II. THEORETICAL AND METHODOLOGICAL PROBLEMS AND TASKS

The theoretical and methodological problems that must be overcome in developing a new field of comparative studies range over a wide area, from the development of typologies and dynamic concepts of evolution and change, to the problem of gathering data and applying quantitative comparative techniques. For purposes of simplification, the discussion will concentrate on three tasks which have always been of primary importance for the growth of new types of comparative work: developing typologies and classifications of political systems; building models; and compiling and evaluating comparative data.

1. Developing Typologies

The classification and typing of communist systems pose special problems for the comparative political scientist.[12] Within the communist world, while there is great diversity, there is no obvious pattern of development which would permit one to point to major sub-groups or distinctive system types, with the exception of the now historical system of pure Stalinism. Communist states are not always easy to identify; Cuba comes to mind as a country whose claim to be communist is still open to question, and some persons would also exclude Yugoslavia from the communist camp.

Global typologies, indispensable when discussing contemporary political systems, are nevertheless difficult to utilize in making distinctions among communist states. All too often, plausible and convenient categories, such as totalitarian or authoritarian systems types, tend to break down when communist states begin to evolve out of the standard Stalinist pattern. If the Yugoslav political system has lost its totalitarian characteristics, for example, what exactly has it become? Is is perhaps now authoritarian? Some discussion hints at this, but the term authoritarian hardly seems appropriate to a modernizing elite or a communist oligarchy of the type that rules Yugoslavia today. Should the country then be designated as a newly emerging nation with a one-party system and a modernizing elite? The objection to this suggestion lies in the fact that communist Yugoslavia has always been a "newly emerging" nation with a one-party system; that is, the reason for the re-classification is not suggested in the new category that is being applied as a result of the changes that have taken place in the system. Nor is Yugoslavia's past revolutionary experience adequately accounted for in this description of the country as a newly emerging nation.

The phenomenon of modernization offers another illustration of the imprecision that surrounds the classification of communist political systems. At what stage in the modernization process does one place communist states in Eastern Europe and the Soviet Union: are they "modern," "mixed," or "traditional"? Even the most advanced communist state has some characteristics of a developing nation, and all share so many features in common regardless of their level of economic development that the significance of differences in degrees of modernization seems much less clear than when dealing with non-communist systems. In an effort to deal with some of these problems of comparison, Professor Brzezinski once referred to the Soviet Union as "quasi-modern,"[13] an interesting observation on the character of Soviet society, but difficult to use for comparative purposes.

Because of these obvious difficulties, the problem of classification of communist systems may have to be dealt with on a common sense basis at first, beginning with an effort to determine what obvious characteristics identify this type of system. What these characteristics are is in itself a debatable point,[14] but it would not seem unreasonable to suggest that certain fundamental traits reappear consistently in our conception of the communist form of rule. Ideology is an obvious common denominator of communist governments; party supremacy and the experience of a period of revolutionary rule in which the pre-communist social order is destroyed are others. A descriptive definition of the limits of the group being considered for comparison might then run something along the following lines: communist states should be considered comparable among themselves, or treated as a distinct category for purposes of comparison with other types of political systems, if they have adopted the Marxist ideology, if they have experienced a revolution which has destroyed the power structure of the earlier system, and if the Party has acquired a monopoly in the decision-making processes of the societies in question, exercising decisive control over all major political, economic and cultural organizations.

This common sense definition admittedly has many deficiencies: it relies heavily on the fact that most communist states have their origins in the Stalinist form of communism; it does not provide an unambiguous guide to which systems should be considered part of the communist world and which should not; and it does not solve the problem of making broad distinctions among types of systems within the communist camp.

In practical comparative work, meanwhile, the significance of being able to utilize precise classifications or typologies varies with the nature of the question being asked. In the case of certain types of elite studies, for example, where the method employed is that of accumulating replicative data, the number of countries utilized and their exact location on a taxonomic chart may not be of crucial importance. On the other hand, if one employs statistical data to develop comparisons among major types of political systems, or to identify the salient characteristics of each type of system (as Banks and Textor have done),[15] the placement of a country in one category rather than another may materially affect the over-all results, especially if the countries being compared are rank-ordered. To cite a more extreme case, the attempt to construct paradigms of systems types based on pairs of mutually exclusive characteristics such as the Parsonian system of pattern-variables, or the modern-traditional dichotomy, makes extraordinary demands on the typologist,[16] far beyond the capabilities of most theoretical work on communist systems undertaken up until the present time.

2. Building Models

Closely related to the development of typologies, but nevertheless a distinct branch of comparative analysis in its own right, is the conceptualization and testing of models of political systems. Models are important for comparative methodology because they seek to establish the central characteristics and interrelationships of a specific type of political system. Out of this work may emerge a variety of comparative insights into functional relationships, stresses and strains characteristic of the system in question, and, hopefully, guidelines for the measurement and comparison of the general performance of the system with other types. Measuring the stability of political systems is a good example of the kind of empirical and comparative analysis that requires some simple model in order to be successful.

Practically all theorizing on communist systems has aimed at creating the elements of a model, and over the years, the number of contending approaches has steadily grown: the totalitarian model (which has received a useful restatement in a comparative context by Harry Eckstein and David Apter);[17] the model of the one party state;[18] the bureaucratic model;[19] and the structural-functional model.[20]

None of these approaches to communist systems has won complete acceptance. The only one of these models which may be said to be the product of contemporary comparative methodology, the structural-functional model, has introduced some new elements into thinking about communist systems, but when applied to specific cases has proven by and large vague and disappointing.[21]

The problem of constructing working models of communist systems in fact involves one in difficult questions concerning the nature of functional relationships in society and the fundamental characteristics of political systems. It is to the credit of the field of communist studies that investigation of this problem began as early as the 1950's when several ambitious projects were undertaken to create systems models of communist societies—models which in turn could be used for locating "vulnerabilities," or strengths and weaknesses of the Soviet system. This research advanced sufficiently to prove the complexity of functional models, but was unfortunately suspended before many of the basic problems could be thoroughly analyzed and essential data collected.[22]

This early experience, combined with the insights of the structural-functional school, nevertheless suggests possible ways of approaching model-building in comparative work with communist states. Functional models, if oriented toward developmental problems, are feasible and much easier to work with than the macro-static type of model implied in the systems approach or by structural-functional concepts.[23] By utilizing a wide range of comparisons and combining them with historical perspectives, the developmental model may be given certain attributes of a static model. For example, through examining the workings of the Stalinist system over time, and under different national conditions, its performance capabilities and functional inter-dependencies can be appraised much more accurately than in the vulnerability studies of the early 1950's. Because Stalinist systems have shown a tendency to excess, forcing certain lines of action to the point of rapidly diminishing returns, functional comparisons might find it useful to experiment with concepts of marginal utility in building models, concentrating on the limits which experience has shown circumscribed the capacities of the Stalinist system under different historical and national conditions. In this way functional analysis might free itself of the difficulties which have resulted from focusing exclusively on "vulnerabilities" (or strengths and weaknesses) or on the systems concept of "total interdependence," when constructing macro-static models.

The generalized notion of systems also contains certain insights which should not go unutilized in comparative work with communist countries. Implicit in the structural-functional model, and explicit in general systems theory, is the distinction between self-regulating social systems in a state of primary equilibrium, and secondary types of systems guided by feedback mechanisms manifest in the activities of the political system. The value of this concept in analyzing the operation of modern governments lies not simply in the emphasis which is thereby placed on the activities of communication and decision-making, but in the suggestion that complex societies can only operate efficiently if the political system performs a feedback function, regulating and sustaining highly specialized and complex activities which in turn may themselves perform important control functions in the society in question. When the state nevertheless seeks to replace these processes and institutions with its own bureaucratic forms of rule, entirely new functional problems are created, about which there has been much speculation, but little methodical comparative analysis aimed at the development of working models.[24]

These exercises in model-building by no means exclude the study of power relationships, and above all, re-examination of the concept of totalitarianism in such a way as to make it more amenable to empirical research. Any comparative study of the Stalinist system would necessarily have as one of its goals the clarification of the dynamics of the totalitarian form of government. This being the case, there does not appear to be any more justification for the position that the comparative approach will replace totalitarian theory than for the thesis that communist systems, because they are (or were) totalitarian, cannot be subjected to comparative forms of analysis.

3. Compiling and Evaluating Comparative Data

Developing a fund of comparative data is perhaps the most crucial of the three tasks facing the field of comparative communist studies. Unless new sources of information can be found and reasonably accurate data accumulated, there is the danger that comparative studies of communist systems will remain suspended in limbo, unable to build on a solid empirical foundation. And while prospects for gathering data on communist countries have improved dramatically in recent years, great problems remain—both in evaluating the extent and reliability of materials originating from communist sources, and in utilizing this information productively in comparative research.

Of the various types of data used for comparative work, statistical materials, or "aggregative data" as Karl Deutsch has called them,[25] are by far the most important. In the communist nations, they are available in widely differing quantities and degrees of reliability. On mainland China, only one census has been carried out (in 1953), and even after its completion, official Chinese figures on the size of the Chinese population varied greatly, sometimes by as much as 24 million in a single year.[26] Chinese data on the size of the state apparatus, social mobility, social stratification and income differentials are limited largely to statistics from the mid-1950s on the number of persons engaged in certain occupations[27] and recently acquired material from the same period on salary scales in non-agricultural occupations.[28] Aggregative data on social, economic and political conditions in other Asian communist countries, and on Cuba, are also sparse or unavailable in a form convenient for comparative research.[29] Information on the Mongolian Peoples Republic is difficult to obtain, although available in somewhat greater amounts than for the communist states of the Far East.[30]

By way of contrast, aggregative data on several Eastern European countries are relatively plentiful and reliable, even by Western standards. In Yugoslavia, three censuses have been held since the communists came to power (in 1948, 1953 and 1961). A wide range of aggregative data are made available through the statistical services of the federal, republic and local governments, and quantitative analyses of such activities as local government, workers councils, problems of urbanization and modernization, the distribution of incomes, size of the bureaucracy and other topics have been carried out by individual scholars and government-sponsored research institutes.[31] Poland and Hungary have developed their statistical reporting rapidly in the last decade, providing valuable information on demographic problems, social stratification, the standard of living, and other areas of interest for comparative work.[32] While other Eastern European countries and the USSR have not equalled this output, they are improving their statistical services steadily and now make available basic information on the population, economy and social structure unobtainable a decade ago.[33]

Many difficulties accompany the use of this data for comparative purposes, and a great deal of cooperation is necessary at the international level if national statistics are to be gathered and presented in a way that permits meaningful comparisons. Communist statistics, while they must be used with great care, do show signs of becoming more truly comparable than in the past. Although the Soviet Union, above all, has displayed great reluctance in cooperating with Western nations in order to make available comparative data in the social sciences—and has produced data comparing communist and Western largely for systems propaganda purposes[34]—there has been an increasing awareness within the bloc that accurate comparative data on common economic and social problems are essential. Through Comecon committees and scholarly conferences, steps are being taken to develop uniform standards for the bloc in the compilation of data on economic problems, the standard of living, and other subjects.[35] At the same time, the fund of Western knowledge on national incomes, levels of consumption and the budgetary expenses of Eastern European countries and the Soviet Union is steadily growing, providing valuable data which are more accessible than that made available in communist countries.[36]

There are obvious drawbacks to using aggregative data from communist countries. Most statistics are not directly concerned with politics (we shall deal with some exceptions shortly), and are restricted largely to Eastern Europe and the Soviet Union. What is available nevertheless constitutes an indispensable basis for comparing both the social determinates of political action and the stages of development through which communist countries are presently passing. Most of this material has until now gone unutilized in the study of communist countries.

In comparative research, aggregative data should be supplemented by sample survey data where possible. Thus, if reliable electoral statistics are not available, survey research may still tell us something about the feelings of people toward their government. Information obtained in this way provides a means of testing for cross-cultural differences on a wide range of political issues, as the work of Almond and Verba has demonstrated.[37] Sample surveys may also be the only way in which to obtain certain types of purely factual information, for example, on consumption habits, or in respect to patterns of communication.

In the study of communist countries, sample survey data have been obtained in several ways. One method has been to interview refugees, escapees, or persons from communist countries who are temporarily abroad. A modest number of projects utilizing this type of information have been organized over the years; the value of such work has varied considerably from the highly respected and influential Harvard study of Soviet refugees to the little utilized data gathered from Hungarian Freedom Fighters by several research teams in 1956 and 1957.[38] Although the number of escapees from Eastern Europe and the Soviet Union has diminished over the years, efforts to question persons who have resided in the Soviet Union continue.[39] At the same time, Radio Free Europe and other organizations interested in the Soviet bloc interview persons temporarily in the West to gain information on public opinion in Eastern European nations.[40] An important pioneering effort in comparative research was carried out by John Armstrong through interviewing West European diplomats and businessmen familiar with Soviet administrative practices, comparing these practices to European methods of public administration.[41]

Sample survey methods have also been employed to gain information on China from Mainland Chinese now residing in Hong Kong. Political obstacles, and the difficulty of administering questionnaires to respondents who are largely illiterate, have nevertheless limited the scope of these projects,[42] and most material gathered from Chinese escapees has been obtained through interviews conducted by individual scholars on a small scale.[43]

Fortunately for comparative communist studies, these limited sources of sample survey data have been augmented in recent years by studies carried out by social scientists in Eastern Europe and the Soviet Union. Their findings, although occasionally suffering from respondent bias and lax methodology (the former has been particularly evident in some Yugoslav projects), are bound to have an impact on both comparative and non-comparative research on communist systems. As a result of extensive polling and interviewing, data on social mobility, the impact of modernization, the attitudes of the younger generation and patterns of communication are becoming available in ever-increasing amounts.[44] Research on many types of institutions characteristic of communist societies such as youth work brigades, or workers councils, is feasible, using cross-national data gathered by sociologists in Eastern Europe. It is now not uncommon for Western and Eastern European scholars to collaborate in studies aimed at testing cross-cultural or cross-national differences; the work of David McClelland in measuring achievement motivation among Polish enterprise managers and American businessmen is an outstanding example of the fruitful results of such cooperations.[45] Research which has been carried out by the University of Pennsylvania on attitudes toward local government, with the cooperation of social scientists from both Yugoslavia and Poland, is a unique effort to test cross-cultural values with a political content.[46] Studies in political sociology in Poland have on occasion tested for cross-cultural differences between Polish and Western societies, replicating Western studies.[47]

Poland and Yugoslavia (especially the former) have taken the lead in gathering sample survey data, while in some cases (Bulgaria, Rumania), public opinion polling is still in its infancy and heavily influenced by political and propaganda considerations.[48] Sample survey work in the Soviet Union stands somewhere between these extremes, having produced what are largely propagandistic studies on attitudes of the youth,[49] but at the same time allowing the advocates of quantitative research in the social sciences to popularize their views and to produce studies of interest on the working class, the use of leisure time, and certain other subjects.[50]

At one time the Chinese communists engaged in a limited amount of polling; rural social surveys were conducted and village histories compiled with the assistance of members of the Young Communist League. The object of this work was, however, not to gather scientific information on conditions in the villages, but to obtain evidence that could be used to convince the peasant that living conditions in the villages had improved under communist rule.[51]

Even in this brief summary it is clear that the situation in respect to the gathering of data on communist countries is changing rapidly, opening new avenues of research which should greatly assist the development of comparative communist studies. The limits to our knowledge are, nevertheless, impressive and sobering. Obviously the fund of data is growing unevenly, and in the case of China (and perhaps Albania) may even be deteriorating in value as time passes. Putting the data that are available into comparative form presents many methodological difficulties, especially when one is working with the results of sample survey studies. Even in areas where the use of comparative data is relatively simple, such as the analysis of elites, great difficulties may arise in obtaining comprehensive and reliable information for all countries under examination.[52] More often than not, the task is beyond the capacities of the lone researcher, and requires a team effort.

Nevertheless, it is to be hoped that the trend toward making increasing amounts of data available will ease the task of applying quantitative techniques to comparative work with communist countries. Information is slowly being made available on political subjects (the social background of party members, for example)[53] which for years were considered sensitive or off limits. There is now a reasonable hope, inconceivable a decade ago, that social scientists in communist countries will assume much of the burden of gathering and analyzing data on such basic problems as social stratification, modernization, and to a limited extent, power elites. Finally, consideration must be given to the existence of great amounts of *unutilized* data, especially in connection with the study of Asian communism; John Lewis has demonstrated that significant results with comparative implications can be gathered from such materials, often of local or regional origin.[54]

The problems of theory and methodology which we have touched on in the preceding pages—classification, model building, and data collection—are clearly of a kind which will challenge the comparative political scientist to the utmost. What success can be expected in these areas is, of course, a highly speculative question, difficult to answer in a field which is still just beginning to explore its potentialities.

On balance, it seems reasonable to conclude that the field of comparative communist studies is not yet in a position to become a quantitative discipline, in the sense that hypotheses will be routinely generated and then confirmed by methods of statistical probability, rank ordering, or other counting techniques. On the other hand, a more modest but no less important goal, that of placing comparative work with communist countries on a firm empirical basis, seems feasible and highly desirable.

Perhaps the chief obstacle to developing a distinctive field of comparative communist studies is no longer the difficulty of obtaining data, but the problem of whether it is possible for comparative work with communist systems to develop a unifying concept with the aid of which the field can develop its own distinctive theories and research strategies. No such concept exists (either as a derivative of totalitarian theory, or of the structural-functional approach) which could win general acceptance among students of communist systems at the present time. It is evident, in this connection, that comparative work with communist systems is developing in a context different from that which characterized the emergence of other areas of comparative work. For it is the departure of communist practice from its unifying concept—the Stalinist pattern of totalitarianism— which is largely responsible for stimulating interest in comparative analysis, rather than the bringing of order out of diversity through the identification of common developmental problems, or structural characteristics (modernization, or democracy).

For this reason, the rapid development of all-inclusive models or typologies seems less likely than the appearance of several different types of models, and perhaps even a number of methods of classifying communist political systems, each serving its own particular purpose. Rather than relying on abstract theory to tie these models together, the comparative study of communist systems must be given a sense of unity through the realization that in communist ideology, party rule, and the experience of totalitarian methods of control (either in the present or in the past), there is combined a distinct and unique response to the demands of contemporary society and the competitive struggle for survival which is the product of the present-day nation-state system.

Values and institutions are still similar enough throughout the communist world that a balance between unity and diversity—admittedly so useful in comparative analysis—is maintained and can be exploited for research purposes. Even in such widely differing systems as those that exist in China and Yugoslavia, for example, there are enough basic forces acting in common to make the comparative study of the two systems (and phenomena within those systems, such as regionalism) a worthwhile and rewarding task.

Does this mean that the comparative study of communist systems will nevertheless remain an ill-defined field of research, seeking but never attaining the theoretical insights associated with the development of comparative studies in other areas? Admittedly one can draw this conclusion from the preceding discussion, although juxtaposing communist and non-communist comparative studies is a deceptive practice, often resulting in an exaggerated estimate of the results which have been achieved in the latter field.

The potentialities of comparative communist studies cannot be accurately gauged, however, without considering all forms of on-going research, both that which is related to the development of typologies, models and the utilization of empirical data, and problem-oriented, or "middle-range" studies. While it is not possible to examine the latter category in as great detail as might be desired, a few observations on the status of middle-range comparative work are indispensable. Out of these remarks may also emerge the hint of a strategy for comparative analysis of communist systems which will make maximum use of the empirical materials now becoming available on communist nations.

III. MIDDLE-RANGE COMPARATIVE STUDIES

It is characteristic of most research in the comparative field—especially that which seeks to utilize empirical materials—that it encompasses both a very small number of truly comparative works and a very large number of studies which are not strictly comparative but provide information in a form which may be utilized for comparative purposes. So it is in the case of middle-range comparative work with communist countries today. The number of comparative empirical studies, uncompromisngly defined, is small, beginning with the pioneering work of R. V. Burks, and including the elite studies now being carried on by Carl Beck,[55] the cross-cultural investigations of Armstrong and the University of Pennsylvania team mentioned earlier, some of the comparative analysis of China and the Soviet Union, and perhaps also the effort of Brzezinski and Huntington to compare the United States and the Soviet Union.

It is a distinctive feature of middle-range research, in addition, that it often approaches its subject matter not with the intent of adding to our knowledge of the political process as a *system*, but through the utilization of elite theory, the investigation of principles of social stratification or modernization, or with the aid of other concepts having a comparative orientation but not concerned with comparing nations or political systems as such. Most of this type of research will be something more than "middle-range," more often than not involving quite complex and fundamental theoretical problems. This, of course, complicates the work of comparative analysis by introducing new theoretical considerations into the picture but, practically speaking, may be the more fruitful approach as long as general political systems theory remains in a state of flux.

If one can accept this approach as part of the natural process of expanding comparative empirical research into a new area, and at the same time agree to consider studies which have evident comparative implications even if they are not, strictly speaking, cross-national in scope, then a rich and varied pattern of middle-range work on communist countries is already discernible, much of it going on within the communist countries themselves.[56]

The study of social stratification and social mobility, of great importance in assessing the impact of ideology and politics on communist societies, is especially advanced in Poland.[57] Materials on social stratification are also appearing in other communist countries and basic data in this field are now available for a majority of the communist systems of Eastern Europe. Although comparative studies of social stratification are still a rarity, valuable work has been done by Western scholars on individual communist states, especially the Soviet Union, Germany and Czechoslovakia.[58] Social mobility in China has recently been treated in the context of the process of industrialization and the impact of the "cultural revolution."[59] Analysis of the distribution of employed persons among various types of occupations has been carried out by both Western and communist social scientists, and serves as a valuable additional source of data on social stratification in communist systems.[60]

Meanwhile, research on elites is being pressed by American political scientists and has been taken up, if cautiously, by the East Europeans.[61] Aggregative and sample survey data on mass communications in communist societies are accumulating in the West and in Eastern Europe, and researchers at the Center for International Studies, MIT, have been using this material and their own data to develop models of communist communication systems.[62] Studies of elections, with all the obvious difficulties they entail, have been carried out in Yugoslavia and Poland, and provide certain insights into political behaviour when used in conjunction with other types of information.[63] In recent years American scholars have turned to the study of interest groups in communist societies, and Eastern European social scientists have been following suit.[64] Finally, the study in Eastern Europe and the Soviet Union of contemporary social problems and trends—urbanization, raising the standard of living, aiding lesser developed regions, to cite a few examples—is growing both in scope and scholarly value.[65]

The appearance of this material signals something of a revolution in the study of communist societies by persons both inside and outside the communist orbit. The fact that these empirical studies do not always live up to the exacting standards required of comparative work is nevertheless apparent. Their shortcomings resemble those discussed earlier: there is far from complete coverage of all communist states (even in Eastern Europe); the quality of individual studies varies widely; and the emphasis is generally on the study of communist societies, rather than political systems.

A further problem, evident in practically all current empirical work carried on both in Eastern Europe and in the West, is the failure of theory to keep up with practical research and the collection of data. The theoretical difficulties that middle-range research has been encountering are actually two-fold: the need to refine theory in the chosen realm of research (interest groups, elites and the like), and the difficulties that arise in taking into account those aspects of communist political systems which set them apart from other systems types. Theorizing on elites in communist systems, for example, has lagged behind the collection of data in recent years, notwithstanding a number of attempts, by Western and Eastern European scholars, to develop a set of theoretical propositions concerning elite structures in communist and non-communist societies.[66]

In the study of interest groups, on the other hand, the difficulty arises that uncritical application to communist systems of comparative concepts developed for the analysis of Western societies may obscure and confuse differences between the two types of systems. Even when the Western concept is tailored to fit the situation prevailing in communist states, it is hard to escape the implication that the barriers separating Western and communist systems are being levelled, even to the extent that there is no longer any essential difference between the two system types. Thus, in the very process of developing methods for comparative communist analysis, the study of the field is robbed of its distinctiveness.

These problems are by and large recognized by those engaged in empirical research on communist countries, and, with greater sophistication and knowledge, it is to be hoped that a satisfactory balance will be struck between emphasizing what is unique to communist political systems and what they share in common with other types of systems. At the same time, growing awareness of the data now available on communist systems should spur the search for new areas of middle-range research, giving the field more balance and depth.

One such area for future work might be that of modernization. Although the concept does pose difficulties when applied to communist states, there is a great deal that can be done by way of clarifying the character of the modernization process in communist systems. This involves the utilization of existing studies of the modernizing process, both theoretical and data-oriented, and material now becoming available in the communist countries themselves (the recent volume, *Yugoslavia, A Multi-National State*, by Jack Fischer, is a pioneer effort in this area).[67]

Another form of middle-range research, relatively neglected in the past, involves the study of historical systems. This approach is applicable not only to the Stalinist-type systems of Eastern Europe and the Soviet Union, but also to the period of the NEP in Russia. Although not strictly comparable to later developments in other communist countries, the NEP produced an interesting body of statistical information and other forms of empirical data. Some of this material, such as the party census of 1927, has utility in conjunction with comparative work on contemporary communist systems.[68]

A different type of approach utilizing quantitative information involves the analysis of relatively clear-cut types of data which pose interesting theoretical and practical problems concerning communist systems. Thus one might wish to ask why party membership in communist countries usually remains within certain more or less well-defined limits, measured as a percentage of the total populations of communist states. Investigation of this problem would require both analysis in depth, and cross-nationally.[69]

In dealing with middle-range research one must consider not only the type of problem to be investigated, but the units to be chosen for comparison. This problem, although we have reserved it for last, is in many ways the most troublesome in middle-range comparative work with communist countries. Not only do the limitations of the analyst in language skills, area competency and so on act as a restraining factor, but the peculiar problems of cross-national work with communist states often place limits on the types of strategies or techniques which may be employed when utilizing comparative data.

Thus research based on comparisons among the thirteen or fourteen communist states now in existence must take into account the small number of units involved; that in respect to any given problem only a certain percentage of these countries will have the right type of data; and that in a still smaller number of cases will the information be utilizable in comparative form.

These problems are not confined to the comparative study of communist systems, but do apply to the communist states with special force. In the case of such quantitative methods as rank-ordering or factor analysis, the small number of nations involved poses an especially serious problem; such techniques have usually dealt with communist states only within the context of broad, global, samples, and even in this case the results have not always been satisfactory.[70]

Under the circumstances, it may be that in whatever area middle-range research choses to work (elites, modernization, or some aspect of the political process), the best results may be achieved by maintaining a flexible frame of reference. Case studies might be used to generate hypotheses and refine existing concepts, and these could be combined with cross-national comparisons at whatever level—national, regional or local—is most convenient under the circumstances. Rank-ordering or regression techniques, if employed, might experiment with intra-national and cross-national regional comparisons of nation-states. Already a certain amount of success has been achieved using this method in the study of regionalism in China.[71] In recent years, the desirability of developing data banks on regional and local differences has been debated;[72] in Poland, regression analysis has actually been applied in a comparative form in the study of local government.[73]

This is only the bare suggestion of a strategy, and one which at that deals with only a single aspect of the comparative study of communist nations. The immediate need is to stress a balanced approach in which middle-range research, basic theoretical work, and the study of communist values and ideologies would all play an equal role. Karl Deutsch aptly described the challenge that lies ahead when he pointed out (in reference to the comparative field generally) that "there is before us an intellectual need and a desperately difficult task, a task which cannot be accomplished in itself by committees or conferences, but can only be pioneered by individuals and then developed by the criticisms, the discussions, and the cooperation of many scientists over many years. It is necessary to put together . . . three types of theory—the broad general perspective, the hard specific findings, and the middle-range models and techniques so that we will eventually get a choice of broad intellectual systems, encompassing a wide range of phenomena and permitting the recognition of rich and complex patterns."[74]

On balance, there is no reason why the comparative analysis of communist systems cannot follow this path sketched for comparative studies in general. We lack convenient typologies and unifying concepts for communist systems, but we are on sound ground in treating these systems as distinctive and separate from other major types of systems, amenable to model-building and other forms of basic comparative research. Not being bound in any way by an "ideal type" or evolutionary model, we are free to assemble building blocs of data applicable to a wide variety of situations (both past and present) and to encourage the broadest possible utilization of new and existing comparative techniques. If the communist systems continue in their present course of widening diversity and (in most cases) evolutionary change, efforts to gather data and develop theory can be subjected to continuous on-going review and validation.

To do all of this, of course, requires confidence and a desire to work on the frontiers of political science. It also seems important to remind ourselves that comparative analysis cannot be considered as "replacing" existing methods of analysis or traditional theoretical frameworks, but rather as reinforcing them, making them more effective. If we can maintain this attitude, and keep the new field broad and flexible so that it may grow, there is no doubt that it will eventually make a major contribution to the study of communist political systems.

Notes

1. H. Gordon Skilling, "Soviet and Communist Politics: A Comparative Approach," *Journal of Politics*, 22 (May, 1960), 300–13; Robert C. Tucker, "On the Comparative Study of Communism," *World Politics*, 19 (Jan., 1967), 242–57; symposium on comparative politics and communist systems in *Slavic Review*, 26 (March, 1967), 1–28. The problems of comparing China and Soviet Russia were the subject of a meeting sponsored by the American Council of Learned Societies in the spring of 1966. Professor Lucian Pye has outlined the problems of comparative research with communist nations in his address, "Comparative Politics and Communist Studies," delivered to the 62nd Annual Meeting of the American Political Science Association, 1966.

2. Hugh Seton Watson, *The East European Revolution* (1951); Ygael Gluckstein, *Stalin's Satellites in Europe* (1952); Alvin Z. Rubinstein (ed.), *Communist Political Systems* (1966).

3. A. Doak Barnett (ed.), *Communist Strategies in Asia: A Comparative Analysis of Governments and Parties* (1963); Robert A. Scalapino, *The Communist Revolution in Asia* (1965).

4. Joseph LaPalombara (ed.), *Bureaucracy and Political Development* (1963); Harold Lasswell, *World Revolutionary Elites: Studies in Coercive Ideological Movements* (1963); Henry W. Ehrmann, *Interest Groups on Four Continents* (1958); Lucian W. Pye and Sidney Verba, *Political Culture and Political Development* (1965); Sigmund Neumann, *Modern Political Parties* (1956).

5. Zbigniew K. Brzezinski, *The Soviet Bloc: Unity and Conflict* (1961); Richard Lowenthal, *World Communism* (1966); Walter Laqueur and Leopold Labedz (eds.), *Communism and Revolution: the Strategic uses of Political Violence* (1964); H. Gordon Skilling, *Communism National and International* (1964). Although primarily concerned with international politics, note should also be made of the series of monographs issued under the auspices of the Hoover Institute on War, Revolution and Peace, Stanford University, which includes studies on the Soviet Union and the world communist system, the Mongolian People's Republic, the Korean People's Republic, and the Chinese People's Republic.

6. A project on the comparative study of the legal systems of the USSR, China, Poland and Yugoslavia has led to the publication of several monographs: Jerome A. Cohen, "The Criminal Process in the People's Republic of China," *Harvard Law Review*, 79 (1966), 469–74; John N. Hazard, "The Soviet Legal Pattern's Spread Abroad," *University of Illinois Law Forum* (Spring, 1964), 277–97; Aleksander W. Rudzinski, "The New Communist Civil Codes of Czechoslovakia and Poland," *Indiana Law Journal*, 41 (Fall, 1965), 33–68. Among many comparative legal studies dealing with communist systems, mention should also be made of Vladimir Gosovski and Kazimierz Grzybowski (eds.), *Government, Law and Courts in the Soviet Union and Eastern Europe* (1959); Ivo Lapenna, *State and Law: Soviet and Yugoslav Theory* (1964); Istvah Szaszy, *Private International Law in the European People's Democracies* (Budapest, 1964). A pioneering work in this field in Samuel Sharp, *New Constitutions in the Soviet Sphere* (1950).

7. Kurt London (ed.), *Unity and Contradiction* (1962); Walter Laqueur and Leopold Labedz (eds.), *The Future of Communist Society* (1962); Franz Shurmann, "Comparative Politics of Russia and China," paper delivered to the 61st Annual Meeting of the American Political Science Association, 1965.

8. Exceptions have included the work of R. V. Burks, *The Dynamics of Communism in Eastern Europe* (1961) and Gordon Skilling, whose recent volume, *The Governments of Communist East Europe* (1966), is a truly comparative text. A pioneering work in comparisons of the United States and the Soviet Union is Zbigniew Brzezinski and Samuel Huntington, *Political Power USA/USSR* (1964).

9. Roy Pierce, "Liberty and Policy as Variables," *American Political Science Review*, 57 (Sept., 1963), 659.

10. Reference to elite studies will be made in more detail in section III of this article.

11. Systems studies of communist states are discussed below.

12. The literature on typologies relevant to communist states includes Carl J. Friedrich and Zbigniew K. Brzezinski, *Totalitarian Dictatorship and Autocracy* (1956); Gabriel A. Almond, "Comparative Political Systems," *Journal of Politics*, 18 (Aug., 1956), 391–409; Gabriel A. Almond and James S. Coleman (eds.), *The Politics of Developing Areas* (1960); Gabriel A. Almond and G. Bingham Powell Jr., *Comparative Politics: a Developmental Approach* (1966); Robert A. Dahl, *Modern Political Analysis* (1963); Karl Lowenstein, *Political Power and the Governmental Process* (1957); Barrington Moore Jr., "Notes on the Acquiring of Political Power," *World Politics*, 8 (Oct., 1955), 1–20; Robert C. Tucker, "Toward a Comparative Politics of Movement Regimes," *American Political Science Review*, 55 (June, 1961), 281–93; David Apter, *The Politics of Modernization* (1965), 22–25.

13. *Political Power USA/USSR*. Edward Shils has called the Soviet Union a "tyrannically deformed manifestations of potentialities which are inherent in the process of modernization." Frederick C. Barghoorn quoting Shils in Lucian Pye and Sidney Verba, *loc. cit.*

14. The problem is discussed by Alfred G. Meyer, "The Comparative Study of Communist Political Systems," *Slavic Review*, 20 (March, 1967), 5–6.

15. Arthur S. Banks and Robert B. Textor, *A Cross-Polity Survey* (1963).

16. For examples of this type of work, see Talcott Parsons and Edward A. Shils, *Toward a General Theory of Action* (1951), p. 185; Barrington Moore, *Terror and Progress* (1954), p. 185; Herbert Spiro, *World Politics: The Global System* (1966), Ch. 3; Gabriel Almond and James S. Coleman, *op. cit.*, 22–23.

17. *Comparative Politics: a Reader* (1963), pp. 433–39.

18. Robert C. Tucker, "Toward a Comparative Politics of Movement Regimes," *op. cit.*

19. Suggested in the works of Bertram Wolfe, *Six Keys to the Soviet System* (1956); David Dallin, *The Changing World of Soviet Russia* (1956); Leon Trotsky, *The Revolution Betrayed* (1937); and Milovan Djilas, *The New Class* (1957). For a restatement of some of the elements of this approach, see Allan Kassof, "The Administered Society: Totalitarianism Without Terror,' *World Politics*, 16 (July, 1964), 558–75 and Alfred Meyer, *op. cit.*

20. Gabriel Almond and James S. Coleman, *op. cit.*; David Easton, *A Systems Analysis of Political Life* (1965) and *A Framework for Political Analysis* (1965); Frederick C. Barghoorn, *Politics in the USSR* (1966).

21. One may take as an example the suggestion by Gabriel Almond that input activities embracing "interest articulation" are universal functional requisites of political systems, when in communist states they are normally largely dysfunctional in effect. David Easton has encountered similar problems in his model which stresses the entrance of "demands" into the political system, with the implication that without such inputs there could be no political system. In Easton's analysis the autonomy of decision-making in totalitarian states is taken into account by speaking of "within puts," but the difference between them and normal "inputs" into the system is never fully clarified. Other elements of Easton's approach put more stress on elite analysis, and as a consequence, have greater applicability to totalitarian states. For further criticisms of the structural-functional approach, see Robert E. Dowse, "A Functionalist's Logic," *World Politics*, 18 (July, 1966), 607–22.

22. Clyde Kluckhohn, Alex Inkeles, and Raymond A. Bauer, "Strategic Psychological and Sociological Strengths and Vulnerabilities of the Soviet Social System," Russian Research Center, Harvard University (Oct., 1954); Barrington Moore, Jr., "The Strengths and Weaknesses of the Soviet System," Air University, Human Resources Research Institute, Maxwell Air Force Base (Dec., 1952); Irwin Sanders,

"Research for Evaluation of Social Systems Analysis," Air Force Personnel and Training Research Center, Randolph Air Force Base, Texas (Sept. 15, 1957); Raymond Bauer *et al.*, *How the Soviet System Works* (1956); William A. Lybrand, "Outline of an Analytic Approach to Predicting Societal System Recovery from Air Attack," AFOSR Technical Note 60-1416, ASTIA AD No. 255770 (March, 1961).

23. The possibilities of developing comparative models based on a dynamic analysis of performance of political systems is dealth with briefly by A. M. Halpern, "Contemporary China as a Problem for Political Science," *World Politics*, 15 (April, 1963), 361–75, and is stressed by Gabriel Almond and G. Bingham Powell, Jr., *op. cit.*, Ch. 8.

24. See Zbigniew Brzezinski and Samuel Huntington, *op. cit.*, 124, where the Soviet political system is described using cybernetic terminology. Also relevant are Ludwig von Bertalanffy, "General Systems Theory," *General Systems Yearbook* (1956), Vol. I, 1–100.

25. See his remarks in Richard L. Merritt and Stein Rokkan, *Comparing Nations: the Use of Quantitative Data in Cross National Research* (1966), p. 41.

26. Amrit Lal, "China's Perennial Census Problem," *Eastern World*, 18 (May, 1964), 10–12. For a useful summary of statistical information available on China, still accurate in most particulars, see Lawrence Kraider and John Aird, "Sources of Demographic Data on Mainland China," *American Sociological Review*, 24 (Oct., 1959), 623.

27. John Philip Emerson, *Non-Agricultural Employment in Mainland China, 1949–1958* (1965).

28. At the time of writing, still in the process of translation. See also Central Intelligence Agency, *Average Annual Money Earnings of Workers and Staff in Communist China, 1949–1950* (Oct. 1960). The most recent source of data on mainland China is U.S. Congress, Joint Economic Committee, *An Economic Profile of Mainland China*, (1967), Vol. II.

29. For data on Cuba, see The Cuban Economic Research Project, *A Study on Cuba* (1965). Sources for North Vietnamese statistical materials are cited in Lê Chaû, *Le Viet Nam Socialiste: Une Économie de Transition* (1966).

30. See G. G. S. Murphy, *Soviet Mongolia* (1966).

31. Some representative materials, ranging from statistical summaries to analyses in depth in which aggregative data have been employed in Yugoslavia, include: Savezni zavod za statistiku, "Narodni odbori srezovi i opština: sastav odbora i izborni rezultati" [Peoples Councils of the Districts and localities: composition of committees and elections results]," No. 134 (1959); Zavod SR Slovenije za statistiku, "Prikazi in študije," No. 6 (1964), which deals with the membership of the workers councils in Yugoslavia; Savezni zavod za statistiku, "Rezultati popisa službenika i-x-1956 [Results of the Census of Functionaries i-x-1956]" (1957); Dušan Čalić, *Industrializacija Jugoslavije* [The Industrialization of Yugoslavia] (1963); Petar J. Marković, *Strukturne promene na selu kao resultat ekonomskog razvitka period 1900–1960* [Structural Changes in the Village as a Result of the Economic Development of the Period 1900–1960] (1963). A guide to decision-making by the federal government is provided by a description of the decisions made by the federal government in Savezna Narodna Skupština, *Izveštaj Savezno Izvršnog Veča* [Report of the Federal Executive Committee], annual report. Incomes are reported by branch of industry and percentage of employees receiving certain levels of income in the Statistical Annual (*Statistički godišnjak*); more methodical and revealing data on income differentials of various segments of society have been gathered by the Slovenian statistical bureau and published in its bulletin, *Statistično Gradivo*. Studies employing sample survey data and analyses of elections will be cited below.

32. A number of the more important Polish works using aggregative data will be cited in the discussion to follow. Of general interest are Andrzej Karpiński *et al.*, *Problemy rozwoju gospodarczego Polski Ludowej 1944–1964* [Problems of the Econ-

omic Development of People's Poland, 1944–1964] (1965); Adam Sarapaty (ed.), *Przemiany spoleczne w Polsce Ludowej* [Social Change in People's Poland] (1965); Ryszard Turski, *Dynamika przemian spolecznych w Polsce* [The Dynamics of Social Change in Poland] (1961); Edward Rossett, *Oblicze demograficzne Polski Ludowej* [The Demographic Face of People's Poland] (1965). Studies issued by the Hungarian Statistical Office, Központi Statistikai O Hivatal, have dealt with a wide variety of social and demographic problems; a number are cited below.

33. Basic data on economic and social activities in the USSR appear in the statistical annual *Narodnoe khozíaistvo SSSR* [The National Economy of the USSR] which resumed publication in 1957 after a lapse of almost two decades. Aggregative data on education, occupational structure, national composition of the population of the USSR and other subjects may be found in the statistical journal *Vestnik Statistiki* and in the annual *SSSR v tsifrakh* (also published for a number of the Union Republics). For a recent study on the Soviet Union giving a compilation of demographic data from Soviet sources, U.S. Congress, Joint Economic Committee, *New Directions in the Soviet Economy*, Part III, *The Human Resources* (1966). All of the remaining East European governments have published statistical yearbooks; all have held one or more censuses in the post-war period.

34. An example of the Soviet approach toward sharing comparative data was provided by the 1958 Prague conference of social scientists sponsored by UNESCO; the American participant remarked that the Soviet social scientists "never quite admit that studies of social and economic conditions, to be truly comparable, must include free and open use of data from the Eastern (Communist) countries, as well as from others. In some deep sense, they regard their case as different": Everett C. Hughes, *Comparative Studies in Society and History*, 1 (March, 1959), 290. For Soviet publications giving comparative statistics on the bloc, *Ekonomika Sotsialisticheskikh stran v tsifrakh* [The Economies of Socialist Countries in Figures] (1965); Ia. Ia. Kotkovskiĭ *et al.*, *Sopostavlenie urovneĭ ekonomicheskogo razvitíia sotsialisticheskikh stran* [Determining the Level of Economic Development of Socialist Countries] (1965). For comparison of the Soviet and American economies with a clear propagandistic intent, "Nauchnaía konferentsíia po voprosam metodologii spostavleníia osnovnykh ekonomicheskikh pokazateleĭ SSSR i S Sh A [Scientific Conference on the Question of Methodology in Establishing the Basic Economic Indicators of the USSR and the USA], *Vestnik Statistika*, No. 1 (1963), 29–73.

35. Publications of Comecon include *Metodologicheskie polozheníia pokazateleĭ statistiki truda stran chlenov SEV* [Methodological Positions Concerning Statistical Indicators of Labor in Member Countries of COMECON] (1963); *Metodologicheskie polozheníia pokazatelei statistiki naseleníia stran chlenov SEV* [Methodological Positions Concerning the Population of the Countries of COMECON]. In another area, see M. Mód (ed.), *The Standard of Living: Some Problems of Analysis and International Comparison* (Budapest, 1962).

36. See the volumes issued under the Research Project on National Income in East Central Europe, Columbia University, *Czechoslovak National Income and Product in 1947–48 and 1955–56* (1962); *Hungarian National Income and Product in 1955* (1963); *Polish National Income and Product, 1954, 1955, and 1956* (1965). Much of this information is summarized by Maurice Ernst, "Postwar Economic Growth in Eastern Europe (A Comparison with Western Europe)," *New Directions in the Soviet Economy, op. cit.*, Part IV, 875–916.

37. *The Civic Culture* (1963).

38. The earliest and most successful of these studies was the Harvard project on the Soviet Union. Its results have been given in Alex Inkeles and Raymond A. Bauer, *The Soviet Citizen: Daily Life in a Totalitarian Society* (1959). Studies on Eastern Europe have included the interviewing of refugees by Siegfried Kracauer, *Satellite Mentality: Political Attitudes and Propaganda Susceptibilities of Non-communists in Hungary, Poland and Czechoslovakia* (1956); the survey of between 500 and 600 refugees from the Hungarian revolution by the Special Operations Research Office

in early 1957, the results of which can be found in Special Operations Research Office, *Socio-Psychological Information on Hungarian Refugees*, 3 vols. (no date); the work on Hungarian Freedom Fighters carried out under the auspices of Columbia University, the results of which have not been published but are on file in the Columbia University Library. Information from this project was utilized by Paul Zinner, *Revolution in Hungary* (1962). Under the auspices of the Free Europe Press, Henry Gleitman and Joseph J. Greenbaum carried out interviews of Hungarian refugees from the 1956 revolution. The results of this study were presented in several articles by the two organizers of the project: "Hungarian Socio-Political Attitudes and Revolutionary Action," *Public Opinion Quarterly*, 24 (Spring, 1960), 64–76; "Attitudes and Personality Patterns of Hungarian Refugees," *Public Opinion Quarterly*, 25 (Fall, 1961), 35–65. A fourth study of Hungarian refugees was carried out by International Research Associates, *Personal Interviews with 1,000 Hungarian Refugees in Austria* (1957).

39. Interviewing of persons from the Soviet Union has been going on under the auspices of the Center for International Studies, Massachusetts Institute of Technology, in connection with the study of communications in communist countries.

For more on the study of communications, see Part III below.

40. In the past six years, Radio Free Europe has interviewed over 20,000 East European citizens visiting in the West, preparing reports on such issues as "The Psycho-Political Climate in Bulgaria" (Dec., 1960); "The Attitude of Young Czechoslovaks Regarding War and Peace" (Feb., 1966); and "Flight Motivation of Refugees from Four Soviet Bloc Countries" (Sept., 1963). A summary of the results of these studies can be found in "What Do East Europeans Think," *East Europe*, 15 (March, 1960), 26–28.

41. John Armstrong, "Sources of Administrative Behavior: Some Soviet and Western European Comparisons," *American Political Science Review*, 59 (Sept., 1965), 643–55.

42. In the Chinese case, the problems facing sample survey work with displaced persons were evaluated as "appalling" at a conference held on the subject in 1962 under the sponsorship of the American Council of Learned Societies. Prior to that time two major studies had been organized. One was under the auspices of the UN and dealt with the problems of refugees, but contained data of interest for the political scientist: Dr. Edvard Hambro, *The Problems of Chinese Refugees in Hong Kong* (1955). The other early study was carried out under the direction of the Special Operations Resarch Office and involved the interviewing of approximately 2,000 Mainland Chinese on various aspects of communications in communist China, especially word of mouth communications. Unclassified results of this study are available through the organizer of the research, Barton Whaley: "Propin China: A Study of Word of Mouth Communications in Communist China." In 1964–65, Paul Hiniker, working under the auspices of the Center for International Studies, Massachusetts Institute of Technology, interviewed over 400 Chinese refugees on the effects of mass communications: "The Effect of Mass Communication in Communist China" (unpublished Ph.D. thesis, MIT June, 1966).

43. For a recent example of this type of work, see A. Doak Barnett, *Cadres, Bureaucracy and Political Power in Communist China* (1967).

44. Polish interest in public opinion sampling dates from 1956; since that time the most active group in the field has been the Public Opinion Research Center (OBOP). The OBOP has worked with a national quota sample of some 3,000 persons and until recently some 25 studies a year were being carried out under its auspices. Despite a reaction against public opinion polling by the Communist leadership in Poland, work of this kind continues. Descriptions of Polish sample survey work include Władyslaw Markiewicz, "Sociological Research in People's Poland," in Stanisław Ehrlich (ed.), *Social and Political Transformations in Poland* (1964), pp. 221–254; Andrzej Siciński, "Public Opinion Surveys in Poland," *International Social Science Journal*, 15 (1963), 91–109; Emilia Wilder, "Sociology in

Eastern Europe: Poland," *Problems of Communism*, 14 (Jan.–Feb., 1965), 62–66. Among the many Polish studies, the following may be noted as genuine contributions to our knowledge of the political attitudes of groups in Poland: Stefan Nowak, "Środowiskowe determinanty ideologii społeczney studentów Warszawy [Environmental Determinants of Social Ideology of Warsaw Students]," *Studia Socjologiczne* (1962), 143–180; Józef Koszek, "Postawy społeczno-polityczne chłopów," [Social-Political Attitudes of the Peasants], *Studia Socjologiczno Polityczne* (1964), 207–249; Stefan Nowak, "Egalitarian Attitudes of Warsaw Students," *American Sociological Review*, 25 (April, 1960), 219–231. Yugoslav sample survey work has been carried out chiefly through the Institute for Social Sciences, Belgrade, and the Institute for Sociology and Philosophy at the University of Ljubljana. Studies have included testing of a national sample for opinions on the Yugoslav constitution, the party congress, and the national question; sampling of local functionaries to gain information on decision-making in local government and in the workers council; studies of mass communications; and polling of the attitudes of the younger generation. Important sources for this material include: Stanislaw Skrzypek, "The Political, Cultural and Social Views of Yugoslav Youth," *Public Opinion Quarterly*, 29 (Spring, 1965), 87–106; publications of the Institute for Social Sciences, including the series *Jugoslovensko javno mnenje* [Yugoslav Public Opinion]; *Javno mnenje o prednacrtu novog Ustava* [Public Opinion on the Draft of the New Constitution] (1964); Vojin Hadžistević *et al.*, *Tendencije i praksa neposrednog upravljanja radnika u ekonomskim jedinicama* [Tendencies and Practice in the Direct Administration of the Workers in Economic Units] (1963); Slavko Milosavljevski, *Saveti narodnih odbora: organizacija i funkcionisanje* [Councils of the People's Committees: Organization and Functioning] (1963). Slovenian studies can be found in Inštitut za Sociologijo in Filizofijo pri univerzi v Ljubljani, *Informativni Bilten*, *passim*. Studies on social mobility, modernization and communications are cited below.

45. David McClelland, *The Achieving Society* (1961).

46. The progress of the study is described in International Social Science Council mimeographed report, "International Studies of Values in Politics: Report of the Third International Roundtable, Warsaw, Poland, July 16–26, 1966" (1966).

47. Antonina Kłoskowska, "National Concepts and Attitudes of Children in a Middle Sized City in Polish Western Territories," *The Polish Sociological Journal*, No. 1–2 (June–Dec., 1961), 43–56 (in which the author applied the questionnaires of O. Klineburg and W. E. Lambert, given in *International Social Science Journal*, 11 (1959), 221–238, on national attitudes to Polish children); Józef Kádzielski, "*Miedzypokoleniowa ruchliwość społeczne mieszkańców Łodzi* [Inter-Generational Mobility of Lodz Inhabitants]," *Przegląd Socjologiczny*, 17 (1963), 114–218, in which aggregate data on mobility in Lodz are compared with similar data for the cities of Indianapolis and Aarhus.

48. The Bulgarians have now set up a "Methodical Research Office" under the Bulgarian State Radio to carry out opinion polls of radio listeners.

Rumania has been calling for greater objectivity in the social sciences, but has been slow to set up any polling organizations. The Hungarians are well-advanced in market research and have carried out time-budget studies, polls on the use of leisure time and of mass media. The Czechs now have established a sociological institute under the Academy of Sciences which is working in this field, and in 1966 an institute for the study of public opinion was formed in Prague. This is in addition to the institute for sociological research in Bratislava, which was the first to carry out sample-survey studies. For some reports on this activity, Ralph K. White, "Social Science Research in the Soviet Bloc," *Public Opinion Quarterly*, 28 (Summer, 1964), 20–26; Edward Taborsky, "Sociology in Eastern Europe: Czechoslovakia," *Problems of Communism*, 14 (Jan.–Feb., 1965), 62–66; Peter C. Ludz, "Sociology in Eastern Europe: East Germany," *ibid.*, 66–67.

49. Boris A. Grushin, V. Chikin, *Ispoved' pokolenii͡a* [Confessions of a Generation] (1962).

50. A useful review of these studies can be found in Elizabeth Ann Weinberg, "Soviet Sociology: 1960–1963," Center for International Studies, MIT, Oct. 11, 1964. For Soviet accounts, Akademiia Nauk SSSR, Institut Filosofii, *Kolichestvennie metodi v sotsiologii* [Quantitative Methods in Sociology] (1966). For opposition to the use of quantitative methods in studying Soviet society, see L. A. Baĭdel'dinov, *Statistika v sotsiologicheskom issledovanii* [Statistics in Sociological Research] (1965).

51. H. Lethbridge, "Classes in Class," *The Far Eastern Economic Review* (Aug. 8, 1963), 333–334; Maurice Freedman, "Sociology in China: A Brief Survey," *British Journal of Sociology*, 13 (June, 1962), 173.

52. Carl Beck, on the basis of his experience with East European elites, has remarked that "Communist statistics on the social composition of the party are unreliable, not comparable, and unavailable for certain periods of time": "Bureaucracy and Political Development in Eastern Europe," in LaPalombara, *op. cit.*, 292.

53. For example, Czechoslovakia did not release data on the party's composition until recently. Although most of this information must be gained from scattered reports of party congresses and plenums, compilations of data are sometimes made available by the communist parties. An excellent example of this type of publication is the valuable volume of the Uzbekistan party, *Kommunisticheskaiā Partiia Uzbekistana v tsifrakh: Sbornik statisticheskikh materialov 1924–1964 gody* [The Communist Party of Uzbekistan in Figures: Collection of Statistical Materials 1924–1964] (Tashkent, 1964). The Soviet party census of 1927 is discussed below.

54. John W. Lewis, "The Study of Chinese Political Culture," *World Politics*, 18 (1966), 503–524.

55. See the discussion of elites that follows.

56. In locating empirical studies originating in communist countries, the following bibliographies are useful: *International Bibliography of the Social Sciences*, series on political science and sociology; U.S. Department of Commerce, Bureau of Census, *Bibliography of Social Science Periodicals and Monograph Series: Foreign Social Science Bibliographies Series* (Poland, Czechoslovakia, North Korea, China, Yugoslavia, and the USSR); Jerzy J. Wiatr, "Political Sociology in Eastern Europe: A Trend Report and a Bibliography," *Current Sociology*, 13 (1965). For recent Soviet works in the Social Sciences: Murray Feshbach, "A Selected Bibliography of Recent Soviet Monographs," Joint Economic Committee, Congress of the United States, *op. cit.*, Part IV, 977–1026. A guide to early empirical work in Yugoslavia is found in the mimeographed report of the Institute for Social Sciences, Belgrade, *Bibliografska anotacija dela empirijskog karaktera iz oblasti drustvenih nauka* [Annotated Bibliography of Materials of an Empirical Character in the Social Sciences] (1964). For East Germany, Peter C. Ludz (ed.), "Studien und Materialen zur Soziologie der DDR," *Kölner Zeitschrift für Soziologie und Sozial-psychologie* (1964), 327–418. Emilia Wilder, *op. cit.*, refers to a bibliographic survey of Polish materials listing 62 books and 871 dissertations in the field of sociology for the period 1958–1961, in *Trybuna Ludu*, April, 29, 1964. For China, see Peter Berton and Eugene Wu, *Contemporary China: A Research Guide* (1967); Hungarian materials listed in Központi Statisztikai Hivatal, Könyvtara, *Magyar Közgazdasági és Statisztikai Irodalom: Bibliografia* ... [Hungarian Bibliography of Economics and Statistics] (1963). For Bulgarian works, L. Dzherova and H. Toteva, *Bibliografiā NA Bulgarskata statisticheskaiā literatura, 1878–1960* [Bibliography of Bulgarian Statistical Literature, 1878–1960] (1961); Czech studies are reported in Karel Kozelka and Čeněk Zatloukal, "Sociologie: Přehled ćeské a slovenské výběr ze zahraničkní literatury [Sociology: A Survey of Czech and Slovak and a selection of Foreign Literature]," *Přehled Literatury*, No. 3 (1965). A partial guide to the NEP period in Russia is provided by *Katalog knig po obshchestvennim Voprosam* [Catalogue of Books on Social Questions] (Moscow, 1926) and *Sistematicheskiĭ ukazatel' sotsial'no-ekonomicheskoĭ literaturi izdannoĭ Gosizdatom za vremiā s 1919 do 1924 gg.* [Systematic Index to Social-Economic Literature Published by Gosizdat from 1919 to 1924] (Moscow, 1924).

57. Outstanding for its concern with empirical analysis of social stratification in Poland has been the series "Z badan klasy robotniczej i inteligencji" [Research on the Working Class and Intelligentsia] edited by Jan Szczepanski, which now runs to 20 volumes. A major contribution to the theoretical literature has been made by Stanslaw Ossowski, *Class Structure in the Social Consciousness* (1963). Other significant Polish works include B. Gateski (ed.), *Społeczno-Ekonomiczna Strukture Wsi* [Social Economic Structure of the Peasantry] (1961); Adam Sarapaty (ed.), *Socjologia Zawodów* [Sociology of Occupations] (1965); ———, *Studia nad uwarstwieniem i ruchliwością społeczną w Polsce* [A Study of Stratification and Social Mobility in Poland] (1965); Antoni Rajkiewicz, *Zatrudnienie w Polsce Ludowej w latach 1950–1970: Dynamika i struktura* [Employment in People's Poland in the Years 1950–1970: Dynamics and Structure] (1965).

58. Among many works, the following may be cited as representative and providing a wide variety of data on social stratification in Eastern Europe and the USSR: Karl Lungwitz, *Über die Klassen Struktur in der Deutschen Demokratischen Republik: eine Sozial-ökonomisch-statistische Untersuchung* (Berlin, 1962); Akademiiā Nauk SSSR, Institut Istorii, *Izmeneniiā v chislennosti i sostave sovetskogo rabochego klassa: Sbornik statei* [Changes in the Number and Composition of the Soviet Working Class: Collection of Articles] (1961); A. Bogarskiĭ, "O tak nazyvaemoĭ 'sotsial'noi mobilnosti'," [On So-Called Social Mobility] *Voprosy Filosofii* (1958), pp. 64–73; Alex Inkeles, "Social Stratification and Mobility in the Soviet Union, 1940–1950," *American Sociological Review*, 15 (1950), 465–473; Janina Markiewicz-Lagneau, "Les Problèmes de Mobilité Sociale en U.R.S.S.," *Cahiers du Monde Russe et Soviétique*, 7 (April–June, 1966), 161–188; *Sčítání lidu, domů a bytů v Československé Socialistické Republice k 1 březnu 1961, Díl. II: Sociální, ekonomická a profesionální skladba obyvatelstva* [Census of Population, Housing and Flats in the Czechoslovak Socialist Republic of 1 March, 1961, Part II: Social, Economic and Professional Composition of the Population]; Daniel Kubat, "Social Mobility in Czechoslovakia," *American Sociological Review*, 28 (1963), 203–212; Központi Statisztikai Hivatal, *Társadalmi Rétegződés Magyarországon (15,000 Háztartás 1963)* [The Social Stratification of Hungary (15,000 Households)] (1966); Republica Populară Romînă, Direcţia Centrală de Statistică, *Recensămîntul Populatiei Din 21 Februarie 1956: Structura Social-Economică A Populaţiei. . . .* [Population Census of 21 February 1956: Social-Economic Structure of the Population] (1960); Miroslav Pecujlić, *Promene u socijalnoj strukturi Jugoslavije* [Changes in the Social Structure of Yugoslavia] (1963), Miloš Ilić *et al.*, *Socijalna struktura i pokretlivost radničke klase Jugoslavije* [Social Structure and Mobility of the Working Class in Yugoslavia] (1963); Marko Markov, *Kam vprosa za klasovite izmenenja NRB* [Problems of Class Changes in the BPR (Bulgarian Peoples Republic)] Sofia, 1960; Pavel Machonin, "Structure Sociale de la Tchechoslovaquie Contemporaine" *Recherches Internationales à la Lumière du Marxisme* (May–June, 1966), 41–58; Petru Dimitriu, "Elemente der Einheit und der Differenzierung in der Klassenstruktur der Ostblockstaaten," *Ost Europa*, 12 (1962), 403–420; R. Lukić and Ljubomir Marković, *Klasni Sastav u socijalističkim zemljama* [The Class Structure in Socialist States] (1960).

59. John W. Lewis, "Political Aspects of Mobility in China's Urban Development," *American Political Science Review*, 60 (Dec., 1966), 899–912.

60. John Philip Emerson, *op. cit.*; Murray S. Weitzman and Andrew Elias, *The Magnitude and Distribution of Civilian Employment in the USSR, 1928–1959* (April, 1961); Gertrude Schroder, "Industrial Wage Differentials in the USSR," *Soviet Studies*, 17 (Jan., 1966), 303–317; J. Pacuraru, "Planned Development and Labour Force Structure in Rumania, 1950–1965," *International Labor Review*, (Dec., 1966), 535–549; János Timár, *Planning the Labour Force in Hungary* (1966); Werner Bosch, *Die Sozialstruktur in West und Mitteldeutschland* (Bonn, 1958); T. Frejka, "Dlouhodobý vývoj odvětvové struktury společenské pracovní síly" [Long-Range Evolution of the Branch Structure of the Society's Working Force]

Politiká Ekonomie, (Aug., 1966), 661–673; Minko Minkov, *Naselenieto i rabotnata sila v Bulgariîa* [Population and the Working Force in Bulgaria] (Sofia, 1966). Polish and Yugoslav works have been cited earlier in connection with social stratification and availability of aggregative data.

61. John A. Armstrong, "Party Bifurcation and Elite Interests," *Soviet Studies*, 17 (April, 1966), 417–30; Grey Hodnett, "The Obkom First Secretaries," *Slavic Review*, 24 (Dec., 1965), 636–52; Zygmunt Bauman, "Economic Growth, Social Structure, Elite Formation: The Case of Poland," *International Social Science Journal* 16 (1964), 203–16; Jeremy R. Azrael, *Managerial Power and Soviet Politics* (1966); John A. Armstrong, *The Soviet Bureaucratic Elite: A Case Study of the Ukranian Apparatus* (1959); Daniel Kubat, "Patterns of Leadership in a Communist State; Czechoslovakia 1946–1958," *Journal of Central European Affairs*, 21 (Oct., 1961), 305–318; K. Valentin Müller, *Die Manager in der Sowjetzone: Eine Empirische Untersuchung zur Soziologie der Wirtschaftlichen und Militärischen Führungsschicht in Mitteldeutschland* (1962); Charles C. Moskos Jr., "From Monarchy to Communism: The Social Transformation of the Albanian Elite," in Herbert R. Barrington *et al., Social Change in Developing Areas* (1965), pp. 205–21; R. C. Angell *et al.,* "Social Values and Foreign Policy Attitudes of Soviet and American Elites," *Journal of Conflict Resolution*, 8 (Dec., 1964), 330–491; Frederick C. Tiewes, *Provincial Party Personnel in Mainland China* 1956–1966 (Columbia University, East Asian Institute, 1967); John W. Lewis, *Leadership in Communist China* (1963); Zygmunt Bauman, "Struktura władzy społeczności lokalnej: Konceptualizacja badań [Pattern of Power in a Local Community: Conceptualization of Research]," *Studia Socjologiczno-Polityczne*, No. 12 (1962), 7–30; J. Jerovšek, "Neformalne strukture odlučanje na nivoj opčine [Informal Structure of Decision Making at the Level of the opstina]," *Sodobnost* (Ljubljana), No. 12, 1964, 1183–94; Radošin Rajović, *Proces stvaranja opštinskih pravnih propsia* [The Process of Creating Opstina Ordinances] (1962). Among on-going research projects whose results were not available for this article, special note should be taken of the study of East European elites using computer techniques at the University of Pittsburgh. Some results are included in Carl Beck, "Bureaucratic Conservatism and Innovation in Eastern Europe," paper delivered to the 1966 Annual Meeting of the American Political Science Association.

62. A sizable literature on communications and propaganda in communist countries now exists. Some studies of relevance for comparative work using empirical data, or relying on sample survey methods, include Richard R. Fagen, "Mass Media Growth: A Comparison of Communist and Other Countries," *Journalism Quarterly*, 41 (Autumn, 1964), 563–67 and 572; Alex Inkeles, *Public Opinion in Soviet Russia* (1958); Raymond Bauer and David B. Gleicher, "Word of Mouth Communication in the Soviet Union" (Maxwell Air Force Base, Human Resources Institute, 1953); Special Operations Research Office, "Propin China: A Study of Word of Mouth Communications in Communist China," *op. cit.*; Paul Hiniker, "The Effects of Mass Communication in Communist China," *op. cit.* Some of the materials produced by the Center of International Studies, MIT, Research Program on Problems of International Communication and Security include Alan P. I. Liu, "Growth and Modernizing Function of Rural Radio in Communist China," *Journalism Quarterly*, 41 (Autumn, 1964), 573–577; ———, "The Use of Traditional Media for Modernization in Communist China," Center for International Studies, MIT (Oct., 1965); F. Gayle Durham, "Radio and Television in the Soviet Union," Center for International Studies, MIT (June, 1965). For Polish materials, see Andrzej Sicinski, "Surveys of Mass Communication of the Public Opinion Research Center," *Polish Sociological Journal*, No. 1–2 (June–Dec., 1961), 97–101. The best work on communications in Yugoslavia has been carried out by the Institute for Sociology and Philosophy at the University of Ljubljana; the results can be found in the bulletin of the institute, Institut z sociologijo, *Informativni Bilten*. See also Institut društvenih nauka, *Sredstva masovnog komuniciranja u Jugoslaviji* [Media of

Mass Communication in Yugoslavia] (1966); and Samuel L. Popkin, "A Model of a Communication System," *The American Behavioral Scientist*, 8 (May, 1965), 8–11.

63. See Austin Ranney (ed.), *Essays on the Behavioral Study of Politics* (1962), 235–51; J. Wiatr, "Niektóre zagadnienia opinii publicznej w świetle wyborów 1957 i 1958 [Several Problems of Public Opinion in the Light of the Elections of 1957 and 1958]," *Studia Socjologiczno Polityczne*, No. 4 (1959); Z. A. Pełczyński and D. E. Butler (ed.), *Elections Abroad* (1969), 119–66; Stanislaw Bereza, "Wybory do Dzielnicowej Rady Narodowej Warszawa-Ochota w roku 1958" [Elections to the Peoples Council of Warsaw-Ochota During 1958], *Studia Socjologiczno Polityczne*, No. 2 (1959), 161–164. These studies have analyzed class and regional participation in Polish elections according to the number of registered voters that participate in elections, and the percentage voting for the front. In addition, the process of "negative selection" in Polish elections, by which it is possible to cross names off the single slate of candidates and thus change the order in which persons are elected from that given on the official list, has been used to determine the popularity of various types of persons as candidates for office. Perhaps the best summary of the economic and social influences on voting detected by these methods, cast in the form of an explicit comparison with assumptions concerning electoral behavior in the West, can be seen in Jerzy J. Wiatr, "Economic and Social Factors of Electoral Behavior," *The Polish Sociological Journal*, No. 3–4 (Jan.–June, 1962), 65–75. In communist countries the presence of two candidates is practically unknown, but when Yugoslavia briefly experimented with such a system in 1953, issues and attitudes began to emerge among the electorate. See Thomas F. Hammond, "Yugoslav Elections: Democracy in Small Doses," *Political Science Quarterly*, 70 (March, 1955), 57–74. For the 1965 elections, Institut društvenih nauka, *Skupštinski izbori 1965* [Parliamentary Elections 1965] (1966).

64. H. Gordon Skilling, "Interest Groups and Communist Politics," *World Politics*, 18 (April, 1966), 435–451; Henry W. Morton (ed.), *Soviet Policy Making: Studies of Communism in Transition* (1966). Włodzimierz Wesełowski, "Class Domination and the Power of Interest Groups," *The Polish Sociological Journal*, No. 3–4 (Jan.–June, 1962), 53–64; Jovan Djordjević, "Interest Groups and the Political System of Yugoslavia," in Henry W. Ehrmann, *Interest Groups on Four Continents* (1958), pp. 197–228; Michael Lakatos, "K niektorým problémom štruktury našej politickej sústavy [On some Problems of the Structure of Our Political System]," *Pravni Obzor*, 1 (1965), 26–36, cited by H. Gordon Skilling, *op. cit.*; T. H. Kuliev, *Problema interesov v Sotsialisticheskom obshchestve* [Problems of Interest in Socialist Society] (1967).

65. For Polish works in this field, see earlier references on aggregative data. Also representative of this type of analysis are Dolfe Vogelnik, *Urbanizacija kao odraz privrednog razvoja FNRJ* [Urbanization as an Expression of the Economic Development of Yugoslavia] (1961); László Lengyel, "Vélemények és Tények as Életszinvonalról [Opinions and Facts About the Living Standard]," *Statisztikai Szemle*, No. 2 (Feb., 1966), 139–57 and No. 3 (March, 1966), 227–244; Branko Kubović, *Regionalno aspekt privrednog razvitka Jugoslavije* [Regional Aspects of Economic Development in Yugoslavia] (1961); M. V. Bakhrakh, "Issledovanie urovinīā ekonomicheskogo ravzitīā raĭona (na primere Moldavskoĭ SSR) [Investigation of the Level of Economic Development of Regions (Using the Example of the Moldavian SSR)]" in Akademiīā Nauk SSSR, *Voprosi Metodiki Issledovaniīā Razmeshcheniīā Proizvodstva* [Questions of Method in Research on the Location of Production] (1965), 26–46; N. M. Rimashevskaīā, *Ekonomicheskii analiz dohodov rabochikh i Sluzhashchikh* [Economic Analysis of the Incomes of Workers and Functionaries] (1965); Stanislaw Ehrlich (ed.), *Social and Political Transformations in Poland* (1964). Western sources on modernization and the standard of living are cited below.

66. Ossowski, *op. cit.*; Suzanne Keller, *Beyond the Ruling Class* (1963); Carl Beck *et al.*, *A Survey of Elite Studies* (Special Operations Research Office Memo 65-3, March, 1965); Raymond Aron, "Social Structure and the Ruling Class," *British*

Journal of Sociology, 1 (March, 1950), 1–16 and 126–43; ———, *La Lutte de Classes* (1964).

67. There are a number of excellent studies in which data for the global analysis of modernization are gathered and analyzed, using information from communist countries as well as non-communist, but the results are not given in a form which can be used for the comparative analysis of communist systems. See Leo F. Schnore, "The Statistical Measurement of Urbanization and Economic Development," *Land Economics*, 37 (Aug., 1961), 229–45; Norton Ginsburg, *Atlas of Economic Development* (1961). Some interesting insights into the pattern of industrialization in communist nations can be gained from Brian J. L. Berry, "An Inductive Approach to the Regionalization of Economic Development" in Norton Ginsburg (ed.), *Geography and Economic Development*, University of Chicago Department of Geography Research Paper No. 62 (1960), 97. Data on relative levels of consumption prior to World War II—and the problems that arise in making such a comparative analysis— are given in M. K. Bennett, "International Disparities in Consumption Levels," *The American Economic Review*, 11 (Sept., 1951), 632–49. Important for comparative analysis of the standard of living in the post-war period are Maria-Elisabeth Ruban, *Die Entwicklung des Lebensstandards in der Sowjetunion* (1965); Central Intelligence Agency, *A Comparison of Consumption in the USSR and the United States* (1964); Václav Holešovský, "Personal Consumption in Czechoslovakia, Hungary and Poland, 1950–1960, A Comparison," *Slavic Review*, 24 (Dec., 1965), 622–35; Janet G. Chapman, *Real Wages in the Soviet Union since 1928* (1963). For other quantitative approaches to measuring development, see Charles K. Wilbur, "A Non-monetary Index of Economic Development," *Soviet Studies*, 17 (April, 1966), 408–416, and Jack Fischer, *op. cit.*

68. Aggregative data appeared in this period on a wide variety of subjects important for cross-national and comparative analysis, including social stratification (class differences and occupational breakdowns), data on communications (mail turnover, number of radio stations, and the like), and economic and demographic data. From this period date some of the few statistics ever published on the size of the party in administrative organs, trade unions, and other important institutions in Soviet society. Statistics on the number of arrests and related information on crime were also published in this period, and data can even be found from the early 1920's on the size of the security organs. Valuable data are also available from the early 1920's on the social composition of the party and local government organs at the local level. Two censuses (in addition to a number of industrial censuses and the party census of 1927) were carried out in 1920 (incomplete) and 1926. The main sources for these data are *Trudy Tsentral'nogo Statisticheskogo Upravleniia* [Works of the Central Statistical Administration] in which the results of the censuses are included; *Statisticheskii ezhegodnik* [Statistical Annual]; *Narodnoe khoziaistvo SSSR* [National Economy of the USSR], published through 1932; Statisticheskii otdel Tsentral'nogo Komiteta Vsesoiuznoi Kommunisticheskoi Partii (Bol'shevikov), *Vsesoiuznaia partiinaia perepis' 1927 goda* [All-Union Party Census for 1927] 8 vols. (1927); Vsesoiuznaia Kommunisticheskaia Partiia (Bol'shevikóv) Tsentral'nyi komitet BKP (b) Organizatsionno-instruktorskii Otdel, *Sostav VKP (b) v tsifrakh* [Composition of the All-Union Communist Party in Figures], 11 Vols.

69. For data on the membership of communist parties, U.S. Department of State, Bureau of Intelligence and Research, *World Strength of Communist Party Organizations*. Compilations of prominent officials in communist countries are available in the State Department volumes, *Intelligence Research Aid*.

70. Philip Cutright, "National Political Development: Measurement and Analysis," *American Sociological Review*, 28 (April, 1963), 253–64; Ivo K. Feierabend, "Correlates of Political Stability," paper delivered to the 1963 Annual Meeting of the American Political Science Association; Phillip M. Gregg and Arthur S. Banks "Dimensions of Political Systems: Factor Analysis of a Cross Polity Survey," *American Political Science Review*, 59 (Sept., 1965), 602–14.

71. See the discussion in John W. Lewis, "The Study of Chinese Political Culture," *op. cit.*

72. Stein Rokkan (ed.), *Data Archives for the Social Sciences* (1965), 122–127.

73. Stanislaw Rokita, "Analiza czynnikowa w badaniach regionalnych [Factor Analysis in Regional Research]," *Przegląd Statystyczny* (1966), 245–60.

74. Richard L. Merritt and Stein Rokkan, *op. cit.*, p. 32.

PART 2

Political Elites
in the Soviet Union
and Eastern Europe

As Paul Shoup has pointed out, one of the major areas in which behavioral research is being conducted concerns the recruitment and behavior of political elites and interest groups in the Soviet Union and Eastern Europe. Rita Mae Kelly and Frederic J. Fleron have examined the importance of ideology in the decision-making process and have applied findings of social psychology research on belief systems and motivation to the problem of discerning the relationships between ideology and basic personal attitudes. They argue that an exclusive focus on interest groups exaggerates the determination of an individual's beliefs and values by his group memberships. More important for an understanding of an individual's attitudes, they maintain, are the specific roles he plays in the society. They conclude that an understanding of the impact of formal ideology on decision-making requires the development of a methodology that recognizes the complexities of human motivation.

Milton Lodge focuses on a related topic: the attitudes of various elite groupings in the Soviet Union. He applies content analysis to the official publications of a number of specialized elites in the Soviet Union—party officials, central economic bureaucrats, the military, the literary elite, and the legal profession—in order to discover any differences in attitudes concerning the decision-making process. He concludes that since 1953 there has developed a gradual group awareness among the Soviet elite, one which has included an increased desire for specialist elites, as opposed to the party officials, to participate in decision-making.

Chapters 4 and 5 deal with the question of co-optation into the party leadership in the Soviet Union. Michael Gehlen and Michael McBride focus on the background characteristics of Central Committee members in order to assess the relative importance of various career characteristics for success. Frederic Fleron, however, deals in more detail with the actual use of co-optation as a means of replenishing the ranks of the elite. He also discusses the relative influence that the co-optation process gives to specialist elites in the policy process.

Joel Schwartz and William Keech turn to a different level in order to examine the influence of a broader public on policy formation in the Soviet Union. They analyze in some detail two decisions in the field of education—the 1958 education act that called for a reorganization of the educational system and the debate in the mid-1960s about post-university work assignments. They show that public opinion in both of these cases did influence policy, in particular since there existed disputes among the top decision-makers. In the Soviet Union, they conclude, public debate on a policy tends to assume the form of proposals concerning *means* to implement a policy rather than policies or *goals* themselves.

Carl Beck, Gerard A. Johnson, and J. Thomas McKechnie have examined the composition of the Central Committee of the Bulgarian Communist Party in 1962 in order to discover the differences in career characteristics of new recruits to the Central Committee, holdovers of the past, and those who were dismissed. By means of factor analysis they attempt to specify the various career patterns within the party and conclude that three sets of distinctions are significant—territorial (regional vs. local), staff (membership or non-membership on a commission), and rank (secretary or non-secretary). The new Central Committee was much more strongly representative of the regional secretariat and central commission than was its predecessor. As the authors indicate, this was related to a struggle within the party between Todor Zhivdov, the First Secretary, whose support was primarily in the provincial party organizations and the Central Committee apparatus, and Premier Anton Yugov, supported mainly by the state apparatus. Within the context of this struggle, certain career patterns were advantageous (or detrimental) to advancement in the party hierarchy.

2

Motivation, Methodology, and Communist Ideology

RITA MAE KELLY AND FREDERIC J. FLERON, JR.

Ever since Western scholars began trying to analyze the political behavior of Communist leaders, they have felt compelled to present some answer to the question: In what ways does the official ideological system affect the actions and decisions of these leaders? After fifty years of Communist rule in the Soviet Union, however, there is no one

The authors wish to express their thanks to the following persons for comments and suggestions on earlier drafts of this article: Lou Jean Fleron, Vincent Kelly, Bernard Morris, and Erik P. Hoffmann. Needless to say, none of them should be held responsible for the views and interpretations contained herein. The article, with minor changes, is reprinted with permission from *Soviet Studies*, XXI (1970), 297–313.

Notes to this selection begin on page 75.

53

consistent answer. Confusion and contradiction still reign.[1] In the literature on the subject one finds that the position a scholar takes is very often related to his particular field of specialization. For example, if one has an anthropological or psychoanalytic bent, then one tends to follow the point of view advocated by Dicks and Leites. The ideology fulfills important functions for the maintenance of the leader's ego and, hence, the official ideology is a strong, dominant motivating force, not easily subject to change.[2] Political scientists, although they vary considerably, tend to take a more pragmatic and cynical point of view. Avid Kremlinologists generally discount the official ideology as a major motivating force and concentrate on "who is doing-in whom." To many of them ideology is almost entirely a polemical and political weapon or a useful opiate for the masses.[3] A geopolitical theorist tends to claim that traditional national and strategic interests constitute the main motivating force for behavior. Ideology is only added verbiage justifying what the leaders would do in any case.[4] Historians emphasize the similarity between contemporary behavior and the traditional Slavic character and institutions, saying that the latter determine most of Soviet behavioral patterns.[5] The social psychologists and sociologists seem to take a more intermediate position, i.e., ideology is sometimes only a polemical tool, and at other times a major determinant of how they think and act.[6]

Rigid compartmentalization of inquiry, whether by academic discipline or geographic area, greatly hampers the construction of empirical theory. Without such theory, we are unable either to explain or to predict phenomena. Previous discussions of the motivational role of ideology in Communist systems illustrate some of the factors contributing to such an outcome. The question of the relationship between Communist ideology and Communist behavior has been discussed in isolation from more general empirical theory. Most students of Communist ideology and behavior have tended to view the relationship between *Communist* thought and action as a unique problem.[7] However, any discussion of the motivational role of *Communist* ideology is merely part of the more general question of the motivational role of ideology in determining or at least influencing behavior in any political system. Therefore, research done on the more general question must be relevant to the specific question.

But there has been felt, in the United States in particular, a special urgency about answering the question of what behavioral consequences the Communist ideology has. This demand for immediate answers has contributed to a tendency to proceed to generalizations about Communist ideology after examining only the available empirical data on Communist systems, and without undertaking the more arduous (but certainly more fruitful) task of studying the motivational role of Communist ideology in the context of general empirical theory. The pronounced policy science orientation of Communist studies in the United States has had serious effects on both the questions asked about ideology in Communist systems and the answers given to those questions. The position taken seems to be: "If we are to be relevant as Soviet or Communist 'experts,' we have to be able to give some immediate answer concerning the motivational role of ideology in Communist systems because, whatever the answer, it has critical implications for U.S. policy decisions." For one reason or another, Communist ideology is viewed as a relevant variable in this context and must be taken into account by American policy makers. So every Communist "specialist" has an answer to this vital question of the motivational role of Communist ideology and seeks to justify it, usually by pointing to certain actions in the past which conformed to his interpretation of the motivational role of Communist ideology. Most frequently these interpretations have been based on very scanty, impressionistic data. Relatively few attempts have been made to apply our rich variety of reliable contemporary research techniques to systematically collected data. The frequently heard argument is that the research methods and techniques of modern social and behavioral science cannot be systematically applied to the study of Communist systems because we do not have open access to those systems. Although this is frequently true, there are many areas which have been left unexplored despite the availability of techniques which would permit us to analyze available data relevant to the testing of basic propositions from empirical theory. The recent study by Triska and Finley is an excellent example of innovation in this regard.[8]

What follows is based on our conviction that scarcity of data concerning relevant variables does not justify sloppy methodology or exclusion of relevant variables. Inaccessibility of data is a frustrating problem, but it is a pragmatic, technical problem. It is not a legitimate excuse for lowering standards for the evaluation of empirical research. Further, absence of available data on relevant variables does not make those variables any less relevant; it merely means that we ought to be more cautious in our conclusions and more restrained in our prognostications to policy makers. The purpose of this article is to discuss some variables which psychological theory suggests are relevant to the relationship between ideology and behavior, but which have been generally absent in previous discussions of the motivational impact of Communist ideology on Communist behavior.

PROBLEMS
OF CONCEPTUALIZATION

Unfortunately, as Nathan Glazer has observed, one of the pressing conceptual problems of social psychology is that "no study of the relation between attitudes and personality has yet . . . solved the problem of distinguishing ideology—the views one picks up—from character— the orientations that are basic to a person."[9] This statement refers to the fact that very few individuals in a society will have a belief and value system that coincides exactly with that of the official ideological system and that many of the variables relating to why such a divergence exists involve the specific personality traits and personality processes of each individual. Although the conceptual problem is still not satisfactorily resolved in the eyes of most psychologists, progress has been made in establishing a framework for what variables and distinctions must be considered in attempts to relate a formal ideology to an individual's or a group's ideology.

In an attempt to clarify the relationship of an ideological system to an individual, Milton Rokeach introduced the concept of beliefdisbelief systems. In his discussion of this concept he points out that, as the term "belief-disbelief system" is applied to individuals and to groups, it necessarily must include "*all* of a person's beliefs and therefore is meant to be more inclusive than what is normally meant by ideology. Ideology refers to a more or less institutionalized set of beliefs—'the belief someone picks up.' Belief-disbelief systems contain these too but, in addition, they contain highly personalized preideological beliefs."[10]

Since the ideological beliefs constitute much less than the total belief-disbelief system of an individual or a group, it obviously is grossly insufficient to study only the content and structure of the ideological system when one is looking for determinants of human behavior.

One must first and foremost look at the content and structure of the individual's entire belief system.

When looking at the belief system of an individual or group, one must be as concerned about the various content levels within that belief system. One way the former distinctions can be made is by presenting a broad definition of beliefs which allows the notion of hierarchy to be built into it. One group of scholars has proposed that beliefs be generally defined as follows: beliefs "are existential propositions held by individual human beings regarding the structure and operation of the social and physical universe and one's place in it . . . ." They are "vectors which bear upon an individual as he confronts a choice of conduct." Within the context of this broad definition, they suggest that four distinctions be made:

1. *Cognitive Standards*: the existential propositions which serve as criteria to establish the validity and/or the applicability of information and are not themselves subject to ultimate verification.
2. *Appreciative Standards*: existential propositions which serve as criteria to evaluate the potential results of an act particularly in reference to its gratificatory significance.
3. *Knowledge*: an existential proposition that an individual accepts as established fact which is subject to further empirical verification.
4. *Power*: an existential proposition regarding man's perception of his relative capacity to influence and/or control the structure and operation of the social and physical world.[11]

These four subdefinitions of beliefs are given because they provide not only useful distinctions for the study of belief-disbelief systems in general (and of Communist ideologies in particular) but also because they introduce the notion of content hierarchy within belief systems. An examination of the four subdefinitions should suggest, for example, that those elements of a belief system or ideology that fall in the categories of (4) Power and (3) Knowledge would be much more susceptible to change through scientific discovery and changing circumstances over time than (1) Cognitive Standards and (2) Appreciative Standards. It is also a feasible and testable hypothesis that Appreciative Standards will change before Cognitive Standards change. Hence, if one could identify in either an individual's or group's belief system (or in the Marxian ideological system) which aspects would fall in which of the above categories, then one could proceed to the formulation and testing of hypotheses regarding them. In addition, one could hypothesize which elements of the belief system in Marxian ideology are set for individuals and groups by (a) the socialization process during child-hood, (b) educational and higher vocational training, (c) indoctrination of Party doctrine, (d) the role individuals perform in society, or (e) any other variable considered relevant. As will be shown below, all of these four variables plus many others help to determine what an individual's, or a group's, or a nation's operative ideology will be.

Once the distinctions in terms of content are understood, one can further try to determine the consistency with which an individual holds specific beliefs at each structural level of the belief-disbelief system. This endeavor can be accomplished by evaluating whether that belief fits into the structure of the individual's belief system at (1) the specific opinionation level, (2) the habitual opinionation level, (3) the attitudinal level, or (4) the ideological level. If beliefs are held at the specific opinionation level, it means that they "are not related in any way to other opinions . . . are not in any way characteristic of a person who makes them . . . and are not reproducible in the sense that if the same or a similar question were asked again under different circumstances, the answer might be different."[12] In other words, such opinions would not be very likely to influence behavior. If they did, they would do so in a random, inconsistent fashion.

The chief characteristic of habitual opinions is that they are re-producible and "form a relatively constant part of an individuals' makeup. In other words these are opinions which are voiced in the same or a similar manner on different occasions, and which are not subject to sudden arbitrary changes, such as are opinions at the lowest level."[13] At the more general attitudinal level, "we find not only that an individual holds a particular opinion with regard to a particular issue with a certain degree of stability; we also find that he holds concurrently a large number of other opinions on the same issue which in combination define his attitude towards that issue."[14]

Finally, at the most general level are found "ideologies" which Eysenck defines as clusterings of attitudes. Beliefs held at these latter three levels are quite likely to influence behavior, with those at the "ideological" level being the most likely to do so. The higher the level the greater value the individual places on the belief and the larger is his vested interest in the belief. Hence, when a decision-making situation arises it is more likely that the individual will decide in these circum-stances he would rather do "this" with "that" than if the belief is held at the lowest level.

Although Eysenck's use of the ubiquitous and ambiguous word *ideologies* is unfortunate in the above context, it should not blur the rather obvious point that is being made, which is: no individual can or does hold all beliefs with equal strengths and no person can simultaneously and consistently act on all his beliefs. Specific circumstances, his own physical and mental limitations, and those of the system in which he operates simply make this impossible. Moreover, some beliefs become more internalized and habitual than others, and some are held more dogmatically than others. In terms of trying to answer questions regarding which beliefs are operative and which are most susceptible to change, attention must be directed to this problem of how beliefs are held and structured.

SOURCES
OF PERSONAL IDEOLOGY

The accompanying map (Fig. 1), created by M. Brewster Smith,[15] provides a paradigm for viewing the many different general classes of variables which can influence personal behavior in general and political behavior in particular. As can readily be seen from this map, three out of the five broad classes of variables involve variables from the social environment, most of which cannot be controlled by the individual. The least controllable class of variables by far is that involving the distal social antecedents, such as the prior history of one's country before one was born and while one was growing up, its existing economic and political system, and other broad social determinants, such as the existence of a formal, established ideological system like Marxism-Leninism-Stalinism. All of these "givens" can affect the motivating forces of an individual, but the extent to which they either can or will do so is largely determined by the variables listed under Roman numeral II, i.e., the more immediate social environment as it affects an individual as he is reared, educated, and socialized into the society and its culture.

It is obvious from the vast literature on socialization that the socioeconomic status of an individual's family will, in part, determine how a child or even an adult will perceive objective reality.[16] It more often than not will partly determine his opportunities for educational and occupational training which, in turn, will also help to determine how much and what forms of the official, formal ideology, he (or she) will be exposed to.

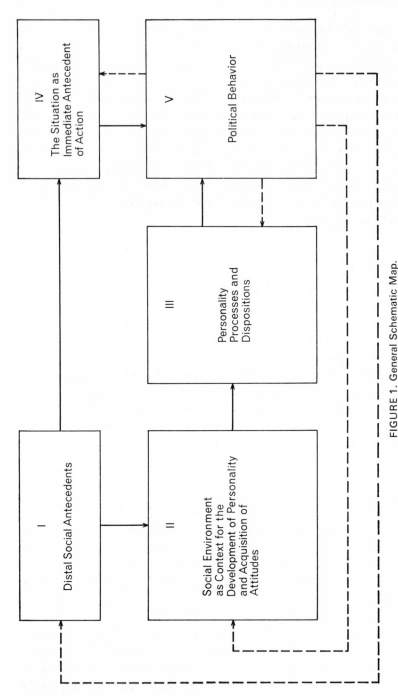

FIGURE 1. General Schematic Map.

Adapted from M. Brewster Smith, "A Map for the Analysis of Personality and Politics," *The Journal of Social Issues*, XXIV, 3 (July 1968), 17. Reprinted by permission of the author and publisher.

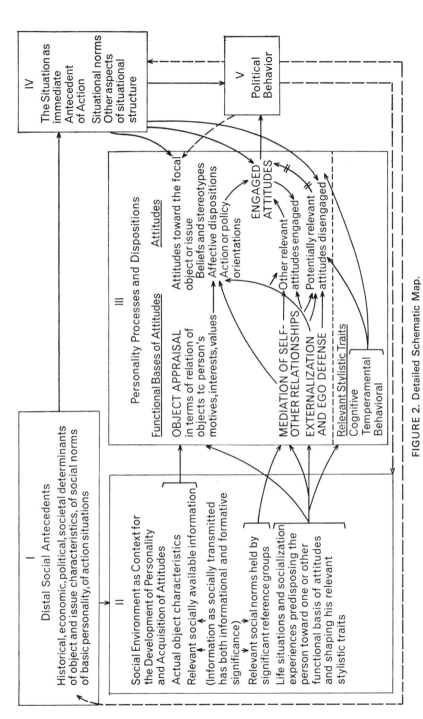

FIGURE 2. Detailed Schematic Map.

Adapted from Smith, *ibid.*, 25. Reprinted by permission of the author and publisher.

61

Obviously, exposure to the formal ideology is a prerequisite to its becoming any sort of a motivational force in behavior. It is true, of course, that most Soviet children are exposed to at least the essential elements of the formal ideology through the school system, the Octobrists, the Pioneers, and the Komsomol organization, but even this exposure does not guarantee that the belief and value systems of the formal ideology will be internalized by the individuals receiving that exposure. It is always possible, and quite likely, that the other socialization experiences and interactions with one's fellow human beings will lead one to internalize and, as an adult, act upon a belief quite different from the one formally taught. For example, while the national or Party ideology may assume that human beings are basically good and perfectable, an individual's early childhood and adult experiences may lead him to believe otherwise. As an adult, he may find it politically necessary and expedient to affirm the official ideological position, but in his decision-making and behavior, he will be motivated by his belief based on experience rather than the stated ideological position.[17]

When one considers not only the socio-economic diversity of families and individuals in the Soviet Union, but also its vast numbers of ethnic, linguistic, and religious groups and traditions, it readily becomes apparent that even among those who become leaders and a part of the elite in the society there is a high probability that whatever part of the written, formal ideology does become a motivating force for them will not be consistent, and the same applies to the whole decision-making group. When one further considers the fact that an individual's personal attitudes, beliefs, and values are often largely determined by the social norms, the beliefs, etc., of his peers and reference groups, the amount of diversity in terms of the degree of internalization of the formal ideology among members of the society and of the elite group becomes even greater. The increasing literature on interest groups in the Soviet Union is largely based on the assumption that membership in such an interest group will coincide with a particular ideological and political emphasis and outlook which is different from that of one belonging to another interest group.[18] Important questions here, however, are to what extent can the members of an interest group be expected to hold similar beliefs and what should scholars look for in trying to answer this question.[19]

Psychologists generally hold that the diversity and conformity of an individual's beliefs and values are limited by the basic psychological and biological limits of *Homo sapiens* in general. The limits to conformity are determined basically by man's biological nature. "As a member of the *Homo sapiens* species man is phsyiologically capable of a wide variety of mutually exclusive responses to given stimuli. This capacity for choice is the essential physio-psychological basis for the development of what we identify as 'values,' namely, standards of the desirable which men apply in making choices."[20] This means that the norms governing the responses of individuals or groups to given stimuli vary widely. Values and beliefs are not, in fact, universally shared phenomena. Individuals deviate from the norm. Moreover, since beliefs and values are learned and, hence, transmitted by one generation to another by socially agreed-upon sysmbols, they are more likely to change than biological phenomena. Communicating an official, ideological system such as Marxism-Leninism-Stalinism can seldom be uniform and precise whether it be from one age group to another, from one occupational elite group to another, or, as polycentralism has revealed, from one nation to another. In addition, whatever is internalized by the individual or the group is interpreted in terms of their own past experiences and is continually re-evaluated and changed as a result of their new experiences. Consequently, even within interest groups, a good deal of diversity can and should be expected.

It is, nonetheless, generally true that a great many of the beliefs and values that influence decision-making are determined for an individual by the groups to which he belongs, for the limits of diversity in beliefs and values are of a psychological and sociological nature. Yet, simple membership in a group (including an interest group) does not seem to be as significant a determination of an individual's beliefs and values as the specific roles he plays in the society. There are a great number of specialized roles in human societies which make individuals dependent and less than self-sufficient and autonomous.

> Each of these specialized roles involves specific rights and obligations on the part of the person to whom they are assigned. These rights and obligations are expectancies held by the person playing the role which, if they are to be adequately filled, must be inculcated in the individual role player as moral imperatives in his socialization into the role. . . . Ultimately, most human norms, especially those which apply to public policy decisions, can be conceived as role expectancies and variations in "value" profiles can be understood as differences in role expectancies.[21]

What this means for students of Communist political systems is that less emphasis should probably be put on studies of interest groups, defined as broad occupational groupings, and more emphasis should be placed on the types of roles individuals play within such groupings.[22] It also seems to indicate that if one really wants to know what importance ideology has in decision-making in the Soviet Union, one would have to identify and specify the role-expectancies of individuals in various decision-making positions in the Soviet Union.[23] If existential propositions from the ideological belief system and normative propositions from the ideology constitute an important and integral part of these role-expectancies, then the chances are high that these role-expectancies are those parts of the ideology that will influence political decision-making.

IDEOLOGY AND BEHAVIOR

In political science, as well as in the field of Communist studies in particular, there is a great tendency to equate values and ideology with supposed purposes of actions or with different outcomes. Following in the tradition of Lasswell and Kaplan in *Power and Society*,[24] many scholars of Communist systems use what can be called a "motive-belief" type of explanation to link ideology, values or belief systems to political behavior and decision-making. The logic of this type of explanation is something as follows: A desired event—or a goal event—often thought to be set by an ideology is said to be the motive or the cause for a certain action or a series of actions. This is very often done when it can be found in a written statement that this or that is part of an action program or this or that is a stated goal and over a period of time this or that actually is fulfilled. In other words it is assumed that "if X values Y, it means that X acts so as to bring about the consummation of Y."[25] At its worst, such types of explanation mean: "Y happened, therefore, X must have valued Y."

Unfortunately, the demonstration of such a causal relationship is not so easily accomplished. Psychologists have known for a long time that neither words nor actions are invariably accurate reflections of underlying beliefs, attitudes, or goals. A person's beliefs and attitudes prejudice an issue by determining his *set*, i.e., his way of reacting to new facts and experiences. They become *mental habits* which, *if aroused*, determine actions. But since attitudes are intervening variables and must be measured indirectly, to assert that a particular attitude regarding a goal, object, or belief motivated a person, one must be able to link that attitude with antecedent conditions and consequent behavior. It is not sufficient to study just the verbal statements of attitudes or just the consequent behavior. One must analyze all of the above, plus the need level and drives of the individual or of the individuals that compose a group.[26] It is known, for example, that two people can hold the same belief with the same degree of strength and intensity, and still behave differently. Obviously, something besides "ideology" is involved even when an individual ostensibly acts as though "ideology is motivating" his behavior.

The utilization of this motive-belief type of explanation causes other problems as well. At the group level of analysis there is the very real problem of determining empirically whether or not a group actually believes that a stated or written goal, such as the withering away of the state, is an operative one, i.e., that it is a goal actually desired and thought possible of achievement. If there is such a thing as a group goal, it can only be a composite of the goals of individuals that constitute the group. It is true that one can speak of a goal as a property of the group without worrying in detail about its origins. However, before one can go further and assert that a particular stated goal is operative, one must determine the extent to which the group members do in fact accept the group goals.

This question of whether or not groups can have properties separate and distinct from the individuals who compose them is one to which scholars of Communist systems should pay more attention. When the issue involves evaluation of an official statement to the effect that the Communist Party represents the "will of the people," even though only one person is generally allowed to run for an office, Western scholars generally follow the principle of Methodological Individualism, i.e., they assert the statement is false because there can be no such group characteristic as "will of the people" unless it can be demonstrated that each and every member of the electorate (the people) has had the opportunity to express this individual will in a truly democratic, secret election. In this context, the group property "will of the people" is said to be dependent upon counting the different "wills" of each person and coming up with a majority. When the issue involves ideology, on the other hand, scholars often disregard the scientific principle of

Methodological Individualism. In this context statements such as "the Party believes," or "the army took the position," or the "economic managers acted on the basis of," etc. are often made. Yet here the basic methodological issue is the same. The "will of the people" refers to the beliefs and values of individuals within a group. The operative beliefs and values of the Party, of the army, etc., also refer to the beliefs and values of individuals within these groups. Since all groups are composed of aggregates of individuals, the characteristics or properties of all groups must be dependent upon the characteristics and properties of the individuals who compose them. Hence, group concepts of the behavior of groups must refer to the complex patterns of descriptive, empirical relations among individuals.[27]

Whether or not the group as such actually has a particular goal or part of the belief system as an operative basis of reference or action will be a function of a number of things. To go back to Smith's map, it depends, first of all, upon how the individual mediates the "self-other" relationships within his own particular group and his perception of society, as well as his objective position, role, and function in society.

A second circumstance affecting whether or not a goal or belief will become operative for a group is the position of the group itself, its habitual pattern of behavior, and its roles and functions in society.[28] A good illustration of how these variables can mediate the possible impact upon a stated belief or goal is the decision-making situation of an economic manager in the Soviet Union. It has often been asserted that the main reason why the profit motive was not introduced into the Soviet economic system was the ideological belief in the superior value of the Marxian theory of surplus value. While historically this may well be true, it is largely irrelevant to a contemporary discussion of decision-making for most Soviet political and economic leaders. The decisions and responses of an economic manager, for example, would more likely be determined by the habit of conforming to "success-indicators" and group norms for managers than they would be by any ideological belief or goal considerations. Even for the planning officials in Gosplan this ideological problem is not an immediate criterion for their decisions. Their goals have already been set for them. Until recently, the vast majority accepted these goals and the supposed rationale behind them without question.[29] The same was probably true even for the Politburo members. The ideological belief only became important for decision-making when economists such as Liberman demonstrated that it had to be questioned in order to enable the economy to perform efficiently, and provided an alternative to it. Once they had demonstrated that the Marxian theory of surplus value was not supported by facts at the knowledge level in the belief system, then the political question arose: do we or do we not accept these findings even though they disprove and reject some of our most basic ideological tenets? An important point must be noted here. Even at this point no part of the written content of the ideology *per se* becomes the criterion for decision-making! What happens is that some other criteria are used to accept or reject this element of Marxian ideology.

Other circumstances which help to determine whether or not a stated goal or belief will become operative for a group are: (1) the motives of each individual for behavior in general; (2) each individual's judgment of the relative positive and negative weights for him of engaging in the activities necessary to achieve the group goal; (3) each individual's subjective estimate of the probability that a group goal can and will be achieved; (4) the clarity of the group goal, and (5) the amount of interdependency and cohesiveness of the group members.[30] Unmentioned still is perhaps the most important consideration, which is what motivated the individual to accept the goal (or belief) to begin with. An individual's motive for accepting the goal or belief will generally be as influential in determining whether or not it affects his political behavior as the actual goal or belief itself.[31]

MOTIVATION

Psychologists generally assert that motivation for human behavior can be broken down into the following categories: (1) Within the human organism itself there exists a variety of internal urges, whims, wishes, feelings, emotions, drives, instincts, wants, desires, demands, purposes, interests, aspirations, needs, and/or "motives"; (2) On the basis of interaction between the organism and his environment there develop incentives, goals, or object values which attract or repell the organism; and (3) There are strictly environmental determinants, i.e., the application of some irresistible force which of necessity leads to a particular response. Categorizing these types of motivation somewhat differently, one finds that some (emotion, force, drive, instinct, need) are at a biological level; others (urge, wish, feeling, impulse, want, striving, desire, demand) have significant "mental" import; and still others (purpose, interests, intention, attitude, aspiration, plan, motive, incentive, goal, value) require interaction with objects or states in the environment.[32] To satisfy any one of these items is, in a sense, to behave in a manner to fulfill a goal, or better, a "need." All are an inherent part of an individual's total personality, and all will at some time or another become the motivation or a part of the motivation for behavior, including political behavior. The questions is: when?

One theory of motivation that has recently gained prominence in the discipline of political science is Abraham Maslow's theory of five main categories of human needs.[33] This theory of motivation, more than any other, makes a clear distinction among the different goals (or needs) of human beings and tackles directly the problem of when various needs are capable of motivating behavior. Hence, although the theory is not empirically proven, it does provide a very useful model and aid for illustrating some of the basic issues involved in the study of motivation.

According to Maslow, all human beings have the following levels of needs: (1) individuals have basic *physical needs*, such as the need for food, for water, and for sex; (2) they also have *safety needs*, that is, a need for order, predictability, and dependability of their environment; (3) they have a *need for belonging*, which includes the need to be loved, to have affection, and friends; (4) they have a *need for self-esteem*, such as feeling equal to others; and (5) they have a *need for self-actualization*, i.e., a need to fulfill themselves. In Maslow's opinion, individuals pursue these five needs for their own sake throughout their lives. The needs are universal to the human organism regardless of the culture in which he lives or the ideology he is said to have embraced. In addition, these needs, which establish "goals" for an individual (consciously or unconsciously) are in a hierarchical arrangement. This notion of hierarchy means the following: until there is a substantial and relatively durable satisfaction of the physical needs, it will not be possible for the second level of needs, the safety needs, to emerge fully. Before the third level of needs, the need for belonging, can manifest itself as a strong force of motivation, the safety needs must be reasonably well met; and before the need for self-esteem can blossom forth, the need for belonging must be fairly well satisfied; and finally, before an individual can attain the highest level of motivation, which falls under the broad category of the need for self-actualization, all of the other four types of needs must be adequately fulfilled.

Maslow's hierarchial theory has many implications for the study of politics and the study of ideology. It helps one realize, for example, that neither politics nor any written, official ideological system necessarily performs any directly significant function in the fulfillment of the more basic needs. To satisfy their physical needs, the needs of belonging, and even basic safety needs, individuals usually turn to the local grocery store and to their family and friends. It is true that the political and economic system and the stage of development of a country will determine how well these needs can be met, but, nonetheless, whether one is a peasant in the Soviet Union or a member of the Politburo, the sources for fulfillment of these needs tend to be one's immediate family, circle of friends, and professional colleagues. In the words of Davies, "It is only when the achievement of these needs is threatened by individuals or groups too powerful to be dealt with privately that people turn to politics to secure their ends. Politics is generally only an indirect and instrumental means to the attainment of these ends. In other words, from a psychological point of view, politics is a form of exceptional, non-routine human behavior."[34] It might be added that in most political systems it would be even more exceptional and non-routine to find that a person's manner and motivation for fulfilling these lower needs were directly influenced by the official ideological system, for when individuals do not have these basic needs met, they tend to withdraw not only from any concern from politics, but also from a formal system of ideology.

Maslow's theory implies (and research on various revolutions tends to support this implication) that extreme deprivation of either the physical or safety needs can and often will lead to depoliticization.[35] There are numerous examples in the history of the Soviet Union to support this contention. Bauer, for example, found that in the 1930s and 1940s the physical and safety needs of the Soviet populace were so severely unfulfilled that most of the people simply withdrew from politics, creating the illusion and, in fact, the reality that the Soviet political system was very stable. It was stable, to a very large extent, simply because the people withdrew from either supporting or opposing it. Marxian ideology and/or any correspondence or discrepancy between that ideology and the practices of the Party were, for all practical purposes, irrelevant to their actual political behavior.[36]

The same can be said for what happened in the Ukraine during Hitler's invasion. Initially the population's hostility to the Soviet system (at perhaps an ideological level) led them to greet the Nazi army joyously. When, however, it was found that the Nazis were quite willing to starve and kill them, the Ukrainians chose to support the Soviet military and to fight Hitler. It does not appear that this was an ideological decision. It was a very basic human necessity of survival.

At the decision-making level these same hierarchical needs apply. It is thought that most individuals who engage in politics have successfully attained the self-actualization level.[37] This means that the most common level of motivation for intense political participation is one in which the other needs have already been well met. In other words, most political actors enjoy intense political participation for its own sake and "not primarily because [they] thereby feed or protect [themselves] or because [they] can give socially acceptable vent to [their] aggressions, gain great deference, or bend people to [their] will."[38] While there are certainly exceptions to this generalization and these will be discussed below, it seems reasonable to assume that many aspects of an ideological belief system can become operative only when the key decision-makers have attained this level. It is highly unlikely, for example, that any political leader will worry about implementing immediately a stated ideological goal or tenet if he thinks his life is in danger (as seems to have often been the case in the Soviet Union, particularly during the various succession crises). It is also highly unlikely that a preference for one version of an ideological position will receive high consideration if a political actor feels his sense of belonging to the in-group and personal self-esteem are being threatened. Under these circumstances ideology is likely to become not a goal or criteria for behavior, but rather a tool, polemical or otherwise, to achieve a more basic human need. What all this means is that before one can successfully analyze the function of ideology in decision-making, one must not only know the content of the ideology and the existing rules and norms of the political game in a system but also at what level of the human need-hierarchy the political actors can act and are acting, for the criteria for making decisions and acting will vary according to these need levels. And to repeat, ideological goal considerations are highly unlikely to become criteria for decision-making until and unless political actors have most of their lower level needs fairly well met and no fear that they will suddenly be unmet.

One very good illustration of how severe deprivation or the fear of such deprivation can lead even the most political members of a society to abandon considerations of principle and ideology in order to satisfy lower level needs is found in the behavior of some of the victims of the Great Purge Trials in the 1930s in the Soviet Union. The individuals who were forced to confess to sins against Marxism, the Party, the government, and the state were severely deprived of the food, sleep, and any order or predictability regarding when they would be fed, allowed to rest, or how they would be treated. They were additionally deprived of any clear sense of belonging, even to a group of persecuted prisoners. Having been cut off from their families and persuasively told they were traitors to the system and to the society, they were further isolated from their fellow victims and allowed to learn of their welfare only from periodical screams and reports that the others had confessed to the alleged crimes. This severe deprivation along with a simultaneous severe lowering of their own feelings of self-esteem and dignity as human beings certainly reduced their physical and mental capability of being strongly motivated by any "orthodox" ideological considerations and, indeed, perhaps even higher level ethical values. As Davies, in somewhat stronger terms, put it:

> At no time did they in any usual sense actually become social or political. They confessed their sins against society not so much because of a sense of social responsibility as to get sleep and bread . . . . In short, they had a stark, naked, physical need to survive, however hopeless, and to gain some sense of identity and worth, however contemptible.[39]

When these basic needs are unmet, a human being ceases to be "political." If they are not ever adequately met, human beings will never become "political." Although it is true that some of the lower level human needs, such as the need for self-preservation can become the main motivating force for political behavior and can obstruct the potential motivating force of an individual's basic beliefs and values, these needs usually are satisfied and play little or no motivating role in often mundane day-to-day political situations.

PERSONALITY PROCESSES
AND MOTIVATION

At the lower left-hand corner of III in Smith's map (Fig. 2) under the heading "Externalization and Ego Defense" one finds, in a somewhat different form, an illustration of how the basic human needs elaborated by Maslow fit into a total motivational framework. Individuals have these needs. However, the manner in which specific individuals will try to cope with threats to the satisfaction of these needs will depend upon their previous life and personality development. Individuals who are more prone to be anxiety-ridden and to have more internal conflicts than others will probably have their belief and value systems as well as their political decisions determined, to a higher degree than other individuals, by their need to defend their ego than by the objective facts.[40] Beliefs and values for them would be more likely to fulfill the function of ego defense than the function of object appraisal. Such individuals may latch onto and subscribe to an ideological system because of these needs. They may also reject the formal ideology for the same reason. (It would be interesting to compare and analyze in these terms the members of Agitprop and the dissident writers and intellectuals in the Soviet Union. Basic personality needs and processes certainly must account for much of the divergence in beliefs, values, and behaviors. While it may be that members of these two groups differ substantially in their basic personality traits and the functions which their beliefs and values fulfill for their personality maintenance, it is equally possible that a similar proportion within each group are using, in differing ways, the official ideological system as a means of justifying a particular manner of satisfying and defending needs and egos.)

The heading "Mediation of Self-Other Relationships" refers not only to the nature and type of interaction one has with others but also to the need an individual has for identifying with and being similar to or different from one's peers and reference groups. The role this personality process can have in motivating political behavior should be fairly obvious. Individuals who have a need to conform or who have habituated themselves to conforming will be more likely to adopt as their own large segments of a formal and official ideological system than those who do not. Also, an intense dislike for a person, or the converse, a strong liking for a person, could lead to either the rejection or the acceptance of a particular ideological point of view in a given situation.

Certainly one of the needs human beings have is the need to know and to feel that the beliefs they hold are based on the "truth." The personality process related to "Object Appraisal" refers to this need. Most individuals, including "Communist" ones, like to assert that they hold this or that belief or opinion because they have objectively analyzed a problem and on the basis of existing knowledge and experience have reached an objective conclusion regarding what means will lead to what ends. If an individual does hold a belief because of this motivation, however, it means only that that particular belief is not a function of his other needs, but rather the end product of what the individual perceives to be the objective situation based upon his previous experience and present knowledge. It does not necessarily mean that the belief held will be any more "operative," i.e., acted upon more consistently, than other beliefs which are held because they fulfill some other function for the maintenance and operation of the personality of the individual concerned.[41]

This point is important to note because when most scholars of Communist systems talk about ideology as a motivating force in decision-making, they do so largely in terms of what seems to them to be a means-end relationship among beliefs, values, and goals. To most scholars an aspect of the ideological system is considered to be "operative" when, ostensibly at least, the actors involved have made something of an objective appraisal of the situation and then take concrete political actions in terms of goal attainment or instrumental action which can be related to some element in the written ideological system. If such a relationship is observed often, it is argued that the political actors actually "believe" in the ideology. It is also sometimes argued that if the leaders act irrationally or inefficiently and a correspondence between this behavior and some element in the ideological system can be seen then they also must "believe" in that ideological tenet. Hence, the question of objective appraisal is very important.

Apparently, it is thought that if and only if significant elements of the official ideology are held as either objective truths or attainable goals and values, will the ideology or elements of it be "operative" for an individual, group, or society. One of the crucial questions here is what is meant and perhaps what should be meant by the term "operative." If that term refers to the functions an official ideological system fulfills, then it should be obvious by now that an official ideology can and probably does fulfill quite different functions for individuals, for groups, and indeed, for nations. While a specific decision-making body may act as though all or most of its members believe in a particular tenet or goal in one circumstance, it may well be that all or sections of the group are acting that way for quite different reasons. In another situation, which ostensibly is similar, the majority of these individuals may take quite a different stand, giving the impression that this aspect of the ideology is not "operative." The reason for taking the different stand could have nothing to do with belief or lack of it in a particular ideological tenet or goal. It could simply mean, and probably often does mean, that in the new situation different motivating forces were at work and the strength of one force simply overrode another.

From this brief discussion of motivation it seems clear that one of the most important reasons for the existing controversy over the motivational role of the Communist official ideological system in political behavior is, indeed, the fact that the positions advocated by different scholars are based on limited methodologies and on limited views of what variables need to be considered. The anthropological and psychoanalytic schools tend to concentrate on character and ego development, which in turn leads them to emphasize temperamental and stylistic traits and ego defenses in the personality. In terms of Smith's map these variables concern primarily only small sections of Roman numerals I, II, and III. Kremlinologists tend to concentrate most on the variables relating to IV, the immediate situational context, and on intense conflict situations. In the past, at least, intense conflict in the Soviet Union has often posed severe dangers to individuals and forced them to be concerned about protecting what Maslow would call their lower level needs. Given this framework, it is not surprising that Kremlinologists are inclined to believe that ideology is primarily a polemical tool. Much the same can be said for the geopolitical theorists, only they tend to pay more attention to the distal social determinants (I) than the Kremlinologists do. The historians obviously study the distal social determinants most intensely. Since the ideological system is only one of numerous variables in this class of variables and historians do not, unless they are doing a study involving biographical data, usually concern themselves with personality dispositions and processes, it would be expected that they would stress the importance of non-ideological determinants of behavior. The social psychologists and sociologists, whose theoretical and methodological orientations encourage them to look to empirical theories of motivation, naturally take a more intermediate position, for as it has been demonstrated, motivation is extremely complex. What will be a strong motivating force in one context will not be in another. Until and unless students of Communist ideologies recognize this fact and also develop a methodological and theoretical orientation which will take into consideration all of the different aspects of the problem, progress will not be made. It is hoped that this paper will stimulate thought in the direction of developing such an orientation.

Notes

1. The best summary of the many different theories which attempt to interpret and explain what determines Soviet political behavior is still Daniel Bell, "Ten Theories in Search of Reality: The Prediction of Soviet Behavior," *World Politics*, X, 3 (April 1958), pp. 327–65. Cf. William Glaser, "Theories of Soviet Foreign Policy: A Classification of the Literature," *World Affairs Quarterly*, XXVII, 2 (July, 1956). A collection of articles which quickly illustrates that the debate has ranged from a complete denial of any motivational impact of ideology to views verging toward ideological determinism; see, "Ideology and Power—A Symposium," in A. Brumberg (ed.), *Russia Under Khrushchev* (New York: Praeger, 1962), pp. 3–68.

2. See Henry V. Dicks, "Observations on Contemporary Russian Behavior," *Human Relations*, V, 2 (1952), pp. 111–75, and Nathan Leites, *A Study of Bolshevism* (New York: Free Press, 1953). Jan Triska, Zbigniew Brzezinski, and others also have held similar positions, even though they are not anthropologists or psychoanalysts by training. See Triska's article, "A Model for Study of Soviet Foreign Policy," in *American Political Science Review*, LII, 2 (March 1958), and any of Brzezinski's articles and books.

3. Examples of Kremlinologists who seem to incline toward this view are Myron Rush, *The Rise of Khrushchev* (Washington, D.C.: Public Affairs Press, 1958), and R. Conquest, *Power and Policy in the USSR: The Study of Soviet Dynastics* (New York: St. Martin's, 1961). Cf. Conquest, *The Politics of Ideas in the USSR* (New York: Praeger, 1967).

4. The clearest spokesman for this position has been Samuel Sharp. See "National Interest: Key to Soviet Politics," in *Russia Under Khrushchev*, pp. 15–26. Barrington Moore in "The Relations of Ideology and Foreign Policy," *Soviet Politics: The Dilemma of Power* (Cambridge: Harvard U.P., 1950), takes a similar but more qualified position. While the ideology did not force the Soviet Union to join or abandon any alliance that it would not have simply on the basis of national interest, in some cases it slowed or speeded up the process.

5. Scholars who have represented this group include Nicholas Berdyaev, Sir Bernard Pares, Sir John Maynard, Edward Crankshaw, Ernest Simmons and Cyril E. Black. A good but brief illustration of how present-day historians tend to view the problem is found in Black, "The Modernization of Russian Society," *The Transformation of Russian Society* (Cambridge: Harvard U.P., 1960), pp. 661–80.

6. See Raymond A. Bauer, Alex Inkeles, and Clyde Kluckhohn, *How the Soviet System Works* (Cambridge: Harvard U.P.), pp. 29–35. Though sociologists tend to be more moderate in the positions they hold with regard to how ideology influences political behavior, a great deal of diversity exists with regard to the question of how ideology influences scientists. For a view which asserts that science and ideology are bound to oppose each other, see Bell's "The End of Ideology in the Soviet Union?" in *Marxist Ideology in the Contemporary World*, edited by Milorad M. Drachkovitch (New York: Praeger, 1966), pp. 76–112. For the opposite position see George Fischer's article "Sociology," in *Science and Ideology in Soviet Society*, edited by George Fischer (New York: Atherton, 1967). Those interested in this issue of how science and ideology are related should also consult David Joravsky, "Soviet Ideology," *Soviet Studies*, XVIII, 1 (July 1966), 2–19, and "Ideology, Science and the Party," *Problems of Communism*, XVI, 1 (Jan.-Feb. 1967), 67–75.

7. For example, see P. B. Reddaway, "Aspects of Ideological Belief in the Soviet Union," *Soviet Studies*, XVII, 4 (April, 1966), 472.

8. Jan F. Triska and David D. Finley, *Soviet Foreign Policy* (New York: Macmillan, 1968).

9. Nathan Glazer, "New Light on The Authoritarian Personality," *Commentary*, XVII (March, 1954), 293.

10. Milton Rokeach, *The Open and Closed Mind* (New York: Basic Books, 1960), p. 35. For a more recent discussion of the relationship between ideology and belief system, see Samuel H. Barnes, "Ideology and the Organization of Conflict: On the Relationship between Political Thought and Behavior," *Journal of Politics*, XXVIII, 3 (Aug. 1966), 513–30.

11. Philip E. Jacob and James J. Flink, "Values and Their Function in Decision-Making," *American Behavioral Scientist*, V, Suppl. 9 (May 1962), 23.

12. H. J. Eysenck, *The Psychology of Politics* (London: Routledge), p. 111.

13. *Ibid.*, pp. 111–12.

14. *Ibid.*, p. 112.

15. A discussion of the main sections of this map and their connections can be found in M. Brewster Smith, "A Map for the Analysis of Personality and Politics," *Journal of Social Issues*, XXIV, 3 (July 1968), 15–28. The other essays in this issue of the *Journal of Social Issues* are relevant to the present discussion, especially the introductory essay by Fred I. Greenstein, "The Need for Systematic Inquiry into Personality and Politics: Introduction and Overview," 1–14. Cf. Fred I. Greenstein, "The Impact of Personality on Politics: An Attempt to Clear Away Underbrush," *American Political Science Review*, LXI, 3 (Sept. 1967), 629–41.

16. Two good studies of political socialization are Herbert H. Hyman, *Political Socialization: A Study in the Psychology of Political Behavior* (New York: Free Press, 1959), and Fred I. Greenstein, *Children and Politics* (New Haven: Yale U.P., 1965).

17. Philip Worchel, in "Social Ideology and Reactions to International Events," *Journal of Conflict Resolution*, XI, 4 (Dec. 1967), 414–31, found, for example, that the ideological orientation toward others developed through the socialization process is definitely related to how a person reacts toward alternative resolutions of international conflict situations.

18. See, for example, the work of Roger Pethybridge, *A Key to Soviet Politics: The Crisis of the Anti-Party Group* (New York: Praeger, 1962). Sidney I. Ploss has found evidence that this split in beliefs and values is reflected in the Soviet press. See his paper "Political Conflict and the Soviet Press," presented at the 1964 Annual Meeting of the American Political Science Association, Chicago, Sept. 1964. For some additional recent research on groups and group values in Soviet politics, see the following: H. Gordon Skilling, "Interest Groups and Communist Politics," *World Politics*, XVIII, 3 (April 1966), 435–51; Milton Lodge, "Soviet Elite Participatory Attitudes in the Post-Stalin Period," *American Political Science Review*, LXII, 3 (Sept. 1968), 827–39; Milton Lodge, " 'Groupism' in the Post-Stalin Period," *Midwest Journal of Political Science*, XII, 3 (Aug. 1968), 330–51; Sidney I. Ploss, "Interest Groups," in Allen Kassof (ed.), *Prospects for Soviet Society* (New York: Praeger, 1968), pp. 76–103.

19. For a further discussion of this point along somewhat different lines, see Frederic J. Fleron, Jr., "Representation of Career Types in the Soviet Political Leadership," in R. Barry Farrell (ed.), *Political Leadership in Eastern Europe and the Soviet Union* (Chicago: Aldine, 1970), pp. 108–39.

20. Jacob and Flink, "Values and Their Function in Decision-Making," *op. cit.*, p. 13.

21. *Ibid.*, p. 14. See also Seymour Lieberman, "The Effects of Changes in Roles on the Attitudes of Role Occupants," and Robert K. Merton, "Occupational Roles: Bureaucratic Structure and Personality," in *Personality and Social Systems*, edited by Neil J. and William T. Smelser (New York: Wiley, 1963), pp. 264–79 and 255–63, respectively.

22. For an excellent discussion related to this point, see John Wilson Lewis, "Chinese Communist Party Leadership and the Succession to Mao-Tse-tung: An Appraisal of Tensions" (Washington, D.C.: U.S. Department of State, Bureau of Intelligence and Research, Policy Research Study, Jan. 1964), esp. p. 2.

23. Cf. Erik P. Hoffmann, "Role Conflict and Role Ambiguity in the Communist Party of the Soviet Union," [in this volume, supra].

24. Harold Lasswell and Abraham Kaplan, *Power and Society* (New Haven: Yale U.P., 1950).

25. An example of the use of the motive-belief type of explanation in Soviet studies can be found in Myron Rush, *Political Succession in the USSR* (New York: Columbia U.P., 1965), p. 67, where he tries to explain why Khrushchev became the leader of the anti-Malenkov group in 1954–55. For an analysis and criticism of Rush's use of motive-belief explanation, see Frederic J. Fleron, Jr., "Soviet Area Studies and the Social Sciences: Some Methological Problems in Communist Studies," *Soviet Studies*, XIX, 3 (Jan. 1968), 336–37. For a more detailed general discussion of motive-belief explanation, see Quentin Gibson, *The Logic of Social Enquiry* (London: Routledge, 1960), Chap. 4.

26. Eysenck, *op. cit.*, pp. 230–39.

27. May Brodbeck, "Methodological Individualism: Definition and Reduction," *Philosophy of Science*, XXV, 1 (Jan. 1958), 1–22.

28. C. N. Cofer and M. H. Appley, *Motivation: Theory and Research* (New York: Wiley, 1963), pp. 779–80.

29. For important discussions of the variables related to density of doctrinal stereotypes, see Triska and Finley, *Soviet Foreign Policy*, pp. 119–27.

30. Cofer and Appley, *op. cit.*, pp. 779–80.

31. Cf. Fred. I. Greenstein, "Personality and Politics: Problems of Evidence, Inference, and Conceptualization," *American Behavioral Scientist*, XI, 11 (Nov. 1967), 38–53.

32. For a good discussion of the different theories of motivation and the extent to which evidence exists to support them, see Cofer and Appley, *op. cit.*

33. Abraham Maslow, "A Theory of Motivation," *Psychological Review*, 50 (1943), 370–96. The theory was applied to political behavior by James C. Davies in *Human Nature in Politics: The Dynamics of Political Behavior* (New York: Wiley, 1963).

34. Davies, *op. cit.*, p. 10.

35. The more empirical studies on revolution consistently show that revolutions based on the masses occurred only after a significant increase in economic development had prevailed for a number of years. The sudden drop in prosperity immediately prior to the revolutions, while perhaps a necessary condition for the occurrence of a revolution, did not constitute severe deprivation. Cf. Crane Brinton, *The Anatomy of Revolution* (New York: Vintage Books, 1952), and Raymond Tanter and Manus Midlarsky, "A Theory of Revolution," *Journal of Conflict Resolution*, XI, 3 (Sept. 1967), 264–80.

36. Bauer, Inkeles, and Kluckhohn, *op. cit.*

37. Davies, *op. cit.*, p. 59.

38. *Ibid.*

39. *Ibid.*, p. 19.

40. Nathan Leites' *A Study of Bolshevism* is a detailed and elaborate application of this generalization to the Soviet leadership group.

41. *Ibid.* Cf. Rokeach, *op. cit.*

3

Soviet Elite Participatory Attitudes in the Post-Stalin Period

MILTON LODGE

This paper, part of a larger study, is a comparative analysis of five Soviet elites—the central Party *apparatchiki*, and four specialist

Reprinted with permission from *American Political Science Review*, LXII (1968), 827–39. An earlier version of this paper was delivered at the 1967 Annual Meeting of the Midwest Conference of Political Scientists, Purdue University, Lafayette, Ind., April 27–29, 1967. The data were collected at the Institute for the Study of the U.S.S.R., Munich, Germany, in the winter of 1965–66, funded by a grant from the University of Michigan Center for Russian and East European Studies. The author is indebted to the Institute's staff for their cooperation, to Professors William Zimmerman and Vernon Van Dyke for helpful criticisms, and to Merrill Shanks and Susan Lawther for methodological assistance.
Notes to the selection begin on page 100.

elites: the central economic bureaucrats, the military, the literary intelligentsia, and the legal profession. By content analyzing representative periodicals for each elite, data are collected on elite attitudes toward participation in the political system. The overall goal is to gain a measure of the direction and scope of Soviet elite attitudinal change since Stalin; more specifically, (1) to measure the extent to which the elites perceive themselves as participants in the policy-making process, (2) to determine whether the elites perceive their participatory role as expanding over time, and (3) to demark changing patterns of Party-specialist elite relations from 1952–65.

To ground this study in a theoretical framework, analytical categories and hypotheses—derived in part from Brzezinski and Huntington's *Political Power: USA/USSR*—are formulated to test the perceived extent of elite participation in the Soviet political process.[1] Synoptically, models of political systems may be built by reducing to essentials the mode of interaction between the regime and society. A key variable in analyzing this interaction between superstructure and base is the role and efficacy of societal groups in influencing policy formation and implementation. Following this tack a descriptive continuum may be set up for classifying political systems. At one end of the continuum are ideological systems (e.g., the USSR), at the other "instrumental" systems (e.g., the United States). In instrumental systems the relationship between the political and social system is characterized by "access and interaction." In an ideological political system—with totalitarianism at the polar extreme—social groups are infiltrated, controlled, manipulated, and denied effective participation in the political process.

Brzezinski, along with a growing number of Western scholars, notes some degree of Soviet systemic change over time, arguing that the central Party apparatus—still dominant in policy-making and implementation—is being forced to tolerate greater elite participation in the political process. The extent to which the specialist elites perceive themselves and are perceived by the other elites as participants is the focal point of this study and the major variable in determining the degree of systemic change along the continuum toward a less ideological political system.

The ideological-instrumental continuum may be graphically portrayed as a five-point scale ranging from perceived Party dominance on the ideological side of the continuum to perceived specialist elite participation at the instrumental end of the continuum, with 3.0 representing joint, relatively equal, Party-specialist elite participation. The analytical categories are comparably scaled and designed to generate data suitable for plotting elite attitudes on the continuum.

The scaled positions within the participatory categories are:

1.0 Party participation solely
2.0 Party participation primarily
3.0 Joint Party-specialist elite participation
4.0 Specialist elite participation primarily
5.0 Specialist elite participation solely
(See Figure 1.)

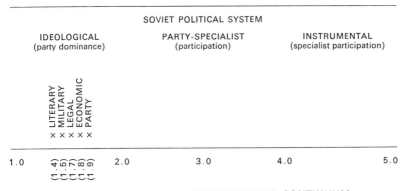

FIGURE 1. IDEOLOGICAL-INSTRUMENTAL CONTINUUM

In this hypothetical situation the Soviet political system is Party-dominant—all the elites are participating within the ideological parameters (1.0–2.9) of the political arena. Instrumentality—operationally defined as specialist elite participation in the political process—would characterize the political system if specialist scores were in the 3.0–5.0 range.

Within the Party's espoused values for the "transition to communism" the knowledge and skills of specialists, it is reasoned, are indispensable. "No single strategic elite," writes Suzanne Keller, "can today know all there is to be known, and none can perform all the functions involved in social leadership."[2] If it is true that the Party and specialists are becoming increasingly interdependent, what, from the Party's perspective, would be the ideal Party-specialist relationship? Ruling out either polar extreme as systemically dysfunctional, a tentative "mix" may be a mini-max postion in which the maximum degree of specialist participation is tolerable which still allows for Party dominance in the policy- and decision-making arena. With 3.0 corresponding to relatively equal Party-specialist participation, the Party's optimal position would be in the 2.5–2.9 range where the Party could capitalize on specialist elite participation without surrendering control.

I. RESEARCH METHOD

Western analyses of Soviet politics must, of necessity, rely heavily on published sources. Both the totalitarian and Kremlinological models typically portray Soviet communication channels as being monopolistically controlled by the central Party *apparat*. Rejecting both approaches, this project is premised on the assumption that Soviet specialist elites— due to their strategic role in society—enjoy sufficient leeway in the system to articulate a range of beliefs and values in their specialist journals.

Soviet spokesmen grudgingly acknowledge and Western analyses have demonstrated that specialist journals are vehicles for the limited articulation of elite attitudes.[3] Representing a functional sphere of activity in the political system, specialist journals primarily perform an *instrumental* role—authors, as experts, elaborate on policies within their sphere of competence, suggest ways and means for improving implementation, mobilize support, and most important of all, criticize shortcomings. The overwhelming majority of sampled articles are achievement oriented, that is, are chiefly concerned with questions of how best to fulfill the plan, increase efficiency, and overcome weaknesses.

Within this orientation authors are predominantly concerned with specifics: a manager of a textile factory in Petropavlosk argues that Party interference in the running of the plant resulted in decreased production; a Marshal complains that criticism of company commanders at Party meetings undermines the officer's authority and reduces troop morale; a jurist warns that a Central Committee decree calling for the exemplary punishment of "parasites" undercuts the Party's campaign to strengthen socialist law; Tvardovsky, editor-in-chief of *Novy mir*, favorably comments on "truthfulness" in literature, while Khrushchev rails against the young writers' emphasis on "decadent" themes. In sum, although specialist journals are rarely vehicles for an open and direct confrontation with the Party, specialist attitudes are articulated through instrumental proposals and criticisms—within the Party's espoused values of productivity, efficiency, and "communism"—without overtly challenging the Party's role in policy integration. In the Soviet context, rejection of the Party's integrative role is opposition, elite participation in the formulation and implementation of specific policies is politics. Direct opposition is rare, politics is ubiquitous. With the decline of terror in the post-Stalin period controversies are no longer zero-sum games.

By content analyzing articles in specialist elite journals and aggregating the frequencies of occurrence, elite attitudinal trends may be compared. Categories are formulated and data collected on elite beliefs—(who is described as actually making decisions), and elite values (preferences on who *should* make decisions). The resultant analysis of elite beliefs and values yields a measure of attitudinal trends toward a more participatory, less ideological, political system. All references to elite participation therefore refer to attitudinal, not actual, participation and may be treated as *indicators* of systemic change.

The Elites

For each elite, "representative" periodical(s) were selected for content analysis:

The Central Party	*Kommunist* (Communist)
Apparat	*Partiinaya zhizn* (Party Life)
The Economic Elite	*Voprosy ekonomiki* (Problems of Economics)
	Ekonomicheskaya gazeta (Economic Gazette)
The Military	*Krasnaya zvezda* (Red Star)
The Legal Profession	*Sovetskoye gosudarstvo i pravo* (Soviet State and Law)
	Sovetskaya yustitsia (Soviet Justice)
The Literary Elite	*Oktyabr* (October)
	Literaturnaya gazeta (Literary Gazette)
	Novy mir (New World)

The Sample

To satisfy the definitional requirement of objectivity in content analysis systematic sampling procedures are required.

I. The unit of analysis is the article. Articles in the sample were chosen from the periodicals on the basis of a quota sample. The issues from each periodical were selected at intervals so as to cover the entire year and avoid the inclusion of any one period, e.g., avoiding every

December issue of journals or Monday issue of newspapers. From the selected issue only the lead article, the first signed article, was coded. (In newspapers the lead article is the first signed article in the upper left hand corner of page two.)

II. The unit of enumeration, what is being coded and counted, is the major theme of a paragraph. When clearly articulating one position in one category, the major theme could be coded once and only once.

III. The size of the sample is equal for each elite each year, 600 paragraphs per elite for each of the eight sampled years—1952, 1953, 1955, 1957, 1959, 1961, 1963, and 1965—a yearly sample of 3,000 paragraphs (600 paragraphs × 5 elites) for a total study sample of 24,000 paragraphs (3,000 paragraphs per year × 8 years).

Categories and Hypotheses

The categories, or value dimensions, are designed to generate data on Soviet elite attitudes toward the policy-making and decision-making process. Policy-making is operationally distinguished from decision-making in terms of the policy decision's impact on society. Policy-making entails decisions which effect a) the entire U.S.S.R. or b) one or more republics. Decision-making refers to policies affecting any one administration unit below the republic level, e.g., a region, territory, district, factory, or farm. Thus a decision affecting all collective farms in a republic is operationally defined as policy-making, while a decision affecting a specific collective is defined as decision-making.

Reliability

Reliability tests were administered to establish a presumption of objectivity. Twenty-five percent of all sampled articles were recoded by a second coder working independently of the first. The articles included in the reliability test were selected by means of an "accidental sample," i.e., chosen randomly for each journal each year. The formula for testing reliability is:

$$\frac{\text{Total number of agreements}}{\text{Total number of paragraphs in the article}} = \text{percentage of reliability}$$

The total study reliability is statistically significant at 89.4 percent.

II. ELITE PARTICIPATORY ATTITUDES IN THE POST-STALIN POLITICAL SYSTEM

The Soviet political system—when conceived as an ideological system—is characterized by central Party *apparat* dominance in the political arena.

I. ON POLICY-MAKING

Hypothesis 1: Over time the specialist elites increasingly describe themselves as participants in the policy-making process.

In operational terms Party primacy will be reflected in mean scores of 1.0–2.9 on Category I—Who is Responsible for Policy-Making?—while higher, participatory scores of 3.0–5.0 in the later years would support the hypothesis that the policy-making process is becoming less ideological over time (Table 1).

TABLE 1

ELITE PERCEPTIONS OF THE POLICY-MAKING ARENA, 1952–1965

Policy-Making Is the Responsibility Of
1.0 the Party leadership solely
2.0 the Party leadership primarily
3.0 both the Party and specialist participating
4.0 the specialists primarily
5.0 the specialists solely[a]

Elites	1952	1953	1955	1957	1959	1961	1963	1965	All Years
Party	1.9	1.9	2.0	1.4	2.9	2.7	1.7	2.3	2.1
Economic	000	2.5	2.3	1.5	3.2	3.0	2.8	3.6	2.5
Legal	000	1.3	2.3	2.9	1.7	4.0	2.5	3.8	2.7
Military	(1.8)[b]	(1.6)	1.6	1.3	000	2.2	3.3	2.7	2.1
Literary	1.8	1.0	1.8	2.9	2.4	2.0	2.5	3.1	2.3
All Elites	1.8	1.6	1.9	2.1	2.5	2.6	2.7	3.2	2.4
Specialists	1.8	1.6	1.9	2.1	2.4	2.8	2.8	3.3	2.4

$F_{(33,106)} = 3.089$, significant at .001

[a] An example of position 5.0, taken from the illustrative material used in training the coders, is:

The formation of our military world view has taken place in a creative atmosphere ... and is the result of the common effort of military theorists and practical military people. Thanks to this, we have developed a body of unified theory on the basis of which a broad state program has been carried out to prepare the country and armed forces for the defense of the Fatherland. *Kommunist Vooruzhennykh sil,* No. 10 (May 1962), 12.

[b] Data for the military were unavailable for 1952 and 1953. The mean score for all elites was assigned the military for these years and noted within the brackets.

The general trend is toward increased specialist elite participation in the policy-making arena. Note, for example, the gradual, rather steady increase in specialist scores from 1953 onward, culminating in 1965 with an instrumental score of 3.3. While the thrust toward greater specialist elite participation is significant, the trend is uneven for each of the individual elites. A zig-zag course is the characteristic pattern, perhaps best described by the un-Leninist notion of *two steps forward one step back*. For the specialist elites, reversals are typically followed by a resurgence which marks an advance beyond the previous low. This dysrhythmic process is a common phenomenon on all the categories and, as will be shown, is a function of Party-specialist elite conflict.

By dividing the eight sampled years into two equal periods, 1952–57 and 1959–65 overall participatory trends are more readily illustrated (Table 2).

TABLE 2

ELITE PERCEPTIONS OF THE POLICY-MAKING
ARENA, 1952–57 TO 1959–65

Elites	1952–57	1959–65	% Change
Party	1.8	2.4	+33%
Economic	1.9	3.3	+74%
Legal	2.4	2.9	+21%
Military	1.6	2.3	+44%
Literary	1.9	2.7	+42%
All Elites	1.9	2.7	+42%
Specialists	1.9	2.8	+47%

With a 47% specialist increase in 1959–65 over the earlier period, hypothesis I is supported—the perceived boundaries of the political arena are expanding over time. As specialist elite participation increases, Party dominance decreases: all the elites recognize greater specialist elite participation, although in 1959–65 the Party at 2.4 defines the parameters of the policy-making arena in more restrictive terms than do the specialists.

Juxtaposed to the belief category—who *is* described as actually making policy—is its counterpart, a value category on who *should* make policy.

Hypothesis 2: The specialist elites are pressing the Party for greater influence in the policy-making arena.

To show the extent of specialist elite pressure on the Party for a larger role in policy-making, three operational prerequisites need be met: 1) specialist scores on the value category (who should participate?) must increase over time, 2) must be demonstrably higher than Party scores, and 3) be appreciably higher, more participatory, than perceptions of actual participation (Table 3).

TABLE 3

ELITE VALUES TOWARD PARTICIPATION IN THE POLICY-MAKING ARENA, 1952–1965

	Policy-Making *Should* Be The Responsibility Of 1.0 the Party leadership solely 2.0 the Party leadership primarily 3.0 both the Party and specialists participating[a] 4.0 the specialists primarily 5.0 the specialists solely								
Elites	1952	1953	1955	1957	1959	1961	1963	1965	All Years
Party	1.9	1.4	1.5	2.1	2.1	2.2	2.0	2.4	1.9
Economic	1.0	1.2	3.0	1.6	2.9	3.4	2.7	3.1	2.2
Legal	1.2	1.4	1.9	2.9	2.7	3.2	3.7	3.3	2.5
Military	(1.3)	(1.3)	1.4	2.8	2.3	2.4	3.2	3.4	2.3
Literary	1.4	1.3	2.9	2.7	2.8	3.0	3.1	3.6	2.6
All Elites	1.3	1.3	2.1	2.5	2.6	2.7	2.9	3.2	2.4
Specialist	1.2	1.3	2.3	2.5	2.7	3.0	3.2	3.4	2.4

$F_{(38,177)} = 7.246$, significant at .001

[a] An example of position 3.0 is contained in a speech by Khrushchev at a meeting of agronomists:

You say "Comrade Khrushchev said thus and so." Am I the highest authority in agricultural science? You are President of the Ukraine Republic Academy of Sciences and I am the Secretary of the Party Central Committee. You must help me in these matters, and not I you. I might be wrong, and if I am, you, as an honest scientist, should say: "Comrade Khrushchev, you do not quite understand the matter." If you explain things to me correctly, I will thank you for it. Let us say I was wrong. But you will say, "Comrade Khrushchev said this and I supported him." What sort of scientist is this comrades? This is toadyism and timeserving. *Pravda*, December 25, 1961.

Again the trend is toward greater specialist elite participation. In 1963 and 1965 the specialists are in the participatory range, and in 1965 only the Party opts for Party dominance. The general trend for specialists is continuous and marks a steady increase from 1952 through 1965. Developments over time are more clearly demonstrated by comparing the 1952–57 period with 1959–65 (Table 4).

In support of the hypothesis that the specialist elites are pressing the Party for greater participation in the policy-making arena, the three requisite conditions are met:

1. Specialist scores increase over time. The instrumental average of 3.1 in 1959–65 marks a 72% increase over 1952–57.

TABLE 4

ELITE VALUES TOWARD POLICY-MAKING
1952–57 TO 1959–65

Elites	1952–57	1959–65	% Change
Party	1.7	2.2	+29%
Economic	1.5	2.9	+93%
Legal	2.0	3.1	+55%
Military	1.7	2.9	+71%
Literary	1.9	3.2	+68%
All Elites	1.8	2.9	+61%
Specialists	1.8	3.1	+72%

2. By 1959–65 all the specialist elites opt for a more participatory role in policy-making than the Party deems desirable. In every year from 1955 through 1965, specialist scores are higher, i.e., more participatory, than are Party scores. Since increased elite participation directly reduces Party dominance, the Party, as expected, claims that actual elite participation in the later period is greater (2.4) than desirable (2.2).

3. Specialist scores on who should make policy are appreciably higher in the 1959–65 period than on the question who *is* described as making policy (Table 5).

TABLE 5

COMPARISON OF SPECIALIST ELITE PERCEPTIONS AND VALUES
OF THE POLICY-MAKING ARENA

Is-Should Categories	1959	1961	1963	1965	1959–1965
Specialist Beliefs (who makes policy?)	2.4	2.8	2.8	3.3	2.8
Specialist Values (who should make policy?)	2.7	3.0	3.2	3.4	3.1
% Should > is	13%	7%	14%	3%	11%

In sum, on the important question of policy-making, a strong participatory trend is manifested by the specialist elites and recognized by the Party. Not denying the Party's ability to check, at least temporarily, elite participation,[4] a distinct feature of the post-Stalin period is this attitudinal development away from strict Party dominance.

2. ON DECISION-MAKING

In an ideological political system the Party is portrayed as dominant in local as well as policy level decisions, reserving for itself the role of final arbiter in disputes over implementation.

Hypothesis 3: Over time the specialist elites increasingly depict themselves as participants in the decision-making process (Table 6).

TABLE 6

ELITE PERCEPTIONS OF THE DECISION-MAKING ARENA, 1952–1965[a]

Elites	1952	1953	1955	1957	1959	1961	1963	1965	All Years
Party	2.4	2.4	2.6	2.6	3.3	4.0	2.1	3.1	2.8
Economic	000	2.5	3.3	2.8	4.2	3.8	2.5	2.2	3.0
Legal	3.0	000	3.1	2.8	2.5	2.8	2.9	2.5	2.8
Military	(2.5)	(2.6)	2.5	2.9	2.2	2.7	3.3	3.0	2.7
Literary	2.1	2.7	4.1	2.9	4.3	2.7	4.0	3.2	3.2
All Elites	2.5	2.6	3.5	2.8	3.1	3.1	2.9	2.8	2.9
Specialists	2.5	2.6	3.2	2.8	3.3	2.9	3.2	2.7	2.9

$F_{(35,154)} = 1.166$, significant at .001

[a] An example of position 5.0 is: "Indeed, if the chief means to be used in war is nuclear missiles, this means that we are obligated to construct both the theory of the art of warfare, the operational tactical training of troops and their indoctrinating with regard for the use, above all, of these weapons. This means that each officer, master sargent, sargent, soldier and sailor must learn to act, to carry out his duties and battle orders, as required by the conditions of nuclear-missile war." *Krasnaya zvezda*, May 11, 1962.

The years 1959 and 1961 represent the high tide of decentralization. Participatory Party scores in these years mirror Party efforts to increase production and efficiency through local initiative. By late 1961, however, the Party line changed as the inevitable consequences—"localism," "family circles," and fraud—threatened economic planning and central Party control.

The third hypothesis—a predicted specialist increase over time—is tenuously supported with an 8% participatory increase in 1959–65 over the earlier period (Table 7).

TABLE 7

ELITE PERCEPTIONS OF THE DECISION-MAKING
ARENA, IN 1952–57 TO 1959–65

Elites	1952–57	1959–65	% Change
Party	2.5	3.1	+23%
Economic	2.9	3.2	+11%
Legal	2.9	2.6	−12%
Military	2.6	2.8	+ 8%
Literary	3.1	3.6	+18%
All Elites	2.8	2.9	+ 5%
Specialists	2.8	3.0	+ 8%

The level of elite participatory attitudes in both periods is high, significantly higher than on policy-making, and seemingly reflects greater tolerance by the Party of specialist elite participation at the local level. With an instrumental score of 3.0 in 1959–65, the specialists perceive themselves as relative equals to the Party in decision-making.

Hypothesis 4: The specialists are pressing the Party for greater influence on the decision-making level (Table 8).

TABLE 8

ELITE VALUES TOWARD PARTICIPATION IN THE DECISION-MAKING
ARENA, 1952–1965[a]

Elites	1952	1953	1955	1957	1959	1961	1963	1965	All Years
Party	3.1	2.8	3.4	2.1	3.7	3.6	2.3	2.1	2.9
Economic	3.3	4.0	4.3	2.2	4.5	3.8	4.0	4.2	3.8
Legal	1.7	3.6	3.3	3.3	4.1	4.1	3.2	3.4	3.4
Military	(2.9)	(3.3)	2.3	4.1	3.0	2.9	2.9	3.2	3.1
Literary	3.8	2.6	3.7	3.2	3.9	4.5	3.2	3.4	3.5
All Elites	2.9	3.0	3.3	3.0	3.9	3.7	3.3	3.3	3.3
Specialists	2.9	3.1	3.3	3.2	3.9	3.8	3.4	3.6	3.4

$F_{(37,194)} = 1.767$, significant at .001

[a] An example of position 5.0, taken from Khrushchev's speech at the Moscow Writers' Union:
I do not think I ought to take up an analysis of your works in my address. I am not a literary critic, as you know, and for that reason do not feel called on to analyze your literary works. *Pravda*, May 22, 1959.

For specialists, instrumental scores on who *should* make decisions are manifested in every year from the death of Stalin onward, and a 16% overall increase is recorded over time (Table 9).

TABLE 9

ELITE VALUES TOWARD DECISION-MAKING
1952–57 TO 1959–65

Elites	1952–57	1959–65	% Change
Party	2.7	2.9	+ 7%
Economic	3.4	4.1	+21%
Legal	3.0	3.7	+23%
Military	3.0	3.0	000%
Literary	3.3	3.6	+ 9%
All Elites	3.1	3.5	+13%
Specialists	3.1	3.6	+16%

In both periods the specialists score in the instrumental range, and in 1959–65 all the specialist elites press for greater participation than the Party believes desirable.

When specialist elite perceptions of the decision-making process (who makes decisions?) are compared to elite values (who should make decisions?) two patterns emerge:

1) Despite ups and downs through the years, in each of the sampled years the specialists opt for greater responsibility in decision-making than they depict themselves as having (Table 10).

TABLE 10

COMPARISON OF SPECIALIST PERCEPTIONS OF THE DECISION-MAKING ARENA TO SPECIALIST PARTICIPATORY VALUES, 1952–65

Should-Is Categories	1952	1953	1955	1957	1959	1961	1963	1965	1952–57	1959–65	All Years
Who Makes Decisions	2.5	2.6	3.2	2.8	3.3	2.9	3.2	2.7	2.8	3.0	2.9
Should Make Decisions	2.9	3.1	3.3	3.2	3.9	3.8	3.4	3.6	3.1	3.6	3.3
% Should > Is	16%	19%	3%	14%	18%	31%	6%	33%	11%	20%	14%

2) Of all the elites in the 1959–65 period, only the Party claims that elite participation (perceived by the Party to be 3.1) is greater than desirable (2.9). If it is true that the Party is seeking a formula for balancing a high level of specialist elite participation with Party control, a comparison of Party and specialist scores on who should make decisions suggests that the specialist elites seek to upset the mini-max formula at the Party's expense (Table 11).

TABLE 11

COMPARISON OF PARTY AND SPECIALIST VALUES TOWARD PARTICIPATION IN DECISION-MAKING (WHO SHOULD MAKE DECISIONS?)

Elites	1952–57	1959–65	All Years
Party	2.7	2.9	2.8
Specialists	3.1	3.6	3.4
% Spec. > Party	15%	24%	21%

Scanning the data on the decision-making categories it appears that the military is closest to the Party's position, but this compliance is, as will be demonstrated in the discussion of Party-specialist conflict, directly traceable to Zhukov's defeat in 1957, and scores in the later years suggest that the military has strengthened its position since the Cuban missile crisis. The economic elite, despite its decline in 1957 following Malenkov's fall and Khrushchev's industrial reorganization, scores in the instrumental range on decision-making, reflecting a degree of success in its drive for greater managerial influence at the factory level. (Scores on the policy level follow a similar course.) The legal elite—the only specialist elite to experience a decline in participation on the decisional level, apparently a result of the Party's post-1958 retreat on socialist legality—topped all elites with a 23% increase over time on who should make decisions, indicating dissatisfaction with Party dominance. (An identical pattern occurred on the policy-making categories.) In both the 1952–57 and 1959–65 periods, the literary elite scored in the participatory range on decision-making and is, predictably, kept from still higher scores by the more Party-oriented attitudes articulated in the conservative journal *Oktyabr*. All in all, specialist elite participation in the decision-making arena is significant at 2.9 for All Years, and pressure to enhance their participatory role (3.4 for All Years) is growing increasingly strong over time.

3. AUTHORITY SOURCES IN PROBLEM SOLVING

A relationship exists between the form of political system and the type of rationalizations used in initiating, defending, and criticizing policy decisions. Historically, the dominance of the Party in the Soviet political system is linked to its claim of ideological supremacy. Certain sources of authority are supportive of CPSU dominance, e.g., the justification of policy decisions based on an appeal to Leninist historical consciousness, whereas other authority sources, for instance, a policy recommendation based on empirical evidence or expert opinion, are more conducive to specialist elite participation in the political process. In the category tapping the authority sources appealed to by the five elites in justifying their position on policies and decisions, lower scores of 1.0–2.9 reflect a Party dominant ideological system, scores in the 3.0–3.9 range are conducive to joint Party-specialist participation, and the higher scores of 4.0–5.0 support a more instrumental environment for specialist elite participation.

Hypothesis 5: Over time, as elite participation increases, the elites will opt for more instrumental forms of justification (Table 12).

TABLE 12

ELITE JUSTIFICATIONS FOR POLICY RECOMMENDATIONS, 1952–1965

What is the authority source appealed to in policy- and decision-making? How are policy decisions justified?
1.0 recommendations are based on an understanding of the laws of historical development/by analogy to a theory or decision of Marx, Lenin, Stalin *in the past*
2.0 recommendation is generally derived from Marxism, Leninism, Stalinism
3.0 recommendation is derived from Marxism, Leninsim, Stalinism, in conjunction with practice/ scientific Marxist-Leninist analysis/Marxism and objective analysis[a]
4.0 recommendation is based on expert opinions/the clash of opinions/discussion
5.0 recommendation is derived from objective investigation/by empirical methods/by scientific findings

Elites	1952	1953	1955	1957	1959	1961	1963	1965	All Years
Party	2.3	2.5	2.8	3.3	3.9	3.4	3.1	2.5	2.9
Economic	2.1	2.6	3.2	2.8	3.1	3.1	3.8	3.6	3.1
Legal	1.5	2.7	3.2	3.8	3.5	3.7	4.0	3.2	3.1
Military	(2.1)	(2.5)	2.3	2.6	2.3	2.3	2.7	2.9	2.5
Literary	2.2	2.2	2.5	3.4	3.3	2.5	3.2	3.1	2.9
All Elites	2.1	2.5	2.8	3.2	3.4	2.9	3.3	3.1	2.9
Specialists	2.0	2.5	2.8	3.1	3.1	2.9	3.4	3.2	2.9

$F_{(38,209)} = 2.661$, significant at .001

[a] An example of position 3.0:
Marxism is not an "universal master key" which can be applied without study practice and without analyzing the data of practice. Authors who construct their conclusions merely on superficial analogies, [position 1.0] or interpretations, comparisons, and "analyses" of quotations [position 2.0] and not on the study of facts—on the study of life—need to be reminded of how the founders of Marxism described the significance of the theory they established. *Kommunist*, No. 7, 1955.

As specialist elite participation increases it is hypothesized that the elites will tend increasingly to justify and criticize policy decisions in more instrumental terms, since appeals to historical consciousness and ideological awareness are more supportive of Party dominance. Comparing the two periods, the trend over time marks a significant change away from strict ideological appeals (Table 13).

TABLE 13

ELITE JUSTIFICATIONS FOR POLICY RECOM-
MENDATIONS, 1952–57 TO 1959–65

Elites	1952–57	1959–65	% Change
Party	2.8	3.2	+14%
Economic	2.6	3.5	+35%
Legal	2.8	3.5	+25%
Military	2.4	2.6	+ 8%
Literary	2.7	3.0	+11%
All Elites	2.6	3.2	+23%
Specialists	2.6	3.2	+23%

With specialists in the instrumental range in four of the last five years and showing a 23% increase over time, the hypothesis is generally affirmed. In the 1959–65 period all elites but the military tend to evaluate policies in instrumental terms more conducive to specialist elite participation. Party scores are high; throughout the Khrushchev years from 1957–1963, the Party scored in the instrumental range. This development may qualify as one indicator of what some observers, notably Barrington Moore, foresee as a Soviet potential for "technical-rational" development.[5]

4. PARTICIPATORY VALUES: AN OVERVIEW

Although the hypotheses and categories are analytically distinct, all relate to the basic question of elite participation. By collapsing the categories into one dimension and averaging each elite's score on all five categories, a Grand Mean score is derived, which may serve as a general indicator of overall participatory trends in the post-Stalin period (Table 14).

TABLE 14

ELITE ATTITUDES TOWARD PARTICIPATION: ALL CATEGORIES
COMBINED 1952–1965

Elites	1952	1953	1955	1957	1959	1961	1963	1965	All Years
Party	2.3	2.2	2.5	2.3	3.2	3.2	2.2	2.5	2.6
Economic	2.2	2.6	3.2	2.2	3.6	3.4	3.1	3.3	2.9
Legal	1.9	2.3	2.8	3.2	2.9	3.6	3.3	3.2	2.9
Military	2.1	2.2	2.0	2.7	2.5	2.5	3.1	3.0	2.5
Literary	2.2	2.0	3.0	3.0	3.4	2.9	3.2	3.3	2.9
All Elites	2.1	2.2	2.5	2.7	3.1	3.0	3.0	3.1	2.8
Specialists	2.1	2.2	2.7	2.8	3.1	3.1	3.2	3.2	2.8

Readily visible at the outset is the year by year instrumental increase for specialists from 1952 through 1965. Participatory trends are manifested by all the elites (Table 15).

A 24% All-Elite increase in the latter period is significant and indicative of the rapidity of change since Stalin. Thru 1959–65 Specialists scores are in the participatory range and in 1963 and 1965 every specialist elite is over 3.0.

TABLE 15

ELITE ATTITUDES TOWARD PARTICIPATION:
ALL CATEGORIES COMBINED, 1952–57 TO
1959–65

Elites	1952–57	1959–65	% Change
Party	2.3	2.8	+22%
Economic	2.5	3.4	+36%
Legal	2.6	3.2	+23%
Military	2.5	2.7	+ 8%
Literary	2.6	3.2	+23%
All Elites	2.5	3.1	+24%
Specialists	2.6	3.1	+19%

The military is perennially low among the specialists and at times below the Party as well. In all probability this reflects Party efforts to exercise exceptionally rigorous political controls over the military. Although not readily apparent from the figures, Marshal Zhukov's removal in 1957 was a crucial development in Party-military relations. By comparing attitudinal scores from an equal sample of articles from *Krasnaya zvezda* for the period immediately preceding and following Zhukov's ouster, the effects of Zhukov's dismissal on the military elite are demonstrated (Table 16).

TABLE 16

MILITARY ATTITUDES SURROUNDING MARSHAL ZHUKOV'S
DISMISSAL

Categories	Pre-Zhukov Ouster	Post-Zhukov Ouster	All 1957
Who Makes Policy?	1.7	1.0	1.3
Who Should Make Policy?	3.6	1.5	2.8
Who Makes Decisions?	3.5	2.0	2.9
Who Should Make Decisions?	4.4	2.8	4.1
Authority Source	2.7	1.9	2.6
All Categories Combined	3.3	1.9	2.7

The "price" Khrushchev paid for the military's support against the anti-Party group was for a time exceedingly high. From the data Zhukov's major thrust was for greater autonomy in the decision-making arena: a score of 4.4 represents a virtual denial of Party influence over local level military affairs. Not until 1963—following the Cuban missile crisis—did the military recover from the post-Zhukov crackdown.[6] The decline in military scores following an open confrontation against the Party is a characteristic pattern for all the specialist elites, again demonstrating the Party's capacity to thwart, temporarily, elite participation in the political process.

While a dysrhythmic pattern of elite behavior is typical for all the categories, 1963 marks a crisis year in Party-elite relations, for contrary to earlier developments the Party's retreat in 1963 to a more Party dominant position was *not*, as in the past, accompanied by a general decline for the specialist elites but by an overall specialist increase to a more instrumental position.[7] In short, Party-elite relations became significantly more conflictful as both Party and elites denied one another a dominant role in the political arena.

III. PARTY-SPECIALIST ELITE RELATIONS

The Party, confronted with more elite participation than it considers desirable and with still higher elite aspirations, finds it increasingly difficult to enforce mini-max boundaries on the specialist elites. Comparing elite beliefs and values, two types of Party-elite relations may be identified: *accommodation* or *conflict*. Accommodation exists when both the Party and specialist elites substantially agree on the allocation or responsibility in policy- and decision-making. Conflict—opting for mutually exclusive values—exists when the Party and elites substantially disagree on the allocation of responsibility in the political arena.[8]

Tentatively:

> *Hypothesis 6: As specialist elite participation increases, Party-elite conflict increases.*

And:

> *Hypothesis 7: As specialist elite participation increases beyond Party dominance, i.e., beyond mini-max boundaries, the intensity of conflict increases.*

Focusing on system-wide trends, Party-elite relations may be typed by comparing differential scores on the combined category (Table 17).

TABLE 17

PARTY-ELITE RELATIONS: ACCOMMODATION OR CONFLICT:
ALL CATEGORIES COMBINED, 1952–65*

Elites	1952	1953	1955	1957	1959	1961	1963	1965	All Years
Economic	− .17	+ .35	+ .73	− .12	+ .36	+ .23	+ .91	+ .88	+ .37
Legal	− .48	+ .07	+ .29	+ .84	− .30	+ .37	+ .03	+ .78	+ .34
Military	− (.20)	+ (.05)	− .47	+ .44	− .74	− .69	+ .80	+ .56	− .03
Literary	− .13	− .22	+ .49	+ .69	+ .16	− .25	+ .97	+ .82	+ .36
Specialists	− .24	+ .02	+ .23	+ .45	− .12	− .10	+ .95	+ .77	+ .27

* Minus scores denote accommodation, plus scores conflict

All-Year differential scores show that the economic, literary, and legal elites are in conflict with the Party. The military, at − .03, is in a "bare bargain" relationship. The years 1952, 1959, and 1961 are periods of accommodation, 1955, 1957, 1963, and 1965 years of conflict. Since 1959 and 1961 are the only two years in which the Party scored in the instrumental range, Party-elite accommodation in these two years is largely due to the Party's permissive definition of the boundaries of the political arena. With + .27 the All-Year conflict score, those years above the mean constitute "crisis years"; rank ordered the crisis years in Party-specialist relations are 1963, 1965, and 1957, notably, all periods related to succession crises, thereby lending support to the notion that when the Party is internally divided elite participation increases.

On scanning the differential scores of the individual elites an interesting pattern emerges: following an open confrontation against the Party, the elite typically moves from conflict to accommodation, then, in the next sampled year back into a conflict relationship with the Party. For example, note the two-steps-forward, one-step-back pattern for the economic elite in the years from 1955 through 1959, the legal elite's 1959 accommodating position following the Party's 1958 retreat on the Fundamental Laws, and the military's 1959 score following Marshal Zhukov's ouster. Accommodation, it appears, is *enforced* accommodation—is a result of successful Party efforts to thwart elite encroachments in the political arena, rather than a sign of a consensual definition of the boundaries of the political system. Within this framework, conflict signifies the Party's inability to control the participatory beliefs and aspirations of the specialist elites.

As predicted in hypothesis 6, Party-elite conflict increases over time (Table 18).

TABLE 18

PARTY-ELITE RELATIONS: AC-
COMMODATION OR CONFLICT:
ALL CATEGORIES COMBINED,
1952–57 TO 1959–65

Elites	1952–57	1959–62
Economic	+ .20	+ .60
Legal	+ .18	+ .47
Military	− .05	− .02
Literary	+ .21	+ .43
Specialists	+ .12	+ .37

A threefold increase in conflict is significant, especially so when it is recalled that All-Elite participation scores on the combined category increased by 2.4%, and the Party moved from 2.3 in the early period to a mini-max score of 2.8 in 1959–65. In the later period, then, Party-elite conflict increases at a sharper rate than does elite participation, thereby supporting the predicted increase in intensity of conflict as Party dominance is threatened by the specialist elites.

Conflict characterizes Party-elite relations in the post-Stalin period and in particular in the later years. This conflict is becoming generalized throughout the system. All the dimensions are in conflict (Table 19).

TABLE 19

PARTY-SPECIALIST RELATIONS: ACCOMMODATION OR CONFLICT,
1952–65

Categories	1952	1953	1955	1957	1959	1961	1963	1965	All Years
Who Makes Policy?	− .14	− .26	− .08	+ .71	− .47	+ .14	+1.13	+1.05	+ .26
Who Should Make Policy?	− .69	− .06	+ .82	− .43	+ .49	+ .75	+1.15	+ .93	+ .48
Who Makes Decisions?	+ .10	+ .23	+ .63	+ .21	− .01	−1.13	+1.10	. −32	+ .10
Who Should Make Decisions?	− .11	+ .25	− .17	+1.08	+ .15	+ .24	+1.02	+1.50	+ .50
Authority Sources	− .36	− .04	− .04	− .18	− .78	+ .50	+ .32	+ .71	+ .02
All Categories	− .24	+ .02	− .23	+ .45	− .12	+ .10	+ .95	+ .77	+ .27

Two inferences may be drawn from this comparison of conflict scores. First, the focus of Party-specialist elite conflict is changing over time: in 1952–57 the question of elite participation on the decision-making level was most in conflict, while in 1959–65 participation in the policy-making arena ranks as the major source of Party-elite conflict. Since specialist elite participation in the policy-making arena threatens the Party's integrative role, this development constitutes a most serious challenge to the Party's position in the Soviet political system.

Secondly, while all dimensions but the perceived boundaries of the decision-making arena are in conflict in 1959–65, this one instance of accommodation is a result of the Party exceeding its mini-max boundaries with a participatory score of 3.1. That responsibility for decision-making is in contention is apparent from the +.73 1959–65 conflict score on who should participate—the Party opting for 2.9 (the absolute maximum level for maintaining dominance in the decision-making arena), the Specialists denying Party dominance with a 3.6 average in 1959–65. Thus, by the later period the 2.5–2.9 mini-max range no longer represents the boundaries of compromise but a *field of conflict*.

IV. CONCLUSION

Three systemic trends emerge from a review of the data:

1. *Elite participatory attitudes show a marked increase over time, reaching the instrumental level in 1959–65.* By plotting All-Elite grand mean scores on the ideological-instrumental continuum this trend is graphically depicted in Figure 2.

IDEOLOGICAL	PARTY-SPECIALIST	INSTRUMENTAL
(party dominance)	(participation)	(specialist participation)

1952	1953	1955	1957	1959	1961	1963	1965	
×	×	×	×	×	×	×	×	

1.0	2.0	3.0	4.0	5.0

FIGURE 2. THE IDEOLOGICAL-INSTRUMENTAL CONTINUUM ALL-ELITE SCORES ON ALL CATEGORIES

With 3.0 corresponding to joint Party-elite participation, the trend is away from Party dominance toward what appears to be a "polyarchical" system,[9] toward what H. Gordon Skilling calls a "pluralism of elites."[10]

2. *Conflict characterizes Party-specialist elite relations in the post-Stalin period.* Party-elite conflict exists in both periods. In 1952–57, with a specialist participation score of 2.5, the extent of Party-elite conflict is +.12, while in 1959–65 the level of specialist participation

climbs to 3.1 and the level of conflict to $+.37$. In short, as specialist elite participatory attitudes increased by one-quarter, Party-elite conflict showed a threefold increase, despite the Party's move from 2.3 to a mini-max position of 2.8.

3. Concomitant with the attitudinal development toward elite participation and the intensification of Party-elite conflict is the trend toward an erosion of the ideological foundations of Party dominance— toward what Almond and Powell call the "secularization of values."[11] *Over the years all the elites, the Party included, increasingly come to rely on scientific knowledge and expert skills as crucial resources in the decision-making process.*

In sum, the Soviet political system is competitive. By 1959–65 participatory elite attitudes and Party-elite conflict reach levels which are incompatible with the totalitarian model. The Party's capacity to dominate what Stalin fondly called the "commanding heights" is an empirical question, not an absolute given in the post-Stalin period. This is not to deny that the Party is more powerful than the elites, but rather that the Party is not omnipotent. Party-specialist elite interdependence, not Party dominance, characterizes Party-elite relations. New models of Soviet politics are obviously needed.[12] The conception of the Soviet political system as a monolith is a myth.

Notes

1. Zbigniew Brzezinski and Samuel Huntington, *Political Power: USA/USSR* (New York: Viking, 1964), Pt. I.

2. *Beyond the Ruling Class: Strategic Elites in Modern Society* (New York: Random, 1963), p. 70; the five elites in this study generally conform to Keller's concept of strategic elites and fulfill the expectation that elite participation will increase over time.

3. Soviet references to this problem are numerous. See, e.g., the authoritative editorial titled "Concerning Discussions in Scholarly Journals," in *Kommunist*, No. 7, 1955, which, after stating that Marxist-Leninism must be the "essential" framework within which specialist discussion should take place, bemoans the fact that scholarly articles "often" by-pass Party formulas and all too frequently attempt "to reverse fundamental theses of the Party." For a general dicussion of the increasing leeway for instrumental criticism in the post-Stalin period, see Sidney Ploss, *Conflict and Decision-Making in Soviet Russia* (Princeton: Princeton U.P., 1965). A quantitative analysis comparing Soviet elite values manifested in journals is found in Robert Angell's "Social Values of Soviet and American Elites," *Journal of Conflict Resolution*, 8 (Dec. 1964), 330–85.

4. Note, e.g., the effect of Khrushchev's 1957 victory over Malenkov and Zhukov on the economic and military elites, and the effect of the 1962–63 anti-parasite

legislation on the legal elite. The zig-zag course for the individual elites is apparently a result of major policy disputes between the Party and specific elite.

5. *Terror and Progress—USSR* (New York, Harper Torchbooks, 1954), Chap. 7.

6. Secondary support marking the missile crisis as a turning point in military-Party relations is found in Thomas Wolfe, *Soviet Strategy at the Crossroads* (Cambridge: Harvard U.P., 1964), and Roman Kolkowicz, *The Soviet Military and the Communist Party* (Princeton: Princeton U.P., 1967).

7. See Carl Linden, *Khrushchev and the Soviet Leadership* (Baltimore: Johns Hopkins U.P., 1966), for a discussion of the Cuban missile crisis as a variable in Khrushchev's fall and as a possible cause for the Party's loss of control over the elites in 1963 and 1965, esp. pp. 146–47.

8. In operational terms, accommodation exists when the Party's score on the participatory categories is higher than the elite's score, i.e., when the specialist score is within the Party's prescribed boundary of the political arena. (E.g., if the Party score is 2.90 and the specialist score 2.50, the extent of accommodation is −.40, the minus sign denoting accommodation.) Conflict exists when the specialist elite score is more participatory than that of the Party. (E.g., if the Party score is 2.50 and the elite score 3.00, the level of conflict is +.50, plus signs denoting conflict.) For clarity all mean scores are carried two decimal places in the accommodation conflict tables.

9. Robert A. Dahl, *Preface to Democratic Theory* (Chicago: U. of Chicago P., 1956), Chap. 3.

10. H. Gordon Skilling, "Interest Groups and Communist Politics," *World Politics*, 18 (June 1966), 449.

11. Gabriel A. Almond and G. Bingham Powell, Jr., *Comparative Politics: A Developmental Approach* (Boston: Little, 1967), pp. 24–5; the secularization of culture is described as: "the process whereby traditional orientations and attitudes give way to more dynamic decision-making processes involving the gathering of information, the evaluation of information, the laying out of alternative courses of action, the selection of a course of action from among these possible courses, and the means whereby one tests whether or not a given course of action is producing the consequences which were intended."

12. See H. Gordon Skilling, *op. cit.*, 449–551; Alex Inkeles, "Models in the Analysis of Soviet Society, *Survey*, No. 60 (July, 1966), 3–12; Joel J. Schwartz and William R. Keech, "Group Influence on the Policy Process in the Soviet Union," *American Political Science Review*, LXII (Sept. 1968), 840–51.

4

The Soviet Central Committee: An Elite Analysis

MICHAEL P. GEHLEN AND MICHAEL MCBRIDE

This paper is a study of the backgrounds of the members of the Central Committee of the Communist Party of the Soviet Union. The purpose of its first part is to present and interpret certain quantitative material concerning the background characteristics of the members of the Central Committee. The conclusion elaborates premises regarding the function of co-optation in the higher Party organs and suggests possible relation-

Reprinted with permission from *American Political Science Review*, LXII (1968), 1232–41.
  Notes to the selection begin on page 124.

ships of this function to the education and career experiences of the Central Committee membership as discussed in the first part. To pursue an ideal study of this type, we recognize that extensive interviews and depth exploration of the sociological histories of the members would be desirable. In the case of the Soviet political elite such a course is obviously not possible at the present time. Nevertheless, sufficient data exist to make a modest beginning toward what we hope will help to lay a foundation for more extensive analysis of elites in the Soviet system in the future.

Two basic assumptions underlie our interest in the backgrounds of the Soviet political elite. First, and more important for this paper, is the premise that persons are co-opted into the Central Committee primarily, though not exclusively, as a result of the group associations they have made during the courses of their careers. These associations are largely career associations, and most of the members become part of the elite of important functional groups before they become members of the Party elite. Educational background, age, Party status, role associations, occupation, and other factors all converge to influence the development of the careers of the members. Our concern is with the general patterns of these and related variables among the total membership of the Central Committee.

A second and corollary premise is that the attitudes and value orientations of individual members are shaped in significant part by these background factors, especially by education, occupation, and role associations. This assumption, of course, opens the Pandora's box of how to determine ideological influence. More to the point here, however, the premise is intended to underscore the belief that many members are co-opted precisely because of their different backgrounds and career associations in order to bring people of varying experience, perceptions, and abilities toward the center of the decisional processes. This premise is predicated on the view that the Central Committee of the CPSU has become a composite of the representatives of key functional groups and is the principal medium, either through individual members or as a collective, through which the members of the °Politburo regularly exchange information with the elites of major interests in the system. Co-operation is viewed here as a rational process of attaining group representation in order to facilitate the communications flow between the principal decision-makers and the functional groups of Soviet society and to integrate group elites into the Party-dominated system. Co-optation, therefore, is interpreted as having both representative and regulatory functions. In short, we see the membership selection and function of the Central Committee as an institutionalization of a high level communications network.

I. FINDINGS
ON BIOGRAPHICAL CHARACTERISTICS

The empirical portion of this study consists of the examination of background factors of members of the Central Committee elected at the 23rd Congress of the Communist Party of the Soviet Union held in 1966. The data were collected from written sources, primarily from *Who's Who in the U.S.S.R.*, other information made available by the Institute for the Study of the U.S.S.R. in Munich, and official Soviet sources.[1] Of the 195 full members, sufficient information was obtained on 184. Of the 165 candidate members, similar information was available on 125. The basic total population of the sample therefore is 309, although in some categories information was available on a larger number of candidates.

The data collected on the 309 members were classified into twenty-eight variables. Among the more important were date of birth, level of education, source of education, the learned occupation, the practiced occupation, date of admission to the CPSU, date of admission to the Central Committee, record of Party work, occupational status before and after 1953, and region of residency. Insufficient data made some variables impossible to use. These were population of place of birth, region of birth, social class of parents, and recent technological education or retooling. Others, which will be considered later, proved of only limited value. After the data were assembled, frequency distributions were made of all variables and their subdivisions. Then, a correlation matrix was employed in order to ascertain patterns of interrelationships between pairs of variables.

AGE AND SEX

Examination of age and sex of the members of the Central Committee (CC) reveals what one might expect. The full members were slightly older than the candidates, but the average age of both groups fell into the 54–60 age category. Thirty-eight and six-tenths percent of the full members and 22.6% of the candidates were born in the decade 1900–09, while 45.7% of the former and 52.4% of the latter were born between 1910 and 1919. Only one person in each group was born after 1930, and only 11 of the full members and 7 of the candidates were born before 1900. In 1967, the average age of the full member was 57 and that of the candidate was slightly under 55. These figures indicate that the newly elected members kept the average age at about the same level as it had been for the CC elected in 1961.[2] (At the time 58.5% of the total membership had been born in the decade of 1900–09.) The overwhelming number of both types of members were male. Only five full members and five candidates were women (two of the candidates for whom biographical data were unavailable were also women).

EDUCATION

The level of education of the CC membership continued to show a gradual increase as did the tendency to co-opt persons who had basically a specialized higher education. Table 1 indicates the level of education

TABLE 1

LEVEL AND TYPES OF EDUCATION

	Full Members		Candidate Members	
University	17	9.3%	11	8.8%
Party School Only	8	4.4	15	12.0
Military Academy	15	8.1	10	8.0
Technical*	120	65.2	64	51.2
Secondary	4	2.2	2	1.6
Other	1	.5	0	0.0
No Data/or None Reported	19	10.3	23	18.4
	184	100 %	125	100 %

"Technical" includes institutes, polytechnical schools, and specialized academics other than military ones.

attained by the members. These figures may be compared with those representing the source of the highest degree attained by the member (Table 2). These two tables indicate a slight decline in the number of persons educated at universities and military academies from the CC elected in 1961. There was a simultaneous increase in the number that had Party schools as their only source of higher education. In regard

TABLE 2

SOURCE OF HIGHEST DEGREE

	Full Members		Candidate Members	
University	14	7.6%	9	7.2%
Party Schools	32	17.4	28	22.4
Military Academy	16	8.7	10	8.0
Technical	100	54.4	49	39.2
Secondary	4	2.2	2	1.6
No Data/None Received	18	9.7	27	21.6
	184	100 %	125	100 %

to the technically trained, there was an increase both in number and percentage in the ranks of the full members—from 58% to 61%. However, there was a substantial decrease in technical education among the candidates. This number dropped from 83 to 64, while the size of the candidate ranks was being increased, The percentage of those so classified declined from 53.4% to 38.8%. The reasons for this shift among the candidate membership toward more exclusive education in party schools and less technical education was probably to provide compensation to the so-called "reds" or more ideologically oriented members, while the "experts" were being rewarded with full membership.

OCCUPATION

An important aspect of education is the learned occupation. The frequency of this variable was also tabulated with the related factor of the occupation practiced by the CC members during the early parts of their careers. Table 3 lists the percentages of the memberships in the

TABLE 3

LEARNED OCCUPATION

	Full Members	Candidates	Total
Engineering	42.1%	30.3%	37.5%
Science & Mathematics	5.6	3.0	4.7
Agronomy	18.5	16.2	17.5
Military	8.3	14.1	10.6
Arts & Letters	12.7	16.2	14.0
Other (mostly Party training)	12.8	20.2	15.7
	100 %	100 %	100 %

principal categories of learned occupations. The information in this table corresponds fairly closely with the occupations practiced by the members of the CC in the early parts of their careers. Table 4 provides

TABLE 4

PRACTICED OCCUPATION

	Full Members	Candidates	Total
Engineering	38.0%	26.7%	33.6%
Science & Mathematics	4.9	2.8	4.2
Agronomy	16.6	19.4	17.5
Military	9.2	13.2	10.8
Arts & Letters	15.3	16.1	15.6
Other (mostly Party work)	16.0	21.8	18.3
	100 %	100 %	100 %

the latter information, indicating the slightly higher percentage of people drawn immediately into Party work than were specifically educated for that purpose. This practice was quite probably the result of the need to fill Party posts that were associated with some productive function (e.g., factory or kolkhoz management) that demanded technical competence.

It is suggestive from the principal occupational lines followed during the bulk of their careers that the "learned" occupations of the CC members were only selectively significant. Scientists had obviously been trained as scientists, for example, but Party workers came from a variety of educational backgrounds. In order to ascertain the career orientations pursued by individuals over a longer term period than was indicated in Table 4, occupational status was examined in two parts: first, the career orientation of each member before 1953 and, second, the career orientation after 1953. The year 1953 was chosen as the dividing line between Stalinist and post-Stalinist Russia so that any significant variation in career patterns and in means of mobility might be more accurately assessed. Career orientation was determined by the number of years a CC member had spent in a particular type of occupation. Table 5 presents the data collected on occupational status of full members while Table 6 presents the corresponding information for the candidate members.

The most striking difference between the occupational associations of the full members before and after 1953 is the sharp increase in apparatus assignments from 40.0% to 54.9%. This very strongly sug-

TABLE 5

OCCUPATIONAL STATUS OF FULL MEMBERS

Occupation	Occupational Status before 1953		Occupational Status after 1953	
Party Apparatchiki	74	37.2%	101	54.9%
High Level Bureaucrats				
(heavy industry)	25	13.6	23	12.5
(light industry)	1	.5	1	.5
(agriculture)	5	2.7	10	5.4
Low Level Bureaucrats				
(heavy industry)	15	8.2	0	0.0
(light industry)	1	.5	0	0.0
(agriculture)	11	6.0	0	0.0
Other Bureaucrats[1]	5	2.7	12	6.5
Indeterminate[2]	3	1.6	5	2.7
Military Officers	15	8.2	14	7.6
Scientists	4	2.2	4	2.2
Writers	3	1.6	3	1.6
Journalists	1	.5	1	.5
Trade Union Officers	4	2.2	6	3.3
Workers	3	1.6	2	1.1
Others	2	1.1	2	1.1
No Data	12	6.5		
	184	100 %	184	100 %

[1] "Other bureaucrats" include those in the cultural, welfare, planning, and security ministries of the government.

[2] "Indeterminate" includes those who spent such equal portions of their careers in both party and state work as to make it impossible to place them in either category.

gests the importance of ties with the apparatus for upward mobility in the higher levels of the Party. Since most of those moving into apparatus posts had devoted most of their careers to economic or cultural activities, the increase also underscores the emphasis placed on experience in a relatively broad range of economic and cultural areas as one condition for the co-optation of nonprofessional apparatchiki into important apparatus positions. The data indicate that about one-third of the members of the Party apparatus in the 1966 Central Committee had built their earlier careers in the economic or cultural bureaucracy or some related unit of Soviet society. In addition, many of those who had been professional apparatchiki from near the outset of their careers had been intensively trained in economic and technological matters in Party schools. As a consequence of these factors, a substantial proportion of the apparatchiki themselves had acquired some measure of expertise or specialization in one or more areas outside of Party administration. The co-optation of such experienced persons into the apparatus suggests an effort on the part of the apparatchiki to enrich their own numbers with highly competent individuals who have succeeded in careers outside the apparatus and to help assure the loyalty of such experienced persons to the role of the apparatus in the system.

TABLE 6

OCCUPATIONAL STATUS OF CANDIDATE MEMBERS

Occupation	Occupational Status before 1953		Occupational Status after 1953	
Party Apparatchiki	50	40.0%	66	50.2%
High-Level Bureaucrats				
(heavy industry)	9	7.2	14	10.6
(light industry)	4	3.2	5	3.8
(agriculture)	4	3.2	5	3.8
Low-Level Bureaucrats				
(heavy industry)	4	3.2	0	0
(light industry)	0	0.0	0	0
(agriculture)	4	3.2	1	0.8
Other bureaucrats[1]	3	2.4	7	5.4
Indeterminate[2]	3	2.4	5	3.8
Military Officers	11	8.8	13	10.0
Scientists	3	2.4	3	2.3
Writers	4	3.2	4	3.1
Journalists	3	2.4	2	1.5
Trade Union Officers	1	.8	4	3.1
Workers	2	1.6	2	1.6
Others	0	0.0	0	0
No Data	20	16.0		
	125	100 %	131	100 %

[1] "Other bureaucrats" include those in the cultural, welfare, planning, and security ministries of the government.
[2] "Indeterminate" includes those who spent such equal portions of their careers in both party and state work as to make it impossible to place them in either category.

The priority given to continuation of the influence of the Party apparatus and to the development of heavy industry is attested to by the paucity of formal representation accorded persons in light industry and in intermediate and lower-level bureaucratic positions. The fact that only one full member was associated with light industry both before and after 1953 indicates that careers in that sector of the economy have afforded little opportunity for upward mobility. On the other hand, it should be noted that a small number of the apparatchiki and of those now in the Council of Ministers have developed special competence in the light industry sector.

The same general pattern exists for the candidate membership as for the full members.

PRIOR POSITIONS

A related point of particular importance is the relationship between the position occupied by an individual and his co-optation into the Central Committee. Examination of the compositions of the Central Committees elected in 1952, 1956, 1961, and 1966 reveals that at least eighty and possibly one hundred of the full members are chosen as a result of their holding particular positions.[3] The figure cannot be more precise, for the size of the Central Committee has tended to increase with each election, thereby making it difficult to ascertain whether the holders of some posts will continue to serve in the CC regardless of their personal identities. In addition to the members of the CPSU Politburo and Secretariat, who are always members of the Central Committee, there are sixty-five or more posts that carry CC membership with them. These include all the first secretaries of the Union Republic Parties, thirty-five or more first secretaries of important provincial Party organizations (Moscow, Leningrad, Kiev, Stalingrad-Volgograd, etc.), and the first secretaries of the Moscow and Leningrad city Party organizations. From the government, the chairman of the All-Union Council of Ministers, also a member of the Politburo, and at least two first deputy chairmen of the Council are members, along with the Ministers and First Deputy Ministers of Defense and Foreign Affairs. Besides these, the chairmen of the Republic Councils of Ministers of the RSFSR, the Ukraine, Byelorussia, and probably Georgia and Uzbekistan are Central Committee members. From the mass organizations, the first secretary of the Komsomols and the chairman of the Trade Union Council are members. Although supporting data come from a rather limited time span, it can be stated that the editor of *Pravda*, the president of the Academy of Sciences, and at least one deputy chairman of the Trade Union Council have probably become positions bringing automatic membership in the Central Committee. There have also regularly been other members of the Council of Ministers represented on the Central Committee, but they have not been associated with any particular ministry.

As yet, candidate membership appears to have no such strong associations with particular positions, although there are some indications of change in this regard. Perhaps as many as twenty-five provincial Party first secretarial posts have reached the point where they carry with them candidate membership. Some particular types of specialists may consistently be given candidate status but thus far there is no indication that they are chosen as a result of positions already held. In general, the Party leaders may be expected to have more flexibility in the selection of candidates.

The remaining members and candidate members of the Central Committee are not commonly associated with any special positions although the great majority of them also seem to be selected as a result of a combination of their reputations and positions. The co-optation of certain military officers, scientists, literary figures, journalists, economic planners and managers of industrial and agricultural enterprises round out the respresentative significance of the institution. Some of these may achieve permanent membership. This is a distinct possibility for marshals in command of crucially stationed troops or the admirals of key fleets. It is certainly less likely for less highly institutionalized professional groups, such as writers and scientists.

The association of some positions with CC membership is undoubtedly a major reason for the relative stability of membership in recent years. Whereas there were at least two fairly sharp turnovers on the CC during the 1950's, the membership has been relatively stable since the election of the CC of 1961. In 1966, 79.4% of the 175 full members from the preceding Central Committee were reelected, although the size was increased to 195 to allow for the co-optation of additional persons. Only twenty-six living members of the previous Central Committee were not returned. Seventy percent of the full members had never served as candidates, having been drawn directly into voting status. Twenty-two (12%) had served as candidates in the preceding committee. Seventy-eight percent were elected in 1956 or later, over one-half of these in 1961.

The candidate membership experienced greater changes in 1966 than the full membership. Here it should be remembered that data were not available on 40 of the 165 candidates. The vast majority of these were new admissions. However, the data referred to in this paragraph consist of references only to 129 candidates for whom information could be collected on those variables dealing with candidate status. Of these, 51 were elected in 1966, 54 in 1961, and 6 in 1956. In short, over 84% of the 129 reached the Central Committee at or after the 20th Party Congress of 1956.

A related matter worthy of attention is that the proportion of apparatchiki and bureaucrats among the full members of the CC of

1966 did not differ significantly from that found in the CC selected at the 22nd Party Congress of 1961. On the other hand, the number of bureaucrats in the candidate membership decreased from 29.0% to 25.6%, while the proportion of apparatchiki increased over 3%. Both the apparatchiki and bureaucrats who were full members immediately prior to the 23rd Party Congress were sufficiently entrenched to discourage a serious turnover. The pressure from the conservatives, who apparently were still anxious to prevent a resurgence of Khrushchev-type reformism, was felt more keenly in the candidate membership, where the percentage of bureaucrats and technocrats declined due to an increase in apparatchiki.

OCCUPATIONAL CHANGES

Of particular interest is the question of who changed occupational classifications after 1953. A total of 54 full members, 41 with technical education, changed job classifications in the post-Stalin years. These figures include 12 for whom there were no data for the years since 1953. Of these 12, nine had assumed career associations with the party apparatus after 1953. Sixteen of the others moved from positions in the lower and intermediary levels of the agricultural and industrial bureaucracies into the ranks of the apparatchiki. All but one of these had records of technical education. Six achieved upward mobility in their initial career areas, moving from low-level to high-level bureaucratic positions. No pattern existed among the remaining 20 full members who changed from one job classification to another.

Of the candidate members, 20 changed kinds of positions and another 20 moved from the unclassified (no data) category before 1953 to identifiable posts after that date. Twelve of the unclassified occupied positions in the apparatchiki after 1953. Nine others moved from the low- or middle-level bureaucracy into the party apparatus, eight of these having had technical education. Eleven others changed kinds of positions without a pattern. Of the 40 candidates, there was no information on the educational backgrounds of 19, while 19 others had technical training and two had nontechnical higher education.

Of those whose occupational associations changed after 1953, there was a primary movement from specialized bureaucratic positions to the party apparatus and a secondary movement from low-level to high-level positions in the same general occupational category. The primary movement indicates a tendency of the party to recruit and promote at least partly on the basis of specialized education and experience. The secondary movement of promotion within the ranks of a particular organization is probably typical of nonparty institutional processes. The primary movement is undoubtedly more important as a means of providing the apparatus with the intelligence necessary to exert effective control over nonparty institutions by giving the apparatus groups of experts with previous or continuing association with those institutions.

PLACE OF RESIDENCE

Although the place-of-residence factor did not have a significant correlation with the other variables considered, it does indicate the shifting living habits of the Soviet elite. Seventy-eight percent of the full members and 63% of the candidates listed their current residences in cities of 500,000 or more. Of the total membership 91% lived in cities of 100,000 or above. Moscow was by far the most widely claimed residence, despite the fact that many who lived there were formally associated with republic Party organizations. Of the full membership, 46% had residencies in Moscow, while 44% of the candidates had the same. Also, 65% of the full members and 62% of the candidates resided in the RSFSR, with the Ukraine and the Central Asian republics following as the next most widely claimed places of residence.

PARTY STATUS

The status of each member in the CPSU is another major area of consideration. Factors examined here are date of admission to the CPSU, the tenure of each member in the Central Committee, and the record of service in the central, republic, and regional Party organs. Then attention will be focused on the backgrounds of the members who were newly elected at the 23rd Party Congress.

The record of the dates of admission to Party membership is found in Table 7. The large percentage of candidates for whom there is no information suggests that those individuals were admitted fairly recently (at least, postwar) and that they are probably younger than the members for whom there is information. Assuming this to be the case, well over one-half the candidates were admitted after the great purges of the

TABLE 7

DATE OF ADMISSION TO THE CPSU

	Full Members		Candidates	
Pre-1917	57	2.7%	0	0.0%
1918–1937	76	41.3	34	27.2
1938–1945	88	47.8	62	49.6
1946–1952	4	2.2	6	4.8
1953 or After	4	2.2	1	.8
No Data	7	3.8	22	17.6
	184	100 %	125	100 %

1930's. In contrast, about 45% of the full members attained membership prior to or during the great purge. Nevertheless, the old Bolsheviks have almost entirely vanished, only five members of the CC having joined the Party prior to the revolution.

Another aspect of Party status concerns the records of those who had worked as apparatchiki in the Party before being co-opted into the Central Committee. Tables 8 and 9 indicate the Party status of the CC members before and after 1953. Party status here refers to the level of official positions held in the organs of the CPSU. Well over one-half

TABLE 8

PARTY OFFICES HELD BY FULL MEMBERS

	Before 1953		After 1953	
Central Apparatus	6	3.4%	8	4.4%
Central & Republic Apparati	1	.5	17	9.2
Republic Apparati	13	7.1	16	8.7
Republic & Regional Apparati	17	9.2	31	16.8
Regional Apparati	42	22.8	43	23.4
All Three Levels	3	1.6	13	7.1
None	102	55.4	56	30.4
	184	100 %	184	100 %

of both the full members and candidates had no record of regular service in Party organs before 1953. In the post-Stalin period this situation was reversed with the reversal being most sharp among the candidates. This information suggests two important possibilities that tend to enforce the findings on occupational backgrounds presented in Tables 5 and 6. First, many members made themselves accessible to co-optation into the apparatchiki as a means of increasing their upward mobility after having already established themselves in other

TABLE 9

PARTY OFFICES HELD BY CANDIDATE MEMBERS

	Before 1953		After 1953	
Central Apparatus	5	4.0%	11	8.8%
Central & Republic Apparati	0	0.0	6	4.8
Republic Apparati	4	3.2	21	16.8
Republic & Regional Apparati	6	4.8	17	13.6
Regional Apparati	34	27.2	36	28.8
All Three Levels	0	0.0	3	2.4
None	76	60.8	31	24.8
	125	100 %	125	100 %

occupational endeavors. This means that a significant portion of the CC who would now be classified as apparatchiki would not have been so classified during most of their careers. For the most part, they appear to be specialists who demonstrated their abilities as engineers or administrators and were only later drawn into full-time Party work. Second, the turnover in candidate membership in 1966 suggests that some individuals who had been members primarily as a result of their specialization and who had not become apparatchiki were removed from candidacy in favor of those who had given more regular administrative service to Party organs in the past.

NEW MEMBERS

Examination of the backgrounds of the newly elected members can be expected to shed further light on patterns of continuity or change in the membership of the Central Committee. Consequently, the educational backgrounds and careers of the 38 new full members and the 51 new candidates are highlighted in Tables 10 and 11. Of the 89 new members

TABLE 10

EDUCATIONAL BACKGROUNDS OF NEW MEMBERS

	Full Members	Candidate Members
Engineering	10	9
Agronomy	7	4
Science	3	2
Military	2	4
Arts & Letters	2	7
Party School Only	3	4
No Data	11	21
	38	51

TABLE 11

OCCUPATIONS OF NEW MEMBERS

| | Full Members | | Candidate Members | |
	Before 1953	After 1953	Before 1953	After 1953
Apparatchiki	17	23	16	27
High-Level Bureaucrats	6	8	2	10
Low-Level Bureaucrats	5	0	1	1
Military Officers	2	2	3	5
Writer	0	0	1	1
Journalists	0	0	2	1
Scientists	3	3	2	2
Trade Union Officers	0	0	1	4
Indeterminate	0	1	0	0
No Data	4	0	23	0
	37	37	51	51

and candidates considered, 50 (56%) had been regularly associated with the Party apparatus after 1953. All but 18 (20%) had had at least periodic occupational association with the apparatus. This suggests a possible effort on the part of the ruling *coalition* of the Party to check the influence of the technocrats and to stabilize, if not accelerate, the influence of the apparatchiki in the hierarchy of the CPSU. At the same time it should be emphasized that this effort had more effect on the candidate membership than on the full membership.

II. CORRELATIONS

AGE

Although there were only about three years separating the average ages of the full and candidate members of the Central Committee, age proved to have statistical importance as a factor influencing other variables and demarking differences between the two classes of membership. Date of birth was related to both the level and to the source of education. Despite the small difference in age, the candidates had had greater access to higher forms of education. The higher correlations for the candidates lead one to assume that a larger number of them were

	Level of Education	Source of Degree	Learned Occupation
Age of Full Members	.3149	.3024	.2932
Age of Candidates	.5279	.4742	.3428

co-opted into the Central Committee on the basis of their specialized training than was the case with the full members, who were often selected on the basis of their positions. In related areas, date of birth had an expectedly high correlation with date of admission to the CPSU, .5608 for the full members and .4682 for the candidates. The lower correlation for the candidates indicates a wider distribution of age of admission, thereby reducing, to a modest extent, the importance of age as a significant determinant to admission.

SEX

Sex is an obvious influence on the selection of members when one considers that only five of the 184 full members and five of the 125 candidates for whom information was available were women. Elite status in the CPSU is clearly reserved largely for males. What, then, are the factors that help to create the exceptions? For the full members no definite pattern was observed. However, two factors stood out in regard to the women candidates. All five of the latter had records as active members of the Komsomols, working in the apparatus of that organization, and four of the five had careers as apparatchiki. Two of the full members had the same backgrounds. The single exception among the candidates was the Minister of Social Security, who was associated with the state bureaucracy. Only one of the five was newly elected to the Central Committee. The foregoing factors indicate that those women who were able to overcome the political obstacle created by their sex have done so largely through their records as political activists in youth organizations and their willingness to seek careers in the Party apparatus rather than through specialization in technical areas. Moreover, it should be noted that the women tended to be younger than the male members, for the eldest was fifty-six and two of the ten were in their thirties.

EDUCATION

Level and source of education proved to be of greater significance for candidates than for full members, although it was important for both. Not only did these two factors have a greater bearing on the learned and practiced occupations of the candidates than of the full members, but the source of the highest degree earned by the candidates had a significance of .3540 with Party office held before 1953. The correlation of the same variables pertaining to full members was only .2820. In

FULL MEMBERS

	Learned Occupation	Practiced Occupation
Level of Education	.3189	.2101
Source of Highest Degree	.3244	.1897

CANDIDATE MEMBERS

	Learned Occupation	Practiced Occupation
Level of Education	.6243	.5848
Source of Highest Degree	.5403	.5370

addition, a similar positive correlation (.3896) existed between the Party office held by candidates after 1953 and occupational status after 1953. Those patterns suggest rather strongly that the candidates were co-opted more for the degree of specialization than the full members. If such is the case, it can be hypothesized that candidate members in the Central Committee elected at the 23rd Party Congress were selected because they were thought to provide a communications input into the higher decision-making centers of the CPSU. It appears that the full members, as distinct from the candidates, became less directly associated with the occupational specialty for which they were educated as they moved to higher positions in the political structure.

REGIONAL FACTORS

There was a correlation of .3956 between candidate status in the Central Committee and the region of birth. This indicates that candidacy is used more to give recognition to the geographic divisions and ethnic groups of the U.S.S.R. than full membership, for which the correlation was only .2053. Related to this is the relationship of experience in a large city Party organization to the levels of the Party apparatus in which members of the CC who had such experience worked. These levels were identified by the Party offices that were held in the central, republic, and regional Party organizations. The correlations suggest that work in a city Party organization was more important for the full members than for the candidates in terms of their movement upward in the Party apparatus. It also suggests that the younger full

PARTY OFFICE HELD

	Full Members		Candidate Members	
	Before 1953	After 1953	Before 1953	After 1953
City Party Work	.4937	.3548	.3018	.3005

members and most of the candidates had found other means of attaining upward mobility in the system. The days of intense rivalry between the Moscow and Leningrad Party organizations are probably about over, and the importance of association with one or the other has apparently declined despite the increasing tendency to move to the larger cities. This indicator, especially when considered in combination with the background of the members in the Party apparatus, bears out the basic contention that factors other than professional associations with the apparatus are of considerable significance in determining the co-optation of persons into the Central Committee, even during a period of conservative reaction to the reformism of the Khrushchev years and even though many of them may be assigned positions in the apparatus after becoming CC members or candidates.

FOREIGN TRAVEL

Among the other relationships examined only two merit attention, and these may be only of passing interest. There was no apparent difference between the number of awards and decorations bestowed upon the two classes of CC members. What difference existed can probably be accounted for by the slight age difference. On the other hand, one curious differential may be construed as indicating the greater status of the full members in comparison with the candidates. This factor is foreign travel. There is a positive correlation of .3544 between full membership and foreign travel and a slight inverse correlation between candidate membership and foreign travel. This may be interpreted as a distinction in status, although it should be pointed out that the number of full members who had had diplomatic experience may have accounted for part of the difference in correlation.

III. SUMMARY AND CONCLUSIONS

The evidence presented indicates the importance of education to members of the Soviet political elite both in terms of influencing how they launched their careers and of influencing their status in the CPSU. Most of this educational preparation was specialized rather than general, with the four largest categories being engineering, agronomy, Party, and military, in that order. Of our sample 65% (120) of the full members and 51% (64) of the candidates had a technical education (excluding military officers and scientists). The career patterns of the members included 55% (101) of the full members and 50% (66) of the candidates who had primary associations in the Party apparatus after 1953. In addition, 25% (46) of the full members and 26% (32) of the candidates had primary associations with the state bureaucracy (excluding the military). Of those in the bureaucratic category, members attached to the heavy industry segment of the state machinery were clearly predominant, with modest representation being given to agricultural administrators and specialists and only token recognition to those associated with light industry.

Despite the fact of considerable experience in the Party apparatus after 1953, a clear majority of both full and candidate members held no Party posts on the central, republic, or regional levels of the apparatus prior to 1953. This was true of 55% (102) of the full members and 60% (64) of the candidates. It was only after 1953—that is, the period during which increasing emphasis was given to co-opting persons into Party leadership positions who had specialized training and experience in some functional service (economics, agronomy, military technology, etc.)—that many of the members were assigned positions, temporarily or otherwise, in various levels of the Party apparatus. During this period all but 30% (56) of the full members and 24% (30) of the candidates held official posts in Party groups.

The correlation study demonstrated a modest though meaningful relationship between degree earned and Party office and between the Party office held by candidates and their occupational status after 1953. These correlations, especially when considered in the light of the data concerning backgrounds in the Party posts, and a general survey of the 1956 and 1961 Central Committees, support the contention that co-optation is developing largely into a rational process and not merely into a device with which to play games of musical chairs. In short, at least a large percentage, though undoubtedly not all, are drawn into the Central Committee as a result of their knowledge, demonstrated abilities, and occupational role associations. Their presence helps to assure an inflow of information from others with whom the members have occupational associations. It is in the sense of accessibility that the members of the Central Committee may be considered representatives, though certainly at this stage of development they are not equal voting deputies.

The role functions of the persons in the Central Committee, especially their representative role, are closely associated with *who* they are and *why* they were co-opted. The question of who they are is partially answered by the foregoing empirical study. They are persons with key occupational assignments, most of whom had acquired reputations as successes in their respective career specializations. Most are also associated with an important functional group in the Soviet system. To be sure, the evidence presented here does not deal with the difficult and important question of the degree of group solidarity and the extent to which the persons of the same group share or contest particular values. The situation of the apparatchiki, who constitute such a significant percentage of the membership, is a case in point. The very fact that some of them have joined the apparatus rather late in their careers, that some are in Party posts that require technical training and special skills as well as administrative ability, and that still others have spent their adult lives in Party administration or in propaganda and security organs indicate the range of experiences and attitudes that they may carry into the Central Committee. The point here is simply that most have been associated with particular functional groups that have particular interests. From these associations and interests they can be expected to have acquired specialized knowledge and abilities that influence their perceptions of systemic goals as well as of their own roles in the system.

The question of why they were co-opted relates to the practice of co-optation and the kind of representation they are able to perform. Philip Selznick has argued that organizations adopt two principal mechanisms of defense as means of enhancing the security of the organization in its relations to the social forces around it.[4] These mechanisms are ideology and co-optation. The use of ideology as a device of political socialization in the Soviet system is widely recognized by Western observers. The rational use of co-optation in the system has been noted but not deeply explored. Selznick suggests that there are two types of co-optation: formal and informal. Informal co-optation involves the actual sharing of power by the old elite with the co-opted persons. While this has occurred in the case of the Central Committee in leadership disputes (e.g., the antiparty crisis of 1957), the actual sharing of power is undoubtedly the exception rather than the rule. On the other hand, the concept of formal co-optation appears to have more meaningful application in analyzing why persons are co-opted into the Central Committee. This mechanism is used to maintain or increase general acceptance of the legitimacy of the Party elite as the highest decision-making authority in the system by establishing definite means of accessibility to key individuals and especially to key groups. This is accomplished by the selection of persons who are part of group elites. Such use of co-optation also consists of selecting persons who are dependable sources of information. The inflow of knowledge that they bring helps the elite to make more effective operational decisions than they otherwise might make. By co-opting persons on the basis of these two factors—accessibility and communications—the ruling elite may have the advantage of increased stability and information without a complementary loss of power.

The sharing of the symbols of authority, however, opens the door to pressure for a transfer of real power to the co-opted parties. The prevention of this development requires some form of control (Selznick contends informal control) over the co-opted elements. These forces —the sharing of symbols of authority and the placement of controls over those with whom authority is seemingly shared—create tension between representation and participation on the one hand and integration and regulation on the other. Such tension is suggested by the addition of apparatus-associated persons to the Central Committee in 1966 (especially among the candidates) and the corresponding decrease in the more diffuse technocratic contingent. The relative stability of the full membership, however, indicates that certain groups and individuals had acquired representation by right and that only a major conflict would overturn the general balance of forces. Candidacy may be a means of giving ostensible authority and recognition to those less firmly entrenched but ambitious to secure recognition to themselves and those with whom they are professionally associated.

These interpretations must, for the present, be tentative, although they are definitely suggested by the history of the Central Committee since 1956 and by the examination of the backgrounds of the members. The paucity of reliable information on informal channels of communications makes the problem of a more comprehensive empirical study virtually insurmountable for the time being. However, it is our hope that the methods used and the hypotheses set forth in this study will be suggestive to others of related and more comprehensive projects that might be developed in the future.

Notes

1. The most accessible source of biographical data is the *Who's Who in the U.S.S.R., 1965–1966*, compiled by the Institute for the Study of the U.S.S.R., Munich, Germany, and published by Scarecrow Press, 1966. Additional information is available in the files of the Institute. Short but current biographical sketches are published in the *Ezhegodnik* of the *Great Soviet Encyclopedia*. More extensive biographies, though sometimes less up-to-date, are found in *Biograficheskii slovar'*, produced at different times by different professional groups (scientists, engineers, etc.) in the U.S.S.R.

2. References to the background characteristics of the Central Committee membership between 1961 and 1966 are based on Michael P. Gehlen, "The Educational Backgrounds and Career Orientations of the Members of the Central Committee of the CPSU," *American Behavioral Scientist*, (April 1966), 11–14.

3. Compilations of the members and their positions at the time of election to the Central Committee are available in *Current Soviet Policies*, vols. I–IV, published by Columbia U.P. and by Praeger.

4. See Philip Selznick, *TVA and the Grassroots*, U. of California Publications in Culture and Society, vol. III, pp. 259–61. For other works involving either elite or group analysis see: Bernard M. Bass, *Leadership, Psychology, and Organizational Behavior* (New York: Harper, 1960); Dorwin Cartwright and Alvin Zander, *Group Dynamics, Research and Theory* (Evanston, Ill.: Row, 1960); Lewis J. Edinger, *Political Leadership of Industrial Societies* (New York: Wiley, 1967); Thomas Gordon, *Group-Centered Leadership* (Boston: Houghton, 1955); Morris Janowitz, *The Professional Soldier* (New York: Free Press, 1960); Harold D. Lasswell, *Power and Personality* (New York: Viking, 1948); Dwaine Marvick, *Political Decision-Makers* (New York: Free Press, 1961); Robert Tannenbaum, *Leadership and Organization: A Behavioral Science Approach* (New York: McGraw, 1961). For one of the few in-depth analyses of an important segment of the Soviet elite, see John A. Armstrong, *The Soviet Bureaucratic Elite* (New York: Praeger, 1959).

5

Co-optation as a Mechanism of Adaption to Change: The Soviet Political Leadership System

FREDERIC J. FLERON, JR.

The major focus of this paper is the manner in which the Soviet political elite has attempted to adapt to its changing environment. In order to maintain its leadership position in an industrialized society, a political elite which does not already possess the skills necessary to manage such a society (especially to the degree of a state-controlled economy) has at least four alternative courses of action. The alternative adaptive

Reprinted with minor corrections by permission from *Polity* II (1969), 176–201. Revised version of a paper presented at the 1968 Annual Meeting of the American Political Science Association, Washington, D.C., Sept. 6, 1968. For helpful suggestions on the earlier draft, the author would like to thank Erik P. Hoffmann, John Gillespie, and R. Barry Farrell.

Notes to the selection begin on page 146.

mechanisms are: (1) to try to get the specialized elites[1] to contribute their skills at no cost or force them to contribute those skills; (2) to retrain some of the members of the political elite or recruit into the system as replacements new young cadres with the necessary skills; (3) to co-opt into the system members of specialized elites who possess the necessary skills; or finally—and this is to relinquish openly at least a portion of its leadership position—(4) to share power with specialized elites on a more-or-less competitive and equal basis as in a pluralistic system.

I have developed a conceptual scheme for the classification of political leadership systems which embodies the above forms of adaption. This typology, based on the nature of group participation, acquisition and utilization of skills, and leadership selection, offers an alternative to the oversimplified totalitarian-pluralistic dichotomy, which is the usual frame of reference for studies of Soviet political "development" or "modernization." Pluralism is most frequently taken to be the only viable form of political development for any industrialized society. Herein two other forms of systemic change are suggested as logical and empirical possibilities.

There is considerable agreement on the proposition that industrialization leads to social pluralism, the sharing of political power among several groups. It is much less certain that social pluralism leads inevitably, or even generally, to political pluralism, in the sense that many groups arise which have skills needed by the society and therefore gain social status. The Soviet Union is one good example of the source of doubt about the truth of the second proposition. This is obvious even in the literature which is within the framework of the totalitarian-pluralistic dichotomy: some say that the Soviet Union has "limited pluralism," or does not have "genuine pluralism"; others give the ominous prognosis of "destruction or breakdown" of the Soviet system unless it achieves political pluralism.

It was for the clarification of this conceptual difficulty that I developed the following scheme (see Table 1).[2] A detailed indictment of the totalitarian-pluralistic conception of Soviet political change and a more elaborate presentation of my classificatory scheme have been presented elsewhere.[3] For present purposes, therefore, only a brief sketch of each type of system needs to be presented. This classificatory scheme has proved to have considerable empirical import and theoretical utility in my own research on the Soviet political leadership system.

The four distinct systems of this typology are as follows. Representing

TABLE 1

CHARACTERISTICS OF POLITICAL LEADERSHIP SYSTEMS

	Monocratic	Adaptive Monocratic	Co-optative	Pluralistic
Professional Politicians in Political Offices	Yes	Yes	Possibly	Possibly
Specialized Elites in Political Offices	No	No	Yes	Yes
Political Elite Responsible to the People	No	No	No	Yes
Institutionalized Advantage for Professional Politicians	Yes	Yes	Yes	No
New Skills Acquired by the Political Elite	No	Yes	Possibly*	Possibly*
Method of Replenishing the Political Elite	Recruitment	Recruitment	Co-optation	Election (also possibly co-optation)

* Possibly = df. an accompanying characteristic, not a defining characteristic, i.e., presence or absence of that characteristic is an empirical, not a definitional matter.

the two extremes on the spectrum are the pluralistic and monocratic systems.[4] Somewhere in between are two intermediate (although not necessarily chronologically intermediate) types.

In a *monocratic system* political offices are held only by an elite of professional (careerist) politicians. There is no structural pluralism in the polity, but there may be pluralism in the rest of society. Where there do exist various independent structured social groups, they are excluded from active (as opposed to passive) participation in the polity. Whatever autonomous groups do exist, therefore, are not independent centers of *political* power, but could very well act as centers of power in other areas of society, e.g., the cultural or economic sectors.

The political elite in a monocratic system may possess the skills necessary to run society, although that is not an essential characteristic of a monocratic system. However, to the extent that the political elite does not possess these skills, it can obtain them at no cost from the various specialized elites in society[5]—that is, it can extract the necessary technical information from the specialized elites without having to exchange it for a voice in the policy-making process.

In a *pluralistic system* various specialized elites compete for political offices and for influence and participation in the policy-making process. To the extent that professional (careerist) politicians exist, they do not possess any special privileges or institutionalized advantages—that is, they have the same status as any other interest group or specialized

elite in terms of their possibilities of getting into office. The political
elite would not be self-perpetuating by heredity, co-optation, or any
other means. The formation of organized (associational) interest groups
is considered to be a legitimate means of acquiring offices and influencing policy. While pluralism is one possible outcome of the industrialization process with its resulting division of labor and structural
differentiation in society, there appear to be at least two additional
possible outcomes. These I shall refer to as the adaptive-monocratic
system and the co-optation system.

An *adaptive-monocratic system* arises from a situation in which the
monocratic elite does not itself have, and cannot freely obtain, the
skills necessary to make and effectively carry out policy in all areas
in which it desires to do so. A very likely example here would be
political control over a complex, industrialized society, and the technical skills necessary to that task. The monocratic political elite may
choose to acquire these skills itself, rather than force (by one means
or another) members of specialized elites to contribute freely these skills
to the political system. To reiterate an important distinction, the political elite in a purely monocratic system does not attempt to change its
skill characteristics, whereas the political elite in an adaptive-monocratic system does attempt to do so. In both systems the distribution
of political power is essentially monocratic. Hence, an adaptive-monocratic system must be viewed in a temporal context where at one time
the monocratic elite does not possess all the skills it needs, and it employs certain methods in acquiring those skills for itself, thus enabling
it to maintain monocratic control without the use of force.

In an adaptive-monocratic system there are two basic methods by
which the political elite can acquire the desired nonpolitical technical
skills: it can retrain existing cadres, or, perhaps more satisfactory
in terms of minimizing administrative disruption, it can recruit into
the lower echelons of the political elite younger cadres who have
already completed the desired technical training.

The fourth political leadership system I have called the *co-optation
system*. Like an adaptive-monocracy, the co-optation system must be
viewed in a temporal context in which at one time the political elite
does not possess all the skills it needs to do what it desires. Here the
similarity ends. Whereas in an adaptive-monocratic system the required
new skills are acquired by the processes of retraining and recruitment,
in the co-optation system these skills are acquired by co-opting into

the political elite members of various specialized elites in society, thus giving those elites direct access to the policy-making process.

What distinguishes this co-optation process from the recruitment procedures in an adaptive-monocratic system is that co-opted specialists are men who had already established a career in one of the non-political sectors of society and, thus, would be entering the political elite midway or late in their careers. They would already have earned a reputation outside the political elite and are co-opted because of their expertise in a particular skill area. We might expect their primary affiliation to be with their nonpolitical professional-vocational group. This is to be contrasted with the process in an adaptive-monocratic system in which young men are recruited into the political elite very early in their careers as specialists. Such recruits would not have already established careers and reputations in the nonpolitical sectors, nor would they have established firm relations with nonpolitical professional-vocational groups.

While the difference between the two systems is made initially in terms of the processes utilized by the political elite in acquiring specialized skills, these processes could lead to other, far-reaching differences. The different socialization processes to which these two distinct types would be subjected seems to warrant such a categorical distinction between recruitment and co-optation.

CLASSIFICATION OF THE SOVIET POLITICAL LEADERSHIP SYSTEM

The data presented here are drawn from a larger study which utilized all known (relevant) elite biographic data on all full members of the Central Committee from 1952 through 1965. Since those data have been reported in detail elsewhere, they need only be summarized here.[6] On the basis of these findings, we can reach some tentative conclusions concerning the nature of the Soviet political leadership system between 1952 and 1965, and then consider the implications of the particular Soviet methods of adaptation to a changing environment. We shall begin by examining the findings in the context of the defining characteristics of the aforementioned systems.

First, the data yielded the unsurprising fact that there were professional politicians in political offices. They comprised 64.8%, 63.9%, and 45.7% of the Central Committees selected at the 19th (1952), 20th (1956), and 22nd (1961) Party Congresses, respectively. They were found in increasing proportions in the Party Congresses, the Central Committees, and the Politburo, as well as in the various types of line and staff agencies in the Central Party Apparatus. This information, by itself, does not enable us to distinguish among the four types of political leadership systems, since the existence of professional politicians in political offices is a defining characteristic of monocratic and adaptive-monocratic systems, and an accompanying characteristic of co-optative and pluralistic systems.

Second, analysis of the composition of the Party Congress, Central Committee, and Politburo indicates that members of specialized elites also occupy political offices. Their representation in the Central Committees was 25.6%, 27.8%, and 44.0% for the years 1952, 1956, and 1961, respectively. According to this criterion, we would have to classify the Soviet political leadership system as co-optative or pluralistic, since only in these two systems is the presence of specialized elites in political offices a defining characteristic; the absence of such elites is a defining characteristic of monocratic and adaptive-monocratic systems.

Third, professional politicians had an institutionalized advantage in the Soviet political leadership system from 1952–65. Two measures of institutionalized advantage yielded this conclusion: (1) the degree of overrepresentation of professional politicians in the Politburo given their representation in the Central Committee and (2) the extent to which professional politicians dominate the "staff" agencies in the Central Party Apparatus, which are relevant to institutionalized advantage because these agencies control (more or less) the composition of other bodies within the political elite.

The direction of change in these two measures is conflicting. According to the former, the trend is toward greater institutionalized advantage for professional politicians (see Table 2), whereas according to the latter, the trend is toward less institutionalized advantage (see Table 3). This contradiction comes about because the numbers of co-opted members of specialized elites are increasing in both Central Party Apparatus staff positions and on the Central Committee, while their numbers in the Politburo have remained relatively constant. One possible explanation of these findings is that the specialized elites in CPA staff agencies have met less resistance in increasing the propor-

TABLE 2

RECRUITMENT AND CO-OPTATION INTO THE POLITICAL ELITE:
POLITBURO AND CENTRAL COMMITTEE

		Central Committee		Politburo		Deviation from Proportional Representation
1952	Recruited	75.4%	(43)	75.0%	(18)	0.0%
	Co-opted	24.6	(14)	25.0	(6)	
1953	Recruited	75.4	(43)	90.0	(9)	+20.0
	Co-opted	24.6	(14)	10.0	(1)	
1956	Recruited	69.9	(65)	92.8	(13)	+32.7
	Co-opted	30.1	(28)	7.2	(1)	
1961	Recruited	49.7	(74)	75.0	(12)	+50.0
	Co-opted	50.3	(75)	25.0	(4)	

TABLE 3

RECRUITMENT AND CO-OPTATION INTO THE POLITICAL ELITE
AMONG CENTRAL PARTY APPARATUS STAFF OFFICIALS IN THE
CENTRAL COMMITTEE BY TIME PERIOD: 1952–65

		All Staff Officials		Cadres and Personnel Staff Officials	
1952–56	Recruited	100.0%	(4)	100.0%	(2)
	Co-opted	0.0	(0)	0.0	(0)
1956–61	Recruited	100.0	(10)	100.0	(5)
	Co-opted	0.0	(0)	0.0	(0)
1961–65	Recruited	66.7	(6)	60.0	(3)
	Co-opted	33.3	(3)	40.0	(2)
1952–65	Recruited	83.3%	(15)	75.0%	(6)
	Co-opted	16.7	(3)	25.0	(2)

tional representation of specialized elites in the Central Committee, while the Politburo has remained impregnable to this trend. An additional or alternative explanation may be that the real power of the Central Committee (esp. vis-à-vis the Politburo) has declined in the past decade such that to increase the representation of specialized elites in the Central Committee permits the professional politicians to share more responsibility with the specialized elites at less risk of sharing power. This point will be elaborated later. Perhaps these slightly contradictory findings can be resolved through future research on other measures of institutionalized advantage: differential rates of upward mobility and lengths of tenure in office for professional politicians and specialized elites.

Despite these differences in direction of change, however, both measures indicate the presence of institutionalized advantage for professional politicians. Therefore, we cannot classify the Soviet political leadership system as pluralistic. Since the monocratic and adaptive-monocratic alternatives have been eliminated according to other criteria, we must classify the Soviet political leadership system as a co-optative political leadership system between 1952 and 1965.[7]

In the Soviet case it is not surprising to find that the development of a pluralistic political leadership system has not come about. It is fairly obvious that the political elite has adapted to the demands of an industrialized society in such a way that it has not abdicated its leading role in Soviet society. In considering the nature of its adaption in my research, I started with the frame of reference of Selznick's TVA study—that organizational behavior is viewed in terms of organizational response to organizational need. For Selznick, "One such need is specified as 'the security of the organization as a whole in relation to social forces in its environment.' "[8]

As noted earlier, industrialization leads to the alteration of the social forces; it produces in society a division of labor, functional specialization, and structural differentiation. As Eckstein has suggested, "This functional differentiation in its very nature fragments society into large numbers of groupings and tends to break the hold on social life of the primary kinship and locality groupings."[9] This is what is generally referred to as social pluralism.[10] We shall now examine, in light of the above conceptual scheme and my research findings on the Soviet Union, the relationship of that condition of social pluralism to political pluralism. In other words, we shall examine some selected adaptive capabilities of a co-optative political leadership system and will focus on the Soviet Union as an illustration of an extant co-optative system.

LEGITIMACY

Parsons has said that the only alternative to pluralistic adaptation in the Soviet Union is "general destruction or breakdown."[11] He was led to this conclusion because he felt that "the basic dilemma of the Communists is that it is not possible in the long run . . . to legitimize dictatorship of the Party. . . ."[12] I should like to suggest, however, that the development of a pluralistic polity is not the only solution to this multi-faceted problem of regime legitimacy.

Bauer and Inkeles conclude, for example, that legitimacy of the Party in the Soviet system may be maintained in the eyes of the specialized elites if there is a kind of "boundary maintenance" within the decision-making process; that is, the Party may legitimately decide political questions; but directives of a technical nature are not so well received by specialized elites. They state:

> there is good reason to believe that the underlying principles of Soviet political control over the *ends* of economic and administrative behavior are accepted by most Soviet engineers and managers, indeed are willingly supported by them. They accept these as "political" decisions to be decided by political specialists. They are, in other words, largely withdrawn from politics, "organization men" similar to their counter-parts in the United States. Their main complaint in the past was not over the principle of directing the economy, but rather over arbitrary political interference in predominantly technical decisions, the unreasonably high goals often set in the face of insufficient resources to meet them, and the treatment of failures in judgment or performance by management as if they were acts of political defiance or criminal negligence. Since Stalin's death such abuse has been tremendously reduced. Soviet managers seem, on the whole, quite satisfied with the situation.[13]

It is also interesting to note that co-optation itself has been used to legitimize the ruling political elite. Selznick has argued that "Co-optation reflects a state of tension between formal authority and social power. . . . Where the formal authority and leadership reflects real social power, its stability is assured. On the other hand, when it becomes divorced from the sources of social power its continued existence is threatened."[14] Lacking the technical skills of real social power in an industrialized society, the Soviet political elite employed the co-optative mechanism to bring those skills into its ranks. To have remained an elite possessing merely political skills—in this case, a monocratic political elite—would undoubtedly have caused it to be viewed as parasitic by the specialized elites. Such a political elite could hardly be viewed as legitimate by those outside it who provided the specialized skills for the construction of an industrialized society in the Soviet Union. Yet both the recruitment and co-optative mechanisms of adaptation have been employed by the Soviet political and Party elites, resulting in the fact that those elites themselves possess the skills necessary to take an active part in the administration of an industrialized society. Recruitment brings technical skills into the political elite. Co-optation has done not only that, but it also allowed active participation of the specialized elites in the political elite. The net result is to increase the legitimacy of the political elite in the eyes of these specialized elites, for the latter have a good many actual and virtual representatives in the political elite. For this reason, I find it difficult to agree with Parsons, Meissner, Brzezinski, and others who argue that the political elite does not have legitimacy in the Soviet system and is "a foreign body in the fabric of the elite structure of an industrialized society."[15] To the extent that the Soviet political elite ever was as they describe it, the data from my research indicate that by the increasing utilization of co-optation the political elite has rejuvenated itself by thus acquiring men with the skills and experience needed to administer a modern, industrialized society.

CIRCULATION OF ELITES

This is all part of the general process of the circulation of elites which has probably come about, Lasswell asserts, because of the "shift of the dialectic of development from the class struggle to the skill struggle."[16] In his book *The Ruling Class* Gaetano Mosca described the factors underlying the circulation of elites.

> What we see is that as soon as there is a shift in the balance of political forces—when, that is, a need is felt that capacities different from the old should assert themselves in the management of the state, when the old capacities, therefore, lose some of their importance or changes in their distribution occur—then the manner in which the ruling class is constituted changes also. If a new source of wealth develops in a society, if the practical importance of knowledge grows . . . if a new current of ideas spreads, then, simultaneously, far-reaching dislocations occur in the ruling class. One might say, indeed, that the whole history of civilized mankind comes down to a conflict between the tendency of dominant elements to monopolize political power and transmit possession of it by inheritance, and the tendency toward a dislocation of old forces and an insurgence of new forces . . . Ruling classes decline inevitably when they cease to find scope for the capacities through which they rose to power, when they can no longer render the social services which they once rendered, or when their talents and the services they render lose in importance in the social environment in which they live.[17]

There are three distinct aspects of the circulation of elites: (1) circulation of individuals, (2) circulation of offices, and (3) circulation of groups or types of individuals. Circulation of individuals refers to the process in every system of replacing individual members of the elite who, by death, retirement, or for other reasons, have left the elite. In such cases of individual replacement, the new member possesses the same skill characteristics as the old member; and, therefore, the characteristics of the elite are not changed. This is true of monocratic as well as co-optative and pluralistic political leadership systems.

The circulation of offices refers to whether new offices replace existing offices to perform similar functions or new functions. (In either case these may or may not be accompanied by circulation of groups.) In the former case there is circulation of offices but continuity in the performance of certain functions within the political system. An example of this type of circulation of offices is the creation of the Comrades' Courts and *Druzhina* (people's volunteer squads) in 1959 to take over some of the functions of the state apparatus, the People's Courts and police.[18] The functions of apprehending and correcting individuals committing certain kinds of "crimes" continued to be performed in the Soviet Union, but after 1959 they were performed by new institutions in Soviet society. The subsequent reversal of this trend must be viewed as another circulation of offices, or perhaps as recirculation of offices.

In the latter case there is circulation of offices with change in the performance of certain functions. An example here is the creation of cabinet positions of urban affairs and transportation in the United States. If, as Brzezinski suggests, there has been in the Soviet Union an institutionalization of mechanisms for dealing with superannuated individuals or those who have been removed from top political positions, this would provide a clue to change in the nature of Soviet politics. "The struggle tends to become less a matter of life or death, and more one in which the price of defeat is simply retirement and some personal disgrace."[19] A reappraisal of such forms of circulation of offices as the dissolution of the Party-State Control Commission, the establishment of the *Sovnarkhozy*, the bifurcation of the regional Party apparatus;[20] the periodic oscillation between the "functional" and "production-branch" bases of organization within the Party and the administrative reforms of 1958, 1962, and 1964 might provide other clues to change in the Soviet political system.

In assessing change which comes in the Soviet political system as a result of change in the leadership system the most important of the three aspects of the circulation of elites is the circulation of groups and types of individuals which constitute the elite. The greatest single potential for change seems to occur when groups circulate. Critics of the hypothesis that there are trends toward liberalization and pluralization in the Soviet polity argue that until inroads are made into the Party's monopoly of power there can be little hope of liberalization.[21] My research has demonstrated that in at least one sector of the political elite—the Central Committee from 1952 through 1965—both political and Party professionals were replaced by members of the technical intelligentsia and other specialized elites. Hence, this particular criticism of the liberalization hypothesis has been answered, and one could argue that perhaps a necessary condition for positive change is coming into existence.[22]

FORMAL AND INFORMAL CO-OPTATION

There are at least five reasons why a political elite might co-opt members of specialized elites: (1) to maintain or increase the legitimacy of the political elite (which was discussed earlier), (2) to utilize the skills of the specialized elites, (3) to have greater access to the specialized elites, (4) to share power, and (5) to share responsibility. While no effort is made here to document the motives of the political elite in co-opting members of specialized elites, we can nevertheless introduce some important hypotheses concerning the relationship of the selectors and the selected. In his pioneering study of co-optation, Selznick introduced a central hypothesis which, when viewed in the context of the above five motives for co-optation, performs an important heuristic function: "Co-optation which results in actual sharing of power will tend to operate informally, and correlatively, co-optation oriented toward legitimization or accessibility will tend to be effected through formal devices."[23]

In the Soviet Union, the Party has employed formal co-optation in that it has publicly absorbed members of specialized elites into the Party Congress, Central Committee, and Politburo. In sharing these forms of power, the Soviet political elite can share responsibility for decisions with the specialized elites, have greater access to the specialized elites through their formal representatives, and probably maintain the legitimacy of the political elite in issuing directives to the specialized elites.

At the same time, the forms of power always carry the threat of acquisition of the substance of power. It seems unlikely that specialized elites are co-opted for purposes of sharing power (or at least not too much of it—the Soviet response to the developments in Czechoslovakia is an interesting indicator of their attitudes on that question), although having been co-opted into political positions these specialized elites' potential influence on the policy-making process certainly increases; and it increases further as they go from the Party Congress to the Central Committee to the Politburo. Hence, in co-opting members of specialized elites into these bodies, the political elite runs the very serious risk of having to share power. The data indicate that the representation of specialized elites decreases as we move from the Party Congress

TABLE 4

LEADERSHIP CADRES, INTELLIGENTSIA, AND WORKERS AND
FARMERS IN THE PARTY CONGRESS, CENTRAL COMMITTEE
AND POLITBURO: 1952–61*

		Party Congress		Central Committee		Politburo	
Oct. 1952	LC	30.1%	(359)	75.2%	(94)	66.7%	(24)
	SECTI	40.6	(484)	15.2	(19)	25.0	(9)
	W & F	29.3	(349)	0.0	(0)	0.0	(0)
Totals		100.0	(1192)	90.4	(125)	91.7	(36)
March 1953	L C	30.1	(359)	75.2	(94)	64.3	(9)
	SECTI	40.6	(484)	15.2	(19)	21.4	(3)
	W & F	29.3	(349)	0.0	(0)	0.0	(0)
Totals		100.0	(1192)	90.4	(125)	85.7	(14)
Feb. 1956	L C	51.8	(702)	77.4	(103)	64.7	(11)
	SECTI	15.9	(215)	14.3	(19)	17.8	(3)
	W & F	32.3	(438)	0.0	(0)	0.0	(0)
Totals		100.0	(1355)	91.7	(133)	82.5	(17)
Nov. 1961	L C	39.2	(1728)	72.0	(126)	100.0	(16)
	SECTI	34.6	(1614)	17.7	(31)	0.0	(0)
	W & F	22.3	(983)	2.3	(4)	0.0	(0)
Totals		96.1	(4408)	92.0	(175)	100.0	(16)

* L C = Leadership Cadres; SECTI = Scientific, Economic, Cultural, and Technical Intelligentsia; W & F = Workers and Farmers. Totals in % columns are based on % of each body included in these three categories. Totals in the (N) columns represent total membership in each body. The discrepancy is accounted for by the fact that the military is excluded from these calculations. Data for this table were obtained primarily from the Credentials Commission Reports of the 19th, 20th, and 22nd Party Congresses.

to the Central Committee to the Politburo (see Tables 2 and 4). Therefore, it appears that the political elite is unwilling to risk too much
sharing of power in order to achieve sharing of responsibility, although
it is important to note that in some areas (the Central Committee), they
are "risking" it more over time (see Table 5).

Furthermore, specialized elites are formally co-opted into staff
positions in the CPA where the officeholders have considerable power
in performing staffing, checking, and administrative functions within
the Party. This evidence appears to be an exception to Selznick's
hypothesis that "co-optation which results in an actual sharing of
power will tend to operate informally."[24]

TABLE 5

RECRUITMENT AND CO-OPTATION INTO POLITICAL ELITE AMONG
LEADERSHIP CADRES AND SCIENTIFIC-TECHNICAL INTELLIGENTSIA
IN CENTRAL COMMITTEE: 1952–61*

	1952 (N = 125)	1956 (N = 133)	1961 (N = 175)
Recruited Leadership Cadres	64.8% (81)	63.9% (85)	45.7% (80)
Co-opted Leadership Cadres plus Scientific, Economic, Cultural, and Technical Intelligentsia	25.6 (32)	27.8 (37)	44.0 (77)

* Columns do not add to 100.0% because the Military, Workers, and Farmers are
excluded from these calculations.

The Schwartz-Keech study of the 1958 education reforms is a clear
example of informal co-optation for purposes of sharing power.[25]
In this case, when members of the Politburo could not resolve policy
conflicts among themselves, they went to the educational elite seeking
expert information with which to bolster their positions. This was an
informal mechanism which resulted, on that issue at least, in sharing
power with a specialized elite.

Certainly there is a problem for the Party in making great concessions
to the technocrats in terms of decision-making and control. The
Soviet type of command economy requires that these technocrats be
kept subservient to, or at least below, the Party. Hence, Wiles suggests,
whenever the Party gets the feeling that it "is doing itself out of a job"
and that "a gradual Thermidor" is setting in, "it can switch to a model
with fewer technocrats in it, or at least with fewer very important
technocrats."[26] The important point here is that it is the professional

politicians within the Party through their control of the channels of co-optation (e.g., staff agencies), rather than "the Party," who are able "to change the model, re-stir the ant-heap, re-create the discrepancy between ideology and fact."[27] In particular, not only can they decide *how many* members of specialized elites (technocrats and others) to let into the critical political positions, they decide *which ones* to admit and *where* to admit them. It is here that the notion of a co-optative political leadership system highlights central variables in the assessment of change in the Soviet political system.

To be sure, the professional politicians are constrained by certain considerations when deciding these "how many," "which," and "where" questions. Soviet policy makers have continually demonstrated their willingness to be impressed by successful realization of the production norms. Success can do more for the technocrats, individually and collectively, than probably anything else. While the professional politicians can permit themselves temporary luxuries such as the decentralization of 1957 which reduced the relative power of the technical specialist elites,[28] over the long run influence will probably accrue to those who demonstrate that they can produce the goods, both literally and figuratively.

SPECIALIST ELITE INTEREST ARTICULATION AND INFLUENCE IN THE POLICY-MAKING PROCESS

Schwartz and Keech in their study of the 1958 education reforms identified one type of situation in which the various specialized elites are able to influence the outcome of events and have their views taken into account. "Under conditions of leadership conflict, unresolved disputes may lead some of the participants to broaden the scope of conflict by involving policy groups who might shift the balance."[29] This tends to confirm the findings of Lodge that "when the Party is internally divided [specialist] elite participation increases"[30] and of Azrael that "the only periods during which they [the technicians] have acquired a certain independence have been those in which the central leadership has been internally split."[31] Insofar as these groups in any way influenced the outcome of events "it was through the communication of their expert judgments to people at the top of the hierarchy who *were* in a position to influence outcomes."[32] Thus, the groups involved became "articulators of expert judgment." Schwartz and Keech hypothesize that "the more and greater the disputes on the top policy making level, the more likely it is that policy groups will be involved and listened to."[33]

While this is one very important part of the political process and interest articulation in the Soviet Union, it must be remembered that it is only a part. It says nothing of the types of individuals at the top who are likely to come into conflict and, thus, provide a situation in which various "expert judgments" are sought out. Furthermore, we should not conclude from this type of approach that under conditions when the top leadership is not in conflict there is no representation of various group interests. Certainly a wide range of interests would be represented among the members of specialized elites who have been co-opted into the political elite, although in no way would I wish to suggest that these individuals constitute a homogeneous category within the political elite.

There are compelling reasons to believe that, because of their entirely different professional socialization, these co-opted specialists probably share a different *Weltanschauung* and approach to problem-solving from that of professional politicians,[34] yet there are undoubtedly many individual differences related to personality, length of time in a specialized elite occupation, etc. Elite membership constitutes one method of access to the political elite in which the various specialized interests receive direct and continuing articulation by those in the political elite who share those views or in some sense represent them. It is unlikely that all specialized interests are represented to the same extent and some may not be represented at all. What the Schwartz-Keech study does in this context is to point out the conditions under which members of the political nonelite are given a greater chance to make their views known to the political elite, and in such cases they are consciously sought out by the political elite. Taken together, these two approaches offer a more complete picture of the avenues of interest articulation and access to the policy-making process than has been demonstrated heretofore.

Both approaches demonstrate that in the Soviet Union points of access exist in the political system for the articulation of interests: through elite representation and providing expert judgments to the decision makers. In neither case does it appear that associational interest groups played any part. Schwartz and Keech found that the views expressed by specialist elites were those of institutional and nonassociational interest groups. Both of these types of interest groups have access to the decision-making process through representation in the political elite. Certainly not all interests can be represented in this way and no attempt is made to argue here that they are. These two studies do, however, indicate that in a co-optative political leadership system mechanisms do exist for the articulation of the interests of various specialized structures in an industrialized society. In this sense, it is certainly possible that a co-optative political leadership system can be fully capable of adapting to its environment. To argue that all interests are not or cannot be represented in such a system is no argument against its adaptability.

After all, democratic pluralism, which many have argued is the only type of system permitting satisfactory adaption, does not allow *equal* representation of interests in the political system nor does it even guarantee representation of *all* interest groups. In fact, as Robert Wolff has convincingly argued, while "pluralism is not explicitly a philosophy of privilege or injustice—it is a philosophy of equality and justice whose *concrete application* supports inequality by ignoring the existence of certain legitimate social groups."

> This ideological function of pluralism helps to explain one of the peculiarities of American politics. There is a very sharp distinction in the public domain between legitimate interests and those which are absolutely beyond the pale. If a group or interest is within the framework of acceptability, then it can be sure of winning some measure of what it seeks, for the process of national politics is distributive and compromising. On the other hand, if an interest falls *outside* the circle of the acceptable, it receives no attention whatsoever and its proponents are treated as crackpots, extremists or foreign agents. . . . According to pluralist theory, every genuine social group has a right to a voice in the making of policy and a share in the benefits. Any policy urged by a group in the system must be given respectful attention, no matter how bizarre. By the same token, a policy or principle which lacks legitimate representation has no place in the society, no matter how reasonable or right it may be. Consequently, the line between acceptable and unacceptable alternatives is very sharp, so that the territory of American politics is like a plateau with steep cliffs on all sides rather than like a pyramid. On the plateau are all the interest groups which are recognized as legitimate; in the deep valley all around lie the outsiders, the fringe groups which are scorned as "extremist."[35]

Wolff concludes that while pluralism may have been an appropriate approach to political and social problems at one point in American history (the Depression), it no longer is a satisfactory approach to human problem solving in America. America is now confronted with enormous "problems of the society as a whole, not of any particular group." These problems "concern the general good, not merely the aggregate of private goods."

> To deal with such problems, there must be some way of constituting the whole society as a genuine group with a group purpose and a conception of the common good. Pluralism rules this out in theory by portraying society as an aggregate of human communities rather than as itself a human community; and it equally rules out a concern for the general good in practice by encouraging a politics of interest-group pressures in which there is no mechanism for the discovery and expression of the common good.[36]

In sum, "the pluralist system of social groups is an obstacle to the general good!"[37]

If Wolff's prescriptions concerning the United States (and presumably other Western industrialized, pluralistic societies) are realized, the social and political character of Western industrialized society will have progressed through phases essentially individualistic, pluralistic, and collectivistic. At that future point in time, "modern" political systems would be those characterized by such a collectivist approach to the problems of society.

If future generations of political development and modernization theorists possess the same type of cultural bias found in the present generation, they would have to argue that in order to adapt successfully to the exigencies of an advanced industrial society a political system would have to conform to the then current collectivist approach to human problem solving. This would require an embarrassing revision of current theories which tend to view pluralism as the only satisfactory direction of adaptive political development. Hence, systems would be viewed as developing toward this post-pluralist higher stage or facing decay and destruction. In this sense, perhaps the Soviet Union is again "skipping historical stages" since it has been guided by a collectivist ideology for several decades.

Yet in both the United States and the Soviet Union there are interesting differences between theory and practice. On the one hand, the official Soviet position is that there is no need for competition in the Soviet system because there is only one legitimate interest. That interest can be and is represented by the CPSU and, hence, there is no need either for more than one party or for programmatic factions within that one party. This interpretation is supported by a collectivist ideology based on the centrality of the good of society, rather than on the competition and accommodation of a variety of selfish interests. At the same time, as the foregoing analysis has demonstrated, there are institutionalized points of access for the representation of various specialized interests in the Soviet political system.

On the other hand, the dominant feeling in America is that the United States is a pluralistic system in which there is free and open competition among various groups. At the same time, as Robert Wolff has pointed out, this interpretation of political life in America is a mythical idealization of reality; such a system does not exist in the United States. Hence, political reality in both systems is quite different from official public representations.

Finally, there are forces at work in both systems advocating change away from the dominant ideologies. In the United States there are those like Wolff who argue that the pluralistic ideology should give way to some form of collectivist ideology based on the common good of society; in the Soviet Union there are those like A. I. Lepeshkin, the Deputy Editor of *Sovetskoe gosudarstvo i pravo*, who argue for increased competition in the collectivist Soviet society.[38]

Wolff's prescriptions are avowedly in the realm of "what ought to be." Other evaluations of political change are based on what Gustav Bergmann would call an ideological statement—a value judgment which is held "not under its proper logical flag as a value judgment but in the disguise of a statement of fact."[39] In discussing the implications of the fact that the Party schools and CPA cadres and personnel staff agencies probably do not encourage "clusters of creativity," Brzezinski writes:

> It is doubtful that any organization can long remain vital if it is so structured that in its personnel policy it becomes, almost knowingly, inimical to talent and hostile to political innovation. Decay is bound to set in, while the stability of the political system may be endangered, if other social institutions succeed in attracting the society's talent and begin to chafe under the restraints imposed by the ruling but increasingly mediocre *apparatchiki*.[40]

Several problems are evident here. First, Brzezinski offers no concrete evidence that the personnel policy of either the Party elite or the more general political elite is in fact "inimical to talent and hostile to political innovation." On the contrary, my research has clearly indicated that the professional politicians and professional Party officials (the latter presumably Brzezinski's "apparatchiki") who have continued to control entrance into these elites through their domination of the Central Party Apparatus cadres and personnel staff agencies have, at least during the period 1952–65, continued to bring men with technical and other specialized skills into the top positions in the political and Party elites by co-opting members of specialized elites.[41] These co-opted specialists have had considerable experience in the specialized sectors of Soviet society, and to say that they are not "talented" would be ludicrous.

Secondly, while it may be the case that the professional politicians and apparatchiki do not encourage (and may even discourage) *political* innovation among those recruited and co-opted into the political and Party elites, this does not mean that they are hostile to individuals possessing other talents. Hence, it does not seem to be the case that "other social institutions succeed in attracting the society's talent" as Brzezinski seems to think. Brzezinski certainly presents no supporting evidence. Admittedly my research to date has dealt only with the top sector of the Soviet political elite, but I have found that many of these individuals have considerable technical skills through both their formal higher education and their pre-political specialized careers. If later studies can show that at the lower levels of the political elite there is the same high proportion of officials with such "talents," it will be quite clear that the Soviet political leadership system will have succeeded in co-opting into its ranks individuals who have been successful in other sectors of society. This would present quite a different picture of the Soviet political leadership system and its ability to adapt to the demands of a modern industrialized society than that presented by Parsons, Brzezinski, and (the even more extreme) Michel Garder.[42]

Furthermore, it is quite possible for change in the Soviet political system to take place through change in the types of individuals who hold offices in the political elite. Such evidence casts doubts on the almost apocalyptic theory of Garder:

Already there exists a de facto opposition within the ruling class between the functionaries of the apparatus and the upper stratum of the technological intelligentsia, i.e., the scientists, the professors, the plant managers, etc. This opposition cannot but become intensified with the emergence of a new generation. . . . Inevitably, there will come the moment when the true elite of the country, the members of the technological intelligentsia, will feel impelled to seize power.[43]

Since we have found that at least the top echelons of the political elite include a sizable proportion of co-opted members of specialized elites in Soviet society, a more reasonable interpretation of change is Schlesinger's statement that "the CPSU might in due course become the Soviet equivalent of the Congress Party of India or the *Partido Revolucionario Institucional* of Mexico—a loose central party, absorbing all the significant political tendencies within the society and working out its own methods of administration and succession."[44] Such a situation could provide ample opportunity for the articulation of various special interests in Soviet society, and the co-optative system seems perfectly suited to creating that condition.

SUMMARY

The establishment of mechanisms both for the articulation and aggregation of various interests and bringing capable, talented individuals into the political elite are factors viewed by most students as being crucial to the adaptability of any political system to a complex, industrialized society. Many of these students argue, or at least imply, that the only way in which these two conditions can be satisfied is through development in the direction of some form of political system approximating the Anglo-American pluralistic variety. The foregoing analysis has sought to demonstrate that there is at least one viable alternative to such a culturally biased interpretation—that these two conditions of adaptability can be satisfied by a political system directed by a co-optative political leadership system which, for reasons stated earlier, is categorically different from a pluralistic political leadership system. This is not to argue that the Soviet Union may not change in the direction of political pluralism; it is merely to suggest that adaption can be accomplished outside the pluralistic mold. It suggests, further, that we can study political change in the U.S.S.R. and other Communist countries in a more theoretically fruitful fashion than merely measuring them with the yardstick of the Anglo-American political culture.

APPENDIX

DEFINITION OF TERMS

Political Leadership System = df. that part of the political system which comprises the rules, institutions, and practices according to which political leaders are selected, assigned, and removed; the descriptive characteristics of those leaders; and the extent of non-leader influence over those leaders.

Political Office = df. any formal position in the Party, government, *Komsomol*, or trade unions.

Political Elite = df. all persons holding political offices.

Specialized Elite = df. any elite from a nonpolitical sector of society.

Recruitment = df. entry into the political elite at a very early stage in one's career, i.e., prior to having spent more than seven years in a nonpolitical career.

Co-optation = df. entry into the political elite mid or late in one's career, i.e., after having spent more than seven years in a nonpolitical career.

Professional Politician = df. an individual who was recruited into the political elite.

Institutionalized Advantage = df. the existence in a political system of formal (or at least regular) arrangements which give one group (or category) of individuals disproportional potential for achieving or maintaining political positions. The following are three measures of institutionalized advantage for professional politicians (the first two direct and the third indirect): (1) the degree of overrepresentation in the Central Committee and their overrepresentation in both of these higher bodies given their representation in the Party Congress, (2) the extent to which professional politicians dominate the "staff" (as opposed to "line") agencies within the Central Party Apparatus, especially those concerned with cadres and personnel assignment, and (3) differential tenure and upward mobility of professional politicians and specialized elites in political offices.

Notes

1. This and other specialized terms used throughout this selection are defined in the Appendix.
2. These categories are mutually exclusive, but I do not mean to suggest that they are jointly exhaustive; further refinement may result in other logical and empirical possibilities.
3. "Toward a Reconceptualization of Political Change in the Soviet Union: The Political Leadership System," *Comparative Politics*, I, 2 (Jan. 1969).

4. The term "monocratic" is not original with this study. It can be found in the writings of Victor A. Thompson, especially *Modern Organization* (New York: Knopf, 1961), and Max Weber. Thompson seems to have picked up the term from Weber (cf. Thompson, *op. cit.*, p. 74) and uses it interchangeably with the term "monistic." This latter term can be found in several places in the literature and is frequently employed as an antonym for pluralism. See H. Gordon Skilling, "Interest Groups and Communist Politics," *World Politics*, XVIII (1966), p. 499; Clark Kerr, *et al.*, *Industrialism and Industrial Man* (New York: Oxford U.P., 1964), p. 232; Franz Neumann, *Behemoth* (New York: Oxford U.P., 1942), pp. 400–01; Peter H. Merkl, *Political Continuity and Change* (New York: Harper, 1967), pp. 69–77. I have chosen "monocracy" and rejected "monism" for the following reasons. (1) While Skilling, Kerr, and Neumann use "monism," it is not at all certain what they mean by it since they do not use it extensively, but only in passing. In order to avoid confusion, therefore, it seems wise to avoid that concept. (2) When commenting on the Soviet Union, Thompson employs the term "monocratic," rather than "monistic" (Thompson, *op. cit.*, pp. 79–80). Nevertheless, in what follows I do not necessarily mean everything by "monocratic" that Thompson does. I shall stipulate my own definition. Where there is no mention of certain aspects of Thompson's concept, the reader should not assume that I am following his usage *in toto*. Boris Meissner has used the term "monocratic" in discussing the Soviet political system. However, he does not indicate the source of the term and does not provide any definition of his usage (see Boris Meissner, "Soviet Democracy and Bolshevik Party Dictatorship," in Henry W. Ehrmann, ed., *Democracy in a Changing Society* [New York: Praeger, 1964], p. 168.

5. Of course, the political elite is also a specialized elite. Throughout this study, however, the term "specialized elite" will be reserved for elites from the various *nonpolitical* sectors of society.

6. Cf. "Change in the Representation of Career Types in the Soviet Political Leadership System, 1952–65" in R. Barry Farrell, ed., *Political Leadership in the USSR and Eastern Europe*; Carl Beck, Frederic J. Fleron, Jr., Milton Lodge, William Welsh, and George Zaninovich, *Comparative Communist Political Leadership*, forth-coming 1971.

7. The choice of seven years as the cutting point between co-optation and recruit-ment was determined by calculating the mean number of years spent in nonpolitical careers prior to entry into the political elite for all members of the study population. While such an objective test seemed desirable in order to dichotomize the variable, it is also important to note that seven years is quite compatible with the theoretical considerations involved in selecting a cutting point. I wanted a figure which would be reasonable in terms of distinguishing between the differential socializing effects of (1) having spent considerable time at the beginning of one's career in a nonpolitical occupation or profession, and thus developing ties with and taking on the attitudes of that occupational or professional group, and (2) not having undergone such early nonpolitical career experience, but rather entering the political elite very early in one's career.

In the case of the Soviet Union, furthermore, seven years seemed reasonable especially because, unlike the somewhat higher figures used in some studies of differential professional socialization, it did not include any educational preparation. Therefore, when the number of years spent in education for a specific career (which is undoubtedly influential in professional socialization) is added, the figure will go as high as 12 or 13 years.

However, the operationalization of the concepts "recruitment" and "co-optation" (and hence, by definition, "professional politician") establishes *logically* (not empiri-cally) the existence of both professional politicians and specialized elites in the political leadership system. The *empirical* determination of that fact is necessary to the classification of a political leadership system. The use of any "arbitrarily" chosen figure which fell within the range of theoretical usefulness would have enabled us to make that determination empirically. I can state as an empirical matter that the choice of any year from one to twenty-five as a cutting point would have yielded the empirical fact that the Soviet political leadership system from 1952 through 1965 included both professional politicians and specialized elites as defined by any of those years. Therefore, the Soviet political leadership system is inescapably (empirically) classified as a co-optative system, since it cannot be classified as a pluralistic system because it does not meet the other definitional requirements of that type of political leadership system.

8. Philip Selznick, *TVA and the Grass Roots* (New York: Harper Torchbooks, 1966), p. 259.

9. Harry Eckstein, "Group Theory and the Comparative Study of Pressure Groups," in Harry Eckstein and David E. Apter, eds., *Comparative Politics: A Reader* (New York: Free Press, 1963), p. 395.

10. For a discussion of social pluralism see Robert A. Dahl and Charles E, Lindblom, *Politics, Economics, and Welfare* (New York: Harper Torchbooks, 1963), esp. pp. 302–09.

11. Talcott Parsons, "Communism and the West: The Sociology of Conflict," in Amitai and Eva Etzioni, *Social Change: Sources, Patterns, and Consequences* (New York: Basic Books, 1964), p. 397.

12. *Ibid.*

13. Alex Inkeles and Raymond A. Bauer, *The Soviet Citizen: Daily Life in a Totalitarian Society* (Cambridge: Harvard U.P.), p. 389.

14. Selznick, *op. cit.*, p. 15.

15. Boris Meissner, "Totalitarian Rule and Social Change," *Problems of Communism*, XV, 6 (Nov.–Dec. 1966), 60.

16. Harold D. Lasswell, *World Politics and Personal Insecurity* (New York: Free Press, 1965), p. vi.

17. Gaetano Mosca, *The Ruling Class* (New York: McGraw, 1939), pp. 65–6.

18. Darrell P. Hammer, "Law Enforcement, Social Control and the Withering Away of the State: Recent Soviet Experience," *Soviet Studies*, XIV, 4 (April 1963), 379–97.

19. Zbigniew K. Brzezinski, "The Soviet Political System: Transformation or Degeneration?" *Problems of Communism*, XV, 1 (Jan.-Feb. 1966), 7.

20. On this point see John A. Armstrong, "Party Bifurcation and Elite Interests," *Soviet Studies*, XVII, 4 (April 1966), 417–30.

21. Alfred G. Meyer, *The Soviet Political System* (New York: Random House, 1965). pp. 468–71.

22. Dahl and Lindblom, *op. cit.*, pp. 315–17.

23. Selznick, *op. cit.*, p. 260.

24. *Ibid.*

25. Joel J. Schwartz and William R. Keech, "Group Influence and the Policy Process in the Soviet Union," *American Political Science Review*, LXII, 3 (Sept. 1968), 840–51.

26. P. J. D. Wiles, *The Political Economy of Communism* (Oxford: Blackwell, 1962), pp. 26–7.

27. *Ibid.*, p. 26.

28. P. J. D. Wiles, review of Zbigniew K. Brzezinski's *Ideology and Power in Soviet Politics*, in *Slavic Review*, XXI, 3 (Sept. 1962), 557. Soviet managerial personnel, as well as some Western scholars, tended to view the 1962 administrative reforms as "a reversal for the technocrats." Cf. an article by V. Stepanov in *Izvestiia*, Dec. 19, 1962. Cited in Sidney I. Ploss, "Mao's Appeal to the Soviet 'Conservative' " (Princeton U., Center of International Studies, Occasional Papers on Soviet Politics, No. 1, March 19, 1963, p. 3).

29. Schwartz and Keech, *op. cit.*, 847.

30. Milton G. Lodge, "Soviet Elite Participatory Attitudes in the Post-Stalin Period" *American Political Science Review*, LXII, 3 (Sept. 1968), 827–39.

31. Jeremy R. Azrael, *Managerial Power and Soviet Politics* (Cambridge: Harvard U.P., 1964), p. 173.

32. Schwartz and Keech, *op. cit.*, 847.

33. *Ibid.*, 848.

34. Percy H. Tannenbaum and Jack M. McLeod, "On the Measurement of Socialization," *Public Opinion Quarterly*, XXXI, 1 (Spring 1967), 27–37, esp. p. 28 and the sources they cite in footnote 3; Morris Rosenberg, *Occupations and Values* (New York: Free Press, 1957); Vernon K. Dibble, "Occupations and Ideologies," *American Journal of Sociology*, XLVIII, 3 (Nov. 1962), 229–41; John A. Armstrong, "Sources of Administrative Behavior: Some Soviet and Western European Comparisons," *American Political Science Review*, LIX, 3 (Sept. 1965), 643–55.

35. Robert Paul Wolff, "Beyond Tolerance," in Wolff, Barrington Moore, Jr., and Herbert Marcuse, *A Critique of Pure Tolerance* (Boston: Beacon, 1965), pp. 43–5.

36. *Ibid.*, p. 50.

37. *Ibid.*, p. 51.

38. A. I. Lepeshkin in *Sovetskoe gosudarstvo i pravo*, 1965, No. 2, 5–15.

39. Gustav Bergmann, "Ideology," *Ethics*, LXI, 3 (April 1951), 210.

40. Brzezinski, *op. cit.*, 5.

41. See references in footnote 6.

42. Michel Garder, *L'Agonie de Regime en Russie Soviétique* (Paris: Le Table Ronde, 1965). Cf. the discussion of this work by Michel Tatu, "The Beginning of the End?" *Problems of Communism*, XV, 2 (March–April 1966), 44–7.

43. Michel Garder, "Liegt das Sowjetsystem in der Agonie?" *Die Welt* (Hamburg), Jan. 9, 1966. Cited by Wolfgang Leonhard, "Notes on an Agonizing Diagnosis," *Problems of Communism*, XV, 4 (July–Aug. 1966), 36–7. Leonhard's article offers additional evidence for rejecting Garder's theory.

44. Arthur Schlesinger, Jr., "'A Muddling Evolution,'" *Problems of Communism*, XV, 4 (July-Aug. 1966), 45.

6

Public Influence
and Educational Policy
in the Soviet Union

JOEL J. SCHWARTZ AND WILLIAM R. KEECH

It has become widely recognized that Soviet officials do not formulate public policy in a vacuum, and that, indeed, their deliberations take into account in some fashion the needs and demands of various elements of the society. Further, it has been observed that social groups of various types play a noticeable, if only rudimentary, role in articulating interests to the top of the hierarchy. In fact one author has gone so far as to

Part of this study is reprinted with permission from "Group Influence and the Policy Process in the Soviet Union," *American Political Science Review*, LXII (1968), 840–851.
  Notes to the selection begin on page 182.

assert that communist policy-making results from a "parallelogram of conflicting forces and interests."[1] While such viewpoints are now far more widely accepted than in the early fifties, relatively little effort has been devoted to illustrating or illuminating how Soviet public policy in general or even a given Soviet policy can be importantly affected by group activity.

We propose here to make a contribution in that direction. Using the Educational Reform Act of 1958 and a dispute about job placements of university graduates as exemplary cases, we intend to show how and through what process groups can affect policy outcomes, and by identifying circumstances under which this takes place to generate some observations and hypotheses about when such influence is most likely to recur.

In their excellent analysis of Soviet policy formation, Professors Brzezinski and Huntington identify what they call "policy groups," which come closest of any nongovernmental groups to participating in policy formation. These groups, such as the military, industrial managers, agricultural experts, and state bureaucrats,

> whose scope of activity is directly dependent on the allocation of national resources and which are directly affected by any shift in the institutional distribution of power ... advocate to the political leadership certain courses of action; they have their own professional or specialized newspapers which, at times and subject to over-all Party control, can become important vehicles for expressing specific points of view.[2]

In this article we will investigate two instances wherein such groups seemed to influence public policy: the first having the result of virtually scuttling one of Khrushchev's own major proposals, and the second affecting a policy outcome on which the top leadership had not taken a position.

We do not mean to challenge the view that ultimate power in the U.S.S.R. resides at the top of the Communist Party hierarchy. Neither do we mean to infer that the top party leadership can be forced by a "policy group" to act against its will. We hope that the major payoff in this chapter will be in showing that publics can influence Soviet policy formation, even in some rare cases when some top political leaders oppose their position.

The first major section will describe a case in which policy groups played a role in resolving a policy dispute at the top level of Soviet leadership. The second will explain why things happened as they did. The third will describe another case which we feel is more typical of the role of groups in the Soviet policy process. The fourth will explain the outcome of that case, while the fifth will report some hypotheses about when such phenomena are likely to recur.

I. THE DEBATE OVER THE 1958 EDUCATION ACT

A prominent feature of post-Stalin Russia has been the nationwide discussion of certain legislative proposals. This does not constitute a totally new innovation in the Soviet Union. During the preceding period such important laws as the constitution of 1936 received nationwide discussion before enactment. A few differences, however, deserve mention. First, the frequency of these discussions has substantially increased. Second and more important, the impact of these discussions on the proposed legislation has in some instances been far more than peripheral. This especially applies to the debate which surrounded the Educational Reform Act of 1958. A closer look at this debate will afford us an opportunity to consider how the opinion of various "publics" can influence the policy process.

There can be little doubt whose initiative lay behind the proposed reform. At the 13th Komsomol Congress in April of 1958, First Party Secretary Khrushchev severely criticized the existing school system and demanded fundamental changes.[3] This attack seems to have been motivated by three problems facing Soviet society in the mid-fifties, the cause of which Khrushchev linked to the existing school system.

First, the Soviet press had unceasingly criticized the denigrative attitudes of the younger generation toward physical labor.[4] In the opinion of the First Secretary, the undue emphasis upon classical academic training and the neglect of the polytechnical side of education were largely responsible for this attitude.

Second, competition for admission to higher education had reached an excessive degree, and this likewise had caused great concern among political leaders.[5] The competition itself had largely been a by-product of changes in the economic and educational systems.

Prior to 1950 the rapid growth of the economy and the under-developed secondary educational facilities maintained the demand for skilled technical cadres at a higher level than the supply. Throughout this period the number of available places in higher education exceeded the number of secondary school graduates. The postwar years, however, witnessed a remarkable acceleration of secondary school facilities and enrollment. In 1949, out of a total enrollment of thirty-three million pupils only about one million were in grades eight to ten. Four years later the number of pupils in secondary education had risen to four and one-half million.[6] Then the annual supply of secondary school graduates greatly exceeded the number of vacancies in higher education. Since the Soviet regime, for reasons of its own, was unwilling to widen the availability of higher education, the gates of universities were closed to millions of youth regardless of their educational attainment.

An inevitable consequence has been the intensification of competition for the available number of places.[7] The pressures for admission became abnormally high because of the widespread notion that a college degree represents the key to individual advancement and entrance into the new class of Soviet intelligentsia. Consequently, those high school graduates initially denied admission refused to accept their fate. Instead of entering the labor force, many of them became perennial college candidates. Very often they applied to schools whose area of specialization was of no genuine interest to them. But in the absence of alternatives they would often enter an agricultural institute just to be able "to study somewhere."[8] Here again Khrushchev charged that the educational system had bred such attitudes. By allowing students to continue their education uninterruptedly and by stressing almost exclusively academic material, the schools naturally generated the expectation that the path to life lay solely through higher education.

The third problem involved the increasing stratification of Soviet society. The notion that higher education was the key to membership in the "new class" had a firm basis in fact. Yet these educational channels for upward social and political mobility were being drastically constricted as a consequence of their preemption by the incumbent political and bureaucratic elites. Khrushchev himself admitted that in the competition for admission to college the influence of parents often proved more important than the merit of the candidates. He further stated that only 30 to 40 percent of the enrolled students in higher education institutions came from worker and peasant backgrounds.[9] The differential access to a prime source of mobility gravely concerned the First Secretary. Both the content and tenor of his statements clearly indicate that Khrushchev sought to eliminate privilege and inequality from the Soviet educational system.[10]

Finally, we should mention an additional factor which may have influenced the reform movement. At the time of the debate some Western scholars argued that the specifics of Khrushchev's proposals owed much to the serious labor shortage the Soviet economy was about to experience.[11] The argument may be summarized briefly as follows. Because of severe war losses and a declining birth rate in the postwar period the Soviet Union would have one-third fewer people entering the labor force during the late fifties and early sixties than normally would have been the case. Consequently, the ambitious economic growth program could be achieved only if the vast majority of young people were channeled into the active labor force instead of higher education. It is important to note, however, that the Soviet press never cited a labor deficit as cause for the reform. Other evidence also casts doubt upon the validity of this thesis.[12]

While there is room for disagreement as to what problems motivated the reform, there is no ambiguity regarding Khrushchev's proposals for dealing with them. In September 1958, the party secretary published his "thesis" on school reorganization.[13] He suggested that continuous academic education be abolished and that all students be required to combine work with study. In effect this meant phasing out the ten-year school which at that time constituted a completed secondary education. After finishing a seven- or eight-year primary school, said Khrushchev, every young person should enter the labor force. Those who wished to prepare themselves for higher education could continue their studies in evening and correspondence schools. Successful students would receive two or three days' released time from work to facilitate studying.

The substitution of part-time work and study for full-time education in secondary day schools had, from Khrushchev's point of view, two advantages. First, it would instill in the younger generation a respectful attitude toward physical labor. Second, it would equalize access to higher education. The secondary day schools had become the province of children from the urban intelligentsia. Evening and correspondence schools, on the other hand, recruited most of their students from worker and peasant families. The difference in the quality of education offered by these two divisions gave the day school graduate an obvious advantage. By fusing the two channels into one undifferentiated system, Khrushchev hoped to eliminate the class bias in Soviet education. The road to a higher education would be the same for all irrespective of the positions or jobs which the parents held in society.

Study in higher educational institutions was also to be put on a part-time basis. The student would acquire the first two or three years of his college education through evening or correspondence courses. Thereafter he could complete his training on a full-time schedule. Moreover, no individual was to be granted permission to higher education unless he had already worked full time after completing secondary school. Once again we see Khrushchev's determination to deemphasize the purely academic side of education and to enhance the importance of work experience.

If we compare Khrushchev's September memorandum with the actual law adopted in December 1958 we find that the two differ not only in detail but in basic principle.[14] To begin with, the old secondary day school was preserved more or less intact both in form and content. Khrushchev's demand that work be combined with study had received token satisfaction by increasing the number of hours devoted to polytechnical training *within* the schools. But the quantity and quality of academic subjects had in no way been sacrificed. The law established an eleven-year day school to replace the old ten-year day school system. The addition of another year permitted greater emphasis upon labor training without simultaneously diluting the quality of academic education. Indeed, the number of hours devoted to purely academic subjects proved to be *exactly the same* under the new system as it had been under the old.[15]

The maintenance of continuous secondary full-time education must be seen as a rebuff to Khrushchev's demands. When the new law went into effect, it became apparent that nearly all the former ten-year schools would continue to operate as part of the new eleven-year system. Some figures also suggest that the number of students enrolled in the new system was comparable in size to the two senior grades of the old ten-year school.[16] It is true that Khrushchev recognized in his memorandum the need for *some* full-time day schools. But he envisaged that they would operate only during a transitional period and he expected their number to be sharply reduced right from the beginning of the reform.

While the eleven-year system might have satisfied the demand that work be combined with study, it could not possibly have achieved Khrushchev's other expressed purpose—the elimination of privilege and inequality. The perpetuation of a bifurcated full-time and part-time school system insured that inequality would persist. Nevertheless the disadvantages faced by the evening and correspondence student might have significantly diminished had the law incorporated Khrushchev's suggestion regarding released time for study. Yet in this area as well, important modifications were made. The reorganization decree left this question open and subsequent legislation resulted in a far less liberal policy.[17] Under these circumstances the vast majority of college students would continue to come from the full-time secondary schools and an inevitable by-product would be the continuation of class bias in higher education.

The provision for admission to and study in higher educational institutions likewise markedly deviated from Khrushchev's suggestions. Instead of *absolutely* requiring full-time work before admission, the law merely stipulated that *priority* would be granted those with the record of employment or military service. But preference for people with production experience already existed before the reorganization of the school system. Thus the wording of the law gave only formal recognition to an ongoing practice. It cannot be interpreted as a "concession" to the demands made by Khrushchev in his memorandum.

His insistence upon part-time study during the first few college years appears to have been more successfully realized. At least the law accepted it in principle. However, even here some important alterations occurred. The law explicitly exempted from this requirement all students in difficult theoretical disciplines. Similarly, the requirement would be inoperative in both nontechnical higher educational institutions and in arts faculties at universities, since "factory work for students cannot in these cases be connected with their future job."[18]

Generally speaking, the education reform failed to implement the most important goals and purposes which Khrushchev had articulated in his memorandum. What factors can account for the observable disparity between the September proposal and the December law? To answer that question we must look briefly at the discussion which ensued during this period of time. The content of that debate clearly revealed that different societal groups, or at least some members of them, opposed Khrushchev's reform.

Teachers and administrators identified with the ten-year school obviously wished to preserve and protect their institutional bailiwicks. But a frontal attack on the First Secretary's ideas would not have been good politics. Instead they opposed the reform more deviously. Essentially they argued that to prepare youth for manual labor it was not necessary to send them after the eighth grade to factories or farms. A much better way would be to bring the factories and farms into the schools by setting up first-class workshops. Under these conditions it would be possible to teach pupils the same skills they could learn by entering the labor force. To substantiate their case the proponents of this approach assumed the initiative even *before* the appearance of Khrushchev's September memorandum. Prior to the opening of the school year in 1958, Y. I. Afanasenko, Minister of Education for the Russian Republic, announced that the number of schools giving training in industrial and agricultural skills would double. He further announced that the Russian Republic had begun to experiment with extending secondary schools from ten to eleven years. Under the extended program students would spend half of their time at school and the other half at jobs on farms, in factories, or at construction sites. He mentioned that fifty schools with this program had operated the last year and this number would increase to two hundred during the present year. Here, in embryonic form, was the eleven-year school system that became law in December 1958. Thus, through work and deed, those occupational groups associated with full-time secondary education sought to protect the organization they had built with effort and care.[19]

Other groups opposed to the reform included higher educational and scientific personnel. Their arguments were perhaps more telling. They warned that it would be impossible under the new system to ensure the supply of highly qualified cadres for economic and societal growth. How can we, they asked, perfect and advance scientific knowledge when new entrants to higher educational schools would have only eight years of regular schooling behind them and who, in the following years, would have forgotten the little they had once learned. Several prominent educators and scientists went so far as to assert that a hiatus between incomplete and complete secondary school, as well as between complete secondary school and higher education, would result in irreparable damage to the state. For creative work in scientific research often manifests itself when the individual has reached his mid-twenties and the acquisition of theoretical knowledge on a large scale demands uninterrupted study.[20]

The warning of experts reinforced grave doubts raised by many parents. The basic argument of the latter was that a shortened basic school program would adversely affect the physical and intellectual maturation of adolescents. Furthermore, it was said that channeling young people into production at an early age does not give them a chance to adequately choose a skill which best suits them.[21] While both of these points had merit, parental views were somewhat suspect because other motives could be readily discerned. As Khrushchev himself pointed out, many parents were determined that their children receive opportunities for maximum education. They saw his plans as a threat to that opportunity and responded by attacking it. To the extent that pedagogical experts echoed parental concerns, as some did, they served as a linkage between public opinion and political decision-makers. By articulating the interests of an amorphous group in technical terms, the experts transformed their claims into a politically relevant issue.

A few words must also be said about the attitudes of factory managers. Although their opposition did not find explicit expression in the debate, their behaviour left few doubts as to where they stood on the issue. Long before the question of reform had arisen, managers had displayed a reluctance to hire and train juvenile workers. Under the new arrangements they would become responsible for all sorts of educational functions for which the factory was ill prepared. Moreover, the large influx of schoolchildren and the necessity to train them would inevitably divert managers from their own duties of production and plan fulfillment. In light of this fact it is not surprising that the reform act failed to implement Khrushchev's suggestions regarding released time from work. That would have greatly complicated the managers' tasks, and we can assume that their views were transmitted to the proper authorities.[22]

II. THE ROLE OF SOCIAL GROUPS IN SHAPING THE ACT

At this point, our task is to account for the role of groups in forming educational policy, in this instance by interpreting a number of facts. The objective facts we must work from are, in summary, that Khrushchev made a far-reaching proposal to deal with a number of educational problems facing the regime, and that the substance of the proposal was radically modified. The major proponent of the reform was obviously Khrushchev himself. The most important—indeed the only—opponents of the changes we can identify are the social groups cited above.

Here we should note that if one quantifies the number of articles which appeared during the debate, the oppositional point of view is clearly a minority. It is quite possible that a "war of memoranda" may have been raging behind the scenes and that during this exchange the minority position was in fact the majority point of view.[23] Whatever may have been the case, it is undeniable that the oppositional arguments were closer to the form of the finally enacted law.

There are several possible interpretations which would explain the outcome of the educational reform debate. One might argue, for example, that the disparity between the September memorandum and the December law resulted from Khrushchev changing his mind. Once the technocratic elites had pointed out the potentially dangerous consequences inherent in Khrushchev's proposals, the First Secretary simply revised his original position. There is no way, of course, to verify or falsify this interpretation. Since we have no knowledge of Khrushchev's preference schedule or to whom he would most likely listen, we must allow for the possibility that anyone who had a position and stated it prior to the outcome might have influenced Khrushchev. If we accept this interpretation, however, we must resolve certain questions which detract from its credibility.

When Khrushchev spoke to the Komsomol Congress in April 1958, he stated that the Party Central Committee had, *for some time*, been discussing the improvement of public education. Presumably, experts had been consulted during the course of such discussions. We might also presume that Khrushchev sounded out experts between April and September when he was preparing a detailed proposal for educational reform. In light of this, it seems unlikely that Khrushchev changed his mind because he had heard convincing arguments which had not been made in the far longer period which preceded publication of his memorandum.

It is also important to recall that Khrushchev clearly identified himself personally with the issue of educational reform. He placed his public prestige squarely upon the line. As Richard Neustadt has pointed out, chief executives cannot afford to make indiscriminate public announcements. If they are sensitive to the prerequisites of power and influence, they must carefully weigh the consequences which flow from what, when, and how they say things.[24] All the evidence we have on Khrushchev's career suggests that he was highly sensitive to the requisites of power and influence. Thus not only did the First Secretary have ample opportunity to consult expert opinion on the educational question, but he also had a vested political interest in doing so before publicly stating his position.

Our own inclination then is to discount, though not categorically reject, the possibility that Khrushchev simply changed his mind between September and December. An alternative interpretation is that bureaucratic groups prevailed over the First Secretary and forced him to act against his will.[25] To accept this, however, would demand a rewriting of the literature on political power and resources in the Soviet Union that we think is neither necessary nor appropriate. It is quite easy on the other hand to imagine more important actors prevailing over Khrushchev, with the social groups associating themselves spuriously, so to speak, with the stronger actors. In suggesting that interpretation we must argue inferentially because the only direct evidence we have about opposition to the proposal relates to the groups. In the following material we will attempt to account for what happened and to assess the role of the social groups in it.

Brzezinski and Huntington express the orthodox interpretation in arguing that the key political resource in the Soviet Union is control of the party organization, and that such control can be shared only at the top.

> Thus, insofar as there are limits on the power of the top leader in the Soviet Union, they stem from his sharing control of the *apparat* with a small number of colleagues . . . the principal limits on the power of the Soviet leader are inside the Kremlin.[26]

We agree, and we feel that those colleagues were crucially important in defeating Khrushchev's proposal. But the opposition of the groups identified above was not coincidental. We submit that the groups were mobilized after the dispute was left unresolved at the top.

Such an argument forces us to take sides in a dispute among Soviet scholars about whether or not there is conflict within the Soviet leadership at times other than succession crises. It is the position of the "conflict" school that policy issues such as those on agriculture, heavy industry, consumer goods, foreign affairs, Stalinism, economic reorganization, and education are continuous sources of dispute among the top leadership. When one issue is resolved, another is likely to take its place. We think there is strong evidence for this viewpoint, which became more compelling than ever with Khrushchev's political demise in October 1964.[27]

In this specific case, Khrushchev stated, in April of 1958, that the Party Central Committee was presently engaged in preparing a resolution on the improvement of public education.[28] But the September "theses" proved to be simply a note by Khrushchev with the "approval" of the Central Committee, instead of a formal resolution by that august body. This suggests that Khrushchev's educational reform was a highly personal document which lacked support among a substantial element of the top political leadership. Esoteric evidence to support this thesis is provided by the unusual silence of the top political leadership during the educational debate. Khrushchev appears to have been the only Praesidium member to have played a significant role in the reform discussions and to have clearly and publicly expressed his attitudes. Sidney Ploss has argued that in the context of Soviet politics the silence of leaders on a topical issue must be construed as disagreement with the expressed viewpoint of their colleagues.[29] It is also significant that major amendments to Khrushchev's plan were reflected in the Central Committee resolution on education reform which was finally issued on November 16, 1958.[30]

If, as we have argued, the important conflict was on the top leadership level, and if the persons on that level have the power to determine policy outcomes, what role did the social groups play? The answer hangs on the nature of conflict among the leaders. It is well known that such conflict involves elements of power struggle and elements of dispute over policy alternative.[31] Sometimes these elements operate independently of one another; more often they intertwine. Since Khrushchev had decisively defeated his rivals for power in 1957, we can assume that in the case of the education reforms of 1958 the elements of power struggle were less important than at almost any time since Stalin's death, and that the elements of unadulterated policy dispute were correspondingly more important. Indeed, it is unlikely that Khrushchev would have survived such a defeat as this had this policy dispute involved much of a power struggle.

Insofar as this was really a policy dispute, it involved numerous problem-solving considerations, as emphasized above. The problems and policy positions associated with them involved a number of questions of judgment about what courses of action would solve the problem, and what the consequences of such action would have for other goals of the regime. It is here that the groups play an important role. Numerous groups have recognized expertise about what problems are in their own area. The ten-year school personnel had an authoritative position for a judgment that students could get work experience without radically changing the school organization and curriculum. The scientific community had good claim to special insight into the needs of training scientists. Parents may be viewed as having some legitimate judgment about the needs of adolescents, although this is less apparently expertise. One student of the reform debate has argued that

> The most important factors responsible for the change in Khrushchev's original proposals probably were the arguments of experts—the function of expert opinion was to point out to the leadership the possibly harmful consequences to Soviet society of the literal adoption of Khrushchev's original plans.[32]

It is hard to identify any concrete resource other than their own recognized expertise which the groups might have used in the dispute. Neither money, votes, nor popularity were relevant to its resolution. Only the expert judgment was clearly relevant. The only reasonable alternative would seem to be that the regime may have accorded the positions of these groups a certain legitimacy just because they were group preferences, much as an American public official might yield to a constituent's demand simply because he views it as legitimate and because he may view his job as one of servicing such demands when they are legitimate and do not conflict with other goals. We have no reason to believe that Soviet officials view their jobs this way. Communist ideology, unlike democratic ideology, supplies its own policy goals, rather than depending on public expressions of preference to define them. Besides, we have already seen that the goals of these groups conflicted with the goals of none other than the First Secretary of the Communist Party. It does seem apparent that insofar as groups influenced the outcome of this issue it was through the communication of their expert judgments to people at the top of the hierarchy who *were* in a position to influence outcomes. The expertise became a resource to be used in making a case that more harm than good would result from the proposed reform.[33] We contend that in the Soviet Union policy issues are often decided on the basis of such debates. If such is the case the arguments of persons who are recognized as being knowledgeable can be an important resource for the proponent or opponent of a policy proposal.

One can see elements of ambiguity in this interpretation of the role of these groups as articulators of expert judgment. It may appear, for example, that the ten-year school personnel are looking out for themselves when they oppose changes in their institution. The position of the parents seems even more transparent. There may even have been some self-interest involved in the position of the scientists. The point is that there is no objective way for either Soviet leaders or American scholars to clearly separate the elements of self-interest from those of expert predictions of dire consequences. We would argue that in Western democracies as well there is often an almost indecipherable mixture of preference and prediction in policy debate. For example, social welfare policies in the United States are commonly defended in terms of the prospects of contraction and recession if welfare funds are not fed into the economy. The very ambiguity between preference and prediction may serve to enhance the prospects of group influence through the pressing of interests with the support of expert judgments. The congruence of one's interests with one's predictions is probably less important than the persuasiveness of the predictions and the acknowledged expertness of predictors, no matter whose interests they seem to support.

This almost inevitable mixture of self-interest and expertise provides a channel through which groups in the Soviet Union *may* influence policy when higher powers seek their judgment. We do not know how common this occurrence is, but we are confident that expertise is not used in this way to resolve all policy disputes.

III. THE DEBATE OVER THE PROBLEM OF WORK ASSIGNMENTS

The following section of this essay continues our research on group influence and the Soviet policy process. Here we propose to identify different circumstances and processes through which group activity affects policy outcomes. In our first study, the role played by groups was essentially that of response and constraint. Once Khrushchev had defined the political issues of educational reform and initiated policy proposals for dealing with those issues, various groups used their acknowledged expertise in making a case that more harm than good would result from Khrushchev's proposals. In the instance we analyze below, the roles are directly reversed. Instead of reacting to policies initiated by the political leadership, groups—or at least prominent individuals associated with certain groups—assumed the active initiating role themselves. It was they who defined the political issue and established the direction of policy debate. Their behavior, in turn, led to a response from the top political leadership.

With this portion of our essay, then, we hope to broaden the parameters we set in the first section concerning the conditions and processes through which groups can affect decision-making in the Soviet Union. We believe these are necessary first steps toward a more general theory of decision-making in Communist political systems.

As in our first study, the situation which precipitated a political issue was related to the educational system. When a Soviet student graduates from a higher educational institution, his first three years of employment are not necessarily in a place of his own choosing. Every specialist, upon completion of his formal training, must work in a position and area of the country assigned to him by a state placement committee. Such committees are established under the auspices of individual universities and institutes.

At the beginning of each academic year the Ministry of Higher and Specialized Secondary Education forwards to each placement committee a list of positions to which its graduates should be assigned. The committee then examines the records of its students and tries to correlate supply with demand. During the selection process students are ordinarily informed of employment opportunities and may express their preferences. Similarly, representatives of economic enterprises may offer inducements to students they especially wish to hire. Preferences of prospective graduates or employers, however, are in no way binding upon the committee. A simple majority vote determines where each student will work.

Once the committee has reached a decision the young specialist is given an assignment paper. If for reasons of health, family situation, or insufficient jobs, the committee does not place a student, the individual receives a permit to find employment himself.[34] The government realizes that the procedure is not flawless and therefore grants the dissatisfied the right of petition. There is no assurance, however, that his appeal will be favorably acted upon and, if it is rejected, the decision of the placement committee becomes final.

The disagreement of the young specialist with his job appointment by the committee on personnel placement does not free him upon graduation from his duty to report to work in accordance with the placement order.[35]

This rule notwithstanding, many graduates have been unwilling to abide by the decisions of placement committees. As a result they resort to a wide array of irregular and illegal practices in order to secure a job which they deem suitable for themselves. "Suitable" normally connotes a position in a large urban center. What most students object to is the *place*, not the *type* of employment assigned them by placement committees. When faced with the prospect of a position in the provincial and rural areas of the country, they use any means possible to avoid what is commonly referred to as an "imprisonment for three years."[36]

The evasion of assignments to the provinces does not always entail outright refusal. To the extent that it is possible, students try to exploit legitimate means for remaining in large urban centers. Marriage with people who have the right to reside in cities offers salvation to some. Occasionally such marriages occur for the most opportunistic and callous reasons. A judge of the Moscow City Court claimed that a substantial percentage of divorces among young people in the capital and its environs was attributable to so-called "marriages of convenience." Individuals entered matrimony only to secure the right to live in Moscow. Once this objective has been achieved, divorce proceedings are begun.[37]

Other students find a solution in the health provisions of the placement law. If no genuine medical problems exist some individuals invent them.[38] Another common technique is to solicit support from influential friends or organizations. The exercise of *blat* (influence) can prove very helpful when the committee must decide the placement of its graduates. Such informal arrangements and pressures have been frequently condemned in the official press.[39]

Although outsiders do attempt to apply undue influence, academic rectors themselves are not always the scrupulous observers of proper placement procedures. Instead of servicing the wider national interests, they often give preference to the needs of their own locality. By their actions, they frustrated the very intent of a centralized placement system—to insure a supply of cadres for economic enterprises in underdeveloped areas which cannot attract and maintain a stable labor force on a voluntary basis.[40]

The preceding evidence suggests that students are not wholly at the mercy of an impartial placement committee. The resourceful or fortunate graduate has ample opportunities to determine his own place of employment. This is not to say, however, that *most* students can legitimately avoid assignment to the provinces. For the vast majority the choice is simply between obeying or refusing the placement order. The available data indicate that a sizable number choose the latter. Exactly how many this included is impossible to say because the Soviet Union has never published any systematic statistical information on this question. Some figures for specific regions suggests a very high percentage of the graduating class.

Thus, it was reported that in 1962 30 percent of the graduates of the Yerevan State University and 60 percent of the graduates of the Yerevan Institute of Foreign Languages did not accept the positions assigned to them.[41] Other union republics have experienced similar mass refusals of students to accept the decision of placement committees.[42]

These figures are probably not representative of the Soviet Union as a whole. If they were, the centralized distribution of specialists in accordance with rational planning would cease to function. Nevertheless, the problem remains a vexing one and requires attention. While there existed a consensus about the need to do something about the problem, there was widespread disagreement as to what that something should be. Indeed, for several years debate raged in the Soviet press over what policy should be adopted to meet the situation. Most prominent in these debates were officials of the higher educational and Komsomol bureaucracies. This is not surprising since both organizations are directly involved in the placement of graduates. A closer look at this debate and its final resolution will reveal interesting insights into the Soviet policy process.

When discussing the placement problem, educational officials offered "soft" solutions. They stressed the improved moral education of students and the perfection of placement procedures as the most effective way of reducing student refusals to accept their assignments. While acknowledging that some students had forgotten their obligation to society, they also noted that defects in the placement system were a prime cause of this attitude. It was claimed, for example, that students had often been given assignments without carefully considering their preparation for the job or their state of health. Similarly little account was taken of their family situation, and the separation of married couples was not a rare occurrence. Elimination of these shortcomings, so it was said, would help to reduce the number of refusals.[43]

Educators also argued for changes in the recruitment of college students. They urged that industrial and agricultural enterprises more vigorously exploit their right to send their own candidates to study in higher educational institutions. This would enable economic units to plan their own requirements for specialized manpower and make them less dependent upon the state placement committees. Students economically supported by a sponsoring unit in this manner would be legally obligated to work for the enterprise which had sent them to school.[44]

Along the same lines, educators suggested changes in the recruitment of students for agricultural institutes. Graduates of these educational establishments had long been chronic violators of the three-year assignment rule. This is not surprising since many students of agriculture never had any intention of working in the countryside. The intense competition for available places in higher education induces some youth to apply for admission to agricultural institutes when they are not accepted elsewhere. As the Soviet press has often remarked, they operate on the principle "just to study somewhere."[45] In the socially stratified Soviet Union of today large numbers of the younger generation denigrate physical labor. The surest way to avoid consignment to that role is to acquire a college diploma, even if one's specific training is not immediately put to use. A higher education confers not only a potentially greater income level, but, more importantly, the much desired social status of membership in the intelligentsia class.

To overcome this problem educators demanded that applicants for agricultural institutes be recruited mainly among rural youth. Having experience and being interested in agricultural work, they would more willingly return to the villages from which they came. Changes in the composition of the student body, it was stated, could be facilitated by the transference of agricultural institutes to areas of agricultural production. It was pointed out that of the ninety-eight institutes in the Soviet Union only thirteen functioned on state farms. The remaining eighty-five had been located on the "asphalt fields" of large cities. As a result their student bodies included an overwhelming number of urban youth who had no special calling for agricultural work and who were reluctant to leave the city after graduation.[46]

On a more general plane educators asserted the need to improve the moral conditioning of Soviet students. They suggested that every student be evaluated every year at a general meeting of his academic group. The collective should consider not only his academic progress, personal behavior, and participation in social work, but also what thoughts he had about the future and how he hoped to contribute to the building of communism. Such an approach would force every student to pass a serious public review not just once but on a continuing basis. Thus, society could more effectively influence the political and social consciousness of the individual and make him more sensitive to his obligations.[47]

The proposals espoused by Komsomol officials were of a quite different nature. Whereas educational experts favored persuasive and educational methods, some members of the Komsomol leadership agitated on behalf of punitive and repressive measures. Foremost among these was Sergei Pavlov, First Secretary of the Komsomol Central Committee. Indeed, he rarely missed an opportunity to disseminate his belief that harsh methods were required to deal with graduates "who know their rights but not their duties." During an interview in January 1964, one of the authors, Joel Schwartz, discussed this problem with him. His comments left little doubt as to where he stood on the issue. If he had his way, he said, he would deprive such individuals of their diplomas and make their actions subject to criminal prosecution. A conviction, he continued, should obligate the guilty party to repay all of the state funds expended on his or her higher education.[48] One month later, at the February Party plenum, Pavlov repeated what we had discussed in his office. He added that personnel managers who knowingly accepted violators of the placement rule should likewise be criminally prosecuted.[49]

This was not the first time Komsomol officials put forth such proposals. At the beginning of 1960 the Moscow regional Komsomol newspaper invited its readers to express their opinion on the problem. Numerous articles subsequently appeared and in January of the following year the editor summarized what he described as the consensus of the overwhelming majority of replies. That summation reflected in exact form the suggestions of First Secretary Pavlov.[50] This is not surprising since Pavlov headed the Moscow regional apparatus before being elevated to his all-Union position. The implementation of such a program would have been tantamount to a resuscitation of the harsh labor laws introduced by Stalin in 1940. At that time all employees, including young graduates, were subject to criminal prosecution for quitting or changing jobs without prior authorization from the management of the employing unit. Judicial procedure was likewise employed in the event of tardiness or absenteeism without a valid reason. The law remained in effect until 1956 when it was repealed by the Supreme Soviet.

Pavlov and his supporters obviously believed that the behavior of college graduates justified a reinstatement of that law or one similar to it. But individuals prominent in the educational field firmly opposed this point of view. At a conference of educational specialists the Minister of Higher Education in the Russian Republic declared

> We have a law which states that every graduate who completes higher education must work on an assigned job for three years. This law has not been repealed. . . . It is a just law. . . . Improved moral education should reduce the number of refusals to take these jobs. We do not feel that recourse to criminal prosecution which has now been lifted will work better than moral persuasion.[51]

The theme received unequivocal support five years later from V. P. Eliutin, the all-Union Minister of Higher Education. In an interview with a reporter of the Moscow Komsomol newspaper, he took the opportunity to rebut the policies which had been defended by the editorial staff of that paper.

> In the press and in particular in the newspaper *Moskovskii Komsomolets* it has been suggested that diplomas be granted to specialists one or two years after they have worked at their assigned job. This, it was said, would reduce the number of cases in which individual students refuse their state assignment. It seems to me that we have far from exhausted other measures for eliminating shortcomings in the placement of specialists. Our students in the overwhelming majority are honest, conscientious people. Therefore, we must emphasize instead the strengthening of educational and Komsomol work in higher educational institutions together with the reasonable perfection of the placement system itself.[52]

As the statements above indicate, the policies of Pavlov and Eliutin were at opposite ends of the pole. The former demanded the application of coercion while the latter urged reliance upon persuasion. The decision of what to do about the placement of young specialists lay beyond the authority of *both* Pavlov and Eliutin. For the debate analyzed here had political implications far beyond the immediate and limited problem. The diametrically opposed proposals reflected a much wider and more significant controversy which has been occurring in the Soviet Union, namely whether that country should continue the process of de-Stalinization or fall back upon procedures which are reminiscent of the Stalinist period. That controversy has affected every aspect of Soviet life. Western observers of the Soviet scene have classified the contestants as "conservatives" and "reformers," imputing to the former a determined resistance to modifications of the Stalinist pattern and to the latter a conviction that the harsh and repressive ways of the great dictator must give way to a more humane system.

Supporters of both views have sat in the highest political bodies of the Soviet Union. It was to them that the "conservative" Pavlov and the "reformer" Eliutin were addressing their arguments. Each used his own prestigious position and the media of communication available to him in order to appeal to elements of the ruling political leadership whose attitudes were consonant with their own. Thus, a systematic reading of the journal of the Ministry of Higher Education (the organization headed by Eliutin) revealed a moderate and balanced discussion of the placement of graduates. Not only was there an absence of "sensational" refusal figures, but only a minimum amount of space was devoted to this issue over a period of ten years.[53] This type of treatment was, in our opinion, not accidental. This seems to have been the ministry's way of asserting that the problem was not serious enough to warrant coercive measures.

Certain parts of the Komsomol press, on the other hand, devoted a great deal of attention to placement. During the decade 1954–64 the number of articles about students who shirk their state obligations or desert their assignments increased with a crescendo-like tempo. Such intensive coverage can be explained partly by the organization's need to mold popular opinion against this type of behavior. A second and perhaps more important cause was the desire of some Komsomol officials to "prove" that the magnitude of the problem justified the severe measures they advocated. In short, they used the press under their immediate control as a functional aid of policy debate. When First Secretary Pavlov stated that 60 percent of the graduates of the Yeveran Foreign Language Institute refused their assignment or that nearly 50 percent of the agricultural experts sent to the Omsk region never worked at their speciality, he was not simply reporting the "news." His purpose was to manipulate the evidence in support of his policy position.

Despite all of Pavlov's efforts, victory went to the educators. The harsh coercive measures advocated by the First Secretary were never implemented. Persuasion continued to be the main weapon for dealing with "students with a diploma but without a conscience." Moreover, several proposals of educational spokesmen received support from the political leadership. The ministry was instructed to transfer sixty-five agricultural institutes to rural localities, leaving only twenty instead of eighty-five in urban centers.[54] Likewise, a concerted effort was made to channel the maximum number of rural youth into agricultural schools.

IV. GROUPS IN THE POLICY PROCESS

The success of Eliutin and other educational officials was attributable ultimately to the fact that their "reformist" political orientation coincided with the attitudes of the dominant political forces in the country at that time. Pavlov's position was further weakened by his inability to achieve wholehearted support from his own organizational base. In the course of Schwartz's interview the First Secretary admitted that many of his Komsomol colleagues did not share his opinion as to how the government could best deal with students who do not abide by the decisions of placement committees. This finds confirmation in the fact that no formal resolution of the Komsomol Central Committee ever embodied the punitive measures for which Pavlov so consistently argued. It is also significant that other Komsomol newspapers during the same time period made no mention of Pavlov's harshest demands, such as criminal prosecution. Only those media *directly under the Secretary's control* faithfully reflected his viewpoint.[55] Of course, the Ministry of Higher Education may also have been rent by disagreement on this issue. If that were the case, however, it did not find reflection in the pages of the ministry's journal.

We would argue, then, that in spite of superficial differences, the two cases we have investigated reflect similar patterns of Soviet political behavior. In both cases policy groups played an important part in expressing the arguments of the debate and in articulating the different positions on the issue of placement of graduates. In both cases the prevailing political force was above the groups and in the top political leadership, the difference being that in the Reform Act the losing side was publicly supported by the First Secretary of the Communist Party. In the placement case, no top political leader was "defeated" in the outcome, because none was publicly identified with either position. The placement issue appears to have been fought out in the lower echelons, after which the top leaders stepped in to resolve it. The Educational Reform Act was fought out on the top level and the scope of conflict was broadened to include the lower echelons after the top stratum had failed to resolve the issue within its ranks.

These two issues would seem to illustrate three or four basic patterns for resolving political issues in the Soviet Union in periods when there is no succession crisis and when policy debates are not too closely bound up with the struggle for power.

1. It is likely that many policy disputes originate among the top leaders and are resolved among them without broadening the scope of conflict. We know very little about the nature and frequency of such disputes, because we are not likely to learn about any disputes in detail unless the scope of conflict is changed and it becomes a topic of semi-public debate. The decision to invade Czechoslovakia in August 1968 may well have been an example.

2. Some splits originate on the top levels, but are resolved only after the scope of conflict is broadened and policy groups are included. The dispute over the Educational Reform Act of 1958 is a leading example of this. It is important to note that the issue is resolved on top, where it originated, but that the policy groups and their expertise may be involved to define the issues and arguments more clearly.

3. Some policy disputes originate below the top echelons, such as this one over job assignments for graduates. It is possible that many of these are resolved when they are raised, but the example of the job placement issue was resolved from above because the political implications of the resolution involved fundamental issues in post-Stalin Russia. It is unlikely, however, that we will learn about these disputes originating in lower echelons unless some positions require patronage by a member of the ruling political hierarchy.

4. There is probably a fourth category of disputes which are raised and resolved on the lower echelons of decision-makers. Like those that are raised and resolved on the top without broadening the scope of conflict, we are not likely to know about them simply because they do not become public issues.

V. SOME OBSERVATIONS
AND HYPOTHESES

The policy process in the Soviet Union has often been described by Western scholars as a unidirectional phenomenon. Brzezinski and Huntington, for example, make a very clear distinction between policy-initiating roles in the United States and the Soviet Union. Their general conclusion is that decision-making "bubbles up" in the U.S. and "trickles down" in the U.S.S.R. Less metaphorically, their position is that private groups, social forces, and lower-ranking governmental agencies in the U.S. initiate almost all policy proposals while it is the top political leadership in the U.S.S.R. which does all the important initiating.[56]

The data analyzed in this paper convince us that such a view is too simplistic and restrictive. The "trickle down" thesis assumes that policy debates in the Soviet Union occur "only after and upon condition of initiative and support from some coalition or individual among the proximate policy makers."[57] We do not dispute that this is *sometimes* the case. But even when the Praesidium does the initiating, the role and influence of "private groups, social forces, and lower ranking governmental agencies" are by no means minimal.

The debate over educational reform clearly emanated from the central and highest power structure. It appears that the original intent was to manipulate the discussion on behalf of Khrushchev's policy objectives and hence to provide him with increased political resources for resolving a factional dispute among the leadership. Once the scope of conflict had widened, however, the policy debate acquired a momentum and direction of its own. The co-opted publics exploited their opportunity to substantially influence and alter the policy outcome.

The public debate over graduate placement is even more difficult to reconcile with the "trickle down" thesis. Here we are confronted with a classic example of what Brzezinski and Huntington have described as bubbling-up decision-making. Bureaucratic officials who are closest to a specific area of life are the ones who initially identify a problem. It is they who generate proposals for dealing with the problem and it is they who build support among individuals and institutions for particular policy alternatives *prior* to the entry of the top leadership into the policy process.[58] This suggests that decision-making in the U.S.S.R.

consists of a far more complex balanced mix of "bubble up" and "trickle down" than existing literature on Soviet politics implies.

We cannot quantify the relative importance of initiatives from below as compared to policies which originate at the top. But we suspect that the former comprises a substantial portion of the decisions which are made in the Soviet Union. What we are prepared to argue is that the opinion of various publics has become an important input for policy outcomes in the U.S.S.R.

> Opinions of policy groups can influence the policy process either in the form of advocacy of or opposition to initiatives from above or in the form of initiation and promotion of policy proposals from below.

The degree to which various "publics" may influence policy outcomes depends upon their ability to build support for or against specific proposals. The identification of a problem and the generation of policies for dealing with it do not guarantee either a hearing or influence. Somehow publics must gain the attention of high-ranking policy-makers. Achieving this type of access may often take the form of interpersonal relationships and communication. Since such behavior is hidden from the public eye, we have no way of measuring its frequency or importance.

The two cases analyzed here, however, suggest alternative resources which are available for building support around specific policy proposals. In both the educational reform and graduate placement debates, competitive publics relied heavily upon the news media for influencing policy outcomes. In light of this evidence it would seem appropriate to revise the list of functions which are traditionally ascribed to the Soviet mass media.

Anthony Buzek, in his book *How the Communist Press Works*, attributes four functions to the communist press—propaganda, agitation, organization, and criticism.[59] Buzek's discussion presumes that the press is wholly an instrument of authority for mobilizing and manipulating the general public. But mobilization and manipulation can work both ways and the press may become an instrument of various publics for articulating their interests to the authority structure in the hope of influencing it. Hence to "propaganda, agitation, organization, and criticism" must be added the function of interest articulation.

> Access and influence in the Soviet Union often occur by the manipulation of news media at the disposal of and under the control of different groups in the society.

Influencing policy-makers through public communication has become a subtle and sensitive art in the Soviet Union. The danger always exists that a policy intent communication will be interpreted as an attack upon the party's authority or a form of disloyal activity. To avoid stigma of this sort, individuals must clothe their policy criticisms, discussions, and proposals in such a way as to persuade the authority structure that their purpose is simply to *improve* party policy and not to challenge it.

In responding to Khrushchev's initiatives on educational reform, opponents of his policy carefully avoided criticizing his general goals. Such direct challenges are normally considered illegitimate in the Soviet Union. Instead the opposition sought and obtained influence by arguing that the First Secretary's basic goals could be achieved more quickly and completely through certain modifications of his proposals.

The debate over graduate placement proceeded within the framework of acceptance of existing policy. Neither Pavlov nor Eliutin questioned the basic premise that all college graduates must work for three years at a place of employment chosen for them by state labor commissions. Each simply argued that the immediate goals of regime policy were unobtainable under existing procedures but would be achievable with the proposed new ones (Pavlov's position); or that the goals could be more completely achieved by slightly modifying existing procedures (Eliutin's position). In both cases, it is clear that policy discussion centered around narrow, specific, and technical means issues rather than broad ends issues. When we speak of "publics" influencing policy in the U.S.S.R., we must recognize that there are definite limitations to the form and content such activity takes.

> Public influence on the Soviet policy process assumes the form of coherent, specific and technically appropriate means proposals rather than broad ends proposals.

Leadership conflict has already been cited as an important factor in leading top officials to look to group expertise. It is more than conceivable that monolithic leadership would itself seek expert advice, *but* we expect that it would do so more surreptitiously than through semipublic debate. More importantly, it could ignore the advice when it chose to rather than in effect be reversed or manipulated by it. Under conditions of leadership conflict, unresolved disputes may lead some of the participants to broaden the scope of conflict by involving policy groups who might shift the balance and alter the policy outcome.[60] Alternatively, lower-level groups may exploit divisions within the leadership by offering proposals that are congruent with the ideological orientations of one or another Praesidium faction.

> The more and greater the disputes on the top policy-making level, the more likely it is that policy groups will be involved and listened to.

Brzezinski and Huntington point out that policy-makers are "more responsive to the demands or aspirations of groups" during a struggle for power, which would seem to bear out our point.[61] They use Khrushchev's struggle as an example, but they themselves point out elsewhere that victors in power struggles often reverse themselves and adopt the policies advocated by their opponent.[62] This pattern would seem to reduce the long-term impact of group influence in a power struggle. Our own examples are of unreversed policies decided in a period when the heat of the struggle for power had diminished, whether it had completely died or not. Indeed the absence of a threat to his power may well have made Khrushchev more willing to yield to critics of his educational reform policy. Brzezinski and Huntington say that while policy is the means to power in succession struggles,

> in stable dictatorial conditions, however, the leader may sometimes exercise power in matters that do not affect the security of his position. Then, as with the education reform of 1958, he can tolerate substantial amendments to his original proposal.[63]

It may be, then, that conditions of tranquility lend themselves more effectively to more or less permanent and far-reaching group influence than do power struggles. Leaders are probably more eager to solicit the support of groups when they are trying to secure power or ward off threats to their position, but group influence may be more permanent and real outside of power struggles. We are not prepared to predict that group influence over policy will be greater under power struggles or more during ordinary policy conflicts, but we are prepared to argue that under either of these conditions of leadership conflict group influence will be greater than when leadership is relatively monolithic. Such an hypothesis is at the core of our whole argument.

Bauer, Inkeles, and Kluckhohn observe that the failure of a policy may lead the Politburo to adopt an approach that they recently op-posed.[64] Our examples do not directly support this observation, although of course, they do not conflict with it, but the important point suggested by it is that the nature of the issue may be an important variable. Pursuing the rationale for our argument of group influence in the educational and graduate placement reforms, it is apparent that the problematic character of these issues and the fact that the consequences of a shift were not known with certainty made the judgment of policy groups more important than they would have been otherwise. The obvious implication of this is that the more problematic the consequences of a given course of action the more likely it is that groups would be involved.

A related point that is derived from interest group politics in Western democracies is that groups are likely to be more influential in policy outcomes when the issue is narrow and technical than when the issue is broad and general.[65] In democratic polities, this is partly because other publics are less likely to be paying any attention or to care when the issue is technical. Thus the field is left relatively open for the interested group. A further rationale would be pertinent in the case of the Soviet Union: It is not so much that other actors are or are not concerned; it is rather that technical advice and opinions are at a premium on technical issues.

> The more problematic and technical the issue, the more dependent on expert judgment elites will be. Consequently they will be more likely to consult policy groups, who will thereby be more influential on such issues.

While we hope that the above hypotheses help account for conditions varying *within* the current post-Stalinist regime which we associated with such group influence as we have illustrated, we do not argue that such influence ever occurred in the Stalin era. We know of no such prominent examples. In this final section we will identify several underlying conditions which in part distinguish the two eras and make groups more important in policy formation, or at least potentially so, at the present.

One important change is that the rigid dictatorial one-man rule of the Stalin period has given way to collective leadership. While there may be one dominant leader, his power is shared among several key figures at the apex of the political structure. Under conditions of a diffused power structure, group influence is far more likely.[66] When power is exercised in an autocratic manner, groups must gain the ear of the all-powerful leader if they are to influence the policy process. During a period of collective leadership the access routes to points of decision-making may become more numerous. Indeed, the very nature of collective leadership may make political leaders more responsive to group demands.

Carl Linden has argued that the transition from autocracy to oligarchy brings with it a constant struggle for political primacy at the very top. Since no individual is automatically assured of predominant power he must secure that position by winning and holding the support of a combination of societal groupings. His actual or potential rivals, on the other hand, can build their own constituency coalitions by identifying with those elements discontented with an incumbent leader's policy. The politics of leadership struggle then intertwine with the politics of group conflict. It is this interdependence which facilitates group influence on the policy process.[67]

> The larger and more collective the top leadership, the greater the prospects for the sort of disputes that can lead to the involvement of social groups in policy formation.

The attitudes of those leaders and their methods of social control will also have an important bearing on the prospects for group influence. Under a system of terror individuals are frightened into silent submissiveness and live in an atomized state. Unaware that others share common attitudes, grievances, and interests, the terrorized citizen accepts his lot and does not attempt to influence the behavior of decision-makers.[68] Only when terror subsides does this condition of "pluralistic ignorance" end and the opportunity for interest articulation emerge. For now communication, both through the formal mass media and through informal personal interaction, assumes a more candid and realistic nature. Under these new conditions the communication process itself facilitates group influence. It serves to generate widespread awareness of commonly shared attitudes which in turn becomes a powerful factor inducing groups to influence policy outcomes in their favor.

The leashing of terror enhances the prospect for group influence in other ways as well. David Easton points out that not all societal claims and demands are converted into policy outputs. Only those which become public issues have this possibility.[69] In any polity this requires the patronage and support of some political authority figure. In a system where terror is no longer all-pervasive individuals may be far more likely to risk identification with unresolved issues since the consequences of poor choices are far less serious. At best it may mean that one's power position remains static. At worst it may mean a diminution in political power and perhaps even demotion. But it does not mean internment or execution as it so often did during the Stalinist period. The individual has lost a political battle but not necessarily the war. He remains on the scene with the possibility of recouping his losses and rising once again to top political positions.

> Groups will be influential as technocratic spokesmen only when terror subsides and the regime accords them legitimacy of expression of their point of view.

The kind of expert judgment involved in the interest articulation we have described is a function of the nature of a society. Harry Eckstein has noted that modernization increases the significance of groups in the political process.[70] We suggest that the modernization of Russia positively relates to potential group influence in several ways. First, it introduces a functional specialization and differentiation into the society, which in turn generates a diffusion of interests competing with one another to write the laws of society to their advantage. During the early stages of Soviet rule the party preempts interest articulation not only because it wants to but also, to some degree, because it has to. The society which the Bolsheviks inherited was largely composed of an undifferentiated mass of peasants who had traditionally played a politically passive role. Thus the task of identifying and articulating interests fell to the party by default.

This is not to say that at the time of Bolshevik ascendancy there were not functionally specialized groups with political experience in the protection of their interests. They existed but they were far fewer and far less significant than in the present period. Furthermore, those groups tended to be stigmatized by their identification with the old regime. Thus any demands put forth by them lacked an essential ingredient for success—the presumption of legitimacy. The a priori belief of the party that such individuals were disloyal deprived them of any political currency which could be used in the process of trading support for recognition of their demands.

The modernization of Russia has fundamentally altered this situation. Not only has it generated a complex economic and social pluralism but it also has provided new cadres to staff these skilled groups.[71] Those who possess scarce technical capabilities are far more likely to exert influence today than in the past. Such technocrats are products of the new system (the new Soviet man) and their loyalty is not impugned. Consequently, their attempt to influence the political process is perceived in legitimized rather than counterrevolutionary terms. The arguments of scientific, educational, managerial, and youth experts may have been motivated by selfish concerns. But, as we noted earlier, these arguments were made in the context of what would best serve the interests of the Soviet Union. Given the fact that these experts are the products of the Soviet period, their counsel cannot be ignored on the grounds that the purveyors of such ideas are politically suspect. The handicap which afflicted old specialists simply does not operate in the contemporary period.

Stalin's transformation of Russia insured the increased importance of groups in the policy process in yet another way, although the full impact of this development had to await the dictator's death. It was during the thirties and forties that the politicization of society reached totalitarian dimensions. As politics came to predominate in all areas of life, individuals realized that the protection of their interests could be achieved only by gaining access to and influencing the political structure. Unlike Western political systems where many issues are resolved in the private sector of society, the struggle over who gets what when and how in the Soviet Union takes place entirely within the public domain.[72] Thus individuals and groups are perforce compelled to focus their attention and pressure on the decision-making process if they hope to maintain or improve their status.

The fourth implication of modernization stems from the fact that a complex technological society requires stable occupational group membership. As we have already suggested, the behavior of managers, teachers, educators, and scientists was motivated in part by their desire to protect interests derived from their occupational roles. Such a phenomenon occurs, however, only when individuals have an opportunity to firmly anchor themselves in one occupational role, so that it becomes for them an important reference group. This connotes, in turn, an absence of the recurring purge so characteristic of the Stalinist period. Stalin purposefully removed leading strata of important groups lest they become too closely identified with the interests of those groups and more specifically lest they use the economic, social, and political resources inherent in those groups for the purpose of delimiting the decision-making power of the leader.

Now this is a very costly procedure and one that a developed society cannot afford to engage in for very long. Managers, teachers, scientists, and other specialists are not created overnight and their summary purge means not only a loss of experienced and skilled personnel but also the forfeiture of scarce economic resources invested in their education and training. As Soviet society has become more complex and sophisticated this type of gross economic waste proved intolerable. We do not imply, of course, that high-ranking Soviet personnel are no longer removed from their positions. The official press is full of accounts concerning the removal of such personnel. We do argue, however, that "the purge" today differs significantly from its Stalinist predecessor. At present leading occupational strata are not removed in the wholesale manner reminiscent of the thirties and forties. More importantly, their removal is seldom if ever accompanied by internment or execution. Most often they seem to be demoted to a less prestigious and influential job but within the same area of expertise.

> The more modern the society, the more dependent it is on technical expertise, which in turn improves the prospects that groups may influence policy when higher powers seek their judgment.[73]

We have attempted in this article to illustrate that under some circumstances social groups can influence policy formation in the Soviet Union. We have specified those circumstances as clearly as we could, providing hypotheses according to which we expect group influence to vary. If our analysis is sound and valid, we hope that it may provide some guidelines for further research on group influence in the comparative study of communist political systems.[74] Indeed, we hope that some parts of our analysis may be relevant to the study of the role of groups in policy formation in noncommunist political systems as well.

Notes

1. H. Gordon Skilling, "Interest Groups and Communist Politics," *World Politics*, 18 (April 1966), 449.

2. Zbigniew Brzezinski and Samuel P. Huntington, *Political Power: U.S.A./ U.S.S.R.* (New York: Viking, 1963), p. 196.

3. Khrushchev's statement can be found in *XIII S"ezd vsesoiuznogo leninskogo kommunisticheskogo souiza molodezhi: stenograficheskii otchet* (Moscow: Gospolitizdat, 1959), pp. 278–82.

4. See, for example, L. Bueva, "Tvorcheskii trud- osnova kommunistichesgoko vospitaniia molodezhi," *Kommunist*, XXXVII, 3 (Feb. 1961), 53, and *Komsomol'-skaia pravda*, March 2, 1956; Feb. 10, 1957.

5. See *XIII S"ezd, op. cit.*, p. 280. See also S. Pavlov, "Sovetskaia molodezh' v bor'be za kommunizm," *Kommunist*, XXXVI, 4 (March 1960), 63.

6. Nicholas DeWitt, *Education and Professional Employment in the U.S.S.R.* (Washington: National Science Foundation, 1961), p. 140.

7. In his speech to the 13th Komsomol Congress, Khrushchev noted that "last year higher educational institutions were able to accept 400,000 new students, half of them for full time study. . . . However, at least 700,000 secondary school graduates failed to gain admission last year to higher or technical school and between 1953–1956 about 2,200,000 failed to gain admission," *XIII S"ezd, op. cit.*, p. 278.

8. *Ibid.*, p. 282.

9. *Pravda*, Sept. 21, 1958.

10. *XIII S"ezd, op. cit.*, p. 280.

11. See, for example, DeWitt, *op. cit.*, p. 15.

12. For a refutation of the labor deficit thesis see "Facts and Figures," *Bulletin of Radio Free Europe*, Sept. 22, 1958.

13. See *Pravda*, Sept. 21, 1958.

14. For a text of the law see *Spravochnik partiinogo rabotnika* (Moscow: Gospolitizdat, 1959), pp. 517–33.

15. For an analysis of this point see an article by Klaus Mehnert in *Die Welt*, July 18, 1959.

16. The actual law left this point unclear, but later developments indicated that just as many children—about a third of the total—would attend full-time schools as had been the case before the reform. See Thomas Bernstein, "Soviet Educational Reform" (Master's thesis, Columbia University, 1962), p. 111, and articles in the *New York Times*, Sept. 2, 1959, and *Wall Street Journal*, June 29, 1960.

17. Instead of the two to three days released time from work, as suggested by Khrushchev, students in evening schools received only one additional free day for study. See A. I. Shebanova, "O l'gotakh dlia lits sovmeshchaiushchikh rabotu s obucheniem," *Sovetskoe gosudarstvo i pravo*, XXX (Nov. 1960), 99–102.

18. This point was made by the Soviet Minister of Higher Education and was reflected in the final law. See V. P. Eliutin, "Soveshchanie rabotnikov vysshei shkoly," *Vestnik vysshei shkoly*, XVI, 10 (Oct. 1958), 9.

19. *Literaturnaia gazeta*, Aug. 30, 1958.

20. For examples of such arguments see *Literaturnaia gazeta*, June 26, 1958; Dec. 20, 1958; *Pravda*, Sept. 24, 1958; Oct. 17, 1958; Nov. 19, 1958. K. Ia Kondrat'ev and P. A. Shi'lov, "O nekotorykh voprosakh universitetskogo obrazovaniia," *Vestnik vysshei shkoly*, XVI, 10 (Oct. 1958), 17–23.

21. See *Pravda*, Nov. 30, 1958; Dec. 2, 1958; *Literaturnaia gazeta*, Dec. 20, 1958.

22. For a scathing criticism of managerial attitudes toward juvenile workers see the lead editorial in *Pravda*, Sept. 25, 1957.

23. There is some evidence that the opposition was far greater than one would gather from simply reading the official press. For example, relatively few parental criticisms found their way into print. But during 1963–64 when the senior author of this chapter was conducting interviews in the Soviet Union, it was learned that a very large number of urban middle-class parents had strongly criticized Khrushchev's proposals at "PTA" meetings held during the reform debate period. Similarly, Professor William Johnson of the University of Pittsburgh told the same author that opposition among educational officials was far more widespread than the official

press revealed. Professor Johnson was in the Soviet Union at the time of the debate and is known to have extensive contacts with Soviet educators.

24. Richard Neustadt, *Presidential Power* (New York: Wiley, 1964).

25. For an analysis of the reform with this type of implication see David Burg, "Some Thoughts on the Soviet Educational Reform," *Bulletin*, VI (March 1959), 32–6.

26. Brzezinski and Huntington, *op. cit.*, p. 145.

27. See for example, Carl A. Linden, *Khrushchev and the Soviet Leadership 1957–1964* (Baltimore: Johns Hopkins, 1966).

28. See *XIII S"ezd, op. cit.*, p. 282.

29. See Sidney Ploss, *Conflict and Decision-Making in Soviet Russia* (Princeton, 1965), pp. 17–18.

30. For an analysis of these amendments see Rudolph Schlesinger, "The Educational Reform," *Soviet Studies*, X (April 1959), 432–44.

31. See Brzezinski and Huntington, *op. cit.*, pp. 267, 269–83, 295–300.

32. Bernstein, *op. cit.*, p. 119. See also Brzezinski and Huntington, *op. cit.*, p. 214.

33. In this instance, many political leaders may have been especially inclined to "believe" these arguments. As primary members of the new class, Communist Party cadres had good reason to support the educational status quo. They were among the chief beneficiaries of the existing system. Their children enjoyed advantageous access to full-time secondary and higher education. There is no question that such cadres hoped to perpetuate the provision of such education for their children. Khrushchev's proposals surely must have caused consternation among party cadres which other top party leaders would readily have been conscious of. In this respect the party itself was probably an important constituent pressure group which reinforced the doubts Khrushchev's colleagues had about the wisdom of his proposals.

34. Legislation on the placement of graduates stipulates that a student who is physically disabled or supports a disabled parent or other member of the immediate family must be assigned to his place of permanent residence or must be granted a permit to find employment for himself. Husbands and wives who graduate simultaneously must be assigned to the same area. If one finished somewhat later, he or she is assigned to the area where the other one is already working. In the event that the committee cannot find a suitable position, the husband or wife receives a self-placement permit. If the placement committee has exhausted all jobs for which it was given responsibility, specialists who have not been assigned have the right to place themselves.

35. L. I. Karpov, *Vysshaia shkola: osnovnye postanovleniia prikazy i instruktsii* (Moscow, 1957), p. 207. Quoted by N. DeWitt, *op. cit.*, pp. 361–2.

36. This was a term frequently used by Soviet students whom the senior author informally interviewed as an exchange scholar at Moscow University in 1963–64.

37. This was stated at a meeting of civil law jurists at Moscow University in Nov. 1963.

38. For comment on these type fabrications see *Moskovskii komsomolets*, Oct. 27, 1955, p. 2.

39. See "Bol'she vnimaniia raspredeleniiu molodykh spetsialistov," *Vestnik vysshei shkoly*, XIII (Feb. 1955), 3, and M. A. Dzhabrailov, "Student okonchil vuz," *Vestnlk vysshei shkoly*, XVI (May 1961), 69–74.

40. M. A. Dzhabrailov, "Student okonchil vuz," *Vestnik vysshei shkoly*, XVI (May 1961), 70.

41. *Moskovskii komsomolets*, July 10, 1963, p. 2.

42. For example, less than 20 of the 359 graduates of the Tblisi Medical Institute abided by the decision of the placement committee in 1956. *Komsomols'kaia pravda*, July 11, 1957, p. 2.

43. "Bol'she vnimaniia raspredeleniiu molodykh spetsialistov," *Vestnik vysshei shkoly*, XIII (Feb. 1955), 2.

44. Dzhabrailov, *op. cit.*, 69–74.

45. R. Dadabaev, "Rukovodstvo partiinykh organizatsii ideino-politicheskim vospitaniem studentov vysshikh uchebnykh zavedenii (1959–1961)," unpublished candidate's dissertation, Academy of Social Sciences, Moscow, 1963, p. 45.

46. See N. K. Masalkin and K. S. Nemets, "Reshennye i nereshennye zadachi sel'skokhoziaistvennykh vuzov," *Vestnik vysshei shkoly*, XVII (Nov. 1959), 13; T. I. Samokhvalova, "Vuz pereezhaet v sovkhoz," *Vestnik vysshei shkoly*, XVI (March 1961), 11–19; "Studenchestvo prizvano stat provoditukom peredovogo opyta v sel'skom khoziastve," *Vestnik vysshei shkoly*, XX (May 1962), 50.

47. Dzhabrailov, *op. cit.*, 69–74.

48. Interview Jan. 29, 1964, with Sergei Pavlov in Moscow.

49. *Komsomol'skaia pravda*, Feb. 14, 1964, p. 3.

50. *Moskovskii komsomolets*, Jan. 19, 1961, p. 3.

51. N. D. Kazmin (ed.), *Vsesoiuznoe soveshchanie po shkolam-internatam* (Moscow 1958), p. 128, quoted by DeWitt, *op. cit.*, p. 363.

52. *Moskovskii komsomolets*, July 15, 1962, p. 2.

53. From 1955 to 1965 only seven articles were in *any way* concerned with the question of graduate placement.

54. Dadabaev, *op. cit.*, p. 44.

55. The senior author systematically read *Molodoi leninets* (newspaper of the Stalingrad Komsomol Regional Executive Committee) and *Molodoi kommunar* (organ of the Voronezh Komsomol Regional Committee) for the years 1954 to 1964 and found no editorial reflection or support for Pavlov's policies.

56. Brzezinski and Huntington, *op. cit.*, pp. 203–4.

57. Philip D. Stewart, "The Soviet Public and the Policy Process: the Case of the Repeal of Production Education," unpublished manuscript, 1968.

58. The debate over graduate placement is not the only case which demonstrates this pattern. Stewart's study of the repeal of production education and the senior author's current research on economic reform in the Soviet Union reveal similar patterns of policy initiatives "bubbling up."

59. Anthony Buzek, *How the Communist Press Works* (New York: Praeger, 1964), pp. 38–54.

60. See Ploss, *op. cit.*, pp. 61, 84, 286, for other examples and a discussion of changes in the scope of conflict in the Soviet Union. See also E. E. Schattschneider, *The Semisovereign People* (New York: Holt, 1960), for a discussion of the impact of other kinds of changes in patterns of conflict in the United States.

61. Brzezinski and Huntington, *op. cit.*, p. 198.

62. *Ibid.*, pp. 193, 240–52.

63. *Ibid.*, p. 270.

64. Raymond A. Bauer, Alex Inkeles, and Clyde Kluckhohn, *How the Soviet System Works* (New York, 1956), p. 98.

65. See Harry Eckstein, *Pressure Group Politics* (Stanford: Stanford U.P., 1960).

66. Dispersion of decision-making can assume a "personalized" as well as an institutional form. Instead of separation of powers between executive, legislative, and judicial groups one may find a separation of powers between leaders at the top of an outwardly monolithic political structure (see Ploss, *op. cit.*, p. 286). On the relationship between group influence and a diffusion of power see Harry Eckstein, "Group Theory and the Comparative Study of Pressure Groups," in *Comparative Politics*, edited by Harry Eckstein and David Apter (New York: Free Press, 1963), p. 396.

67. Linden, *op. cit.*, pp. 20–1.

68. This condition of "pluralistic ignorance" is discussed in Bauer and others, *op. cit.*, p. 263.

69. David Easton, "The Analysis of Political Systems," in *Comparative Politics: Notes and Readings*, edited by Roy C. Macridis and Bernard E. Brown (Homewood: Darsey, 1964), pp. 94–5.

70. Eckstein, *op. cit.*, p. 395.

71. For an interesting and suggestive article on the growth of pluralism in Russian society see Henry L. Roberts, "The Succession to Khrushchev in Perspective," *Proceedings of the Academy of Political Science*, XXVIII (April 1965), 2–12.

72. We are identifying here a difference of degree. As Eckstein notes, pressure groups have become very active and significant in the postwar political systems of Britain, France, etc., for similar reasons. "One rather obvious reason for this development is the growth of the social service state—of positive government regulating, planning, directing, or entirely drawing into itself all sorts of social activities. This trend has given social groups a greater stake in politics and therefore mobilized them to a much greater extent while making government increasingly dependent on the collaboration and advice, technical or otherwise, of the groups," *op. cit.*, p. 395.

73. See S. N. Eisenstadt, *The Political Systems of Empires* (New York: Free Press, 1963), for a suggestive analysis of the role of skill groups in historical bureaucratic empires.

74. See Robert C. Tucker, "On the Study of Comparative Communism," *World Politics*, XIX (Jan. 1967), 242–57.

7

Party Careers: A Case Study of Bulgarian Central Committee Members, 1962

CARL BECK, GERARD A. JOHNSON, AND J. THOMAS McKECHNIE

At the 8th Party Congress of the Bulgarian Communist Party in November 1962, the composition of the Central Committee was changed. Forty new members of the Committee were recruited; twenty-eight incumbents were dismissed; and sixty-one retained their positions. This paper explores the differences between those who were recruited, dismissed, and held over in terms of their careers within the

Notes to the selection begin on page 202.

Communist Party, including the Party youth organization. We will begin by presenting statistics on discrete Party positions held by those persons composing the three groups. We will then use factor analysis to locate the systematic relationships among positions. These factors can be viewed as the configurations of Party career development common to the individuals making up the three groups.[1]

In a previous paper one of the authors has pointed out that in terms of general career patterns, including experiences outside the Party as well as inside it, the Party bureaucrat official has tended to dominate the Central Committee not only of Bulgaria, but of Czechoslovakia, Hungary, Poland, and Rumania as well. Of those persons who were members of the Bulgarian Central Committee any time from January 14, 1957, when the Party began to stress the need for reconsolidation, to January 1, 1966, 53 percent can be classified as Party bureaucrat officials. It was also pointed out that this characteristic tends to hold for all members of the Bulgarian Central Committee from 1945 to 1966.[2] In this chapter we are concerned with the dynamics of Party positions as reflected in those recruited, dismissed, and held over as a consequence of the 8th Party Congress.

The four years between the 7th and 8th Party Congresses were a period marked by struggle for Party leadership in the context of attempted policy changes. The 7th Party Congress (June 1958) seemed rather placid. There were no apparent signs of factionalism within the Party. The Party continued to stress its role, first declared in 1954, as the leading coordinator in an alliance with the politically conscious elements of the working class, peasantry, and intelligentsia.[3] Premier Anton Yugov outlined a new Five Year Plan which called only for incremental increases in production within the existing administrative framework. This plan was adopted with a minimum of discussion and without known objection.[4]

Within a matter of months, Todor Zhivkov, First Secretary of the Bulgarian Communist Party since 1954, announced a dramatic new economic program. If implemented, the Zhivkov Theses would have replaced the Five Year Plan and substituted for it a program of rapid transformation of the administrative and economic character of Bulgaria.[5] Even after the goals of this program were scaled down, opposition to the Zhivkov Theses continued to come from within the Party.[6] In the wake of this opposition, one of the leading critics, Boris Taskov, Minister of Trade and Politburo member, was dismissed from most of his official positions.[7]

By mid-1960 it was obvious that the new economic program had not succeeded. Purges took place at the lower levels of the Party against those who were charged with sabotaging the program. Old factional disputes that had been treated gingerly with the first de-Stalinization campaign reemerged.[8] A Central Committee Plenum was held in November 1961, following the 22nd Congress of the Communist Party of the Soviet Union. At that Plenum, Vullko Chervenkov, formerly First Secretary of the Party and Premier during the days of Stalinism, was dismissed from the Politburo and shortly thereafter from the Council of Ministers. According to J. F. Brown, Chervenkov still had supporters particularly in the provincial Party apparatus. Yugov, whose basis of support rested in the state apparatus, sought to exploit the old Chervenkov conservatives for his own advantage. However, Yugov could not count on the support of the provincial apparatchiks. He also had little strength in the Central Committee. Zhivkov seized the opportunity of the CPSU's second de-Stalinization campaign to purge the followers of both Yugov and Chervenkov, using the symbols of de-Stalinization and the struggle against the cult of personality. At the same time, he sought to court the support of the provincial party leaders in order to consolidate his position.[9] It is within this context that the Bulgarian Communist Party met to elect a new Central Committee. The selection of new committee members must have been viewed by Zhivkov as a matter of major concern. Our analysis is aimed at showing which configurations of Party career development were detrimental or advantageous during this period.

THE ANALYSIS OF CAREER DEVELOPMENT
BY DISCRETE PARTY POSITIONS HELD

Table 1 presents the proportion of recruits, dismissed, and holdovers who have held the Party positions listed.

A greater proportion of holdovers than dismissed were local secretaries, regional secretaries, Central Committee commission officials and employees, and candidate members of the Central Committee. In contrast, a higher proportion of dismissed were members of Central Committee commissions. The difference between dismissed and holdovers can be viewed as a distinction between lower and higher official positions. Throughout the local, regional, and central territorial units of the Party, holdovers held the higher official positions.

More recruits than dismissed held positions in the regional structure of the Party. The dismissed tended to hold positions in the local structure of the Party. Within the regional structure, recruits tended to have been secretaries. When recruits are compared to holdovers, these distinctions still hold.

Table 2 presents similar statistics using Party youth positions.

Approximately three-fourths of all recruits did not belong to the Party youth organization prior to 1962, compared with approximately one-half of both dismissed and holdovers. The striking finding is that a larger proportion of recruits, when compared to both dismissed and holdovers, held positions at the central level of the youth hierarchy.

TABLE 1

PARTY POSITIONS HELD PRIOR TO THE 8TH BCP CONGRESS[a]

Party Positions	Recruits (N = 40)	Dismissed (N = 28)	Holdovers (N = 61)	Total (N = 129)
		(percentages)		
Member Local Committee	5	21	10	11
Local Official	3	7	3	4
Local Secretary	3	11	15	10
Local Deputy 1st Secretary	0	0	3	2
Local 1st Secretary	5	0	5	4
Member Regional Committee	13	29	20	19
Regional Official	10	7	7	8
Regional Secretary	58	29	34	40
Regional Deputy 1st Secretary	5	4	3	4
Regional 1st Secretary	40	25	26	30
Employee Central Committee Commission	3	7	15	9
Member Central Committee Commission	10	21	13	14
Section Chief Central Committee Commission	10	7	21	15
Deputy Chairman Central Committee Commission	0	0	2	1
Chairman Central Committee Commission	3	7	15	9
Employee Central Committee	3	7	3	4
Candidate Member Central Committee	50	54	66	58
No Party Positions[b]	20	18	5	12

[a] For the purposes of both the discrete and the pattern analysis a total of seventeen Party and fourteen youth organizational positions were examined. Each person is tagged but once for each position regardless of the number of times he held the position. The data are drawn from the machine readable biographical file of the Archive on Political Elites in Eastern Europe, University of Pittsburgh.

[b] It is interesting to note the dominant career of those in this category. Of the eight recruits four had government careers, three had military careers, and one was a journalist. Of those who were dismissed one was a trade unionist and the remainder had military careers. In the third group two had careers in mass organizations and one had a military career.

TABLE 2

POSITIONS HELD IN PARTY YOUTH PRIOR TO 1962

Party Youth	Recruits (N = 40)	Dismissed (N = 28)	Holdovers (N = 61)	Total (N = 129)
		(percentages)		
Member	28	46	49	42
Local Official	0	4	5	3
Local Secretary	3	7	5	5
Local 1st Secretary	0	0	3	1
University Secretary	0	4	0	1
Regional Official	0	0	7	3
Regional Secretary	3	7	8	6
Regional 1st Secretary	5	0	5	4
Employee Central Committee	5	0	3	3
Member Central Committee	15	7	11	12
Section Chief Central Committee Department	0	4	5	3
Member Secretariat	13	7	9	10
National Leader	3	4	5	4
Youth Organizer	0	0	7	3

Of the total recruits, 15 percent were members of the Central Committee and 13 percent were members of the Secretariat, compared with 11 and 9 percent respectively, for those who were held over and 7 percent for both positions for those who were dismissed. Of the three groups, holdovers had the highest proportion of membership, regional official, regional secretary, and youth organizer positions within the Party organization. Dismissed had a slightly higher proportion of local secretaries only. The major finding is that recruits had the highest proportion of membership of the three groups in the Central Committee and Secretariat, although they had the lowest proportion of youth members.

Another difference between dismissed and holdovers emerges when we compare type of Party offices acquired by the two groups in the time between their original appointment to the Central Committee and the 8th Party Congress (Table 3).

Holdovers in greater proportion than dismissed acquired positions in Central Committee commissions. Dismissed in greater proportions than holdovers acquired positions at the local and regional levels of the Party. None of the dismissed or holdovers acquired additional positions in the youth organization after they entered the Central Committee.

The analysis of discrete positions held by recruits, dismissed, and holdovers indicates that a greater proportion of recruits were regional Party secretaries and members of the Secretariat or Central Committee

TABLE 3

PARTY AND YOUTH POSITIONS ACQUIRED FROM ORIGINAL ENTRY INTO CENTRAL COMMITTEE TO NOVEMBER 1962

Position	Dismissed ($N = 28$)	Holdovers ($N = 61$)
	(percentages)	
Member Local Committee	11	2
Local Official	4	0
Local Secretary	4	0
Local Deputy 1st Secretary	0	0
Local 1st Secretary	0	3
Member Regional Committee	0	2
Regional Official	0	0
Regional Secretary	11	3
Regional Deputy 1st Secretary	0	0
Regional 1st Secretary	14	8
Employee Central Committee Commission	0	2
Member Central Committee Commission	11	5
Section Chief Central Committee Commission	4	16
Deputy Chairman Central Committee Commission	0	2
Chairman Central Committee Commission	7	20
Employee Central Committee	0	0
Central Committee Candidate	0	0
All Party Youth	0	0

of the Party youth organization than either dismissed or holdovers. A greater proportion of dismissed were members of local or regional Party committees and members of commissions of the Party Central Committee than either recruits or holdovers. A higher proportion of holdovers were local Party secretaries and employees, section chiefs, and chairmen of commissions of the Party Central Committee than were recruits or dismissed. It is all too easy to argue that these findings demonstrate career channels distinct to each of these groups. This position lacks validity because the data do not tell us anything about how such positions relate to each other to form a channel.

ANALYSIS OF CAREER DEVELOPMENT BY PATTERN OF PARTY POSITIONS HELD

Up to this point our investigation has focused on discrete positions or categories of positions, such as local first secretary or regional official. The emphasis in this part of the chapter is upon relationships between positions. The objective is twofold: to identify which positions coalesce or cluster to form empirical career patterns, and to assess the three groups of Central Committee members in terms of these patterns.

Formal organizations are often thought of as based upon subordinate and superordinate relationships. Do Central Committee members actually progress through a well-defined hierarchy? They may, indeed, evaluate their achievement in terms of their movement up or down such a hierarchy, but just as the "chain of command" does not necessarily reflect the pattern of control in an organization, neither does it necessarily reveal the pattern of promotions and demotions within an organization. Deliberate policies may and often do intrude upon progression through a hierarchy. Some organizations, for example, prefer to recruit at certain levels from outside the organization, and the slogan "Revolution from above" suggests a similar policy in Communist states.

We attempted to identify career patterns by specifying the existing combinations of organizational positions reflected in the data and tabulating the frequency with which these combinations occur.[10] Given the seventeen Party positions and the fourteen youth positions, there are $N(N-1)$ possible combinations for each set of positions. In addition, there is a null pattern for each set of positions. Those persons who fit the null pattern held none of these positions prior to November 1962.

There are 77 empirical combinations of Party positions out of a possible 273, but only 14 patterns can be identified with more than one person (Table 4).

TABLE 4

CAREER PATTERNS IN PARTY ORGANIZATION
($N = 129$)

Null Pattern	($N = 16$)
Candidate Only Pattern	($N = 14$)
12 Replicated Patterns	($N = 36$; $2 \leq N$ per pattern ≤ 5)
63 Unique Patterns	($N = 63$; N per pattern $= 1$)

TABLE 5

CAREER PATTERNS IN YOUTH ORGANIZATION
($N = 129$)

Null Pattern	($N = 75$)
Member Only Pattern	($N = 25$)
3 Replicated Patterns	($N = 7$; $2 \leq N$ per pattern ≤ 3)
25 Unique Patterns	($N = 22$; N per pattern $= 1$)

Out of a possible 183 patterns among positions in the youth organization, 30 empirical patterns exist; of these only 5 are replicated (Table 5).

The diversity and complexity of relationships among respective positions is readily seen. Given the variety of patterns, this technique is of little utility. There is virtually no possibility of comprehensive comparison of the three groups regarding the prevalence of one or another pattern. However, one comparison is of interest. Although fewer recruits were associated with the youth organization (Table 6), among all the Central Committee members more recruits held positions above the member level (Table 7).

TABLE 6

YOUTH ORGANIZATION

	Recruits (N = 40)	Dismissed (N = 28)	Holdovers (N = 61)
Not Members (Null Pattern)	29 (73%)	15 (54%)	31 (51%)
Members	11 (28%)	13 (47%)	30 (49%)

$x^2 = 4.972$, $C = .150$, $df = 2$, $.10 > p > .05$

TABLE 7

YOUTH ORGANIZATION

	Recruits (N = 11)	Dismissed (N = 13)	Holdovers (N = 30)
Members Only	4 (36%)	8 (62%)	13 (43%)
Those Who Held One or More Positions Above the Level of Member	7 (64%)	5 (39%)	17 (57%)

$x^2 = 1.757$, $C = .178$, $df = 2$, $.50 > p > .30$

This finding holds absolutely when recruits are compared with dismissed, and proportionally when recruits are compared with holdovers. It is congruent with our findings when discrete positions are used as a basis of comparison (see Table 2). However, the low values of the descriptive statistics, especially in Table 7, caution us against giving undue emphasis to this finding.

Confronted with a diversity of configurations, we turned to factor analysis to locate replicated empirical relationships among organizational positions. Factor analysis defines dimensions to which the variation in variables are systematically related.[11] The degree of relationship is specified by factor loadings which measure the degree of association between the variables and the factors. The factor loading squared indicates the proportion of total variation in a particular variable which is accounted for by a factor. In our analysis the units of observation were individuals ($N = 129$). The variables are based on dichotomous responses to the question, "Has individual X held position Y at least once in his lifetime before November 1962?"[12] When factors are mathematically defined for dichotomized variables, the resulting factor loadings are conservative. Error, if any, is in the direction of underestimation, rather than overestimation, of the relationship. For this reason we feel justified in choosing to discuss in our analysis of the factors extracted and rotated all those variables with a factor loading greater than $\pm.300$.[13]

In deciding which factors are to be rotated, one convention is to include all those whose eigenvalues are greater than 1.0.[14] We include all factors which accounted for at least 5 percent of the total variance. Therefore, six factors for the Party organization and four factors for youth organization were orthogonally rotated according to Varimax criteria. Each set of factors accounted for between 55 and 60 percent of the total variance in the initial variables.

Each individual can be measured on the dimensions defined by factor analysis. Basically, an individual's score on the initial variables is weighted, using factor loadings of these variables on a given factor to determine his score on that factor. Factors thereby become indices.

On the party factor which accounts for the highest proportion of total variance, the three local Party secretariat variables load highly (Table 8). We have called this factor local/secretariat. A careful comparison of the squared loadings on this factor and the communality[15] of these

TABLE 8

PARTY FACTOR 1—LOCAL/SECRETARIAT

Variable No.	Description	Factor Loading	Factor Loading Squared	Communality
5	Local 1st Secretary	.814	.663	.700
4	Local Deputy 1st Secretary	.802	.643	.763
3	Local Secretary	.611	.373	.688
7	Regional Official	.442	.195	.284
2	Local Official	.372	.138	.737

Proportion of Total Variance   12.7%
Proportion of Common Variance   22.2%

three variables reveal that only approximately one-half of the variance in the local secretary variable accounted for by our six Party factors is associated with this factor—37 percent vs. 69 percent. Most of the remainder is associated with factor 4. In addition, two non-secretariat positions, local official and regional official, are related to this career pattern, although only to a small degree. The factor defines a pattern of positions important in terms of rank, yet not confined to the secretariat, and which are predominantly at the lowest territorial level—the local level.

The second Party factor locates a regional career pattern (Table 9).

TABLE 9

PARTY FACTOR 2—REGIONAL/SECRETARIAT

Variable No.	Description	Factor Loading	Factor Loading Squared	Communality
8	Regional Secretary	.796	.634	.710
10	Regional 1st Secretary	.738	.545	.597
9	Regional Deputy 1st Secretary	.536	.287	.531
6	Member Regional Committee	.323	.104	.554

Proportion of Total Variance   10.9%
Proportion of Common Variance 19.1%

The only variables loading greater than .300 on factor 2 are regional. They include four of the five regional variables used. Just as in the case of the first factor, we find one of the secretariat variables incompletely associated with the factor. A non-secretariat position is part of this career pattern only to a small degree. From factors 1 and 2 it is clear that a local/regional distinction is important in career development. The generally high loadings of secretariat variables, in contrast to the low loadings of non-secretariat variables, indicate less clearly a secretary/non-secretary distinction.

The highest loadings on factors 3 and 4 belong to central level, non-secretary variables. Of the eight variables in factors 3 and 4 (Tables 10 and 11), only one pertains to a secretariat position. When these factors are contrasted to the previous two factors, the presence of a secretary/non-secretary distinction in career development is more evident.

Between factors 3 and 4 the distinction is twofold. Associated with factor 3 are Central Committee commission positions: section chief,

TABLE 10

PARTY FACTOR 3—NON-SECRETARIAT/CENTRAL
COMMISSION/REGIONAL

Variable No.	Description	Factor Loading	Factor Loading Squared	Communality
13	Section Chief Central Committee Commission	.683	.466	.512
6	Member Regional Committee	.577	.333	.554
11	Employee Central Committee Commission	.491	.241	.273
2	Local Official	−.408	.166	.739
12	Member Central Committee Commission	.358	.128	.404

Proportion of Total Variance   9.7%
Proportion of Common Variance   17.0%

TABLE 11

PARTY FACTOR 4—NON-SECRETARIAT/CENTRAL
NON-COMMISSION/LOCAL

Variable No	Description	Factor Loading	Factor Loading Squared	Communality
16	Employee Central Committee	.766	.587	.635
1	Member Local Committee	.754	.569	.631
3	Local Secretary	.430	.185	.688

Proportion of Total Variance   9.2%
Proportion of Common Variance   16.1%

member, employee; whereas on factor 4 we find only employee of the Central Committee. This indicates a distinction in staff positions at the central level. Territoriality also differentiates factor 3 from factor 4. The only local-level variable correlated with factor 3 has a negative loading. At the same time, a regional-level variable has a positive loading on this factor. For factor 4, two local-level variables have positive loadings.

These cleavages of a territorial and commission/non-commission nature in career patterns suggest that regional units had greater access to the locus of administrative decision-making, if we assume that this function in a bureaucratic organization gravitates to those with technical competence in a specific area. When we compare the three groups, we find that the new Central Committee reflected this dominance of the regional over the local.

In order to compare the three groups—recruits, dismissed, and holdovers—we have placed side by side (Table 12) the percentages indicating the proportion of each which have positive scores on these first four factors.[16]

TABLE 12

PROPORTIONS OF POSITIVE SCORES ON THE FIRST FOUR FACTORS COMPARING RECRUITS, DISMISSED, AND HOLDOVERS*

	Recruits (N = 40)	Dismissed (N = 28)	Holdovers (N = 61)
Local/Secretariat	28	47	51
Regional/Secretariat	75	57	71
Non-Secretariat/Central Commission/Regional	60	50	72
Non-Secretariat/Central Non-Commission/Local	25	50	43

* An individual can have a positive score on two or more dimensions. Therefore, career development within the Party can be a composite of several career patterns. The percentages in the table indicate that the Party career profile of some individuals included in our analysis is a composite. If space permitted, a presentation of the complete set of factor scores would more clearly illustrate this.

It should be remembered that these factors are blends of three sets of distinctions: local/regional; secretary/non-secretary; commission/non-commission. Despite this blend it is easy to see the greater importance of the regional level, as opposed to the local level career to the recruits. This is also true of the holdovers, but to a lesser degree. The effect of the change in Central Committee membership at the 8th Party Congress was to give greater prominence to the regional levels of the Party at the expense of the local levels.

Factors 5 and 6 delineate systematic yet less important relationships among the positions in the Party organizations (Tables 13 and 14).[17]

TABLE 13

PARTY FACTOR 5

Variable No.	Description	Factor Loading	Factor Loading Squared	Communality
17	Candidate Member Central Committee	−.795	.632	.662
2	Local Official	.553	.306	.739
15	Chairman Central Committee Commission	.499	.249	.406

Proportion of Total Variance   8.2%
Proportion of Common Variance   14.3%

TABLE 14

PARTY FACTOR 6

Variable No.	Description	Factor Loading	Factor Loading Squared	Communality
14	Deputy Chairman Central Committee Commission	− .784	.615	.635
9	Regional Deputy 1st Secretary	.447	.200	.531
12	Member Central Committee Commission	.361	.130	.404

Proportion of Total Variance   6.5%
Proportion of Common Variance   11.3%

These factors have not been named by us because they are difficult to categorize. We can describe the career patterns which they define. Factor 5 indicates that an individual who was not a candidate member of the Central Committee was more probably either a local official or a chairman of a commission of the Central Committee than an individual who was a candidate member of the Central Committee.[18] Factor 6 tells us that those who were regional deputy first secretaries or members of commissions of the Central Committee were most probably not deputy chairmen of Central Committee commissions.

The youth career patterns of these 129 persons are more difficult to identify completely. Distinctions in youth career developments are less manifest. Factor 1 (Table 15) is best interpreted as a central leadership

TABLE 15

YOUTH FACTOR 1—CENTRAL LEADERSHIP

Variable No.	Description	Factor Loading	Factor Loading Squared	Communality
13	National Leader	.768	.584	.644
12	Member Secretariat	.764	.584	.671
8	Regional 1st Secretary	.617	.381	.487
10	Member Central Committee	.562	.316	.660
1	Member	.484	.234	.444
9	Employee Central Committee	.484	.234	.250

Proportion of Total Variance   18.0%
Proportion of Common Variance   31.8%

dimension. On factor 2 (Table 16) we find an array of variables which are impossible to categorize, although they seem related to organizational function. In contrast to the previous two youth career patterns, factor

TABLE 16

YOUTH FACTOR 2—ORGANIZATIONAL FUNCTION

Variable No.	Description	Factor Loading	Factor Loading Squared	Communality
14	Youth Organizer	.884	.781	.783
6	Regional Official	.748	.560	.580
7	Regional Secretary	.608	.370	.708
10	Member Central Committee	.567	.321	.660
11	Section Chief Central Committee Department	.416	.173	.435
1	Member	.337	.114	.444

Proportion of Total Variance   17.0%
Proportion of Common Variance   30.1%

TABLE 17

YOUTH FACTOR 3—LOCAL

Variable No.	Description	Factor Loading	Factor Loading Squared	Communality
2	Local Official	.880	.774	.776
4	Local 1st Secretary	.813	.661	.667

Proportion of Total Variance   11.4%
Proportion of Common Variance   20.1%

TABLE 18

YOUTH FACTOR 4

Variable No.	Description	Factor Loading	Factor Loading Squared	Communality
3	Local Secretary	.808	.653	.683
7	Regional Secretary	.485	.235	.708
11	Section Chief Central Committee Department	.440	.194	.660
5	University Secretary	−.337	.114	.136
8	Regional 1st Secretary	−.321	.103	.486

Proportion of Total Variance   10.1%
Proportion of Common Variance   17.8%

3 (Table 17) clearly defines a local dimension. Yet, it is not clear what the two local positions which load very highly on this factor have in common besides territoriality. On the youth factor, which accounts for the smallest proportion of variance, local secretary dominates a set of variables whose relationship cannot be interpreted (Table 18).

These factors seem to substantiate a local/central distinction in youth; but they do not substantiate or disavow the other distinctions noted in the Party organization.

The small proportion of recruits who held any positions in the youth organization renders a comparison of the three groups in terms of these patterns impossible. The proportion of holdovers and of dismissed who had positive scores on these dimensions differs very little.

CONCLUSION

Members of the Central Committee simultaneously pursue a number of careers. An individual's career in the Party is only one dimension of his total career profile. Within the Party an individual's career profile is also a composite of various career patterns. We have used factor analysis to specify these various career patterns within the Party. The career patterns are replicated empirical relationships among organizational positions. These relationships would most likely be overlooked by an analysis of biographies of this large a number of persons and would be obscured by reliance solely upon a distribution of Party positions held.

Our analysis shows that three sets of distinctions within Party career patterns are real. They are distinctions of territoriality, staff, and rank. The territorial distinctions are local, regional, and central. The staff distinctions are commission and non-commission. The rank distinctions are secretary and non-secretary. These distinctions are blended in the empirical career patterns of the members of the Central Committee which we have investigated. The blends indicate that all secretaries are not the same: that there are distinctions between secretary, deputy first secretary, and first secretary. They further indicate that career development is not linear through local and regional to central positions. For purposes of explaining career development these blends are analytically more powerful than the often posited view of the Party as a positional or functional hierarchy.

When we evaluate the three groups in terms of these blends, the following conclusions are warranted. To a large majority of recruits the regional secretariat and central commission career distinctions are relevant. The opposites of these, local secretariat and non-commission at the central level, are relevant to only one-fourth of the recruits. In contrast, the dismissed are equally distributed on these dimensions.

Holdovers are similar to recruits in that to a large majority of them the regional secretariat and central commission career distinctions are relevant. They are similar to dismissed and distinct from recruits in that they are equally distributed on the local secretariat and central non-commission dimensions. The 8th Party Congress created a Central Committee that was less diffuse in terms of Party careers than that which preceded the Congress. The new Committee was biased in terms of secretariat-type positions toward the regional level and in terms of non-secretariat positions toward commissions of the Committee.

Notes

1. For examples of various analyses of Party career data see Frederic J. Fleron, Jr., "Co-optation as a Mechanism of Adaption to Change: The Soviet Political Leadership System," *Polity*, II, 176–201 (1969); Michael P. Gehlen and Michael McBride, "The Soviet Central Committee: An Elite Analysis," *American Political Science Review*, LXII, 4 (Dec. 1968), 1232–41; Robert Bass, "East European Communist Elites: Their Character and History," *Journal of International Affairs*, XX, 1 (1966), 107–17; Carl Beck, *Aggregative Career Characteristics of East European Political Leaders* (Pittsburgh: Archive on Political Elites in Eastern Europe, U. of Pittsburgh, 1968).

2. Beck, *op. cit.*

3. The Bulgarian Communist Party has redefined its role at least four times in the post-World War II era. In 1945 its major role was the rallying point of all democratic and progressive forces. In 1948 it emphasized its task as the vanguard, the highest organization of the Bulgarian working class. At the sixth Party Congress in March 1954 it adopted a new definition, as the leading coordinator of the politically conscious elements of society. This definition remained in force until 1962, when the emphasis changed once more to the vanguard as the most conscious representative of the workers, peasants, and the people's intelligentsia. See "RFE Background Report," October 19, 1962, Radio Free Europe, Munich, Germany.

4. For a political analysis of this period see J. F. Brown, *The New Eastern Europe: The Khrushchev Era and After* (New York: Praeger, 1966), pp. 4–19.

5. For the first official announcement of the Zhivkov Theses see *Rabotnichesko Delo*, Jan. 20, 1959. Zhivkov had, however, at least since October 1958 been preparing the Party for the new economic plan. See *Rabotnichesko Delo*, Oct. 26, 1958. For an analysis of the administrative and economic implications see John Kalo, "The Bulgarian Economy," *Survey*, 39 (Dec. 1961), 86–95, and Boris A. Christoff, "The Bulgarian Leap Forward," *Problems of Communism*, VIII, 5 (Sept.–Oct. 1959), 15–20.

6. For analysis of the different motives behind Bulgaria's "great leap forward" and its effects on Party factionalism see Brown, *op. cit.*, especially pp. 11–14. For evidence of the amount and character of opposition see Christoff, *op. cit.*, 18–19.

7. Boris Taskov had lost his ministerial post on March 14, 1959, and was dismissed from the Politburo on April 20, 1959. On the same date he was demoted from full to candidate membership in the Central Committee. He held the position of candidate member of the Committee from April 20, 1959, to November 5, 1962.

8. For the particular character of the de-Stalinization and "New Course" policies

in Bulgaria see E. O. Stillman and R. H. Bass, "Bulgaria: A Study in Satellite Non-Conformity," *Problems of Communism*, IV, 6 (Nov.–Dec. 1955), 26–33.

9. Brown, *op. cit.*, pp. 15–16.

10. For the analyses in this part, computer programs in the BMD series were utilized. For a description of these programs see W. J. Dixon (ed.), *Biomedical Computer Programs* (Berkeley & Los Angeles: U. of California P., 1967), pp. 132–9, 169–84.

11. The term "principal components analysis" is more accurate than "factor analysis" because unities were inserted in the diagonal of the factor matrix. The latter term is used more frequently in the field of political science. For an excellent, concise discussion of factor analysis see R. J. Rummel, "Understanding Factor Analysis," *Journal of Conflict Resolution*, XI, 4 (Dec. 1967), 444–80. For an in-depth treatment see Harry Harman, *Modern Factor Analysis* (2d rev. ed.; Chicago: U. of Chicago P., 1967).

12. The specific positions for the Party and youth organizations are listed in Tables 1 and 2, respectively. The two sets of variables were factor analyzed separately.

13. Rotation enables different variables to cluster on separate factors.

14. The eigenvalue of a factor is equal to the sum of the squared loadings on that factor. It is one measure of the amount of variation accounted for by a factor.

15. The communality, sometimes designated h^2, indicates the proportion of variance in a given variable which is accounted for cumulatively by the factors rotated. It is calculated by summing the squares of the variable's loadings on each of the rotated factors.

16. In calculation, factor scores are standardized, i.e., scaled to have a mean of 0.0 and a standard deviation of 1.0. For this reason the individual who had a null pattern and therefore a 0 value on every variable included in the factor analysis would not necessarily receive a factor score of zero. For instance, on Party factor 1 the null pattern individual received a score of $-.21$, while on Party factor 5 the same individual received a $+.42$. By "positive scores" we mean all the scores on a given factor which were higher than the factor score of a null pattern individual. In effect, we have rescaled the factor scores so that a null pattern individual always has a factor score of zero.

17. The proportion of total variance accounted for by a factor is a measure of the relative importance of a particular pattern.

18. The following cross-tabulation of data pertaining to the three positions to which factor 5 systematically relates helps demonstrate the correspondence between the concrete reality and the map of it provided by factor analysis.

	Candidate Member Central Committee (N = 76)	Never Candidate Member Central Committee (N = 53)
Local Official (N = 4)	0	4
Chairman Central Committee Commission (N = 12)	3	9
Those Who Held Neither of the Above Two Positions	73	40

Of the sixteen persons who held either the position of local official or chairman of a Central Committee commission, only three were candidate members of the Central Committee. This is reflected in the signs of the factor loadings of the three variables (Table 13). Not one of the twelve individuals who were chairmen of a Central Committee was ever a local official. The squared factor loadings indicate this. Factor 5 accounts for less than 50 percent of the variation in these two variables. Therefore, they are related to each other only through their common relationship to the variable with a factor loading greater than $\pm.700$.

PART 3

Policy Implementation and Bureaucracy in Russia and the Soviet Union

The studies in the previous section of this text dealt primarily with the policy-making or input side of the political process, in particular with methods of elite recruitment and influence. We turn now to questions of policy implementation. Don Karl Rowney examines the Imperial Russian Ministry of Internal Affairs to determine its capability to achieve the goals assigned it. He first points to the applicability of contemporary organization theory to a study of the ministry and then analyzes aggregate career data on ministry personnel and budgetary allocations in order to provide a partial answer to this question.

Erik Hoffman also deals with bureaucracy, but with the ideological sectors of the Communist Party apparatus, rather than the imperial ministries. He is concerned with the problems facing Agitprop workers under Khrushchev who had no clear concept of what was expected of them, since their roles were not clearly defined—or, in some cases, were defined in contradictory ways. Hoffmann shows how Khrushchev's successors have attempted to solve this problem, by both a de-emphasis of nonideological rules and a press campaign to communicate role expectations. Hoffmann also indicates that concepts from role theory can be fruitfully applied to the study of bureaucratic behavior in the Soviet Union.

Although Robert Sharlet is also concerned with the output side of the political process, he emphasises the use of law rather than the operations of the bureaucracy. He begins with the argument that Soviet political history can be understood best from a developmental perspective and points out that law was used by the Soviets in the development of the Soviet state and that at different stages of development, law has performed different functions. He concludes with a number of general hypotheses concerning the use of law in the developmental process.

8

The Study of the Imperial Ministry
of Internal Affairs
in the Light of Organization Theory

DON KARL ROWNEY

INTRODUCTION

The purpose of this study is to describe a plan of historical research
and analysis. As a means to this end, part of the study refers to a specific
historical problem as an example of the application of such a research
plan. The historical subject is the central administration of the Imperial

This paper was prepared in part under a Younger Scholars' Fellowship from
the National Endowment on the Humanities. In addition, thanks for assistance
are due to the Center for Research on Social Behavior, Bowling Green State
University, and the National Endowment on the Humanities.
Notes to the selection begin on page 229.

Russian Ministry of Internal Affairs (*Ministerstvo Vnutrennykh Del*) from 1904 to 1916, the second half of Emperor Nicholas II's reign, the last twelve years of the Russian monarchy. A comprehensive study of the ministry during this period is being conducted by the author according to the plan of analysis and with the data described herein.

This chapter begins with a survey of major historical studies of state administration in the Russian Empire and then attempts to show how the study of Russian administration might be rendered less idiosyncratic by borrowing theory and methodology from the study of organizational behavior. To this end there follows a short discussion of relevant aspects of organization theory and then an extended formulation of strategies for the historical analysis of organizations, so that the reader may judge their utility for himself. This discussion is rendered less abstract by the fact that it uses as its example an actual study which is in progress, together with actual data appropriate to the study.

The author believes that the analytic formats to be discussed markedly extend and improve the research options open to the historian. In particular, they offer three advantages: (1) they should produce better descriptive historical studies of this class of social and political phenomena, since description is both more detailed and more cohesive; (2) they should provide some continuity and comparability of research in history and other social sciences, since this discussion tries to explicate common dimensions of theory and methodology; (3) they should provide an improved analytic frame for asking "how" and "why", since classes of data, their significance, and the patterns developed for their arrangement and analysis are made explicit and put into quantifiable form.

PREVIOUS STUDIES
OF RUSSIAN ADMINISTRATION

One way of illustrating the aims of a study of the Ministry of Internal Affairs is by reviewing previously completed studies of similar institutions or groups of institutions in Russia and the Soviet Union. Such an exercise should help sketch the boundaries of what is known about the subject, thereby clarifying the challenges for additional research in the area. There are obviously several possible schemes for classifying a century of research on a subject as broad and important as Russian administration. This review uses a threefold division based on the methodological and substantive emphasis of the studies.

The first group will be called biographical. It includes biographical and autobiographical works about major figures in the imperial administrative apparatus.[1] The influence which such works have had on our attitude toward the Russian past has been profound both because of their number and because they necessarily reinforce the historian's tendency to focus on most visible personalities, to the exclusion of other phenomena (such as systems and procedure, structure, less visible personalities, actual policy outputs, actual resource inputs). Moreover, whether they are critical of their subject or not, these works see the organization and the society in which it functions from the viewpoint of their subject—the scope and penetration of their vision colored or foreshortened by the intensive study of those documents which so clearly reveal their subject to them. In addition to these frankly biographical studies, there is another type of history of Russian administration which should also be classed as biographical. These studies tend to be biographies of organizations in the sense that they emphasize the position of a small number of individuals, together with their policies and, perhaps, their public and personal relations to selected segments of the society—all this to the exclusion of a study of the organization per se.[2]

The second group is characterized by an overwhelmingly legalistic approach which emphasizes the structure of the organization as part of a legal and formal hierarchy. The typical independent variables in such studies are what may be termed formal policy inputs which take the form of laws, decrees, directives, etc. The dependency relationship of the functional variables within the organization being studied (i.e., the dependent variables) is generally taken for granted.[3] Szeftel, for example, states that because of legislation in 1864 "a delegation of power took place that established local self-government" and that this, together with the obligation imposed, in the same year, on the judiciary to interpret the letter of the law under certain circumstances, constituted real limitations on exercise of autocratic power.[4] Implicit in this view is the assumption of mechanical operation of a state apparatus (i.e., extreme instrumentality) which apparatus accepts blindly, if somewhat inefficiently, the allocation of values and the implementation of policies from on high. A large body of studies dealing with aspects or organizational control and dating back to "Bureaucratic Structure and

Personality"[5] at least casts doubt on this assumption. Szeftel's assertion
that "the very existence of these [independent] courts and zemstvos
kept alive the principle of supremacy of law and of government by the
people . . ."[6] is, at best, an oversimplification. Without at least some
verification on the point there is no reason to believe that court or
zemstvo organizations would be significantly more prone to an impartial servitude to the law or obeisance to the public interest than
other official organizations. Various studies[7] have shown that the aims
which any organization pursues are determined by many extraorganizational factors, including the groups or individuals to which
the organization is subordinate, with which it competes, or whose
support it requires. Surely it is simplistic to assume that if an organ
of Russian administration did not serve the interests of the tsars and
their advisers, it served those of law or "the people."

At another extreme, one historian has dealt with the complexities
of evaluating autocratic power in competition with bureaucratic
procedure by simply denying the existence of bureaucratic administration.[8] While he thereby becomes free to assert the independence of the
monarch as a policy-maker, denying the existence of a Russian bureaucracy is a feat of some magnitude. How shall we explain, for example,
the carrying out of millions of daily official acts in the Russian Empire?

Certain studies, which may be classified as legalistic in approach,
appear to be more straightforward than those already described. Two
of these rank among the best studies of state administration in Imperial
Russia.[9] Reading either one, it is possible to acquire a grasp of the
formal pattern of organized state administration, the development of
policy, and organizational responses to it. On the other hand, neither
work goes far beyond the formal dimensions of organizational structure
or into the area of function. They do make the crucial contribution
of showing the *size* and *shape* of the universe with which we are concerned and of identifying some of the data appropriate to a
historical organizational analysis.

The third general group of studies of Russian administration may
go under the title of either collective biographies or elite studies. In
principle these two are quite different approaches. Collective biographies
typically focus on specific variables which describe a homogeneous
group of persons. Although some of the sources and methods may be
different from those used in biographies of individuals, the goals of
the collective and individual biographies are not dissimilar. Basically,

they describe the subject. Elite studies, on the other hand, have a characteristic theoretical underpinning which emphasizes the critical importance of the background and careers of specific groups (elites and sub-elites) on the assumption that this will reveal patterns of functioning of the entire system whether it be political, economic, military, or social.[10] In practice, at least in the historiography of Russian administration, the two approaches have tended to be rather indistinguishable.[11] While one may speculate that elite theory has not proved viable enough to mark off a distinctive, operationalized analysis, it is sufficient to observe the tendency of elite studies merely to describe historical phenomena.

ORGANIZATION THEORY AND HISTORICAL RESEARCH

Like other social scientists, historians may be principally concerned with the rationalization of data (theory of the discipline and interpretation), with data as such (experimentation, survey research, documentary collections), or they may proceed from a consideration of one to the other. For example, the collection and classification of data on events of a major political revolution may lead to formulation of hypotheses about the behavior of individuals and groups under revolutionary conditions. On the other hand, consideration of psychological or sociological hypotheses about conflict may stimulate a collection of data about violent upheavals such as revolutions. Assuming broad familiarity with the "history" of a given society at a given time and assuming a detailed familiarity with the range of resources available for further analysis of social behavior at that time (e.g., memoirs, diaries, the public press, social and economic statistics, to mention a few), it seems economical to be guided in the selection, classification, and interpretation of these data not only by judgments based on one's own experience but by whatever hypotheses and methods seem relevant from other, related disciplines. Such hypotheses may be regarded as series of narrow questions addressed to and made relevant to a given set of data. Of course, it is expected that the answers obtained from an analysis depend to some degree on the questions asked, their appropriateness and their exhaustiveness. On the other hand, it is expected that the kind of data which are available—e.g., experimental, survey,

historical-documentary—will prejudice the sort of questions one asks
and the results one anticipates.

To write that the Ministry of Internal Affairs was an organization
is to make a highly general statement, but it implies more than may be
apparent at first. It specifies the ministry as an *organization*, as distinct
from several other class terms, such as "bureaucracy" or "public
administration." The usefulness of this specification is simply
that it lends scale and significance, and sets boundaries to the
object of the study. Accordingly, the ministry is thought of as a specific
example of a broad class of phenomena nominally defined as "social
units oriented to the realization of specific goals."[12] It is then related
to General Motors, the BBC, the Roman Catholic Church, or the
NKVD, depending on one's level of generalization. In particular, by
avoiding the more common term "bureaucracy," one avoids identification with a particular tradition of scholarship to which organization
theory is indebted but not limited. Moreover, this description affirms
that we expect to draw upon insights which the numerous studies of
organizations in various disciplines have produced. To speak of
"organization theory," however, implies a more cohesive body of
research and conclusions regarding organizational phenomena than
actually exists. In fact, there are several schools of organizational
studies which sometimes yield distressingly different points of view with
regard to similar organizational phenomena. What is more common,
as Etzioni and others have pointed out, is that the hypotheses and empirical studies of organizations are often not comparable. The fact
that "organization theory" is a meaningful term is largely due to
efforts of students of organizations to bring theory and empirical
research together in a comprehensive pattern.[13] It will be apparent,
then, that there is no theory of organizations or organizational behavior
which the study can follow explicitly. There are, however, relatively
cohesive theoretical and methodological points of view. Here, an attempt
is made to analyze the ministry consistently from what has been called
a structural-functional point of view. That is, the variables which are
of interest are related to the structure of the organization and certain
dimensions of its internal function, especially the distribution of
resources.

The structural-functional school of organizational studies has tended
to explicate relationships between formal and informal organization.
Here, "formal organization" is taken to refer to those parts of an

organization which would be described by hierarchical administrative charts, production flow charts, official budgets, standards and rules for job performance, and the like. "Informal organization," on the other hand, emphasizes actual relations as they are observed within the functioning organization—whether this involves resource allocation or social relations among workers—as well as the real relations which obtain between the organization and its environment. This implies that there is often some discrepancy between the formal and informal organizations and the observation of the nature and intensity of such discrepancies may be helpful in understanding how individuals behave in an organizational environment and how they may be expected to behave if we assume certain changes within or outside the organization.

A researcher who approaches organizational study with this assumption and who limits himself to historical data will find it much easier to reconstruct formal patterns of organization than informal ones: formal patterns are more likely to have been recorded than informal ones. As we shall show, however, this does not obviate the analysis of informal structure and function and their relation to formal organization. Indeed, it is by searching out or interpolating data on informal organization that a historian may utilize all his professional skill as an analyst of documentary germaneness and accuracy. Nevertheless, a historian, unlike some other researchers, will ultimately confront the fact that his data are limited by the vagaries of time and whatever other factors cause some documents to be preserved while others are lost. The analysis described here is designed to overcome some of these limitations. The characteristics of historical data, together with the theoretical and methodological potential of organizational analysis, have suggested the analytic structure described in the remainder of this study. Although the final step of conducting the actual analysis is not taken, discussion of the analysis is intended to illustrate and substantiate the advantages of the approach.

The analysis of the Ministry of Internal Affairs is described as being structured in three phases. The first phase is description of the organization as a formal, abstract whole. Such description aims to explicate the formal dimensions and boundaries of the ministry, who constitute its participants and how they can be differentiated formally, and its formal goals and the resources available for their attainment. The second phase describes the organization in terms of the real function of selected organizational parts. As we describe it in this study, and in actual practice, such an analysis would be selective principally because of the unavailability of data. Nevertheless, analysis of a few critically important areas, such as choice and promotion of personnel, affords the opportunity to expose details of actual organizational function and to observe the interplay of formal and informal patterns. The third phase describes the organization in terms of its relation to its environments, e.g., other organizations, society or segments of society. Data which are comparable over a period of years are available to make it feasible to study how organizational change is associated with selected environmental variables. This makes possible a valid, though partial, analysis which will specify conditions of interaction with environment and will, at the same time, allow one to treat the organization as a whole, in process of change—increasing its independence vis-à-vis the environment, maintaining systemic stability, or retarding entropy.

DATA FOR THE MINISTRY
OF INTERNAL AFFAIRS STUDY

The documentary resources appropriate to the study of the ministry may be thought of as forming a single "data file," although they are used in several different forms and for various purposes. The file is divided into materials concerning ministerial structure and those concerning function, including the allocation of resources. Both collections of materials provide information concerning formal and informal aspects of organization. The *Code of Laws* of the Russian Empire and, especially, the *Adres-Kalendar*'[14] provide the basis for information concerning the formal organizational structure of the ministry. The second item is especially useful since it names organizational subdivisions down to the subdepartmental level and provides a means of calculating the number of officials in each unit for each year covered by the study.

The principal source of data concerning organizational function is a file which consists of observations on a total of fifty-three biographic and career variables for persons with officer rank (i.e., "officials") in the ministry.[15] The biographical career records are, in turn, based upon two collections of government documents, the *List of Higher Officials* and the *List of Individuals Serving*.[16] Taken together, the data in the documents describe the careers of officials in the ministry for virtually any length of time and include information on position held during any given year as well as salary paid. In addition, details are provided on such items as the participants' extraministerial interests; their education, religion, and social class of birth;[17] wife's maiden name; and so on. An additional source of data concerning organizational function are detailed (i.e., line item) budgets for the ministry. These include information on operating and capital expenditures in ministerial departments. These data are compiled from *Estimates of Income* and *Reports of the Budget Commission*.[18]

DIMENSIONS
OF MINISTERIAL STRUCTURE

FORMAL GOALS

To what extent can we specify the formal goals of the ministry in, say, 1904? By combining information from several sources[19] we can specify some of the organization's formal goals without, however, achieving a completely satisfactory series of statements. One problem is that certain goals may not be apparent from the literature to which we have access; presumably, in an organization of this sort, some goals were secret, while others may have been reformulated in secret. In either case such goals would still be formal, even though unknown to us. Equally serious is the difficulty of defining the goals operationally. This involves formulating goals so that it is fairly clear what systematic steps must be taken to attain them; it may include a rather precise description of the contribution of small units within larger subdivisions. The advantage of such a formulation to us is simply that it renders our understanding of the relationship of means to ends less interpretive and more factual. It is true that under any circumstances, the higher the level of organization the more difficult operationalizing organizational goals becomes. At the highest policy-making levels no matter how they are formulated, goals will be operationally vague. A formulation, published in the 1890s, which states the objectives of the entire ministry, is a fair example of this vagueness. According to this statement, the ministry was "allotted the very extensive task of caring for the universal welfare of the people, the peace, quiet and good order of the whole Empire."[20] The documents available make it possible to identify ministerial units as to nominal functions and goals. From these sources it is possible to infer "unit goals" which will differ from one department to another and, often, within departments. Table 1 shows all ministerial departments grouped according to four nominal functions for the year 1904. It also shows the pattern of distribution of personnel resources for the same year. This is discussed below.

MEANS TO FORMAL GOALS

How can we determine whether the formal means or resources existed to fulfill these goals in 1904? One can establish (1) the proportion of personnel allocation to given organizational subdivisions and (2) the proportion of budgetary allocations. For the time being it may be assumed that items which have bearing on the *value* of resource or means allocation are roughly equal throughout the organization. These might include items such as the *quality* and *type* of education or the time in service in a specialized area. At a later point, additional attention is given to variations in these items. Here we distinguish whether or not means exist within broad limits of variability by preparing "resource matrices" for each group of unit goals or each organizational department. These include values for such items as the proportion of ministerial personnel allocated per unit or the amount of operating budget allocated per capita in each unit. Such distributions will not distinguish among goals which were inherently "cheaper" to attain or goals which might be more efficiently obtained with one kind of resource combination than another. Rather, they indicate whether the availability of personnel and the allocation of other resources were comparable among units of varying sizes and goals. Since goals and resources are also related to organizational subdivisions, this analysis will permit us to state to what extent (1) diverse goals are served by one single organizational unit; (2) operationally similar goals are served by more than one unit; (3) goals and means to goals are mutually dependent or independent (i.e., the functioning of one department depends upon the functioning of another, and successful attainment of one set of goals provides means for attaining others in a different organizational unit). This last relationship is often described as a means-ends hierarchy and in organization theory, applied to modern Western organizations, it is seen as having important implications for relations among persons and subgroups in the organization.[21]

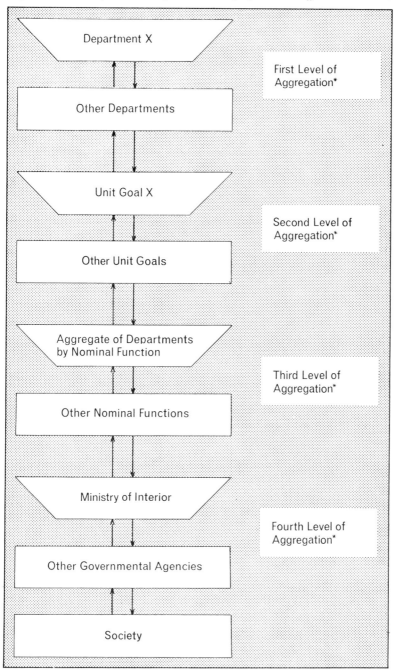

FIGURE 1. Organizational Aggregates and Organizational Environments.

*Levels of aggregation are not necessarily sequential.

TABLE 1

MINISTERIAL DEPARTMENTS GROUPED BY NOMINAL FUNCTION, 1904

								I. General Administration
	Office of Minister and Deputy Ministers	Council of the Minister	Officials Specially Assigned	Chancellory of the Minister	Dept. of General Affairs	Dept. of Clergy Affairs	Economic Dept.	Conference on Zemstvo Affairs
Officials or Official Positions	5	31	58	3	39	212	32	7
% of Total Officials or Official Positions in Ministry	0.5	2.9	5.3	0.3	3.6	19.5	2.9	0.6

	III. Propaganda, Communication, and Education							
	Council and Main Administration for Affairs of Press	Central Committee for Foreign Censorship	Refuge of Prince Oldenburg	Total	Insurance Committee	Medical Dept.	Medical Council	Veterinary Committee
Officials or Official Positions	17	15	28	60	13	24	43	26
% of Total Officials or Official Positions in Ministry	1.6	1.4	2.6	5.6	1.2	2.2	3.9	2.3

Zemstvo Division	Migration Administration	Main Administration for Posts and Telegraph	Administration for Postal Shipment by Railway	Postal-Telegraphic Regional Administration	Total	II. Police-Coercive		
						Dept. of Police	Administration for Military Conscription	Total
44	69	79	23	73	675	44	14	58
4.0	6.3	7.3	2.1	6.7	62.0	4.0	1.3	5.3

IV. Technical								
Veterinary Administration	Statistical Council	Central Statistical Committee	Electro-Technical Institute	Technical Building Committee	Institute of Civil Engineers	Imperial Institute of Experimental Medicine	Total	Total for Ministry
5	17	19	46	16	68	17	294	1,087
0.5	1.6	1.7	4.2	1.5	6.3	1.6	27.0	99.9

BOUNDARIES AND ENVIRONMENTS

For analytic purposes the whole universe must be divided into two parts: (1) the organization and (2) everything else. To that end two interrelated questions must be asked: How can the boundaries of the organization be defined? and What are the environments in which the organization exists? Generally, we are free to determine boundaries in any of several ways.[22] It seems most convenient here to regard as participants only those persons legally specified as employees of the Ministry of Internal Affairs (e.g., the minister, a clerk in the department of civil engineering, local police and, perhaps, guards, charwomen, etc.). Indeed, a large portion of this group will be irrelevant since our interest is confined to individuals with one or another of the official ranks in the Table of Ranks. A more exhaustive definition seems appropriate only for a more extensive analysis than is proposed here.

The definition of organizational environment is equally arbitrary. To begin, we adopt the definition of Hall and Fagen.

> For a given system [organization] *the environment* is the set of all objects, a change in whose attributes affects the system [organization] and also those objects whose attributes are changed by the behavior of the system [organization].[23]

To this we add the modification suggested by Blegen and others and formulated here by Blegen:

> Where the boundary shall be drawn will be dependent on the restriction and assumptions applying for the problem of current interest. The system (S_1) may be considered as composed of hierarchically built up sub-systems $(Ss_1 \ldots n)$ where the system (S_1) is part of the environment. At the same time the system (S_1) may be a sub-system in several more extensive systems $(Se_1 \ldots n)$.[24]

For our purposes, then, we may describe the ministerial environment on different levels. For example, if we consider the organization as a whole, its environment would consist of all social units external to the ministry which affect it or are affected by it. Of course, these will be related in varying orders of superordination and subordination, and involvement with the ministry. On the other hand, if we wish to focus principally on a ministerial department, an organizational subdivision which lies just below the ministry in level of authority, the environment may also include other subdivisions, the entire ministry, extraministerial units, and so on.

The analysis of components of formal organization for the ministry thus yields hierarchies of means-ends and hierarchies of boundaries and environments. We will call these latter hierarchies "levels of aggregation." They are illustrated in Figure 1. The next series of statements will show that there were hierarchies of participants as well.

FORMAL HIERARCHIES OF PARTICIPANTS

Another dimension of the organization which the data reveal is the formal hierarchies of participants, which, in turn, indicate patterns of formal interrelationships among participants. A number of options are open for specifying hierarchies of participants. Factors such as social status outside the organization, religion and national background, amount and type of education, secondary professions, and principal career specialization are all relevant for distinguishing and comparing participants. Since we are concerned only with formal criteria at this point, however, our interest is confined to the following formal factors: official rank and honorary status; official post or posts; salary; seniority.

Rank was a formal means of distinguishing members of the Russian civil service at least from the time of Peter I.[25] An official correlation was established between the level or grade of a given post in the civil service and the rank which its incumbent was expected to hold.[26] Formally, at any rate, appointments which did not conform to these correlations were temporary and could not be confirmed. "Honorary status" refers to certain titles or decorations (*nagrady*) which, together with a pension, or cash prize, were granted as special rewards.[27] Although salary was officially correlated with the organizational position occupied, actual remuneration could vary somewhat. In addition to income from pensions, other factors affected remuneration; these included grants for housing or subsistence and the possibility of holding more than one official position. The term "seniority," finally, here includes total years in service as well as total years in a given rank and position.

A list of the titles of official positions for the Ministry of Internal Affairs alone would consume more than a page of fine print. A sample of such positions is given in Table 2. Groupings are based on the scope or extension of formal authority apparently attached to the position

TABLE 2

SAMPLE OF OFFICIAL MINISTERIAL POSITIONS

Authority Level	Organization Level	Official Position
First (broadest)	Ministerial (includes Council of the Minister)	Minister Vice-Minister member of council
Second	Departmental (includes departments, main administrations, administrative councils other than Council of the Minister; interministerial councils; and committees; Land Division; scientific institutes)	Director Vice-Director Head Vice-Head President Vice-President
Third	Divisions (other than the Land Division; includes departmental secretariates, business offices [deloproizvodstva])	Director Vice-Director Head Vice-Head Expediters Senior and Junior vice-Expediters Secretaries Learned secretaries Expediter-Managers, etc.
Fourth (narrowest)	Nonmanagerial	Clerk Clerk-chancellorist
Temporary or Special Assignments	Specially Assigned	Official with special assignment

as given in the *Adres-Kalendar'*.[28] This system of classification was adopted as an alternative to the official system which classified positions ordinally but which did so incompletely. All levels of formal assignment for participants with any of the official ranks are represented. In addition, all levels of authority from the broadest to the narrowest are represented. Such a distribution provides a suitable format for relating such as *actual* educational experience, career experience, career specialization, social origins, seniority, and salary to *actual* levels of authority. We are, accordingly, in a position to move beyond the purely formal hierarchies of personnel and to make comparisons or correlations which will illustrate the kinds of career patterns and biographic characteristics which, in practice, were associated with various classes of positions in the organization. This leads to the next step in our research design: a discussion of aspects of informal organization as compared with formal organization which emphasizes observed patterns of selection, promotion, demotion, and dismissal of personnel.

SUMMARY

In this section we have identified the resources available for studying the Ministry of Internal Affairs as a formal organization. In addition we have formulated a frame for analyzing these data. In doing so, attention was given to the following factors: formal goals and the means available, roughly defined, to attain these goals; boundaries and environments of the ministry, together with identification of participants; and formal criteria for distinguishing participants from one another on the basis of the scope of their formal, organizational authority.

DIMENSIONS
OF MINISTERIAL FUNCTION

The principal question to be dealt with here is how to formulate an analytic format that permits comparison of the ministry's formal characteristics with actual participant behavior. Such an analysis could center on one or more of a range of substantive categories. These might include formal authority as compared to actual leadership,[29] organizational conflict as related to formal organizational structure,[30] conflict between the goals of organizational professionals (e.g., medical doctors, engineers, or veterinarians) as compared to those of other (i.e., "line") participants.[31] The example used here is limited to a discussion of selection and promotion of participants as these bear on formal organizational structure and the relation of organizational units to one another.

The data supply the following factors on participant qualification based on the formal criteria of education and experience.

   I. Education Cluster
     A. Total years of formal education for each participant.
     B. Participant education experience directly related to unit function.
  II. Experience Cluster
     A. Total years of previous employment for participants.
     B. Total previous years in government or military service for participants.
     C. Total previous years in ministry for participants.
     D. Total previous years in present area of specialization for participants.

Qualifications may be expressed as "unit resources," since distributions may be generated which distinguish among organizational units by showing the extent to which they attracted personnel more or less specially qualified to function in the unit. Obviously such an analysis can be repeated at any level of aggregation within the organization; this permits judgment on the extent to which these factors were relevant for selection and promotion of participants.

If we confine our interest to the 12 or 15 percent of participants occupying the highest authority levels in the organization, the analysis of participant qualifications is further refined and extended to factors associated with promotion.[32] Here, in addition to the formal criteria outlined above, groups of extraorganizational characteristics are also included. The following clusters are considered:

1. Extraorganizational Statuses
   A. Legal class-of-birth designation of participant.
   B. Legal class-of-birth designation of participant's wife.
   C. Prestige level of participant's formal schooling (e.g., attended the Imperial Corps of Pages in St. Petersburg or the Vilno Military Secondary School).
   D. Property held by participant (e.g., total land acreage held by participant's immediate family).
2. Extraorganizational Affiliations
   A. Professional associations and appointments (e.g., "Distinguished Professor of Medicine").
   B. Public service and eleemosynary associations (e.g., Red Cross, school boards).
   C. Elected public offices (e.g., member of State Duma, Justice of the Peace).
   D. Other associations.

Extraorganizational Statuses refers to a cluster of characteristics which are assumed to have been socially significant in Russian society before the 1917 Revolution. What is asked here is whether they were politically or organizationally significant. Extraorganizational Affiliations includes factors bearing on a broad range of activities by participants. These, too, are factors which may have been socially significant. We are asking whether they were organizationally or professionally significant for higher ministry participants. These factors may be analyzed with respect to organizational units at any level of aggregation. Similarly, they may be related to authority levels, posing the question of how the factors are associated with promotion.

Additional analytic formats could be elaborated. We have not considered, for instance, the importance of self-selection by participants. In addition, we should consider variations in remuneration, demotion, lack of promotion, transfer, resignation, and dismissal. We could also extend our consideration of selection and promotion to the subject of organizational control. This includes a consideration of the means available to the organization to secure participant compliance with organizational goals. As Etzioni and others have shown, these patterns differ from one level of an organization to another, and in the case of a highly complex organization such as the ministry, they might be expected to change from one organizational unit to another.

SUMMARY

Our principal concern here has been with aspects of selection and promotion of participants and the way in which these may functionally distinguish organizational units and groups of participants from one another. Factors we have used to illustrate these analyses are educational and professional experience, extraorganizational statuses, and activities of participants.

PATTERNS OF CHANGE: MINISTERIAL INTERACTION WITH ENVIRONMENTS

We may now turn to the problem of organizational change. Our approach is to ascertain and interrelate values for the variables described above for each of the years from 1904 to 1916. Such an approach will not only produce additional descriptive historical material but will also allow us to judge the extent to which the organization interacted with its environments and how their interactions affected organizational structure and function.

We have already shown that we can consider the organization at different levels of aggregation: the whole organization, functional subdivisions, officially established departments, or as an aggregate comprised of unit goals. In each case the environments vary as a function of the level of aggregation with which we are concerned; thus, at the departmental level, we consider departments and similar subdivisions as part of the environment, together with more comprehensive organizational and extraorganizational aggregates which appear to be relevant. This pattern is illustrated in Figure 1, where it was assumed that all of these relationships are potentially reversible. The historical perspectives from which we view organizational interaction with environments influence the format of our analysis as well as whatever specific hypotheses we might wish to test. Our data concerning the ministry encompass approximately 148 continuous months of Russian social and political life. During that time the Russian Empire was directly involved in two major wars (1904–05, 1914–17), a period of peace (1905–14), and a series of civil uprisings (the Revolution of 1905). In addition, the society experienced rapid growth of a class of agrarian freeholders, continued expansion of an industrial-technical establishment, and the establishment of a popularly elected national legislature possessing, in practice, vaguely defined powers. The judgment of historians of virtually all schools is that the ministry was directly and importantly involved with each of these phenomena. Whether the ministry was subject to influence from its environments, however, is an open, empirical question. To the extent that it was, these historical phenomena, among others, should influence our hypotheses concerning organizational change. At the same time we will assume that it exhibited a number of characteristics which organization theory accepts as common to Western, complex, modern organizations. These characteristics, very broadly, include organizational efforts to maintain or increase the resources available to it, to maintain or secure a congruent compliance structure, to maintain its means-goals structure.[33] We will assume that lower levels of organizational aggregation exhibited these same characteristics. These perspectives (i.e., historical phenomena and organizational characteristics) may be formed into hypotheses which specify our expectations of the patterns of organizational change, and which may be evaluated by the data available.

The formulation of formats for the analysis of change in the ministry over time is a relatively simple process, since it consists of an extension, from year to year, of the formats already described. Thus, we record changes in formal means-ends structures by inserting the appropriate new values for each variable each year. The same process may be used for recording frequencies in the authority class-experience-education clusters, and so on. Participant careers may also be analyzed independently of the assumption that they are organizational resources. Here the most useful and comprehensive format is that of stochastic analysis as described by Vroom and MacCrimmon and others.[34]

The formulation of hypotheses which reflect our perspective on the ministerial environment and on organizational characteristics is more complicated. For example, we might specify the following in view of the expansion of a technical industrial establishment:

Formal Structural Change
1. Resource matrix values will be maintained or increased for technically oriented unit goals as compared to their environments in the ministry.
2. Since prestige and remuneration are directly related to authority level, the rate of vertical mobility and the number of participants in high authority levels will be maintained or increased for technically oriented unit goals as compared to their environments in the ministry.
3. Patterns (1) and (2), above, will be repeated for technical departments as compared to their environments in the ministry.

Similar specifications may be formulated for formal-informal relations across time in the ministry. Findings which appear to support the hypotheses should also support the view, for example, that the ministry was subject to influence by environmental variables which did not immediately conflict with its authority structure, did not contribute to the incongruence of its compliance structure, and maintained or increased the resources available to it. On the other hand, findings which support the hypotheses and which indicate, for example, that a rapid improvement in the position of the technical areas was coupled with a relative decline in, say, administrative or security areas lead us to question (1) whether the organization in fact preserved its authority and resource-goals structures and (2) the appropriateness of postulates regarding organizational "characteristics."

Findings which do not appear to support the hypotheses might suggest a broader range of alternatives. (1) They might require a further refinement of hypotheses. For example, the rapid expansion of a unit-goal level might be accompanied by a relative increase in lower participant ranks and a stabilization of higher ranks. Such a state of affairs would then show a curvilinear relationship between rank and time which would fail to support hypothesis (2) *as it is stated* but not in principle. (2) They may suggest intervening variables. For example, the presence of additional personnel possessing certain characteristics or performing certain tasks may be perceived as a threat by an existing authority structure. (3) They may suggest that the ministry was relatively impervious, or was becoming impervious, to environmental variables related to the growth of an industrial technical establishment.

SUMMARY

Our aim has been to describe a plan for the quantitative analysis of a historical subject, the Russian Ministry of Internal Affairs between 1904 and 1916. In developing this analysis we have taken the view that the ministry may nominally be described as an organization and that we are therefore justified in using theoretical and methodological applications from organization theory. Limitations on the use of this theory and methodology were recognized. First, we observed that historical analysis within this or any quantitative format was strictly limited by the data available for carrying out the analysis and that, consequently, theoretical and methodological applications from other areas of the social sciences must take the form of an interchange rather than an application without appropriate adjustment. Second, we observed that one of the most important questions with which we have to deal is whether and to what extent the ministry as an organizational type differed in structure and function from modern Western types. Since this question was open, consequently, it became necessary to apply even verified organization theory, as it now exists, hypothetically.

We have attempted to show that the rather elaborate analytic procedures adopted here were justified on three main grounds:

First, if we look at the ministry as a unique historical subject and our problem as one of historical description, then we argue that the techniques used here are effective devices for marshaling quantitative, descriptive resources—resources which our survey of the historiography of the subject showed are often neglected or badly used.

Second, we argue that the historical approach to the study of organizations—i.e., the ministry as an example of a class of phenomena—has a special contribution to make to the social sciences. Not only does it provide the cross-cultural dimension which is admittedly so important to the study of human behavior, but it also adds a temporal perspective missing from so much of the research of the modern social sciences. In this respect, we argue that the study of the Ministry of Internal Affairs as an organization offers a means of escape from what Stephan Thernstrom has called a "parochialism of time," characteristic of so much research in the social sciences.[35]

Third, we argue that the analysis has not only descriptive value but explanatory value as well. That is, it provides an appropriate frame for answering "how" and "why" questions. Here, explicitness in the use of data and the development of explanatory hypotheses are important factors which contribute to the general pattern of explanation. Moreover, the quantitative characteristics of the analysis provide a means for evaluating the explanatory power of the data. Such evaluations may be conducted by the original researcher as well as by anyone else, since the study may be easily replicated using different quantitative procedures.

Notes

1. The number of autobiographies, memoirs, diaries, and the like exceeds the number of well-done biographies. Relevant examples of both would include: Robert F. Byrnes, *Pobedonostsev: His Life and Thought* (Bloomington: Indiana U. P., 1968); V. I. Gurko, *Features and Figures of the Past: Government and Opinion in the Reign of Nicholas II* (Stanford: Stanford U. P., 1939); Vladimir N. Kokovtsov, *Iz moego proshlogo: vospominaniia, 1903–1919 gg.* [*Out of My Past: Memoirs, 1903–1919*] (Paris: Illiustrirovannaia Rossiia, 1933); Marc Raeff, *Michael Speransky, Statesman of Imperial Russia, 1772–1839* (The Hague: Mouton, 1957); S. D. Urussov, *Memoirs of a Russian Governor* (London: Harper, 1908); Theodore H. Von Laue, *Sergei Witte and the Industrialization of Russia* (New York: Columbia U. P., 1963); S. Iu. Witte, *Tsarstvovanie Nikolaia II* [The Reign of Nicholas II], volumes 2 and 3 of his *Vospominaniia* (Moscow: Izdatel'stvo Sotsial'no-ekonomicheskoi Literatury, 1960). Additional memoirial sources pertaining to the Ministry of Internal Affairs are to be found in the standard bibliographical and bio-bibliographical sources; of particular note, however, is Edward Ellis Smith, *"The Okhrana:" The Russian Department of Police. A Bibliography.* (Stanford: Hoover Institution on War, Revolution and Peace, 1967).

2. Sidney Monas, *The Third Section: Police and Society in Russia under Nicholas I* (Cambridge, Harvard U. P., 1961), is an example of this approach. Others are Leonid Dashkevich, *Nashe ministerstvo vnutrennykh del* [Our Ministry of Internal Affairs] (Berlin: Izdanie Shtura, 1895); *Ministerstvo Vnutrennykh Del: Istoricheskii ocherk* [The Ministry of Internal Affairs: An Historical Sketch] (St. Petersburg: Tipografiia Ministerstva Vnutrennykh Del, 1901), as well as several studies by the close student of nineteenth-century police and censorship, Mikhail Lemke.

3. Included here is the work of legal or constitutional historians: Nikolai M. Korkunov, *Russkoe gosudarstvennoe pravo* [Russian Public Law] (6th ed., 2 vols.; St. Petersburg: Tipografiia Stasiulevicha, 1908–1909); V. E. Romanovskii, *Gosudarstvennoe uchrezhdeniia drevnei i novoi Rossii* [State Administration in Ancient and Modern Russia] (3d ed.; Moscow: I. Knebel', 1911); Genrikh B. Sloizberg, *Dorevoliutsionnyi stroi Rossii* [The Pre-Revolutionary Structure of Russia] (Paris: 1933); G. V. Vernadskii, *Ocherk istorii prava ruskago gosudarstva XVIII–XIX vv.: period imperii* [Outline of the History of the Law of the Russian State in the XVIII–XIXth Centuries: The Period of the Empire] (Prague: Izdatel'stvo Plamia, 1924). A discussion of the resource material available for study of the formal constitutional apparatus is found in Mikhail I. Akhun, "Istochniki dlia izuchenii a istorii gosudarstvennykh uchrezhdenii tsarskoi Rossii (XIX–XX vv.), [Sources for Study of State Administration of Tsarist Russia (XIX-XX Centuries)]," *Arkhivnoe delo*, XLIX (1939), 76–91.

4. Marc Szeftel, "The Form of Government of the Russian Empire Prior to the

Constitutional Reforms of 1905–06." in John Shelton Curtiss (ed.), *Essays in Russian and Soviet History* (New York: Columbia U. P., 1965), p. 117.

5. Robert K. Merton, "Bureaucratic Structure and Personality," *Social Forces*, XVIII (1940), 560–68.

6. Szeftel, *op. cit.*, p. 119. Elsewhere (pp. 117–18) Szeftel states that the principle of delegation of authority to municipalities and zemstvos "counter-balanced the hierarchically organized bureaucratic administration"—not a very useful distinction, since the zemstvos and municipalities were themselves hierarchic and bureaucratic.

7. For example, Henry W. Ehrmann, "French Bureaucracy and Organized Interest," *Administrative Science Quarterly*, V (1961), 535–55; and John Maniha and Charles Perros, "The Reluctant Organization and the Aggressive Environment," *ibid.*, X (1965), 238–57. For additional discussion see Robert L. Peabody and Francis E. Rourke, "Public Bureaucracies," in James G. March (ed.), *Handbook of Organizations* (Chicago: Rand, 1965), pp. 802–37, esp. p. 824; and William R. Dill, "Environment as an Influence on Managerial Autonomy," in James D. Thompson, Peter B. Hammond, Robert W. Hawkes, Buford H. Junker, and Arthur Tuden (eds.), *Comparative Studies in Administration* (Pittsburgh: U. of Pittsburgh P., 1959), pp. 131–61.

8. Marc Raeff, "The Russian Autocracy and Its Officials," *Harvard Slavic Studies*, IV (1967), 77–91.

9. Erik Amburger, *Geschichte der Behördenorganization Russlands von Peter dem Grossen bis 1917* (Leiden: Brill, 1966), and Nikolai Petrovich Eroshkin, *Ocherki istorii gosudarstvennykh uchrezhdenii dorevoliutsionoi Rossii: posobie dlia uchitelia* [Sketch of the History of State Administration in Pre-Revolutionary Russia: A Handbook for Teachers] (Moscow: Gosudarstvennoe Uchebno-pedagogicheskoe Izdatel'stvo, 1960).

10. The most important theoretical sources would include Harold D. Lasswell, Daniel Lerner, and C. Easton Rothwell, *The Comparative Study of Elites: An Introduction and Bibliography* (Stanford: Stanford U. P., 1952); Gaetano Mosca, *The Ruling Class* (New York: McGraw, 1939); Vilfredo Pareto, *The Mind and Society: A Treatise on General Sociology* (New York: Harcourt, 1935), esp. vol. 3.

11. See, for example, John A. Armstrong, *The Soviet Bureaucratic Elite: A Case Study of the Ukrainian Apparatus* (New York: Praeger, 1959), and George K. Schueller, *The Politburo* (Stanford: Stanford U. P., 1951).

12. Amitai Etzioni, *A Comparative Analysis of Complex Organizations: On Power, Involvement and Their Correlates* (New York: Free Press, 1961), p. 79.

13. For an amusing, useful discussion of seminal, synthetic works in the field see James G. March, "Introduction," in March (ed.), *op. cit.* Notable summary treatments are Etzioni, *op. cit.*, and March and Herbert A. Simon, *Organizations* (New York: Wiley, 1958).

14. *Svod zakonov*, Tom I, Chast' 2, Izdanie 1892 (St. Petersburg: Gosudarstvennaia Tipografiia, 1892). *Adres-Kalendar': Obshchaia rospis' nachal'stvuiushchikh i prochikh dolzhnostnykh lits po vsem upravleniiam v Rossiiskoi Imperii na —god. Chast' I: vlasti i mesta tsentral'nago upravleniia i vedomstva ikh* (St. Petersburg: Senatskaia Tipografiia), published annually; see columns 133–62 of the 1904 ed. for material dealing with the Ministry of Internal Affairs.

15. For additional information concerning rank see note 26 below. To facilitate analysis, these records have been coded and stored on IBM-type punched cards.

16. *Spisok vysshikh chinov tsentral'nykh i mestnykh ustanovlenii Ministerstva Vnytrennykh Del. Chast' I* (St. Petersburg: Tipografiia Ministerstva Vnutrennykh Del) *Spisok lits sluzhashchikh po vedomstvu Ministerstva Vnytrennykh Del.* (St. Petersburg), both published annually.

17. Class is taken to mean here the established classes of pre-Revolutionary Russia. Although the classes had a basis in law, the legal definition of the concept and the differentiation of one class from another are not clear. In practice we are able to distinguish the following legal class designation: (1) gentry (hereditary and

personal); (2) clergy; (3) hereditary honored citizens; (4) burghers (five subdivisions); (5) peasantry. See N. I. Lazarevskii, "Sosloviia," *Entsiklopedicheskii Slovar'*; Vol. 30 (St. Petersburg: Brokgaus-Efron, 1900), pp. 911–13.

18. *Smeta raskhodov ministerstva vnutrennykh del na—god* (St. Petersburg), published annually, and *Doklady Biudzhetnoi Komissii po proektu rospisi na — god* (St. Petersburg: Gosudarstvennaia Duma). Whether the latter item was published each year beginning with 1906 is unknown. The author has seen those issued from 1907 to 1914.

19. The sources include *Svod zakonov, op. cit., Ves' Peterburg na 1904 god: Adresnaia i spravochnaia kniga g. S.-Peterburga* (St. Petersburg, 1904), which includes a description of the goals, responsibilities, and authority of ministerial departments, and *The Statesman's Handbook for Russia* (two vols.; St. Petersburg: Chancellory of the Committee of Ministers, 1896).

20. *Statesman's Handbook, op. cit.,* p. 307.

21. See March and Simon, *op. cit.,* pp. 190–91, for a general discussion; Christer Wallroth, "An Analysis of Means-end Structures," *Acta Sociologica,* XI (1968), 110–18, is an example of a study which analyzes an organization in terms of means-ends hierarchies.

22. In fact there are several viable alternatives. Etzioni, *op. cit.,* pp. 20–1, states that those who score "high on at least one of the three dimensions of participation: involvement, subordination, and performance" may be regarded as participants within the organization boundaries. This procedure enables him to regard inmates in prisons and parishioners in churches as participants. On the other hand, March and Simon, *op. cit.,* pp. 89–90, use criteria which would exclude those groups but include others.

23. A. D. Hall and R. E. Fagen, "Definition of a System," *General Systems,* Vol. 1 (1956), quoted in Hans Marius Blegen, "The Systems Approach to the Study of Organizations," *Acta Sociologica,* XI (1968), 13–14.

24. Blegen, *op. cit.,* p. 14.

25. The Table of Ranks, which coordinated civil, military, and court ranks, was issued in 1722, from which time until the Revolution of 1917 it underwent minor revisions. Traditionally, the civil ranks extended through fourteen grades, two of which were inactive. Details are to be found in L. M. Rogovin (compiler), *Ustav o Sluzhbe* [The Manual on Service] (Petrograd: Anisimov, 1915), esp. Part II, pp. 119–215.

26. *Ibid.,* Part I, pp. 54–101.

27. *Ibid.,* Part II, pp. 277–93.

28. *Adres-Kalendar', op. cit.* (1904), columns 133–62.

29. See Etzioni, *op. cit.,* pp. 90–1, 118–19. An attempt to approach such a comparison by analyzing the concepts of power and influence will be found in Dorwin Cartwright, "Influence, Leadership, Control," in March, (ed.), *op. cit.,* pp. 1–47.

30. See March and Simon, *op. cit.,* pp. 121–29.

31. See Mark Abrahamson (ed.), *The Professional in the Organization* (Chicago: Rand, 1967).

32. The *Spisok vysshikh chinov,* which lists only managerial-level civil servants, provides the additional data.

33. Stanley H. Udy, Jr., "The Comparative Analysis of Organizations," in March (ed.), *op. cit.,* pp. 690–705, gives a summary of propositions, together with a discussion of the literature which supports them.

34. Victor H. Vroom and Kenneth R. MacCrimmons, "Toward a Stochastic Model of Managerial Careers," *Administrative Science Quarterly,* XIII (1968), 26–46.

35. "Notes on the Historical Study of Social Mobility," *Comparative Studies in Society and History,* X (1968), 162 ff.

9

Role Conflict and Ambiguity in the Communist Party of the Soviet Union

ERIK P. HOFFMANN

"Role theory" is not really a theory in any strict sense of the term. It is primarily a set of interrelated definitions.[1] The central concept of "role" has been used in the same general way for the past decade. Three basic ideas which appear in most conceptualizations are that "individuals: (1) in *social locations* (2) *behave* (3) with reference to *expectations*."[2] Roles, then, consist of expectations—cognitions con-

The author wishes to thank Alvin Magid, Paul Bernstein, Frederic J. Fleron, Jr., Joseph Hennessy, and Michael Hooper for their valuable comments on an earlier draft of this chapter.

Notes to the selection begin on page 256.

234   ERIK P. HOFFMANN

cerning the appropriate conduct for persons occupying a particular position. Expectations are *communicated* among individuals and groups and generally pertain to the goal orientation, task orientation, or task requirements associated with a specific position.

Few well-confirmed generalizations are contained in this body of theory, and even these are somewhat suspect, due to the shortcomings of the concept of "role." The activities or "potential behaviors" associated with a specific position are often ill-defined and may vary considerably over time. They also vary greatly within and among social systems.[3]

One bothers with role and role-related concepts because they seem to indicate important dimensions of social and organizational behavior. *Role conflict*, for example, is a common phenomenon in most organizations. A person may experience role conflict when the demands of a superior are unreasonable or incompatible, or when some members of his organization expect him to perform in certain ways, while others believe his job entails different rights and responsibilities. An employee may also experience role conflict when demands on his time are so great that he is forced to make difficult decisions concerning priorities, or when he is asked to perform tasks that contradict his religious beliefs, personal values, or expectations from nonprofessional roles— such as father, friend, or club member.[4]

Role ambiguity is another common characteristic of organizational life. A person may experience role ambiguity when he does not know what his supervisor thinks of his work, what criteria are being used to evaluate his performance, and why he is not being treated according to officially accepted rules. A person may also experience role ambiguity when he is uncertain about the scope of his responsibilities, about opportunities for advancement, and about the expectations of others regarding his performance.[5]

Role conflict and ambiguity exist in actual fact ("objective" role conflict and ambiguity) and in the minds of men who fill organizational positions ("experienced" or "perceived" role conflict and ambiguity). These factors may significantly affect administrative behavior and merit careful study as both independent and dependent variables.

Perhaps the most useful paradigm for examining organizational roles is the one Robert Kahn and his associates utilize in a major book on role relationships (see Figure 1).[6] What distinguishes this paradigm is its emphasis on communication. "Role senders" transmit expectations

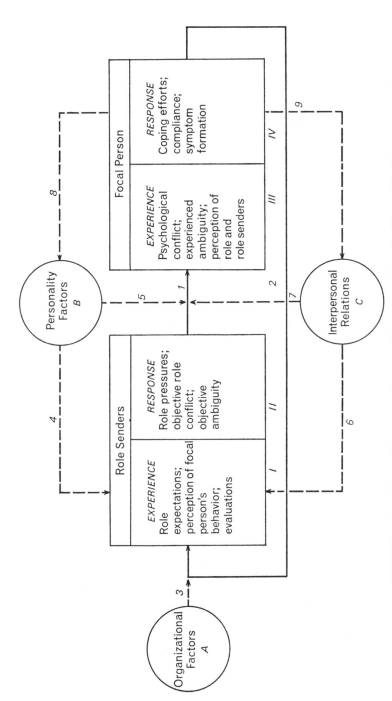

FIGURE 1. A Paradigm of Factors Involved in Adjustment to Role Conflict and Ambiguity.

235

to "focal persons" who respond according to their respective personality characteristics and interpersonal relations. Key variables and clusters of variables are identified, and probable relationships among them are suggested. However, this paradigm is not a theory. It warrants serious study because it provides "a way of thinking about a large set of factors and conditions in complex interaction. The model becomes a theory when the specific variables in each panel are delineated and the causal connections among them are specified."[7]

To say that some organizational, personal, and interpersonal factors affect adjustment to role conflict and ambiguity is not to say very much. But these gross dimensions are a useful starting point for analyzing role behavior in any organization. The paradigm indicates general topics for study; it suggests the kinds of facts that may become data and the ways they may relate to one another.

What contribution can role theory make to the study of Soviet politics? And to what extent can Soviet data help to develop role theory? These are the central questions to be explored. To assist in this endeavor, several descriptive propositions will be examined. They were formulated after careful study of the literature on role theory and on Soviet bureaucracy. Though not derived from a formal model, these propositions seem important and interesting.

1. Role conflict and ambiguity are quite common in the Communist Party of the Soviet Union, especially in the regional Party apparatus.

2. The Brezhnev-Kosygin administration has made significant efforts to alter role expectations and to reduce role conflict and ambiguity.

3. The Brezhnev-Kosygin administration is making considerable use of the central press in these efforts. Party leaders have attempted to redefine and clarify the roles of various types of officials and to prescribe proper behavior in certain ambiguous and tension-filled situations. Moreover, Party leaders are using the press to elicit from lower-level officials information about the origins and consequences of role conflict and ambiguity. They are using the press to stimulate discussion of these problems and to facilitate feedback of accurate information to upper and middle levels of the Party.

4. Increased public discussion about the work of Party functionaries and greater opportunities for interviewing responsible officials make possible the serious study of role relationships in Soviet administration.

I. IDENTIFYING ROLE CONFLICT
AND AMBIGUITY

There is considerable evidence of apparent role conflict and ambiguity in Soviet administration. Here are some recent examples reported in the Party press:

1. The duties of each official on his job are usually clearly defined. But consider the functionary of the Party apparatus, and you will see that his duties are not clear-cut at all. Whereas skills so practiced as to be automatic are a sign of perfection in many fields of work, for the Party functionary automatism is tantamount to formalism, to loss of the sense of the new; it generally leads to mistakes and failures....

The Party apparatus functionary must be an organizer first and foremost. This is axiomatic. But how is he to perform his role of organizer? It is no secret that the functionary of the Party apparatus used to be oriented frequently toward matters which should not have been his concern, that he was required to intervene directly in deciding economic questions. Rural Party functionaries had an especially difficult job. Each time the current agricultural campaign started, they would turn into authorized agents, expediters, investigators, etc. They had to exert pressure and to push all the time. Essentially, dictatorial methods replaced organizational work. What is saddest, the Party apparatus functionary often acted contrary to his own convictions and to common sense. . . .

A. Kuznetsov, assistant head of
the department of Party-organization
work, Odessa Oblast Party
Committee, 1965.[8]

2. At Party meetings of the nonferrous metals processing plant the progress of the enterprise's technical retooling was discussed three times last year, and each time the very same shortcomings were noted. And this is not surprising. The resolutions adopted on the subject . . . failed to pose specific tasks for the shop organizations, the Party groups, and the Communists. The work of the plant Party bureau in essence boiled down to merely formal supervision over the economic activity of the administration. It did not conduct organizational work directly with the men. Many Party members did not know exactly what they were supposed to be doing as Communists. Formally, everything seemed to be democratic. Discussions were held and the administration was criticized. But in essence this discussion was of little benefit.

G. Popov, First Secretary of the
Leningrad City Party Committee,
1966.[9]

3. In reference to work with propagandists, one cannot pass over the fact that many of them are excessively overburdened (*chrezmerno nagruzhaiutsiia*) with all kinds of public duties (*obshchestvennye porucheniia*). [In addition to or in lieu of his regular Party work, a propagandist may also be a member of the people's militia, a frequent participant in a comrades' court, a member of the editorial board of a local radio or newspaper, etc.] Propagandists must be freed from other duties so that they have the time to prepare for classes, study literature, and collect and generalize concrete materials about life in the factory, collective farm, *raion*, *oblast*, etc.

> *Anonymous author of a 28-page*
> *lead article*, V pomoshch'
> politicheskomu samoobrazovaniiu,
> *1958.*[10]

4. The two-year experience of work with the Party agencies organized "according to the production principle" [Khrushchev's bifurcation of the Party apparatus, November 1962 to November 1964] showed the impracticality of the reorganization that was carried out, which often gave rise to confusion in the localities, the jumbling (*smeshenie*) of Party, state, and production functions, and a reduction in the political role of Party organizations. Our Party is a governing Party, and its agencies and organizations are called upon not only to guide production—this is very important—but all social, political, and ideological life. The reorganization violated the territorial-production principle of Party organization worked out during Lenin's time, which had passed the test of many decades of practice and better suited the characteristics and tasks of the Party.

> *V. Stepanov, Editor-in-Chief of*
> Kommunist, *1965.*[11]

5. Many instances of a bureaucratic attitude to the cause are engendered by serious shortcomings in the structure of certain branches of the [state] administrative apparatus, by its unwieldiness and multitude of hierarchical levels. This is often exacerbated by a lack of precise delineation of functions and obligations in administration. All this leads to lack of discipline or even to direct irresponsibility. . . .

It must be admitted that Soviet legislation does not provide with sufficient clarity for specific liability for bureaucratism. However, an inveterate bureaucrat must be severely punished, not only for what he has done, but also for what he *should have* done but did not do, covering himself with formal excuses. . . .

> *V. Zaluzhnyi, position not given,*
> *1965.*[12]

Statements of this kind illustrate many of the methodological problems confronting the student of Soviet politics. Problems of reliability and validity are perhaps the most important. Upon examination these statements reveal a potpourri of information about actual and expected behavior, attitudes and opinions, and purposeful efforts to alter sub-elite behavior. But what is one really measuring with evidence of this kind? How does one gauge the prevalence and distribution of the variables under investigation, and relationships among them? How does one use these "data" to verify hypotheses in some body of theory?

These questions raise fundamental issues concerning the use of written documents in role analysis. Granted, the Soviet central and regional press contain much important information about the expectations, attitudes, and beliefs of various officials and about their political and administrative behavior. But the study of documents "permits generalization only to the universe of document-producers, not to the population at large."[13] Moreover, written sources rarely reveal all or most of the expectations focal persons consider legitimate, to say nothing of expectations considered illegitimate.[14]

How much, then, can the student of role relationships hope to learn from officially regulated communications media? It is relatively easy to discern kinds of behavior leading Party officials consider appropriate in various circumstances. But it is much more difficult to learn whose expectations have the greatest impact on the occupants of middle- and lower-level Party positions, and what these psychological and sociological effects are—especially for cadres who do not contribute to the national, regional, or specialized presses. Moreover, it cannot be assumed that objective role conflict necessarily leads to perceived or experienced role conflict. Administrators and other focal persons are often very skillful in bargaining among competing demands and influences.[15] Objective role conflict may actually *reduce* experienced conflict in some situations. For example, provincial officials may feel that conflicting directives increase their freedom of choice. In short, it is difficult even to describe existing role relationships in Soviet administration. Information yielded from written sources must be considered highly tentative.

With these reservations in mind, let us examine one position in the CPSU in greater detail—that of the staff propaganda worker in, say, an *oblast* or *raion* Party committee. It is known that each year the Communist Party spends millions of rubles on domestic political education, and that "ideological activities" are considered a major aspect of Party work. But what do CPSU leaders expect to receive in return for this investment? What do they expect propagandists to accomplish? How do they determine the success of various programs?

These questions seem to have produced considerable confusion at the highest levels of the Party in the Khrushchev era. Much of this confusion may have stemmed from the fact that Party leaders were unable to agree on what constitutes "effective" ideological work and how to measure it. "Are there scales on which to weigh the fruits of ideological work?" asked Leonid Ilichev rhetorically in 1961, addressing a national conference of propagandists. "There are, comrades," he replied, "and I hope this will not sound like a paradox. They are the same scales on which we weigh our daily needs, our cotton, steel, pig iron, and meat—in short, all the material values created by man."[16]

An editorial in *Politicheskoe samoobrazovanie*, January 1962, expressed the same ideas in the following way:

> A propangadist is a political organizer. He must remember that the results of propaganda can be measured only in practical terms (*prakticheskimi delami*). What good does it do if circles meet regularly at a factory, workers listen to lectures about communism, but the production plan is not fulfilled month after month and the quality of goods is low? We need propaganda that is effective, propaganda that elevates people to heroic deeds, inspires them.[17]

These statements help to document the fact that Soviet leaders desire "effective" propaganda. But what is "effective" propaganda? Shortly after making the statements quoted above, Ilichev went on to declare that the "effectiveness" of Party propaganda cannot be evaluated without also taking into consideration its "ideological (*ideinye*) and moral results."[18] In other words, he stated that the economic achievements of a collective do not necessarily indicate a satisfactory state of affairs in all areas of Party work. An enterprise or *kolkhoz* may fulfill or even exceed its production norms but still tolerate flagrant "violations of labor discipline, money-grubbing, hooliganism, and sectarianism."[19]

Ilichev's speech clearly illustrates the difficulties involved in measuring "effective" propaganda while simultaneously emphasizing the political and production aspects of ideological work. Ilichev asserts that the fruits of Party propaganda must be weighed on the same "scales" as cotton, steel, pig iron, and meat; yet he acknowledges that the influence of propaganda and agitation cannot be measured only by production results. Are the yardsticks or "success indicators" used to measure economic accomplishments always valid when used to evaluate the "effectiveness" of ideological work? Apparently not—and this major problem confronted Party theoreticians and *apparatchiki* throughout the Khrushchev era. Ilichev, for one, sometimes faced up to the dilemma and other times ignored it.

Similar inconsistencies appear in the important Central Committee decree of January 9, 1960. Cadres are told that "the effectiveness of Party propaganda is manifested above all in concrete production results."[20] At the same time the Central Committee criticized unnamed Party, soviet, and economic officials who, "citing satisfactory general indices in the economic work of a province, district, enterprise, or *kolkhoz*, do not pay sufficient attention to rearing the working people in a communist spirit."[21] In effect, Party leaders acknowledged that the fulfillment of production norms does not automatically attest to the high quality of a collective's ideological work.

Yet some leading Party officials—in their public statements, at least—continued to view ideological work as a panacea for social ills. K. T. Mazurov, for example, repeated a familiar but significant assertion in June 1963: "In our country we have no social basis for loafers, hooligans, speculators, and criminals. The fact that . . . such elements exist is to be explained *solely* by the weakness of ideological work in one sector or another, in one or another segment of the population."[22] Similar views were expressed by N. G. Egorychev and A. D. Skaba, also in June 1963:

> Today Party organizations are striving to improve the education of workers in production collectives. However, as a result of (*iz-za*) insufficient attention to educational work at places of residence, one can observe an increased quantity of antisocial behavior. . . . Especially alarming is the increasing amount of drunkenness, and the hooliganism and even serious crimes it causes.[23]
>
> The abundant cases of hooliganism, parasitism, stealing, and production of poor quality goods can be primarily explained by shortcomings in ideological work.[24]

Statements such as these are impeccably orthodox, but evade fundamental issues. Those who maintain that crime and parasitism persist "because" of poor ideological work tell us nothing about the underlying causes of antisocial behavior; they merely describe some of the Party's ultimate goals. To say that good ideological work must achieve certain ends is simply to define "good ideological work"; the real problem lies in devising methods to achieve these goals.

In some respects Khrushchev and Ilichev were great pragmatists—men whose overriding goal was to transform the Communist Party into a more efficient agent of modernization. They ousted many incompetent indoctrination officials, ordered Party committees to recruit numerous technical specialists into part-time propaganda activities, and declared that the fruits of ideological work should be measured primarily by production output. Also, by dividing the Party into industrial and agricultural branches, Khrushchev forced many propaganda officials to participate directly in production work.

On the other hand, Khrushchev and Ilichev sometimes displayed an unrealistic attitude toward ideology and ideological workers. In 1959 and 1960 they initiated a major campaign to expand the scope of domestic propaganda activities, apparently in hopes that the ideas of Marx and Lenin, if clearly explained, could inspire greater economic achievements and significant changes in social relations. Propagandists, disseminators of the creed, were expected to play a major part in this campaign. However, the expectations and demands of central Party officials were simply not realistic. Many mistakenly believed that professional propagandists could assimilate a vast amount of technical information, significantly improve their verbal skills, and quickly acquire the prestige needed to reshape the values and beliefs of their fellow citizens.

Moreover, Khrushchev's expectations of ideological workers appear to have undergone significant changes between 1956 and 1964. Addressing the 20th Party Congress in 1956, he succinctly summarized his views on the role of Party propagandists:

> We must never cease to propagate Marxism-Leninism, to disseminate the theoretical principles of building communism, but we cannot limit ourselves to this. Soviet people expect practical assistance from our propagandists and agitators, too, detailed exposition of advanced experience, sound advice on how to apply this experience at a given enterprise or on a given farm. And to provide this, the propagandists and agitators must not only know theoretical principles but also applied economics. They must speak not in generalities, but with specific knowledge. This is the heart of the matter.[25]

Reporting to the 21st Party Congress, shortly after the unprecedented agricultural achievements of 1958, Khrushchev placed considerably greater emphasis on political propaganda and initiated his well-publicized campaign to create "the new Soviet man." But mounting economic problems in 1961 and 1962 were accompanied by increasing demands for "effective" production propaganda. With the bifurcation of the Party apparatus in November 1962, Khrushchev made it very clear that propagandists were expected to make a tangible contribution to the nation's economic growth. Khrushchev's hopes appear to have given way to frustration and anger. At the June 1963 Central Committee plenum he delivered an insulting speech to a group of Party ideological workers and reportedly remarked: "They do not sow and do not reap, but only munch on (*zhevat'*) bread."[26]

In short, Party leaders' changing, inconsistent, and ambiguous statements about the propaganda profession are an important, though probably unintended, characteristic of official policy throughout the Khrushchev period. Conflicting expectations of Soviet leaders and inconsistencies in official policy pronouncements do not necessarily reflect intellectual sloppiness or inability to cope with complex problems. These discrepancies often reflect conflict and compromise among leading Party officials who do not share the same views on policy alternatives. Some may have advocated substantive role changes, whereas others merely wanted shifts of emphasis within a role.

What effect did all of this have on role relationships among professional propagandists? What did propagandists think their jobs entailed? To what extent did propagandists experience role conflict and ambiguity? These are much more difficult—and for purposes of role analysis, more important—questions to ask.

One can glean relevant information from journals such as *Partiinaia zhizn'*, *Politicheskoe samoobrazovanie*, and *Agitator*, and from the national and regional press. But the constraints on propagandists contributing to these media must constantly be kept in mind. After the bifurcation of the Party apparatus in November 1962, for example, numerous propagandists were probably genuinely confused about their role in the Communist Party. Many were unable to adapt to the new authoritative demands because they lacked the necessary technical and administrative skills to do so. But propaganda cadres were unable or unwilling to express publicly their confusion, frustration, and anxiety. Only after the ouster of Khrushchev did they do so, and then they overdid it to such an extent that it is difficult to determine what they had actually experienced between November 1962 and October 1964. Excessive praise of existing administrative practices and excessive criticism of past practices are common characteristics of public communication in the U.S.S.R., and are an important stumbling block for students of role relationships in Soviet bureaucracy.

Another difficulty for the researcher is to sort out or distinguish among "role expectations," "attitudes," "beliefs," and "opinions" of top-level Soviet officials. Furthermore, it is virtually impossible to learn from written sources which officials various types of ideological workers consider authoritative role senders. Without interview data it is equally difficult to acquire information about objective or experienced role conflict and ambiguity among regional Party cadres.

The researcher's problems become even more complicated when he recalls the top-level confusion concerning ideological work during the Khrushchev administration. Greater disagreements at the highest policy-making level probably increase middle-level autonomy in the CPSU. And greater autonomy probably produces more diverse administrative practices. The more and greater the divisions at the national and republic levels, the greater the probable importance of middle- and lower-level role senders.[27] And the clearer and more uniform the expectations of *obkom* and *raikom* officials, the less likely that propaganda cadres were subjected to or experienced role conflict and ambiguity. Thus the role of the propagandist may have been very clearly defined in some provincial Party organizations, and in others not.

However, the intensity and effects of these phenomena depend not only on organizational factors but on personality factors and interpersonal relations as well. Reexamination of the model presented earlier reveals just how much vital information the student of Soviet role relationships lacks.

In sum, the role of professional propagandists does not seem to have been clearly delineated by top-level officials during the Khrushchev era. This surely enabled provincial Party committees to play a more important part in shaping the expectations and behavior of local propaganda cadres—despite the efforts of *Agitprop*, despite national and regional conferences for indoctrination officials, and despite a series of detailed Central Committee decrees on ideological work.

II. EFFORTS TO REDUCE ROLE CONFLICT AND AMBIGUITY

Under Brezhnev and Kosygin, Party leaders have tried to clarify and redefine many role relationships and to reduce role conflict and ambiguity in several areas. Let us examine, for example, (1) the role of the propagandist and (2) relations among Party organs and the press.[28]

(1) What kinds of economic knowledge was the propaganda cadre expected to acquire? And for what purposes? To the best of my knowledge, the basic issues raised by these questions were not candidly discussed in the Party press until February 1965. Writing in *Partiinaia zhizn'*, A. Klimov and P. Svechnikov affirmed that economic problems could not be resolved merely by increasing the quality and quantity of ideological work. "In order to avoid utopianism and hare-brained schemes," Party bureaus were urged to note that some areas of "communist construction" could be "directly" influenced by ideological activities, and other areas could not.[29]

The terms "direct" and "indirect" influence have taken on a very specific meaning under the Brezhnev-Kosygin administration. Workers with technical skills and "professional training" influence production "directly"; propagandists with verbal skills and the ability to instill "socialist consciousness" (e.g., increase a worker's love of labor, desire for "political self-education," willingness to participate in the activities of his collective) influence the economy "indirectly."

Klimov and Svechnikov acknowledge that some Party workers should be trained to disseminate technical information. But they emphatically reject the idea that propagandists should seek solutions to complex production and supply problems. They also reject the view that economic accomplishments can be directly attributed to the efforts of study circles and political education programs. Acidly observing that some propagandists apparently believe this myth, Klimov and Svechnikov clearly imply that the economic growth of the U.S.S.R. primarily depends on the technical and administrative abilities of leading Party and state officials, not on the exemplary behavior or exhortations of propagandists.

These views contrast sharply with the rhetoric of the Khrushchev era. Party leaders often stated that economic development was "directly dependent" on the political attitudes of Soviet citizens; that there was a "profound interdependence" (*glubokaia vzaimosviaz'*) between production successes and the general level of ideological-educational work; and that the Party's ideological efforts "directly and immediately" affected all political and economic activities. In contrast, Klimov and Svechnikov explicitly stated that "to recognize the enormous signi-

ficance of ideological work clearly does not mean that it can do everything and that all tasks can be entrusted to it."[30]

Brezhnev and Kosygin have certainly not de-emphasized or abandoned domestic political education activities. On the contrary, they are
urging that it be improved, especially through increased use of empirical
sociological research. But they have made it clear that propagandists
are not expected to perform tasks for which they do not have the
necessary skills. Also, they have emphasized that there *is* a place for
propaganda cadres in all Party organizations.

What, then, is the role of the propagandist as it has been redefined
by leading officials in the Brezhnev-Kosygin administration? In public
statements Party leaders have had more to say about what it is *not*
than what it is. However, V. Stepakov, until recently the head of *Agitprop*,
has made several very clear statements on the subject. For example:

> Excellent mastery of theoretical material and skill not only in
> imparting its content to each student but in evoking his profound interest
> in the subject and teaching him how to work independently with politi-
> cal literature—this today is the major requirement of the propagandist.[31]

Moreover, Brezhnev himself has suggested that the main responsibility
of the propagandist is to inculcate "conscious discipline" in all members of society—that is, to increase respect for law and order, to
strengthen labor discipline, and to instill "a sense of thrift"(!) in Soviet
citizens.[32] In short, the propagandist is now expected to be a specialist
in "moral incentives" and political rather than production propaganda.

Most important, propaganda and agitation departments seem to be
held increasingly responsible for the social behavior of people *when
they are off the job*. With workers enjoying more leisure time and Party
leaders showing no signs of abandoning their "commitment" to minister
to the "spiritual needs" of all citizens, the propaganda cadre has a
challenging job indeed. Though this charge is still not defined precisely,
Party officials no longer stress that ideological work should be brought
"nearer to production," and it seems quite possible that fewer future
propagandists will work in fields or factories.

(2) The Brezhnev-Kosygin regime has also attempted to redefine and
clarify the functions of the national and provincial press. These efforts
were consummated in a major Central Committee decree of September
17, 1967.[33]

Most of the problems discussed in this decree have been raised many
times before in the Party press. Individual citizens continuously send

letters to their provincial and local newspapers. Newspaper editors publish readers' suggestions and criticisms, and forward most letters to the appropriate Party, state, or economic organization. Journalists sometimes investigate complaints, publish exposés and constructive criticism, and privately inform Party and state agencies of their findings.

But often these letters and "signals" go unanswered. This is apparently common at all levels of the Party. According to a *Pravda* correspondent, the Party bureau of the Kharkhov *obkom* did not discuss any of the numerous central and republic newspaper articles that had criticized the province's work for over a two-year period.[34] On the other hand, even a Politburo member has made sardonic comments about the "armchair criticism" of professional journalists. K. T. Mazurov remarked in 1965:

> In our press, critical materials on various shortcomings are presented in such a way that they direct the fire of criticism not at the concrete causes of shortcomings, but at Party organs and Party guidance; this does not increase the authority of the Party and undermines our work.[35]

Efforts to clarify official expectations were initiated under Khrushchev. In 1962, for example, the Leningrad *gorkom* noted that local newspapers and radio stations had received "hundreds" of letters from citizens and that the editorial boards of the press and broadcasting media had assumed the role of a "clearinghouse"—evaluating, screening, and relaying feedback information to appropriate Party and government organs. However, political and administrative officials seem to have responded icily to this practice, and many simply ignored these "signals" or replied to public criticism only after several months had elapsed. In short, communication between journalists and Party workers was said to be increasing in only one direction, which, according to the *gorkom* bureau, "lowers the organizational role of the press substantially and confuses public opinion."[36]

In hopes of changing this pattern, the Leningrad *gorkom* urged all *raion* and primary Party organizations "to support" constructive criticism in the press and to cooperate in putting pressure on negligent officials exposed in unsolicited letters. The bureau also ordered leaders of all Party, state, economic, and mass organizations to respond quickly to unpublished letters forwarded privately by the press and to "signals" communicated via newspapers, radio, and television. Officials were instructed to reply promptly to the editorial boards of the broadcasting media *and* to individual letter-writers.

The Central Committee decree of September 17, 1967, acknowledged the existence of many of these problems:

> Many Party, soviet, trade union, and economic bodies do not analyze the substance and nature of letters, do not take effective measures to eliminate the causes and conditions which give rise to the public's complaints and show little concern for the timely examination of valuable proposals.
>
> An inattentive attitude toward requests and complaints gives rise to the dissatisfaction of the letter-writers and compels them to turn to central Party and state bodies on questions that can and should be resolved locally.[37]

The decree also emphasized the "clearinghouse" role of the press and attempted to formalize procedures for processing letters from the public. The Central Committee even demanded that enterprises and other institutions extend and strictly observe established hours for granting personal interviews to the public. In short, Party leaders affirmed the responsibility of the individual to speak his mind, of central and local newspapers to solicit ideas and constructive criticism, and of *oblast*, city, and *raion* Party committees to circulate and utilize this information.

Khrushchev once told a group of journalists: "You are really always at hand to assist the Party. As soon as any decision must be explained and carried out, we turn to you, and you, as the most faithful transmission belt, take the Party's decision and carry it into the very midst of our people."[38] In contrast, the present Party leadership has emphasized that the press is a multidimensional channel of communication. A *Pravda* correspondent recently observed: "The *obkom*'s mail is not only an important means of studying the state of affairs in the localities and public opinion, but it is also a means of influencing this opinion, generalizing advanced experience, and eliminating various shortcomings."[39] The function of the press is to participate actively in all aspects of this work.

III. THE PRESS AS AN INSTRUMENT FOR COMMUNICATING ROLE EXPECTATIONS

Leading Party officials use the press to communicate role expectations. The present leaders, however, have not issued countless directives and proscriptions—that is, they have not rigidly prescribed what actions different types of officials may, must, and must not perform under various conditions.[40] Instead, the Brezhnev-Kosygin administration has encouraged Party, state, and economic officials to discuss publicly the problems they confront in their work. The response has been generally enthusiastic, and as a result Party organizations have accumulated and exchanged considerable information about the sources and consequences of role conflict and ambiguity.[41]

Party leaders have frequently published their views on important questions such as the functions of the Communist Party in Soviet society and role relationships within the CPSU. Here are two recent examples:

> At one time the incorrect opinion held sway that the only task worthy of the attention of Party organizations was economic management and that Party work as such did not exist outside of this. The management of the economy is one of the necessary functions of Party organizations, but it does not exhaust all the aspects of Party work. A one-sided understanding of the role of Party organizations led to the neglect of intra-Party political work. Having adopted such a viewpoint, the Party committees as a rule stood above the economic organizations, supplanted them or became their appendages, relinquishing their own role as political agencies of leadership, and did a poor job of dealing with the economy. This gave rise to turmoil and parallelism.
>
> Even at Party meetings it was mainly economic questions, in the narrow production-technical sense, that were discussed. This is necessary at times, but the main thing—people, their feelings and thoughts and their world outlook—cannot be forgotten. The Party meeting is a school for the ideological and political molding of the Communist as a Party fighter. Here he speaks his views frankly on all the questions of life and receives a correct, Party elucidation of these questions. Public opinion, which plays a major role in our life, is created and channeled through the meetings of Communists. Party organizations are called upon to teach people to see beyond all the petty details of day-to-day specific matters to the broad horizons of communist construction taken as a whole. . . .
>
> *V. Stepanov, Editor-in-Chief of*
> Kommunist, *May 1965.*[42]

> We have many instances in which production specialists have become remarkable Party workers. . . .
> But a knowledge of production is not the only qualification that a

Party worker must have. He is, first and foremost, obliged to be a political functionary, an organizer, a leader, an educator of the masses, able to influence production through people, relying on their experience and initiative and always and in all things taking the long view and understanding the profound connection between day-to-day matters and decisions and the highest Party ideals.

The promotion of specialists to the leadership of Party organizations does not at all mean that attention to Party-political and Party-organization work can be slackened and that the traditions, forms and methods of Party leadership that have been tested and verified by life can be abandoned. Unfortunately, some Party agencies have begun to forget this, regarding a knowledge of production, and sometimes simply the fact of a diploma in specialized education, as the main criterion in the selection of cadres. But, after all, a Party leader with an engineer's diploma is not worth a farthing unless he is at the same time an engineer of human souls, possesses a political approach to the resolution of tasks and is able to work with people. . . .

The Party leader is obliged to be a spiritual mentor; his outlook is broad and he is versed in literature and the arts. And, first of all, he profoundly and thoroughly studies the treasures of Marxism-Leninism and is "on friendly terms" with Party literature. The higher the worker's ideological level and theoretical preparation are, the more fruitful his work will be. His primary duty is constantly to master the theory of Marxism-Leninism, to study intensively the pattern of the development of the socialist economy and to perfect the forms and methods of political work among the masses.

G. Popov, First Secretary of the
Leningrad Gorkom, May 1965.[43]

Stepanov and Popov raise familiar but important issues. Both men are attempting to alter the activities of the Party and role relationships within it. Both are communicating role expectations to various audiences. What these audiences are we can only guess, and how these sent roles affect the behavior of focal persons we do not know. But Stepanov and Popov clearly maintain that CPSU officials need administrative as well as technical skills, and that they should reduce their involvement in day-to-day economic affairs. Administrators should be able to deal with people, and to do so they must be "cultured," respected, and have sound ideological training. Under Khrushchev there was a vast influx of production specialists into Party work, and technical expertise was highly valued. In contrast, Popov hypothesizes that "the higher the worker's ideological level and theoretical preparation are, the more fruitful his work will be."

Many middle- and lower-level officials have publicly stated their views on these issues, especially in forums initiated by the editors of *Pravda* and *Partiinaia zhizn'*. An almost year-long discussion in *Pravda* is a case in point. In February 1967 the First Secretary of the Nizhny Tagil Gorkom noted two "gratifying" trends in Party work in his city:

> First, the desire of Party organizations to get away from so-called "trivia" and examine more profoundly long-range questions of the development of the city's industry. And second, the desire to eliminate the practice of "pressure," to repudiate administrative fiat and firmly to establish the genuinely collective discussion of topical problems and the working out of recommendations based on a profound analysis of the specific situation and the experience of life. . . . [44]

But he went on to observe:

> Everyone knows that politics and economics are inseparable. This proposition is clear in principle. But how is it carried out in practice? In miniature, so to speak, in the conditions of the city and the *raion*, in the primary organization? In general the answer is not difficult: exercise political leadership and decide economic questions in Party fashion. But life sometimes poses tasks over which even an experienced worker racks his brains. Where does the border separating Party work from economic work lie? In fact, does such a border exist?
>
> Take a situation, say, in which we were short of building materials, and it happened that builders were standing idle. The technical and economic council under the city Party committee attempted to come to grips with this problem and make proposals. An especially important one was to unite a number of enterprises producing building materials. It was estimated that this should yield important results. A month went by, then another, but neither the construction trusts nor the Chief Central Urals Construction Administration reacted to this proposal in any way. What was the city Party committee to do?
>
> The bureau of the city Party committee adopted a decision and sent it to the province organizations, enclosing the calculations of the technical and economic council. They listened to us. A specialized Reinforced Concrete Trust was set up, and things were set to rights. Did we act correctly? After all, the subject at hand was a "purely" economic measure; the decision did not even mention the primary Party organizations. Possibly there was another way, but we did not find it. [45]

This is a classic example of perceived role ambiguity. Moreover, the writer states that secretaries of primary Party organizations—many of whom may be uncertain about their own role under the new economic reforms—"can do a great deal to help each [technical specialist] define his role in the implementation of the collective's tasks."[46] Is this the blind helping the blind? Not surprisingly, the *gorkom* secretary concluded on a gloomy note:

> Active searches are under way in Party organizations for new forms and methods of Party influence on the economy and on the spiritual life of collectives, searches for a style of work in the new conditions. But as yet practical experience is still being generalized very poorly and inefficiently. Extremely few recommendations based on the profound study of practice exist. In our view, the Academy of Social Sciences and the Higher Party School, our scientific Party centers, should show more concern about this. Information on the forms and methods of work with the masses should be made more widely available.[47]

In short, the author suggests that central Party and state organs have failed to live up to their obligation to define roles, prescribe proper behavior, and provide adequate technical assistance.

Party leaders have responded by seeking to elicit additional information from provincial officials and by encouraging public discussion of administrative role relationships. For example, the editor of *Pravda* invited readers to respond to the Nizhny Tagil *gorkom* secretary, and "to voice their own opinions" on Party work in the present phase of economic reform.

Published responses expressed a wide variety of views, and many were frank and to the point. For example, an *obkom* first secretary described his expectations of industrial branch department officials. They should "perceive their chief task to lie in profound study of experience, in rendering assistance to Party organizations on the spot, in personnel work in depth, and in checking on performance."[48] In turn, branch department cadres were to play "a considerable role . . . in inculcating in economic managers a sense of personal responsibility for the assigned sector of work."[49] A *gorkom* secretary took this opportunity to complain about factory managers. He said in effect: "Leave us alone, and solve your own problems. Our work is limited to general economic planning and ideological activities."[50] In contrast, a letter from a factory director called for improved communication among local Party organs and heads of enterprises. Noting that *gorkom* and *raikom* directives were often highly critical, he maintained that this reduced the quantity of accurate information primary Party organizations and factories communicate upward.[51] A primary Party organization secretary also discussed this problem, suggesting that conditions would change only when *gorkom* and *raikom* officials offered advice and assistance instead of endless warnings and reprimands:

> Given such an atmosphere, any secretary on his own initiative and at the dictates of his conscience will speak out frankly about all shortcomings and urgent questions. There will scarcely be a need to send commissions to the localities so often, and what is more, their role will change: they will not only be people checking up on things and registering shortcomings, but rather advisers, solicitous disseminators of experience.[52]

In short, the Brezhnev-Kosygin regime has made considerable use of the central press as a forum for discussing role conflict and ambiguity. But Party leaders have been rather reluctant to define precisely the content and parameters of various roles. They have also been reluctant to prescribe proper behavior in situations when officials are forced to choose among conflicting and contradictory expectations. As a result many Party, government, and economic officials probably do not know whether their expectations of others are legitimate in the eyes of Party leaders, whether others' expectations of them are legitimate, and what sanctions, if any, will be brought to bear under various circumstances.

Yet present Party leaders seem to be making a serious attempt to study ambiguous and tension-producing situations. Presumably they are gathering information to anticipate conditions and events, and to categorize classes of situations and patterns of response. To be sure, CPSU leaders may not desire internally consistent directives from central Party and government organs. Consistency may be only a formal goal, and leading officials may actually strive for inconsistency in certain situations. Through action or inaction, intentionally or unintentionally, Party leaders may be unable to avoid communicating inconsistent and ambiguous expectations. But once experience indicates the kinds of situations likely to develop, and assuming Politburo members can agree on basic policy, Central Committee directives will probably have more to say about the specific content of various roles. To the extent that central Party and government officials communicate more specific and uniform expectations, regional Party secretaries will be confronted with an increasing number of "*pre*formed" decisions— decisions that have been made for them in advance of specific situations requiring choice.[53]

IV. THE STUDY OF
ROLE CONFLICT AND AMBIGUITY

Upon reflection, does it really make sense to study role behavior in the Soviet Union without interview data? Perhaps not. Problems of validity and reliability are troublesome under any circumstances. And difficulties are compounded when one seeks to infer expectations and responses solely, or even primarily, from written sources. The Soviet press does contain revealing information about the attitudes and beliefs of various officials.[54] But to describe the behavior associated with different positions and to discover the expectations that actually shape behavior is not an easy undertaking.

Since it is difficult to determine the patterns of behavior that any Soviet "group," let alone Soviet "society," ascribes to a particular position, and since it is even more difficult to determine whose expectations have the greatest influence on occupants of various positions,[55] perhaps the most promising research strategy is to study the ways in which certain *types* of officials perceive or define their own roles. From the statements of focal persons occupying the same position, it is possible to generalize about the role senders they consider important, role pressures they must cope with, and ways in which they apparently respond to different expectations and combinations of expectations.

With the aid of content analysis, one can partially reconstruct from written sources (e.g., *Partiinaia zhizn'* and *Politicheskoe samoobrazovanie*) an official's definition of his professional role. This is not to suggest that articles in the Party press are in any sense "representative" or that they may not have been carefully selected for a specific purpose. But this purpose is not simply to describe desired, rather than existing, conditions. Since one finds significant variations of opinion in *Pravda* and elsewhere, it seems clear that the Brezhnev-Kosygin administration has decided to disseminate widely many kinds of problem-related information. For the student of role relationships this is an encouraging development.

Nevertheless, interview data would significantly advance the study of role relationships in Soviet bureaucracy. Kahn and his associates developed questionnaires that relied heavily on known dimensions of role behavior. Respondents were asked to indicate where along a continuum they would expect the focal person's behavior to lie.[56] To be sure, this method predetermines the kinds of data that will be elicited. But by presenting respondents with a fixed range of alternative answers—that is, by asking whether they think a person or situation has "more or less" of a certain quality, characteristic, or property—the researcher obtains data that can be meaningfully compared. For example, the expectations of role senders and focal persons in similar positions can be classified and contrasted. Data of this kind is particularly useful for cross-national comparison and for testing general propositions of role theory.[57]

Thus, it is important to know certain basic dimensions of role behavior for purposes of verification and comparison. Role theory does not encompass all critical variables that affect administrative behavior, and many relationships among variables have not been tested. But role theory does suggest some of these dimensions and, despite its lack of operationally defined concepts, is of considerable heuristic value. Even the general concept of "role sender" is useful to the student of Soviet politics. Identifying the role senders for certain focal persons or types of focal persons—that is, describing empirically, rather than merely postulating, "role sets"—would be a major scholarly contribution. Measuring the extent to which the press actually defines roles and determines role behavior would also be a significant contribution. Just how important is the press in reinforcing or reducing the influence of *other* role senders? What is the relative importance of central and regional headquarters, face-to-face work groups, local interests, and personality characteristics of middle- and lower-level Party officials in influencing decisions and behavior?[58]

With questions such as these unanswered, it is hardly surprising that students of Soviet politics have contributed virtually nothing to the new and developing field of role theory. To state that certain environmental factors or styles of political leadership affect role conflict and ambiguity is to say very little. What one needs to know is which factors, in what way, and how much.[59] The problem is to learn what factors produce what kinds of role conflict and ambiguity, and, in turn, what effects different types of role conflict and ambiguity have on various personality, organizational, and environmental variables. One must agree that

> Role theory will become a part of scientific theory when it sheds conceptual ambiguity and includes a body of testable and tested generalizations. Until then, to cite the words of Eckstein out of context, it will

"call our attention to the 'real forces' in political [and administrative] processes and to the need for better definitions and operations for dealing with these forces."[60]

Lack of data and theory does not make the study of role relationships any less important. Because role conflict and ambiguity are common characteristics of Soviet bureaucracy, Russian and Western social scientists can make a significant contribution to empirical theory construction in several fields—particularly role theory, organization theory, and comparative administration. The use of "role" and role-related concepts could prove to be a theoretically fruitful way of advancing existing knowledge in these fields. The pitfalls are great, but so is the promise.

Notes

1. For an excellent statement on the differences among "theories," "conceptual frameworks," and "approaches," see Arthur Kalleberg, "The Logic of Comparison: A Methodological Note on the Comparative Study of Political Systems," *World Politics*, XIX (1966), 72. On the nature and functions of theories, see Abraham Kaplan, *The Conduct of Inquiry* (San Francisco: Chandler, 1964); Ernest Nagel, *The Structure of Science* (New York: Harcourt, 1961); Hans Zetterberg, *On Theory and Verification in Sociology* (Totowa: Bedminster, 1965); Quentin Gibson, *The Logic of Social Enquiry* (London: Routledge, 1960); Carl Hempel, *Philosophy of Natural Science* (Englewood Cliffs: Prentice, 1964). On methodological problems of Soviet studies, see Frederic J. Fleron, Jr. (ed.), *Communist Studies and the Social Sciences: Essays on Methodology and Empirical Theory* (Chicago: Rand, 1969).
2. Neal Gross, Ward Mason, and Alexander McEachern, *Explorations in Role Analysis: Studies of the School Superintendency Role* (New York: Wiley, 1958), p. 17. See also Theodore Sarbin and Vernon Allen, "Role Theory," in Gardner Lindzey and Elliot Aronson (eds.), *The Handbook of Social Psychology* (2d ed.; Reading: Addison, 1968), pp. 488–567; Bruce Biddle and Edwin Thomas (eds.), *Role Theory: Concepts and Research* (New York: Wiley, 1966); Roger Brown, *Social Psychology* (New York: Free Press, 1965); Robert Merton, *Social Theory and Social Structure* (New York: Free Press, 1957).
3. See Harry Levinson, a book review of Robert Kahn *et al.*, *Organizational Stress: Studies in Role Conflict and Ambiguity*, in *Administrative Science Quarterly*, X (1965), esp. 127.
4. These definitions are similar to those used in a major study of role relationships in American industrial organizations—Robert Kahn *et al.*, *Organizational Stress: Studies in Role Conflict and Ambiguity* (New York: Wiley, 1964), pp. 11–26 and *passim*.
5. *Ibid.*, pp. 11–26, 380, and *passim*.
6. Adapted from *ibid.*, pp. 26, 30. See also pp. 26–35, 375–98.
7. *Ibid.*, p. 34.
8. A. Kuznetsov, "Rabotnik partiinogo apparata," *Partiinaia zhizn'*, No. 12 (June 1965), 33–4.

9. G. Popov, "Demokratiia i distsiplina," *Pravda*, January 28, 1966, p. 2.

10. "O tvorcheskom izuchenii ekonomicheskoi nauki v seti partiinogo pros-veshcheniia," *V pomoshch' politicheskomu samoobrazovaniiu*, No. 1 (Jan. 1958), 29. p. 2.

12. V. Zaluzhnyi, "Biurokratizmu ne mesto v apparate upravleniia," *Pravda*, Sept. 8, 1965, p. 3.

13. Claire Selltiz *et al.*, *Research Methods in Social Relations* (rev. ed.; New York: Holt, 1959), p. 329.

14. See Alvin Magid, *District Councilorship in an African Society: A Study in Role and Conflict Resolution*, unpublished Ph.D. dissertation, Department of Political Science, Michigan State U., 1965.

15. I am indebted to Professor Roger Kanet for his observations on this point.

16. Leonid Ilichev, Address to the All-Union Conference on Questions of Ideological Work, Dec. 25–28, 1961, *Dvadtsat' vtoroi s'ezd KPSS i voprosy ideologicheskoi raboty* (Moscow: Gospolitizdat, 1962), p. 22.

17. "Nash partiinyi propagandist," *Politicheskoe samoobrazovanie*, No. 1 (Jan. 1962), 6.

18. Ilichev, *op. cit.*, p. 33.

19. *Ibid.*, pp. 33–4.

20. "On the Tasks of Party Propaganda in Present-day Conditions," Central Committee decree of Jan. 9, 1960, *Pravda*, Jan. 10, 1960, pp. 1–2, in Leo Gruliow (ed.), *Current Digest of the Soviet Press*, XII, no. 2 (1960), 19.

21. *Ibid.*, 18.

22. K. T. Mazurov, Speech to the June 1963 Plenary Session of the CPSU Central Committee, in *Plenum Tsentral'nogo komiteta Kommunisticheskoi partii Sovetskogo Soiuza, 18–21 iiunia 1963 goda—stenograficheskii otchet* (Moscow: Politizdat, 1964), p. 203. (Italics mine.)

23. N. G. Egorychev, Speech to the June 1963 Plenary Session of the CPSU Central Committee, in *ibid.*, p. 74.

24. A. D. Skaba, Speech to the June 1963 Plenary Session of the CPSU Central Committee, in *ibid.*, p. 86.

25. Nikita Khrushchev, Report of the CPSU Central Committee to the Twentieth Party Congress, *Pravda*, Feb. 15, 1956, pp. 1–11, in Leo Gruliow (ed.), *Current Soviet Policies*, II (1957), 60.

26. F. S. Goriachev, Address to the March 1965 Plenary Session of the CPSU Central Committee, in *Plenum Tsentral'nogo komiteta Kommunisticheskoi partii Sovetskogo Soiuza, 24–26 marta 1965 goda—stenograficheskii otchet* (Moscow: Politizdat, 1965), p. 83. I am indebted to Dr. Sidney Ploss for bringing this passage to my attention.

27. For similar reasoning in a different context, see Joel Schwartz and William Keech, "Group Influence and the Policy Process in the Soviet Union," *American Political Science Review*, LXII (1968), 847–51.

28. Similar efforts have been repeatedly made in the area of economic reform. See, for example, A. N. Kosygin, "Ob uluchshenii upravleniia promyshlennost'iu, sovershenstvovanii planirovaniia i usilenii ekonomicheskogo stimulirovaniia promyshlennogo proizvodstva," *Pravda*, Sept. 28, 1965, p. 4. See, also, Karl Ryavec, "Soviet Industrial Managers, Their Superiors and the Economic Reform: A Study of an Attempt at Planned Behavioural Change," *Soviet Studies*, XXI (1969), 208–9.

29. A. Klimov and P. Svechnikov, "Zametki o propagande i vospitannii," *Partiinaia zhizn'*, No. 3 (Feb. 1965), 59–60.

30. *Ibid.*, 59.

31. V. Stepakov, "Ovladevat' velikim ucheniem marksizma-leninizma," *Pravda*, Aug. 4, 1965, p. 2.

32. Leonid Brezhnev, Report of the CPSU Central Committee to the Twenty-Third Party Congress, *Pravda*, March 30, 1966, pp. 2–9, in Leo Gruliow (ed.), *Current Digest of the Soviet Press*, XVIII, No. 13 (1966), 4.

33. "Ob uluchshenii raboty po rassmotreniiu pisem i organizatsii priema trudia-shchikhsia," Central Committee decree, *Pravda*, Sept. 17, 1967, p. 2.

34. F. Kozhukhov, "Sovremenno i pravil'no reagirovat' na kritiku," *Pravda*, Aug. 28, 1965, p. 2.

35. K. T. Mazurov, Address to the March 1965 Plenary Session of the CPSU Central Committee, in *Plenum Tsentral'nogo komiteta Kommunisticheskoi partii Sovetskogo Soiuza, 24–26 marta 1965 goda—stenograficheskii otchet*, p. 79.

36. "Vsemerno podderzhivat' printsipal'nuiu kritiku v pechati," *Pravda*, July 16, 1962, p. 2.

37. "Ob uluchshenii raboty po rassmotreniiu pisem i organizatsii priema trudia-shchikhsia," *op. cit.*, p. 2.

38. Quoted in A. Romanov, "Journalism—A Most Important Province of Party and Public Activity," *Partiinaia zhizn'*, May 1961, pp. 17–24, in Leo Gruliow (ed.), *Current Digest of the Soviet Press*, XIII, No. 17 (1961), 10.

39. M. Buzhkevich, "Obrashchaiutsia liudi v obkom," *Pravda*, Aug. 9, 1967, p. 2.

40. These distinctions are discussed in some detail in Herbert Kaufman, *The Forest Ranger: A Study in Administrative Behavior* (Baltimore: Johns Hopkins, 1967), pp. 91–125.

41. See, for example, the many articles in *Partiinaia zhizn'* written in response to A. Kuznetsov, "Rabotnik partiinogo apparata," *Partiinaia zhizn'*, No. 12 (June 1965), 33–7; and the very large number of responses in *Pravda* to G. Kolbin, "Vremia i stil' raboty," *Pravda*, Feb. 6, 1967, pp. 2–3.

42. V. Stepanov, "Vysshie idealy i povsednevnye zaboty partii," *Pravda*, May 17, 1965, p. 2.

43. G. Popov, "Partiinyi rabotnik," *Pravda*, May 30, 1965, p. 2.

44. G. Kolbin, "Vremia i stil' raboty," *op. cit.*, p. 2.

45. *Ibid.*

46. *Ibid.*, p. 3.

47. *Ibid.*

48. A. Yeshtokin, "Otraslevoi otdel obkoma," *Pravda*, Feb. 26, 1967, p. 2.

49. *Ibid.*

50. P. Gundyrin, "Gde nachinaetsia podmena," *Pravda*, June 29, 1967, p. 2.

51. V. Tkach, "O podmene i kontaktakh," *Pravda*, July 3, 1967, p. 2.

52. S. Gushchin, "Otkrovennost' i ob'ektivnost'," *Pravda*, May 23, 1967, p. 4.

53. For a good discussion of "preformed" decisions, see Kaufman, *op. cit.*, esp. p. 91.

54. See Milton Lodge, "Soviet Elite Participatory Attitudes in the Post-Stalin Period," *American Political Science Review*, LXII (1968), 827–39; and Milton Lodge, " 'Groupism' in the Post-Stalin Period," *Midwest Journal of Political Science*, XII (1968), 330–51.

55. See Philip Stewart, *Political Power in the Soviet Union: A Study of Decision-Making in Stalingrad* (Indianapolis: Bobbs, 1968), esp. Chap. 1 and 9.

56. Kahn *et al.*, *op. cit.*, pp. 41–3.

57. See Arthur Kalleberg, "The Logic of Comparison: A Methodological Note on the Comparative Study of Political Systems," *World Politics*, XIX (1966), 69–82; and Hans Zetterberg, *On Theory and Verification in Sociology* (Totowa: Bedminster, 1965).

58. See Kaufman, *op. cit.*, p. 219 and *passim*.

59. Fred Riggs, *Administration in Developing Countries* (Boston: Houghton, 1964), p. 405. For a general discussion of methodological problems in the study of comparative administration, see pp. 399–429.

60. Alvin Magid, "Dimensions of Administrative Role and Conflict Resolution among Local Officials in Northern Nigeria," *Administrative Science Quarterly*, XII (1967), 321–2.

10

Law in the Political Development of a Communist System: Conceptualizing from the Soviet Experience

ROBERT SHARLET

INTRODUCTION

For years, the paramount approach to the study of Soviet political behavior has been distributive analysis.[1] However, because of the necessity of reliable data on the decision-making inputs, this approach has yielded relatively little systematic knowledge about Soviet political behavior.[2] More recently, group theory is being adopted by Soviet

This is a revision of a paper delivered at the 1967 Annual Meeting of the American Political Science Association, Chicago, Sept. 7, 1967.
Notes on this selection begin on page 270.

specialists, but the same problem of a paucity of hard input data persists.[3]

An approach that has not yet received critical attention among Soviet specialists is general systems theory. This is especially adaptable to a developmental perspective on the Soviet political system and can utilize the abundant, available output data. I am referring to the enormous amount of law generated by the Soviet national decision-making process since 1917. These legal data have barely been explored by political scientists; yet, it represents the most reliable and accessible index available of the developmental changes that have produced the Soviet political system.[4] It is time to call attention to these data, the analysis of which from a developmental perspective (within a general systems theory approach) may well yield the kind of systematic generalizations which could be used in the comparative study of political behavior.

PROBLEM

The purpose of this essay is to attempt to conceptualize the functions of law in Soviet political development. Specifically, what systemic functions are performed by law in the development of the Soviet system? More broadly, this inquiry is concerned with how a communist system develops. I shall try to answer the first question and, hopefully, suggest an approach to the second.[5]

TERMS OF REFERENCE

First, it is necessary to define the terms of reference. The term "law" is used in the sense of positive law, or those general rules of external human behavior declared by organs of the state and enforced by its coercive authority. This usage is consistent with Soviet legal theory and practice.[6]

The term "function" is meant to designate the consequences of a component of a system for the system as a whole. As such, this involves no commitment to a distinctive functional approach, and is intended to be analytically distinct from Merton's definition of functions as "those observed consequences which make for the adaptation or adjustment of a given system."[7]

Finally, since "function" is a relational term, the systemic context in which it is used must be discussed. We may begin with the defining characteristics of the concept "Soviet political system." These are:

1. Political resources are highly concentrated and under effective control of the narrow elite stratum of the ruling Communist Party.
2. Access to the policy-making process is severely restricted.
3. Systemic processes are subject to Party control and manipulation.
4. Structures and roles are not highly differentiated (relative to industrialized, noncommunist political systems).
5. Boundaries between the political system and the social system are weak or nonexistent.[8]

In the course of Soviet political development, the Party, through its command of the major political resources and control over the policy-making process, formulates policies that shape the systemic processes in order to facilitate realization of the goals of the system as prescribed by the official ideology of Marxism-Leninism. The systemic processes of the Soviet system are: (1) political socialization, (2) social regulation, (3) political mobilization, and (4) economic development. Overlapping and intermeshing, these processes place at the Party's disposal a matrix of political instruments and social mechanisms for the attainment of its hierarchy of goals.

Political socialization is the process by which the individual is inducted into the political culture, and incessantly indoctrinated through his formative and mature years by a number of agents, including the family, educational system, *komsomol*, mass media, judiciary, comrades' courts, and the individual's *kollektiv* or production team.[9] *Social regulation* is the process by which the norms of interpersonal relations and the relations between citizen and state are defined, sanctioned, and regulated by the legal system, administrative-control apparatus, and officially sponsored peer group controls. Through *political mobilization*, the individual is recruited for participation in the policy execution process through an inclusive network of intermediate groups, including the trade unions, *komsomol*, local soviets, civilian paramilitary organizations, sports societies, professional associations for writers, composers, engineers, and so forth. *Economic development* is the process of constructing and managing the national economy by means of planning agencies, industrial and agricultural administrations, specialized inspectorates, and a number of devices such as wage, price, and taxation structures.

The Party's hierarchy of prescriptive goals includes the preliminary one of preparing the society for heavy industrialization following the Communist political revolution. When this goal was basically achieved by the late 1920s, the first five-year plan was launched and the intermediate goal of carrying out rapid, heavy industrialization assumed the highest priority. The Party's contemporary emphasis on building the "material-technical base of communism" indicates that industrialization is still the predominant systemic goal, although the ultimate normative goal of creating the "new man" by revolutionizing human behavior has been receiving increased attention during the last decade.[10]

To summarize, the concept of "Soviet political development" is used in this essay to describe the process by which the ruling stratum of the Communist Party, in its role as a modernizing elite, constructs, controls, manipulates, and integrates the systemic processes of political socialization, social regulation, political mobilization, and economic development into a system designed to achieve, as rapidly as possible, a hierarchy of prescriptive ideological goals, culminating in the ultimate systemic goal of creating the "new Soviet man" by revolutionizing human behavior.

CONCEPTUALIZATION

Turning now to conceptualization, Soviet law performs the general function of translating Party policy into the more explicit and precise language necessary for policy execution. However, the law also performs a series of more specialized functions by translating into action major Party policies intended to mold and shape the systemic processes of Soviet political development. I shall try to conceptualize these systemic functions of Soviet law, using for examples Soviet economic, criminal, and family law.[11]

FIRST PHASE
OF SOVIET POLITICAL DEVELOPMENT

In the first phase of Soviet political development, the Party prepared the society for a program of heavy industrialization. During the 1920s, Soviet law performed the functions, to borrow J. W. Hurst's typology, of controlling the environment, balancing power, and releasing energy.[12] In controlling the social environment, Soviet economic law, by nationalizing private property in industry, appropriated its economic base for the Party. In balancing between conflicting social forces, Soviet criminal law, by extending legal protection to newly acquired public property, consolidated the economic base. Finally, in releasing the social energy of individuals, Soviet family law, by secularizing marriage and divorce, helped disrupt the prerevolutionary social system, creating the possibility for mobilizing the society.

The scope of nationalization was expressed in a Soviet statute of 1918 entitled:

> On nationalization of the largest enterprises in the mining, metallurgy and metal-working, textile, electro-technical, sawing and timber processing, tobacco, glass, ceramic, leather, cement industries, and so forth; steam plants of local public utilities, and enterprises connected with the railroad industry.[13]

By transferring ownership of the largest part of the industrial economy to the state, this statute fulfilled its declared "purpose of consolidating the dictatorship of the working class and the village poor..."[14] by giving the state "a decisive position in the economy...."[15]

This sweeping nationalization law was deemed essential because "the new State had to make a revolutionary change in the economic structure...."[16] Consequently, nationalization made the Soviet state the largest industrial property owner in the society, necessitating the creation of a bureaucratic apparatus to administer the vast holdings. The emerging administrative apparatus for industry soon became the major component of the economic development process.

Soviet criminal law extended legal protection against theft to the new forms of public property, a term which is used here to include socialist, state, cooperative, and collective farm property. Prerevolutionary criminal law, which had, of course, included penalties for stealing private property, provided less adequate (if any) legal protection for the new forms of public property. The problem as seen by Soviet jurists in 1919 was that "bourgeois law [had been conceived] as a system of norms... of organized force for maintaining the balance of class interests in favor of the ruling class (of the bourgeoisie and landowners)." The task for the proletariat, according to the first Marxist statement of principles for criminal law, was to "work out

rules for curbing its class enemies" by using the state apparatus to
create a new balance of social forces which would be advantageous to
the new ruling class.[17]

Since Marxist jurists regard property as the "key to power,"[18] Soviet
criminal law was first used to correct the imbalance of legal protection
in the prerevolutionary criminal codes. The first Soviet Criminal Code
of 1922 provided adequate legal protection against theft of both public
and private property, with sanctions twice as heavy for stealing public
property.[19] These new legal rules on crimes against property portended
the emergence of a communist legal system within the social regulation
process during the first phase of Soviet political development.

During the formative years of the Soviet system, Soviet economic and
criminal law were used to seize and secure the economic basis for rapid
industrialization. At the same time, it was necessary to disrupt those
prerevolutionary social patterns obstructing the preparation of the
society for an ambitious program of industrialization.

Soviet family law was used to undermine one of the foundations of
the prerevolutionary social system by secularizing and liberalizing
marriage and, especially, divorce within a few months after the Bolshevik Revolution. (Family law, of course, deals with marriage,
divorce, alimony, child support, guardianship, abortion, and so forth,
but it is possible to discuss only one of these aspects in this short
article.) The Soviet divorce statute began with the words "Marriage is
annulled by the petition of both or even one of the parties." This
statement had the effect of revolutionizing social relations throughout
the country, especially in Soviet Central Asia.[20] These changes had a
profound impact on the status of women within the family and in the
society at large. The right to civil divorce, along with other family law
reforms, liberated women for greater social and political participation.
For instance, they became available for recruitment into the growing
labor force by the trade unions as a component of the developing
political mobilization process.

Generally, the availability of easy divorce weakened the family
structure, creating more fluid social relations and contributing, in part,
to the burgeoning juvenile delinquency problem. However, the net
result was positive from the modernizing elite's perspective, since the
family was regarded as a stronghold of the prerevolutionary political
culture, and as a rival competitor of the embryonic communist educational system within the political socialization process.

To summarize, the functions of law in contributing to the preparation for industrialization during the first phase of Soviet political development were: (1) controlling the social environment, exemplified by Soviet law on the ownership and administration of industry; (2) balancing between conflicting social forces, exemplified by Soviet law on crimes against property; and (3) releasing the social energy of the individual, exemplified by Soviet law on divorce.

SECOND PHASE
OF SOVIET POLITICAL DEVELOPMENT

The second phase of Soviet political development began with the launching of the first five-year plan in 1928. Accordingly, law was used to reconstruct the systemic processes, consistent with attaining the new priority goal of rapid industrialization. These changes, for the most part, began to occur in the Soviet Union during the early 1930's.

While Soviet law continued to perform its initial functions, it simultaneously assumed the additional functions, as I would conceptualize them, of transforming the environment, maximizing power, and harnessing energy.[21] In transforming the social environment, Soviet economic law, by implementing long-range, central planning, eliminated the market and institutionalized the Party's command over the direction of the national economy. In maximizing the power of the state, Soviet criminal law, by assigning to public property the highest priority for legal protection, assured control over all social forces in the society. And in harnessing the social energy of the individual, Soviet family law, by strengthening the family structure, consolidated the social foundations of the system. These additional new functions of Soviet law contributed to the rapid industrialization of the Soviet Union.

The systemic implications of centralized, long-range planning were laid out in the preamble of the 1929 Soviet law on the first five-year plan, which

> sets out an expanded program of socialist reconstruction of the national economy, accords with the general course of the Soviet authority toward industrialization of the USSR, socialist reorganization of the village, repression of the capitalist elements in the economic order of the country, and raising the defensive capabilities of the USSR.[22]

The systemic processes had to be substantially reconstructed to accommodate the new heavy demands imposed by the plan as law. The need for incentives, rewards, and strict individual responsibility for decisions led to a reorganization of industrial management and the wage structure in order to facilitate economic development. The demand for a highly skilled labor force and trained executives necessitated restructuring the educational system and changing substantially the emphasis of political socialization. The need for more workers to fill new jobs, and for generally higher labor productivity, led to the incorporation of the trade union system into the state apparatus, enhancing the former's role in political mobilization. Finally, the need for greater labor and contract discipline required strengthening labor law and reviving civil law, thereby enlarging the role of the legal system in social regulation during the second phase of Soviet political development.[23]

The changeover to a planned economy meant the full utilization of existing production facilities and the construction of new productive capacity. Public property became not only the key to power but the key to the future. As a result, Soviet law on crimes against public property was revised, providing for redoubled protection guaranteed by draconian penalties, as stealing public property came to be regarded as something quite different from stealing the property of a private individual.

A Soviet statute of 1932 reflected the increased importance attached to public property, which was described as "sacred and inviolable" as well as the "foundation of the Soviet system." Further, "all persons making attempts on its integrity" were to be regarded as "enemies of the people." Finally, the preamble to the law concluded,

> It is the foremost duty of the Soviet authorities to wage a decisive struggle against misappropriation of property [for which] . . . the courts shall . . . apply the supreme measure of social defense—shooting with confiscation of all property.[24]

Clearly, the Party placed a high value on public property in its various forms, an emphasis that had implications for social regulation and, indirectly, for political socialization during the second phase of Soviet political development.[25]

With the industrial economy growing rapidly and its property foundations protected by formidable legal penalties, Soviet family law was used to strengthen the structure of the family and stabilize the social system. New legislation was enacted on the premise that the family was now expected to strengthen the social order, especially through the "socialist education" of children.

In the Soviet Union, easy divorce was permitted until the 1936 family law, which, "with the aim of combatting light-minded attitudes towards the family," made divorce more expensive and inconvenient.[26] The 1944 family law went even further, making divorce extremely cumbersome, difficult, and expensive to obtain. The new procedures, partially inspired by the Soviet Union's heavy wartime population losses, were clearly designed to discourage divorce. These procedures included a filing fee, several court appearances by both parties, witnesses, an expensive newspaper notice, and, if the divorce was finally granted, a substantial fee that could be charged to either or both parties.[27]

The stricter legal policy on divorce in the Soviet Union led to the more effective integration of the family into the political socialization, social regulation, and political mobilization processes. The reestablished family became a more positive force in political socialization, contributed to the social regulation of juvenile delinquency, and became an agent of political mobilization by strengthening the linkage between state and individual, thereby helping to reduce high labor turnover during a time of great social change.

To summarize, the functions of law in contributing to rapid industrialization during the second phase of Soviet political development are: (1) transforming the social environment, exemplified by planning law; (2) maximizing the Party's power over all social forces, exemplified by the sharply increased sanctions for crimes against public property; and (3) harnessing the social energy of the individual to the goal of industrialization, exemplified by the stricter family law on divorce.

THIRD PHASE
OF SOVIET POLITICAL DEVELOPMENT

It would be premature at this time to attempt to discuss the third phase of Soviet political development. Although it is apparent that during the last ten years the Party leadership as the modernizing elite has begun to devote more attention to the ultimate goal of creating a "new man," the actual results, as well as the rhetoric, seem to indicate that the "new man" is, at best, still only secondary in the contemporary

scale of values. Further development of the Soviet economy still appears
to have primacy.

Soviet law continues to perform its diverse systemic functions in the
ongoing development of the Soviet political system. However, economic, criminal, and family law have been in a state of flux since the
late 1950s. The modernizing elite has been continuously experimenting
in an effort to increase economic efficiency while enlarging the human
dimensions of the system without, however, diminishing the Party's
control in the process, a rather ambitious task. Soviet economic law
has been utilized to decentralize, gradually recentralize, and, recently,
once again partially decentralize the administration of industry, all
during the past decade.[28] The law on crimes against public property
has been reformed, counterreformed, and partially liberalized again
during the same period.[29] And, family law, although it has remained
basically unchanged since 1944, is now the subject of a major discussion
on whether divorce should be liberalized, the family further strengthened, or the status quo simply maintained.[30] Whether or not new
functions of Soviet law will emerge from this period of experimentation
remains to be seen in the future.

THEORETICAL SIGNIFICANCE

By integrating the proposed conceptualization of the functions of
law into the conceptual framework for Soviet political development
outlined in this article, it is possible to formulate a number of regulative
and predictive hypotheses relevant to the political development of
communist systems.[31]

Regulative hypotheses, which can be used to orient research on
certain aspects of the gross political behavior of communist modernizing elites, are:

1. A modernizing elite uses law for converting Communist Party policy
   into the more precise, operational directives necessary for policy
   implementation and execution.
2. A modernizing elite uses the individual branches of law as one of its
   principal instruments for constructing, controlling, integrating, and
   manipulating the systemic processes in order to facilitate the achievement of systemic goals:[32]
   A. Economic law for controlling and transforming the social envir-

onment by converting Communist Party policy on the ownership and administration of property for implementation and
execution within the economic development process.

B. Criminal law for balancing between conflicting social forces
and, subsequently, maximizing the power of the state over all
social forces, by converting Communist Party policy on the protection of property for implementation and execution within the
social regulation process.

C. Family law for releasing and harnessing the social energy of the
individual, especially the woman, by converting Communist
Party policy on divorce for implementation and execution within
the political socialization process.

a. Secularization and liberalization of divorce increases the
woman's availability for recruitment by intermediate groups
such as the *komsomol* and the trade union system within the
political mobilization process.

More specifically, the integrated conceptual framework of the functions of law in the political development of a communist system can
generate narrow-gauge predictive hypotheses which can be operationalized and verified with the abundant, available legal data of the European
communist systems.[33]

These *predictive hypotheses* are:

1. If a Communist Party's systemic goal is to prepare a society for
heavy industrialization, then the modernizing elite will use:

A. Nationalization law for obtaining control of existing industrial
property.

B. The law on crimes against property for providing legal protection
for the expropriated property.

a. The penalties for the crimes against public property tend to be
heavier than the penalties for the same crimes committed against
private property.

C. The law on divorce to secularize and liberalize the rules for the
legal dissolution of marriage.

2. If a Communist Party's systemic goal is to carry out rapid, heavy
industrialization, then the modernizing elite will use:

A. Planning law for centrally directing and administering the
development of the national economy.

B. The law on crimes against property to make crimes against public
property under certain aggravating circumstances punishable by
death.

C. The law on divorce to make the process of legally dissolving marriage much more complicated and difficult.

The preceding regulative and predictive hypotheses, which by no means exhaust the possibilities, should be sufficient to demonstrate that the proposed conceptualization of the functions of law has significance for the broader theoretical task of explaining how a communist political system develops.

Notes

1. The distributive approach to the analysis of Soviet political behavior was originally inspired by Lasswell's work and, accordingly, concentrated on the Communist Party elite. For representative studies using this approach see George K. Schueller, *The Politburo* (Stanford: Stanford U. P., 1951), recently reprinted in Harold D. Lasswell and Daniel Lerner (eds.), *World Revolutionary Elites* (Cambridge: M.I.T. Press, 1966); Nathan Leites, *A Study of Bolshevism* (New York: Free Press, 1953); Robert Conquest, *Power and Policy in the U.S.S.R.* (New York: St. Martin's, 1962); Sidney Ploss, *Conflict and Decision-Making in Soviet Russia* (Princeton: Princeton U. P., 1965); and Carl A. Linden, *Khrushchev and the Soviet Leadership, 1957–1964* (Baltimore: Johns Hopkins, 1966).

2. In addition to the prevailing paucity of reliable data, the distributive approach to political analysis has failed to produce empirical generalizations about Soviet political behavior because Soviet specialists have generally neglected to equip themselves with the methodology of behavioral social science. A fundamental problem has been the absence of a consensus on even such basic concepts as "totalitarianism." See Frederic J. Fleron, Jr., "Soviet Area Studies and the Social Sciences: Some Methodological Problems in Communist Studies," *Soviet Studies*, XIX (1968), 326–27. Another basic problem has been the mechanical reception by Soviet specialists of concepts with empirical referents in American political behavior. See Robert Sharlet, "Concept Formation in Political Science and Communist Studies," *Canadian Slavic Studies*, I (1967), 640–49; and Sharlet, "Systematic Political Science and Communist Systems," *Slavic Review*, XXVI (1967), 22–6.

3. For two interesting examples of the group theory approach to Soviet political behavior, see Milton A. Lodge, "Soviet Elite Participatory Attitudes in the Post-Stalin Period," and Joel J. Schwartz and William R. Keech, "Group Influence on the Policy Process in the Soviet Union." Both articles appeared in *American Political Science Review*, LXII (1968), 827–39 and 840–51, respectively. For a critical analysis of certain methodological and substantive problems of the group theory approach to Soviet political behavior, see Sharlet, "The Soviet Union As a Developing Country," *Journal of Developing Areas*, II (1968), 270–6.

4. However, two legal scientists have made outstanding contributions to our understanding of the relationship between Soviet law and politics. See John N. Hazard, *Law and Social Change in the USSR* (London: Steven, 1953); and Harold J. Berman, *Justice in the USSR*, Vintage Books (rev. ed. enlarged; New York: Random, 1963). For a legal *and* political analysis of Soviet law and politics, see Zigurds L. Zile, Robert Sharlet, and Jean F. Love, *Legal Aspects of Verification in the USSR* (Washington: U.S. Arms Control and Disarmament Agency, 1967), Part I, Ch. 1.

5. The approach to the broader question, partially outlined under "Terms of Reference," is part of a conceptual framework which is more fully elaborated and developed in the author's study *Soviet Modernization* (New York: Pegasus, forthcoming).

6. The only significant exception in Soviet legal theory was E. B. Pashukanis's sociological definition of law, which was current from 1924 through 1930, when Pashukanis made his first "self-criticism" [*samokritika*]. See his *The General Theory of Law and Marxism* and "The Situation on the Legal Theory Front," in *Soviet Legal Philosophy*, translated by Hugh W. Babb and edited by John N. Hazard (Cambridge: Harvard U. P., 1951). For the positivist definition of law that has generally prevailed in Soviet jurisprudence since the 1930s, see A. Ia. Vyshinskii, "The Fundamental Tasks of the Science of Soviet Socialist Law," *ibid*, pp. 336–7. The status of "Soviet" legal positivism in the current period is discussed in Sharlet, "A Survey of Soviet Legal Theory since World War Two, 1947–1966," *Canadian Slavic Studies*, II, 3 (1968), 43–7 (*Bibliography*). For the purposes of this essay, I shall use for data only major Soviet legislation, "because the form and methods of legislation exemplify more boldly than most judicial opinions the law's contribution ... to general social structure," James Willard Hurst, *Law and Social Process in United States History* (Ann Arbor: U. of Michigan Law School, 1960), p. 169.

7. Robert K. Merton, *Social Theory and Social Structure* (rev. and enlarged ed.; New York: Free Press, 1957), p. 50. The distinction between the usage of "function" in this article and Merton's is made by Ernest Nagel, *The Structure of Science* (New York: Harcourt, 1961), pp. 525–6. The present usage of the concept is consistent with "eclectic functionalism," which "involves no commitment to a distinctive functional approach, and the theoretical implications of including the concept of 'function' among the categories of analysis are quite limited." William Flanigan and Edwin Fogelman, "Functionalism in Political Science," in Don Martindale (ed.), *Functionalism in the Social Sciences* (Philadelphia: American Academy of Political and Social Science, 1965), p. 112.

8. For "function" as a relational concept, see Fred M. Frohock, *The Nature of Political Inquiry* (Homewood: Dorsey, 1967), p. 63. For the author's elaboration and analysis of the five defining characteristics of the concept of "Soviet political system," see Sharlet, "Concept Formation in Political Science and Communist Studies," *Canadian Slavic Studies*, I (1967), 644–9; and the same author's "The Soviet Union as a Developing Country," *Journal of Developing Areas*, II (1968), 270–6. In point No. 1, the "narrow elite stratum of the ruling Communist Party," which is conceptualized *infra* as the "modernizing elite," is essentially a locative concept based on positional criteria. On the problems of denoting the concept "elite" in the Soviet system in behavior-functional terms, see Frederic J. Fleron, Jr., "Note on the Explication of the Concept 'Elite' in the Study of Soviet Politics," *Canadian Slavic Studies*, II (1968), 111–15.

9. The general definition of political socialization as induction into the political culture is from Gabriel A. Almond and G. Bingham Powell, Jr., *Comparative Politics: A Developmental Approach* (Boston: Little, 1966), p. 64. For a conceptualization of "mass political socialization" in Soviet political development, see Sharlet "Political Socialization and Soviet Political Development," in Roger E. Kanet and Ivan Volgyes (eds.), *Essays on Soviet Politics* (Lawrence: U.P. of Kansas, forthcoming).

10. The goal of creating the "new man," along with the goal of building the "material-technical base of communism," has a prominent place in the *Program of the Communist Party of the Soviet Union* of 1961. As used in this context, the concept of the "new man" tends to mean "essentially a blend of Bolshevik militancy and Victorian respectability, a disciplined, clean-living, neat, cooperative, patriotic citizen thinking as much of the public good as his own advancement and an intransigent Leninist." Theodore H. Von Laue, *Why Lenin? Why Stalin?: A Reappraisal of the Russian Revolution, 1900–1930*, Preceptor Books (Philadelphia: Lippincott,

1964), p. 218. For the development of the operational concept of the "new man," see Raymond A. Bauer, *The New Man in Soviet Psychology* (Cambridge: Harvard U. P., 1952).

11. The term "economic law" is used in this article to designate those Soviet legal rules, including the five-year plans, which are concerned with the administration of the national economy. This stipulated meaning should not be confused with the highly controversial concept of economic law advocated by A. G. Goikhbarg and P. I. Stuchka in the 1920s, by E. B. Pashukanis and L. Ia. Gintsburg in the 1930s, and revived by V. S. Tadevosian and other Soviet jurists in the late 1950s. See S. N. Bratus', *Predmet i sistema sovetskogo grazhdanskogo prava* [The Subject Matter and System of Soviet Civil Law] (Moscow: Gosiurizdat, 1963), Chap. 9. On the relationship between Soviet politics and law, an authoritative Soviet jurist wrote that "politics" is the "driving belt which sets in motion the state and law and creates their interaction and interdependence." I. P. Trainin, "The Relationship Between State and Law," in *Soviet Legal Philosophy* (Cambridge: Harvard U. P., 1951), translated by Hugh W. Babb, p. 456. On Soviet law as an instrument of social change, an American jurist has written that "Soviet legal theories are predicated upon the idea of progress and are identified with the Soviet policy of transforming, according to a predetermined plan, the economic and social order into that of an industrial civilization." Kazimierz Grzybowski, *Soviet Legal Institutions* (Ann Arbor: U. of Michigan P., 1962), p. 23.

12. See James Willard Hurst, *Law and the Conditions of Freedom in the Nineteenth Century United States* (Evanston: Northwestern U. P., 1956) and Hurst, *op. cit.*; I have followed Hurst's usage of the "release of energy" concept, and have adapted his concepts of "control of the environment" and "balance of power" for the purpose of describing the functions of Soviet law. In contrast, Marxist conceptions of the functions of law tend to be either too specific for use in developmental analysis or too broad to be operationalized. For an example of the former, see V. G. Smirnov, *Funktsii sovetskogo ugolovnogo prava* [The Functions of Soviet Criminal Law] (Leningrad: Izd. LGU, 1965). For an example of the latter, see P. I. Stuchka, *Revoliutsionnaia rol' prava i gosudarstva* (1921) [The Revolutionary Role of Law and State] translated in *Soviet Legal Philosophy, op. cit.* Stuchka's conception basically means that laws "are intended to help construct and consolidate the socialist organization of society." Grzegorz Leopold Seidler, "Marxist Legal Thought in Poland," edited and with an intro. by Robert Sharlet, *Slavic Review*, XXVI (1967), 384. Finally, Berman's concept of "parental law" is useful for a general understanding of Soviet law and an operational analysis of criminal law, but it was not intended for an analysis of the modernizing elite's various uses of law to achieve changing goals in the different phases of Soviet political development. See Berman, *op. cit.*, esp. Chaps. 10 and 16.

13. Ministerstvo Iustitsii RSFSR, *Khronologicheskoe sobranie zakonov, ukazov prezidiuma verkhovnogo soveta i postanovlenii pravitel'stva RSFSR* [Chronological Collection of the Laws and Edicts of the Presidium of the Supreme Soviet and the Decrees of the Government of the RSFSR], Vol. 1: 1917–1928 (Moscow: Gosiurizdat 1959), No. 10, pp. 16–23. The terms "law" or "statute," "edict," and "decree" each have a specific meaning in Soviet jurisprudence, but for purposes of clarity in this brief article the terms "law" or "statute" will be used to designate all three types of legislation.

14. Zigurds L. Zile (ed. and trans.), *Ideas and Forces in Soviet Legal History: Statutes, Decisions and Other Materials on the Development and Processes of Soviet Law* (Madison: College Printing & Typing Co., 1967), p. 17. See Zile (pp. 17–18) for a partial translation of the nationalization statute cited in the preceding note.

15. N. N. Razumovich, *Organizatsionno-pravovye formy sotsialisticheskogo obobshchestvleniia promyshlennosti v SSSR 1917–1920 g.g.* [Organizational and Legal Forms of Socialist Socialized Industry in the USSR, 1917–1920] (Moscow, Izd. AN SSSR, 1959), p. 70.

16. Dimitar Pop-Georgiev, "Foreword," in *Collection of Yugoslav Laws*, Vol. 3: *Nationalization and Expropriation*, edited by Borislav T. Blagojevic (Belgrade: Institute of Comparative Law, 1962), p. 3. Similar statements abound in Soviet literature on nationalization. For a comparison with Communist East European legislation, see A. N. Iodkovskii, *Natsionalizatsiia v Evropeiskikh stranakh narodnoi demokratii: Sravnitel'nyi obzor zakonodatel'stva* [Nationalization in the European People's Democracies: A Comparative Survey of Legislation] (Moscow: AN SSSR, 1956).

17. "Rukovodiashchie nachala po ugolovnomu pravu RSFSR" (1919) [Guiding Principles of the Criminal Law of the RSFSR] in P. I. Stuchka, *Izbrannye proizvedeniia po marksistsko-leninskoi teorii prava* [Selected Works on the Marxist-Leninist Theory of Law], compiled by G. Ia. Kliava (Riga: Latviiskoe gos. izd., 1964), pp. 701–2.

18. This is Hazard's phrase. Hazard, *op. cit.*, p. 1.

19. See Chapter VI, Article 180, of the 1922 Criminal Code of the RSFSR in James H. Meisel and Edward S. Kozera (eds.), *Materials for the Study of the Soviet System: State and Party Constitutions: Laws, Decrees, Decisions and Official Statements of the Leaders in Translation* (2d rev. and enlarged ed.; Ann Arbor: Wahr, 1953), pp. 144–5. For example, "simple theft" from a private person was punishable by imprisonment of up to six months while "simple theft" from the state was punishable by imprisonment of up to one year. The respective penalties for "aggravated theft" were imprisonment of up to two years and imprisonment for not less than three years. For a comparison with Communist East European criminal legislation on crimes against property, see N. S. Alekseev, *Osnovy ugolovnogo prava Germanskoi Demokraticheskoi Respubliki* [Fundamentals of Criminal Law of the German Democratic Republic] (Leningrad: Izd. LGU, 1960); M. A. Gel'fer, *Ugolovnoe pravo Chekhoslovatskoi Narodnoi Respubliki* [Criminal Law of the Czechoslovak People's Republic] (Moscow: Gosiurizdat, 1955); M. A. Gel'fer, *Osnovnye cherty ugolovnogo prava Federativnoi Narodnoi Respubliki Iugoslavii* [Basic Features of the Criminal Law of the Federal People's Republic of Yugoslavia] (Moscow: Gosiurizdat, 1956); S. G. Kelina, *Osnovnye voprosy ugolovnogo prava Vengerskoi Narodnoi Respubliki* [Basic Questions of the Criminal Law of the Hungarian People's Republic] (Moscow: Gosiurizdat, 1960); M. A. Krasnopolina, *Osnovnye voprosy ugolovnogo prava Narodnoi Respubliki Bolgarii* [Basic Questions of the Criminal Law of the People's Republic of Bulgaria] (Moscow: Gosiurizdat, 1960); V. A. Stanik, *Ugolovnoe pravo Polskoi Narodnoi Respubliki* [Criminal Law of the Polish People's Republic] (Moscow: Gosiurizdat, 1955).

20. See "Dekret o rastorzhenii braka" (1917) [Decree on the Dissolution of Marriage] translated in Meisel and Kozera (eds.), *op. cit.*, pp. 41–3. On the impact of divorce in Soviet Central Asia, see Gregory J. Massell, "Law as an Instrument of Revolutionary Change in a Traditional Milieu: The Case of Soviet Central Asia" (paper presented at the 1967 Annual Meeting of the American Political Science Association, Chicago, September 8, 1967). For a comparison with Communist East European family legislation on divorce, see G. M. Sverdlov, *Semeinoe pravo Evropeiskikh stran narodnoi demokratii* [Family Law of the European People's Democracies] (Moscow: Gosiurizdat, 1961), Chap. 4.

21. The relationship between the different sets of functions used by the modernizing elite in the first and second phases of Soviet political development can best be understood by reference to Hurst's "leverage" and "support" functions of law which "refer to use of law's compulsion or of means assembled by law to give a push toward action, either in new directions [e.g., leverage] or along already established lines of motion [e.g., support]." In this sense, the first phase functions of Soviet law performed "support" during the second phase of Soviet political development by sustaining "values already formed" while the second phase functions performed "leverage" by giving impetus to the creation of new values. Hurst, *Law and Social Process* pp. 168 and 182. This is based on the assumption that a single law can perform several functions simultaneously. See Hurst, *ibid.*, p. 174, and David Ries-

man, "Toward an Anthropological Science of Law and the Legal Profession," *American Journal of Sociology*, LVII (1951), 124.

22. Quoted from "Decree of the Fifth Congress of Soviets of the USSR, May 28, 1929, 'On the Five-Year Plan of National Economic Development,' " in Zile, *op. cit.*, p. 147.

23. Hurst uses the concept of the "multiplier" effect of law to describe the systemic impact of a single law (e.g., the "plan" as law). See Hurst, *op. cit.*, p. 172. For example, on the reorganization of industrial management and the wage structure, see Stalin's speech "New Conditions—New Tasks in Economic Development, June 23, 1931," in Stalin, *Works*, Vol. 13 (Moscow: Foreign Languages Publishing House, 1955), pp. 53–82. For legislation on the restructuring of the educational system and the reorientation of political socialization emphasis from 1932 to 1934, see *Sbornik dokumentov i materialov po istorii SSSR: Sovetskogo perioda* [A Collection of Documents and Materials on the History of the USSR: The Soviet Period] (Moscow: Izd. Mosk. univ., 1966), pp. 333–4. For the legislation on the incorporation of the trade union system into the state apparatus and the strengthening of labor discipline, see Documents Nos. 88, 89, and 92 in Meisel and Kozera (eds.), *op. cit.*, pp. 190–2 and 195–6. For the principal legislation on the strengthening of contract discipline, see "Decree of the Central Executive Committee and the Council of People's Commissars of the USSR, February 18, 1931, 'On Liability for Nonperformance of Contracted Work and Deliveries within the Socialist Sector of the National Economy,' " in Zile, *op. cit.*, p. 178.

24. Quoted from "Decree of the Central Executive Committee and the Council of People's Commissars of the USSR, August 7, 1932, 'On the Protection of the Property of State Enterprises, Collective Farms and Cooperatives and on the Strengthening of Public (Socialist) Property,' " in Zile, *op. cit.*, p. 228.

25. On the "educational role" of Soviet law, see Berman, *op. cit.*, pp. 282–4. For cases of law as a political socialization agent, see George Feifer, *Justice in Moscow* (New York: Simon, 1964) and Sharlet, "The Trial of Ushakova," Milwaukee *Journal*, Feb. 8, 1965, p. 12, cols. 1–8.

26. Quoted from the "Decree of the Central Executive Committee and the Council of People's Commissars of the USSR, June 27, 1936, 'On the Prohibition of Abortions, the Improvement of Material Aid to Women in Childbirth, the Establishment of State Assistance to Parents of Large Families, and the Extension of the Network of Lying-in Homes, Creches and Kindergartens; the Tightening-up of Criminal Punishment for the Non-payment of Alimony; and on Certain Modifications in Divorce Legislation,' " in Rudolf Schlesinger (ed.), *Changing Attitudes in Soviet Russia*, Vol. 1: *The Family in the USSR: Documents and Readings* (London: Routledge, 1949), p. 278.

27. See the "Decree of the Presidium of the Supreme Soviet of the USSR, July 8, 1944, 'On Improving State Aid to Pregnant Women, Mothers of Large Families and Unwed Mothers; on Strengthening Measures for the Protection of Motherhood and Children; on the Establishment of the Title "Heroine Mother"; and on Establishment of the Order of the Medal of the Glorious Mother and the Order of the Medal of Motherhood,' " in Schlesinger, *op. cit.*, pp. 374–400.

28. On the initial economic decentralization of 1957, see the partial translation of the "Law on Further Improvement of the Organization of Industrial and Construction Administration, May 10, 1957" in John N. Hazard and Isaac Shapiro (eds.), *The Soviet Legal System: Post-Stalin Documentation and Historical Commentary*. Part 2: *Administering Soviet Socialism* (Dobbs Ferry: Oceana, 1962), pp. 56–60. No single statute can be cited for the gradual economic recentralization which took place from approximately 1958 to 1964. On the most recent decentralization see "O sotsialisticheskom gosudarstvennom proizvodstvennom predpriiatii, October 4, 1965" [On the Socialist State Production Enterprise, October 4, 1965] in *Spravochnik partiinogo rabotnika: Vypusk shestoi* [Handbook for the Party Worker: Vol. 6] (Moscow: Izd. Politichskoi literatury, 1966), pp. 200–18.

29. On the liberalization of the law on crimes against property, see the 1960 "Criminal Code of the RSFSR" as amended to July 3, 1965, Articles 89, 90, 93, and 96, translated in Harold J. Berman (ed.), *Soviet Criminal Law and Procedure: The RSFSR Codes* (Cambridge: Harvard U. P., 1966), pp. 186–90. For the assignment of certain cases involving crimes against property to comrades' courts, see the 1960 "Code of Criminal Procedure of the RSFSR," as amended to July 3, 1965, Articles 7, 10, 108, 113, 209, 234, and 321; and the 1960 "Criminal Code of the RSFSR," Articles 51 and 62 in Berman, *ibid.*, pp. 254, 256, 292, 294–5, 337–8, and 380; pp. 168–9 and 176–7. For a translation and annotation of the 1961 RSFSR "Statute on Comrades' Courts," see Harold J. Berman and James W. Spindler, "Soviet Comrades' Courts," *Washington Law Review*, XXXVIII (1963), 857–95. On the counter-reform of the law on crimes against property, see the "Edict of the Presidium of the Supreme Soviet of the USSR, May 5, 1961, 'On Intensifying the Struggle Against Especially Dangerous Crimes,' " partially translated in Zile, *op. cit.*, p. 359. This edict amended the 1960 "Criminal Code of the RSFSR," Article 93–1 by providing for death by shooting and confiscation of property as an alternate penalty for theft of public property on a large scale. See Berman, *op. cit.*, p. 188. For partial re-liberalization of the law on crimes against property, see the 1965 amendment to the 1960 "Criminal Code of the RSFSR," Article 93–2, which permits the substitution of a fine for the jail sentence for first offenders convicted of stealing public property in a small amount. Berman, *ibid.*, p. 189. For another aspect of this partial re-liberalization, see the 1963 amendment to the 1961 RSFSR "Statute on Comrade's Courts," which broadened the jurisdiction of comrades' courts over certain cases involving crimes against property. Berman and Spindler, *op. cit.*, 864; and Sharlet, "Russia's Courts of Public Pressure," *The Nation*, Jan. 18, 1965, pp. 55–7 and 68.

30. For the basic Soviet text on family law, see G. M. Sverdlov, *Sovetskoe semeinoe pravo* [Soviet Family Law] (Moscow: Gosiurizdat, 1958), esp. Chap. 9 on the dissolution of marriage. Although the 1944 family law basically remains in force, a 1965 amendment "on some changes in the procedure for hearing divorce cases in court," simplified the procedure for obtaining divorce. New fundamental principles of family legislation are now in the process of being drafted. For an analysis of the discussion about family law reform, see Peter H. Juviler, "Family Reforms on the Road to Communism," in Peter H. Juviler and Henry W. Morton (eds.), *Soviet Policy-Making: Studies of Communism in Transition* (New York: Praeger, 1967), Chap. 2. For a survey in translation of the various positions taken in the discussion, see Hazard and Shapiro (eds.), *op. cit.*, Part 3: *Legal Relations between Soviet Citizens*, Chap. 21.

31. On the distinction between "regulative" and "predictive" hypotheses, Lasswell and Kaplan have written that regulative hypotheses "are intended to serve the functions of directing the search for significant data, not of predicting what the data will be found to disclose." Harold D. Lasswell and Abraham Kaplan, *Power and Society: A Framework for Political Inquiry* (New Haven: Yale U. P., 1950), p. xxiii.

32. In addition to law, other instruments used by the modernizing elite for constructing, controlling, integrating, or manipulating the systemic processes include unconverted party resolutions and directives, joint Party-state resolutions and decrees, the party secretariat, and the Party's power [*nomenklatura*] over the appointment of key personnel to the strategic positions in the four systemic processes.

33. In addition to the legal data available in East European languages, a considerable amount of material, including translations of Communist East European law codes, is available in Russian. For a selection of some of the Russian materials relevant to this article, see notes 16, 19, and 20. There is also a growing number of studies on, and translations of, Communist East European law in English. Hazard's *Communists and Their Law* (Chicago: Chicago U.P., 1969) is a major contribution to this body of literature.

PART 4

The Soviet Union in World Affairs

Besides questions of policy-making and implementation on the domestic level, there are also those of a state's involvement in the international political system. In these last chapters the authors provide analyses of specific aspects of Soviet relations with the outside world. Charles Gati presents a detailed analysis of press coverage according to geographical region as one indicator of Soviet interest in an area and of the relative importance of the area to Soviet decision-makers. He shows that over time (1954–1968) the relative interest of the Soviet elite, as measured by amount of press coverage in *Pravda* and *Izvestia*, has remained stable. The only significant change in rankings has occurred with regard to Africa, which has received much more attention in the past few years.

278

P. Terrence Hopmann examines the effect of international crisis and detente on the cohesion of the communist system. He views the communist countries as members of an international subsystem. In order to examine the question of cohesion, Hopmann has conducted a content analysis of statements of communist leaders in order to test the applicability of a model of group cohesion adopted from the literature on social psychology. Hopmann measured the perceptions of nine communist countries of U.S. behavior during each of the four time periods. The results support the initial hypothesis that during periods of crisis there exists more internal cohesion within the communist system.

Dan Heldman is concerned with the relationships among bilateral relations between the Soviet Union and the African countries, the presence and activities of communist-oriented groups in those countries, and the variation between Soviet and African voting behavior in the United Nations. In order to analyze these relationships, he has employed various statistical measures, including analysis of variance and correlation analysis. In addition, he tests a number of causal models in order to determine the reasons for the relationships that he finds. One of his major conclusions is that the closeness of Soviet relations with individual African countries, as well as Soviet voting positions in the UN, is the result of Soviet perceptions of the progressive or reactionary nature of African countries.

11

Soviet Elite
Perception of
International Regions:
A Research Note

CHARLES GATI

I. INTRODUCTION

The extent and nature of Soviet interest in world politics have long perplexed students of Soviet foreign policy. Our studies have featured reflections about the apparent contrast between the ideologically promoted notion of Soviet globalism, on the one hand—largely verbal

The author is indebted to Messrs. Sung-Il Choi and Paul R. Falzer of the University of Kansas for their competent and valuable research assistance. He also wishes to thank the Computation Center of the University of Kansas for use of its facilities.
Notes to the selection begin on page 299.

Soviet commitments to unlimited or undifferentiating engagement in all areas of the world—and the more selective actual performance, on the other. For the latter, Soviet performance, seems to have confirmed the leadership's recognition that limited Soviet resources require limited foreign involvement and that some geographic regions of the world must therefore be considered more important than others. If so, the analysis of Soviet performance raises the question, Which international region or regions occupy the attention and interest of Soviet foreign policy makers?

Based on traditional modes of analysis, the answer usually given by Western scholars and commentators in recent years points toward a trend in the direction of gradually increasing Soviet interest in the developing countries of Africa, Asia, and Latin America. That such trends can also be subjected to empirical investigation becomes evident if we consider the possibility of systematically studying—individually or within the framework of multivariate analysis—such empirical indicators of Soviet interest in international regions as (1) Soviet trade commitments, (2) economic and military aid, (3) the number of accredited Soviet diplomats in the region, (4) the length of Radio Moscow's broadcasts directed to the area, (5) the scope of cultural exchanges, (6) the frequency of visits by top Soviet political leaders, and (7) the quantity of press coverage devoted to the region. Even if some of these indicators are less revealing than others—insofar as economic aid, for example, is granted only to the developing countries—they still provide useful factual information for the analysis of the relative importance the Soviet leadership attaches to various international regions.

In this chapter, part of a larger study, the purpose is more modest: we propose to study the frequency of items (words)—i.e., news reports and commentaries—appearing in *Pravda* and *Izvestia* about international developments, *with a view toward exploring the relative weight the Soviet foreign policy elite assigns to various geographic regions or subsystems of the world.* We are not concerned with the precise content of such news items and commentaries, only with their geographic focus and quantity, recognizing at the same time that the publication of certain items depends on events whose importance the elite cannot deny and whose reporting in *Pravda* and *Izvestia* thus becomes compelling. We also assume that the frequency and geographic orientation of items published in the two leading Soviet dailies are not necessarily indicative of Soviet foreign policy *behavior*; they are suggested to be indicative of the Soviet elite's *perception* of the environment in which foreign policy is made. As J. David Singer has noted in a slightly different context, "the frequency with which particular items are discussed reflects the relative importance of these items to the people who formulate and articulate [Soviet] foreign policy."[1]

II. RESEARCH METHOD

A. PROBLEM OF REGIONALIZATION

For purposes of this chapter, the world beyond the frontiers of the Soviet Union had to be divided into several geographic regions. We have sought a pattern of regionalization that would be recognized easily and at the same time conform to the Soviet perception of the international system as well.

Accordingly, we first considered the regionalization implicit in the organization of the U.S.S.R. Ministry of Foreign Affairs. Not counting its functional divisions, the ministry was split into sixteen geographic divisions as of 1968: six European ones—one of which included the United Kingdom as well as Australia, Canada, and New Zealand—three African, and one division each for the United States, Latin America, the Near East, the Middle East, South Asia, Southeast Asia, and the Far East. It would have been tempting to follow the ministry's pattern of regionalization without change; however, our data required fewer geographic subdivisions.

Second, we considered regionalization along the lines of UN statistical publications which tend to conform to popular notions about geographic regions. The primary difficulty here was their persistent lack of consistency. Third, we considered the possibility of a complex scheme based more on political, social, and economic data than on geography, one of the patterns offered by students of political integration. We concluded, however, that the utilization of one of Russett's schemes, for example, would result in an unduly complicated and unmanageable pattern of regionalization.[2]

Relying primarily on the organization of the Soviet Ministry of Foreign Affairs and on UN statistical publications, then, we delineated seven international regions as follows: (1) Africa; (2) Eastern Europe;

(3) Far East and Pacific; (4) Latin America; (5) Near and Middle East and South Asia; (6) North America; and (7) Western Europe. Although these regions—as seen in Table 1—are not easily comparable in terms

TABLE 1

BASIC DATA ON SEVEN INTERNATIONAL REGIONS AS OF
1966–67 (IN PERCENTAGE)*

Region (No. of independent countries)		Territory	Population	GNP	Communist Party Membership
Africa	(39)	24.2	8.8	5.7	neg.
Eastern Europe	(8)	1.1	3.7	6.2	24.4
Far East & Pacific	(19)	22.4	36.7	10.8	63.2
Latin America	(24)	19.1	8.1	13.5	.8
Near and Middle East & South Asia	(24)	11.6	25.0	10.9	.5
North America	(2)	18.3	7.0	13.8	neg.
Western Europe	(19)	3.3	10.7	39.1	11.1
World Totals	(135)	100.0	100.0	100.0	100.0

* Data exclude the Soviet Union, countries with an estimated population of less than 100,000, and all nonsovereign countries.

Sources: United Nations Statistical Office, Statistical Yearbook; Bureau of Intelligence and Research (U.S. Department of State), World Strength of the Communist Party Organizations.

of their territory, population size, level of economic development or GNP, or the strength of Communist Parties in the area, they do represent easily identifiable geographic entities; coincide, though in a simplified fashion, with the organization of the Soviet Ministry of Foreign Affairs; and provide a convenient pattern for the collection of press data.

B. METHOD OF DATA COLLECTION

Each issue of the Current Digest of the Soviet Press (CDSP) prints a complete record of the content of Pravda and Izvestia. Articles appearing in the two leading dailies are listed in the CDSP weekly index, where their substance and length in words are identified. (Reflecting the style of the Soviet press, distinction is seldom made between news reports and editorials.) Much of the foreign news thus noted is arranged according to the article's geographic focus. As for items without a clear geographic orientation, CDSP lists them under various headings, such as "World Politics," "Disarmament," "International Law," or simply "Miscellany."

Concerned as we were with items which fell under one of our geographic categories, we first counted the number of words in these articles. Next, we added them up year by year and region by region, covering the ten selected years 1954–58 and 1964–68, i.e., the formative years of the Khrushchev era and of the post-Khrushchev era, respectively. Finally, when the actual number of words were thus added and arranged regionally, we "translated" them into percentages.

III. SOVIET PRESS COVERAGE OF INTERNATIONAL REGIONS

In the process of analyzing the data, we asked three major questions.

A. *Which regions have been covered extensively over the years?*

For an overview of the coverage of international regions in *Pravda* and *Izvestia*, two types of averages were calculated. The first was the overall mean and that of the two periods under consideration, producing the results shown in Table 2.

TABLE 2

MEANS OF REGIONAL PRESS COVERAGE (PERCENTAGE, WITH RANK)

Region	1954–58			1964–68	Overall	
Western Europe	32.6	(1)	(2)	23.6	28.1	(1)
Far East & Pacific	26.0	(2)	(1)	24.8	25.4	(2)
Eastern Europe	21.8	(3)	(3)	16.7	19.2	(3)
Near and Middle East & South Asia	10.4	(4)	(6)	9.2	9.8	(4)
North America	6.8	(5)	(5)	9.4	8.1	(5)
Latin America	1.4	(6)	(7)	6.4	3.9	(7)
Africa	1.0	(7)	(4)	9.9	5.5	(6)
Totals	100.0			100.0	100.0	

The second average, the median rank, was calculated on the basis of the relative rank the regions obtained in each of the ten years, producing the results shown in Table 3.

TABLE 3

MEDIANS OF RELATIVE RANK

Region	1954–58	1964–68	Overall
Western Europe	1.0	2.0	2.0
Far East & Pacific	2.0	1.0	2.0
Eastern Europe	3.0	3.0	3.0
Near and Middle East & South Asia	4.0	7.0	5.0
North America	5.0	5.0	5.0
Latin America	6.0	6.0	6.0
Africa	7.0	4.0	5.5

Taken together, the two averages point to the heavy emphasis in *Pravda* and *Izvestia* on such traditional areas of concern for Soviet foreign policy as Western Europe and the Far East and the Pacific. One of every two words printed in the two Soviet dailies about foreign affairs with an area-orientation has been devoted to the two regions. By both counts, Eastern Europe has been a close third. On the other hand, only one of every four words in *Pravda* and *Izvestia* has dealt with the remaining four regions of the world even though they include, among others, such important countries as the United States, India, and the United Arab Republic.

> B. *Is there any trend in the quantity of press coverage of international regions? Specifically, taking 1954-58 as the formative years of the Khrushchev era and 1964-68 as the formative years of the post-Khrushchev era, what similarities and differences can be discerned? What are some of the short-term and long-term trends?*

We shall seek to identify and discuss here (1) *regional trends* (including trends of the Khrushchev and post-Khrushchev eras as well as short-term and long-term trends) and (2) *general trends.*

Regional trends

Of the seven regions, Western Europe has ranked first 4 times and second 6 times; an average of 28.1 percent of foreign news in *Pravda* and *Izvestia* has been devoted to Western Europe. The region reached its peak in 1955 (46.5 percent), the year of the Geneva summit conference and of the conclusion of the Austrian peace treaty. Since then, as Figure 1 shows, coverage of the region has steadily decreased to 21.5 percent by 1968. Thus, our data suggest a substantial short-term and

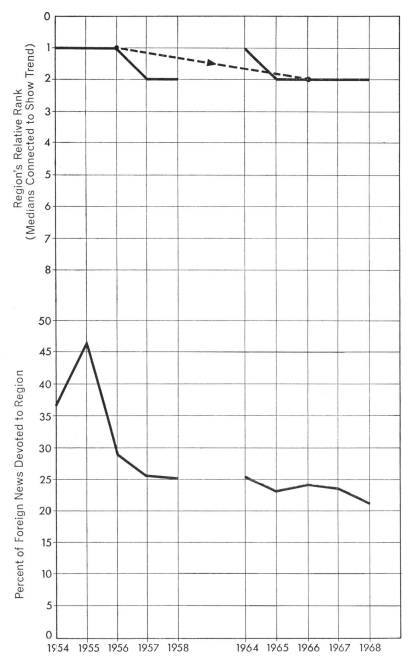

FIGURE 1. Press Coverage of Western Europe.

287

long-term decline, begun during the Khrushchev era and continued
ever since. This downward trend is further confirmed by the comparison
of averages: while 32.6 percent of foreign news focused on Western
Europe under Khrushchev, the average dropped to a mere 23.6 percent
under the post-Khrushchev leadership. The region's median rank has
also declined (from 1 to 2). Thus, while Western Europe's relative
significance continues and remains impressive, the overwhelming preoccupation with Western Europe in earlier years has all but disappeared.

The Far East and the Pacific has ranked first 4 times, and second
and third 3 times each; an average of 25.4 percent of foreign news in
the two dailies has been devoted to the region. The curve reached its
peak in 1966, when news and comment about Vietnam occupied considerable space in the Soviet press. While the Khrushchev era, on the
whole, registered a slight short-term decline in the coverage of the Far
East, it is not possible to discern any comparable or contrary trend
under Brezhnev and Kosygin. The long-term trend, however, is clearer:
the region's median rank has risen from 2 to 1 and the two means are
almost even (26.0 percent vs. 24.8 percent). Accordingly, the region's
vast coverage, despite remarkable fluctuations, supports the view that
the Far East remains an area of profound—and possibly increasing—
interest to the Soviet leadership.

Eastern Europe has ranked first twice, second once, third 6 times,
and fourth once; an average of 19.2 percent of foreign news in *Pravda*
and *Izvestia* has been devoted to the region. The 1956 events in Poland
and particularly in Hungary resulted in the very extensive coverage of
East Europe in that year and which, significantly, further increased in
1957 and 1958. As to the 1960s, coverage of the area showed a marked
and steady decline until 1968, the year of Soviet intervention in Czechoslovakia. It may be that the new Soviet leadership would have preferred
to assign a somewhat lower priority to the region, only to find it
imperative to defend its interests again. At any rate, while press coverage has declined from an average of 21.8 percent in the 1950s to 16.7
percent in the 1960s, Eastern Europe's high and steady median ranks
of 3 signify continuing Soviet preoccupation with the region.

The Near and Middle East and South Asia has ranked third once,
and fourth, fifth, and seventh 3 times each; an average of 9.8 percent
of foreign news in the two dailies has been devoted to the region.
As expected, the Suez crisis of 1956 and the Arab-Israeli war of 1967
received thorough coverage. Unexpectedly, however, neither crisis was

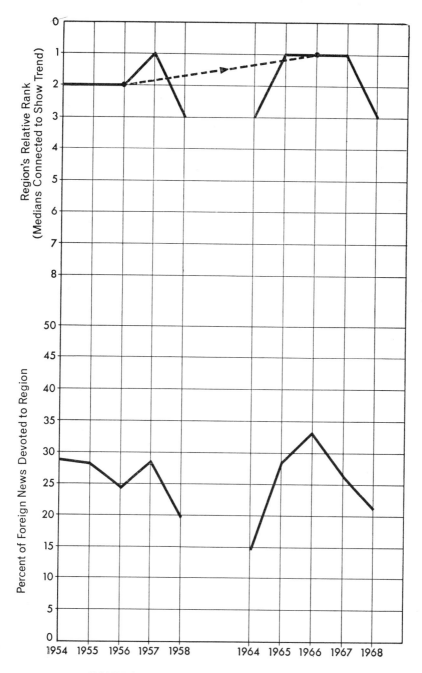

FIGURE 2. Press Coverage of Far East and Pacific.

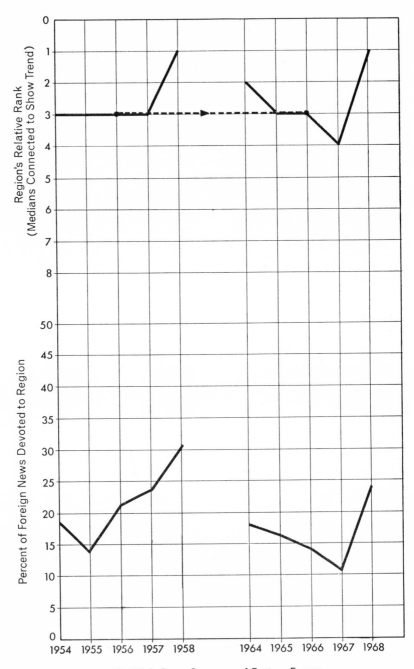

FIGURE 3. Press Coverage of Eastern Europe.

followed up by the kind of rising curve Eastern Europe, for example, experienced after 1956. Indeed, the region's median rank dropped from a midposition of 4 under Khrushchev to a bottom position of 7 in the post-Khrushchev era, and its mean declined from 10.4 percent to 9.2 percent. Our data, therefore, tend to contradict all available indications pointing to a growing Soviet appreciation for the region as the quantity of press coverage over the years reveals a pointedly declining long-term trend. We can only speculate that, perhaps, it is the subregion of South Asia rather than the Arab Middle East to which the Soviet leadership has decided to pay less attention in recent years.

North America has ranked fourth twice and fifth 8 times; an average of 8.1 percent of foreign news in *Pravda* and *Izvestia* has been devoted to the region. The curve reached its peak in 1968 when the average of previous years was doubled: the American presidential campaign and possibly the growing role of the United States in world politics account for the increase. The region's relative rank remains steady, however, even though the mean of the Khrushchev era (6.8 percent) rose to 9.4 percent in the more recent period. On the whole, North America's comparatively low rank of 5 appears firm, with the possibility of a rising short-term trend.

Latin America has ranked sixth 7 times and seventh 3 times; an average of 3.9 percent of foreign news published in the two Soviet dailies has been devoted to the region. In the immediate aftermath of the Cuban revolution, coverage of Latin America greatly increased—from an average of a mere 1.4 percent in the 1950s to 6.4 percent in the 1960s. Since reaching a high of 10.3 percent in 1964, however, coverage of the region has dwindled every year, and the region's median rank dropped from 6 to 7 (or last). Thus, the very low and even declining priority assigned to Latin America in the Soviet press seems fixed in the short run and in the long run as well.

Africa has ranked fourth and sixth 3 times each, and seventh 4 times; an average of 5.5 percent of foreign news in *Pravda* and *Izvestia* has been devoted to the region. Like Latin America, the African curve reached its peak in 1964 and it has steadily declined every year since. However, the African pattern is different in that the region's median rank jumped from a bottom position of 7 under Khrushchev to a midposition of 4 in the 1960s. Thus, while the short-term trend in the Brezhnev-Kosygin period displays a declining curve, the substantial difference between the two means (1.0 percent vs. 9.9

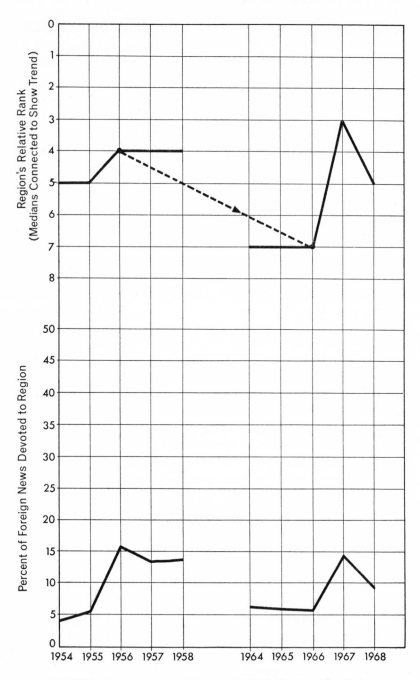

FIGURE 4. Press Coverage of Near and Middle East and South Asia.

292

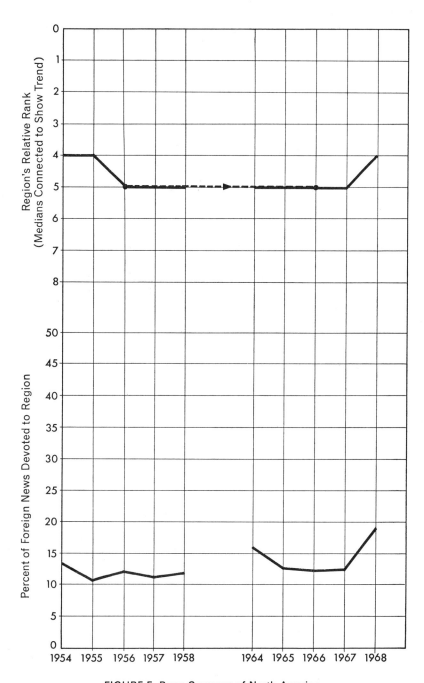

FIGURE 5. Press Coverage of North America.

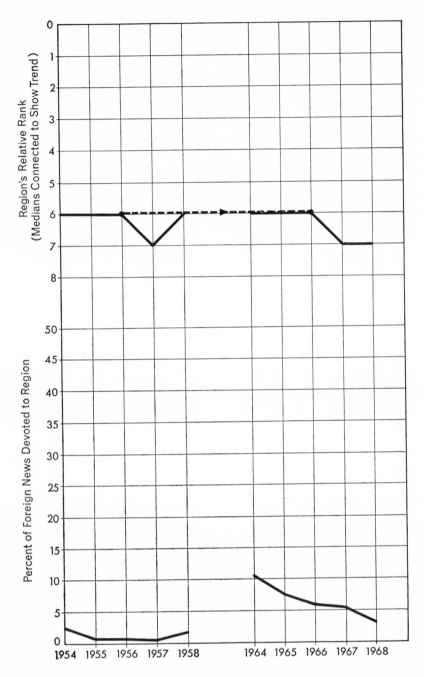

FIGURE 6. Press Coverage of Latin America.

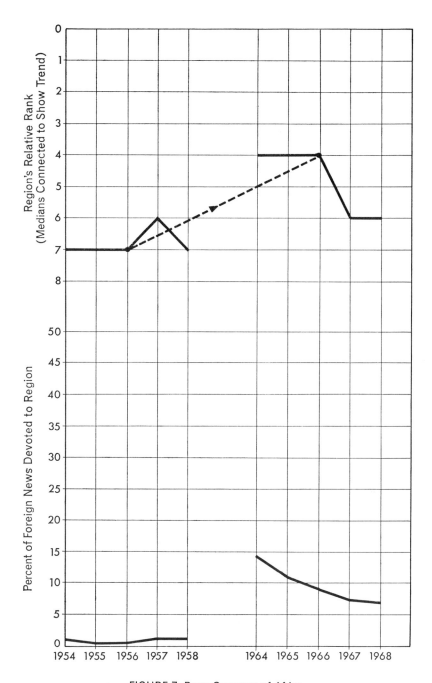

FIGURE 7. Press Coverage of Africa.

percent) and between the two median ranks signifies a growing long-term Soviet interest in the region.

General trends

Detailed interpretation of our data for the seven international regions focused on a rising curve in one region, a declining curve in another; a steady pattern here, no evident pattern there. However, considering the medians of relative rank for overall trends, we can note only two changes occurring during the periods under consideration (see Table 3). First, Africa and the Near East exchanged their respective positions, with the former moving up from its seventh rank to the fourth rank and the latter doing the opposite. Second, the Far East replaced Western Europe in the leading position, while Western Europe dropped to second place. Beyond these two changes, of which the latter seems marginal, *the remaining regions have retained their relative ranks over the years: their degree of consistency is remarkable.*

In *absolute* terms, our data show increased coverage of three "distant" regions: Africa, Latin America, and North America. Their cumulative means nearly tripled between the two periods, from 9.2 percent to 25.7 percent. Conversely, coverage of the four remaining regions—all of which are situated "closer" to the Soviet Union—has declined, from a total of 90.8 percent to 74.3 percent. It may be concluded, therefore, that *Soviet interest in the outside world has become more widespread and comprehensive in recent years.* The rather extreme averages characteristic of the Khrushchev era—ranging from Western Europe's 32.6 percent to Africa's meager 1.0 percent—have given way to a more even distribution of foreign news coverage in the Soviet press. Simply put, the Soviet Union has become more aware of regions it had once considered remote; its perspective has thus broadened. On the other hand, this process of equalization has not resulted in the diminution of the three leading regions of the Far East, Western Europe, and Eastern Europe. What with the impressive interest particularly in the Far East, these three regions can be said to remain high on the Soviet agenda.

> C. *Does the Soviet press merely reflect the regional foci of world developments? Alternatively, does the analysis of press coverage entitle us to speak of the "Soviet perception" of international regions?*

In order to assess the geographic orientation of the Soviet foreign elite, we chose to study a single indicator—the Soviet press. We assumed, first, that the two leading Soviet dailies accurately reflect the elite's perception of the outside world and, second, that a study of the quantity of press coverage would indicate the relative importance assigned to international regions.

The first assumption seems beyond serious challenge; foreign correspondents and editors of *Pravda* and *Izvestia* are members of the Soviet political elite and must be considered authoritative spokesmen for the Communist Party and the government. With qualifications which are "generally comparable to those of members of the Soviet diplomatic service," they can and do "assure alert sensitivity to variations of the current Party line."[3] As to the second assumption, we suggest that newspapers everywhere print foreign news according to the level of national involvement in the particular event. While we have found no comparative empirical investigation to support our proposition, casual reading of, say, *The Times* (London), *Le Monde*, the *New York Times*, and *Pravda* demonstrates that what results in "very extensive" coverage in one may result in "extensive" or only "limited" coverage in the other. Newspapers engaged in the reporting of international developments are "slanted" in terms of the quantity and very possibly the quality of their coverage. For in the daily process of selection, editors tend to apply one criterion: the extent of *national* curiosity about, or involvement with, the event at hand. Given, in addition, the intertwined tasks of information *and* persuasion the Communist Party has consistently assigned to editors of the Soviet press, the conclusion seems compelling: *the quantity of coverage of international regions in* Pravda *and* Izvestia *is less an indication of the "absolute" importance of particular world developments than that of the importance of the region and the event to the Soviet leadership.*

If so, we are still left with a difficult question about Soviet priorities and motivation: *Why* does the Soviet foreign policy elite consider, say, the Far East so crucial and Latin America relatively unimportant? In our search for statistical causality, we correlated Soviet press coverage of the seven geographic regions with the latter's (1) territory, (2) population size, (3) GNP, and (4) Communist Party membership (see relevant data for 1966–67 in Table 1). Is the Soviet elite interested in a particular region because of its large territory or population? Because of its level of economic development? Because of large Communist Parties in the area? Not unexpectedly, we found a set of negative correlations indicating that no causal relationship could be posited between the extent of Soviet press coverage of international regions, on the one hand, and the four variables, on the other. However, when we calculated the combined mean of the same four variables for 1966–67—the last year for which complete data were available—and contrasted it with the quantity of press coverage, the two rankings turned out to be rather similar (see Table 4). Comparable similarity was subsequently found for four of the seven years for which we had data.

TABLE 4

COMBINED MEAN OF FOUR VARIABLES (TERRITORY, POPULATION, GNP, AND CP MEMBERSHIP) AND PRESS COVERAGE FOR 1966–67 (PERCENTAGE, WITH RANK)

Region	Mean of Press Coverage	Combined Mean of Four Variables
Far East & Pacific	26.6 (1)	(1) 33.2
Western Europe	23.4 (2)	(2) 16.0
Near and Middle East & South Asia	19.1 (3)	(3) 12.0
Eastern Europe	10.5 (4)	(7) 8.8
North America	7.6 (5)	(5) 9.7
Africa	7.4 (6)	(6) 9.6
Latin America	5.1 (7)	(4) 10.3
Totals	99.7	99.6

Accordingly, our conclusion regarding the reason or reasons for Soviet priorities among international regions must be cautious, and, unless we test additional variables, it cannot be based on statistical causality. For what we have found is that *the extent of Soviet interest in international regions depends partly on the aggregate of such known, variables as territory, size of population, GNP, and Communist Party membership; partly, however, it depends on other, as yet unknown, variables.* Of such "other" variables, the region's proximity to the Soviet Union, as concluded earlier, appears to have lost some, though by no means all, of its significance.

Thus, while we do not yet have fully adequate statistical information to explain *why* the Soviet leadership assigns high or low priorities to the various regions, we do know that it *does*. We also know of the remarkable consistency which has characterized the Soviet elite's perception of the relative importance of international regions over the years. Further, we have ascertained trends and directions in the leadership's priorities pointing, as they do, to a process of equalization: that while the Far East, Western Europe, and Eastern Europe continue to enjoy the primary attention of the Soviet foreign policy elite, Soviet interest in the outside world has recently widened to include areas once considered far beyond the limits of Soviet interest.

Notes

1. J. David Singer, "Soviet and American Foreign Policy Attitudes: Content Analysis of Elite Articulations, *Journal of Conflict Resolution*, VIII, 4 (Dec. 1964), 425.

2. See Bruce M. Russett, *International Regions and the International System: A Study in Political Ecology* (Chicago: Rand, 1967).

3. Jan F. Triska and David D. Finley, *Soviet Foreign Policy* (New York: Macmillan, 1968), p. 105. See also Theodore E. Kruglak, *The Two Faces of TASS* (Minneapolis: U. of Minnesota P., 1962; New York: McGraw, 1963).

12

The Effects of International Conflict and Détente on Cohesion in the Communist System

P. TERRENCE HOPMANN

I. INTRODUCTION

The changes which have occurred in the communist system in recent years have provided students of international politics with an interesting

This is a revised and expanded version using new data of an article entitled "International Conflict and Cohesion in the Communist System," *International Studies Quarterly*, XI (1967), 212–36. The author would like to express his thanks to Kuan Lee and Andrew L. Haines for programming assistance, to the Stanford University Computation Center for grants of time on the IBM 360/67 to analyze data, and to Ole R. Hosti for his assistance and advice throughout this research project.

Notes to the selection begin on page 339.

subject for theorizing and research. The occurrence of that process which Togliatti has described as "polycentrism," accompanied by a similar process which appears to be at work in the North Atlantic community, is indicative of some major changes which have taken place in the international system throughout the postwar period. Therefore, it is important to theorists interested not only in the communist system but also to those interested in studying the dynamic processes of international politics to be able to explain some of these changes which have made such a dramatic impact on world events in recent years.

This project is intended to take a small step in that direction. Theoretically, it has started with the assumption that the communist system may be treated as an example of an international political coalition, a union of states undertaking certain common purposes. In an abstract sense it also may be treated as a system, which is composed of subsystems, the nation-state members ruled by the Communist Party, and being itself a component within a larger international supra-system. Indeed, the communist bloc has been one of two major systems within an essentially bipolar international system throughout the postwar period, although the rise of a nonaligned system of former colonial nations has brought about a substantial decrease in the tightness of the bipolarity of that supra-system during the same time. By treating the communist system in this manner, we could view some of the relationships among its components and its exchanges with its environment in terms of international interactions. In this project, we were concerned primarily with the nature of the relationship between conflict and détente in the communist system's interactions with its external environment, on the one hand, and the impact of these external factors on the internal cohesion of the communist system, on the other.

In addition, in order to examine their value in the analysis of significant processes occurring within the communist system, this project has employed some of the models and techniques currently being used by social scientists. Thus we have applied in this study a model of group processes which has been derived primarily from work in the fields of social psychology and communications. In addition, we have employed the techniques of computer content analysis as a tool for measuring the degree of cohesion within the communist system. Therefore, one of the purposes of this project is to evaluate tentatively the value of this particular quantitative research technique in analyzing this type of substantive problem.

In brief, this study is an attempt to explain some major trends which have occurred in the structure of the communist system by looking at it within a general systems framework of international interactions. In addition, it is an attempt to examine the value and relevance for the analysis of these changes in the communist system of models and research techniques which have recently been employed by behavioral scientists in the study of international politics. Therefore, throughout, we will be looking for factors which originate in the international environment within which the communist system operates and which may help to explain internal relations among the Communist Party states. This in no way is meant to imply that internal factors, both in the relations among the communist nations themselves and in the domestic politics of these nations, are irrelevant to the process of change which we want to investigate. We have simply elected for the purposes of this project to focus our analysis largely at the level of interaction between the entire international system and the communist system, and thus to look at the former as a factor which may help to explain changes in cohesion within the latter.

II. THE INTERACTION BETWEEN THE INTERNATIONAL SYSTEM AND THE COMMUNIST SYSTEM: THEORETICAL FOUNDATIONS

The central subject for investigation in this study is the impact of the international system on cohesion within the communist system during several events in the postwar years. Thus in general terms we are concerned with the interaction between the external environment and the relations among system components. The basic hypothesis of this study thus predicts that there will be a relationship between East-West conflict and cohesion within the communist system. In general terms, it may be phrased as follows:

> *Hypothesis 1: The greater the intersystem conflict, the greater the intrasystem cohesion.*

The basic foundation for this hypothesis is derived from the writing of Georg Simmel, especially as reformulated by Lewis Coser, on the integrative functions of conflict. In particular, Simmel has argued that, so long as the basic values of a group are intact, conflict with other groups tends to strengthen the internal unity of the group. He summarizes this proposition as follows:

> In short: the group in a state of peace can permit antagonistic members within it to live with one another in an undecided situation because each of them can go his own way and avoid collisions. A state of conflict, however, pulls the members so tightly together and subjects them to such a uniform impulse that they either must completely get along with, or completely repel, one another.[1]

Simmel further argues that, where there is no central sovereign power, a coalition will tend to disintegrate unless all members share a common external danger. Thus, conflict increases the centralization of existing groups and blurs the boundaries between individual group members. Also it may bring actors together who would otherwise have nothing to do with one another.

Coser, in his expansion of Simmel's theory, hypothesizes basically that "outside conflict will strengthen the internal cohesion of the group and increase centralization."[2] His argument suggests that external conflict has a variety of unifying effects on a group. First, it enhances the group's sense of identity by clarifying the boundaries separating it from the surrounding world.[3] Second, conflict with another group mobilizes the energies of the group and causes it to increase its efforts in its own defense, again requiring increased cohesion. This does not mean, however, that all components of the group will respond by performing the same functions in the face of a common enemy or that their behavior will consequently be similar in most respects. On the contrary, in highly complex groups there is likely to be a high degree of role differentiation and a related division of labor in the face of the external threat. Substantial centralization may be required to coordinate the various group components which are performing their own specialized functions.[4] Therefore, the major impact of the external threat may be evidenced in the realm of attitudes and values, inasmuch as conflict frequently affects a group by creating a "reaffirmation of their value system against the outside enemy."[5]

A third aspect of the effect of external conflict is that the group tends to be more intolerant of internal dissent. This may even be carried so far as to search for internal enemies in the form of dissenters, who may then be removed, either voluntarily or involuntarily, from the group.[6]

A fourth, and perhaps most important, aspect is that external conflict may bring together otherwise unrelated units, especially when their pragmatic interests coincide in the formation of such a coalition. In addition, the formation of one coalition in response to a perceived conflictual relationship may often lead to the formation of a symmetrical coalition in opposition. Since the formation of one alliance may be perceived by the units with which a competitive relation exists as a threatening act in itself, this frequently may lead to the formation of counter alliances.[7] The result is a tendency toward highly polarized configurations. In addition, such coalitions may be highly unstable. As Coser suggests:

> Alliances for the purpose of a specific conflict only, may be said to be inherently unstable types of sociation; either they will dissolve after the accomplishment of the purposes for which they were created, or they will grow into more enduring relations through the gradual adjustment of compromise and the emergence of group purposes, group loyalties and group norms.[8]

Coser also suggests one major qualification for the hypothesis that external conflict enhances internal cohesion. Conflict may be functional for the cohesion of a group only when it concerns values, beliefs, and goals which do not contradict the basic assumptions or consensual values upon which group unity is based. In this connection, the pre-existing structure of conflict within the group is an essential variable. If the group is torn by many, but still crosscutting, cleavages, then conflict may help alleviate or reduce the intensity of these conflicts. On the other hand, if the group is divided by one primary line of internal cleavage, especially when that cleavage embraces its basic consensual values, then external conflict may split rather than unify that group. Coser thus concludes:

> The degree of consensus prior to the outbreak of the conflict seems to be the most important factor affecting cohesion. If a group is lacking in basic consensus, outside threat leads not to increased cohesion, but to general apathy, and the group is consequently threatened with disintegration.[9]

This hypothesis that international conflict enhances the cohesion of international alliances is an outgrowth of this general theoretical foundation in group sociology, although it is also one of the most frequent hypotheses appearing in the literature of international relations. For example, this basic hypothesis plays a prominent role in one of the most significant works on international alliances to date, Liska's

Nations in Alliance. In the first place, Liska argues that a common enemy is perhaps the single most important cause for the formation of an alliance. In the absence of an external threat, small powers are unlikely to attempt to ally with larger powers out of fear that their identity will be abridged. In a similar manner, greater powers will normally be unlikely to seek out allies so as not to overextend their commitments and resources. As a result, Liska concludes that:

> Movement towards alignment sets in only when another state intervenes as a threat. The weaker state rallies then to one stronger power as a reaction against the threat from another strong power. The stronger state assumes the role of a protective ally, interested mainly in keeping the resources of the potential victim out of the adversary's control.[10]

Several significant modifications and additions to this basic hypothesis may be found in the international relations literature:

1. The effects of intersystem conflict will tend to have a symmetrical impact on both conflicting alliance systems. Once a coalition is formed within the international system, there is a general tendency also for an opposing coalition to be formed in response to the increased threat now presented by a unified opponent. This proposition too is summarized by Liska: "Whatever may be the effect of one side's exerting pressure on the other side, reciprocal pressures between roughly equal alliance systems tend to consolidate both."[11]

This hypothesis seems to have generally held true in the postwar period in which, for example, the establishment of NATO and especially the inclusion of a rearmed West Germany into its membership seems to have largely prompted the formation of the Warsaw Pact among the communist states of Eastern Europe. This pact has in many ways developed virtually as a mirror image of that coalition, NATO, against which it was intended to defend the communist system.[12] This process may take the form of a mutual strengthening of each coalition to keep pace with the other in a type of reciprocal escalation. In both the communist system and NATO there have also been symmetrical processes of disintegration due to the nonconforming behavior of one major ally, France and China. Thus Kaiser has suggested that there may be mutual weakening as well as mutual strengthening of alliances, resulting in a gradual decrease of the strength of each bloc and a reduction of their mutual threat.[13]

2. Intersystem conflict will tend to increase the hierarchical nature

of alliances, increasing the degree of centralized directiveness. Kaplan sets forth this proposition as follows: "Great external dangers will increase the organizational rigidities of the blocs, whereas a period of distinct international ease might loosen them and tend to make the blocs less hierarchical."[14]

In addition, it has been suggested that second-ranking members of a coalition during periods of relative détente may not only refuse to be dependent upon the bloc leader, but they may increase their contacts with the opposing coalition to enhance their negotiating position vis-à-vis the hegemonic power of their own bloc leader.[15] Recent overtures between France and Rumania are perhaps illustrative of this type of cross-system interaction during periods of relative international détente.

3. Coalitions which derive their cohesion from the threat of a common enemy may disintegrate rapidly when that threat is removed. If the basis for cohesion in an alliance is defense against a common enemy, when that threat is removed it follows that alliance cohesion is also likely to decline. Of course, there may be a certain spillover if integrative habits are learned during periods of external conflict and are then carried on even after the threat has disappeared. However, as Wolfers observes, when the initial basis for an alliance or coalition is defense against an external enemy, "any diminution of the external threat or of the will to meet it will tend to undermine cohesion and render futile any attempts to save the alliance by inward-directed 'diversions.' "[16]

4. External conflict may not necessarily have an integrative effect on an alliance if the threat is perceived as directed at only one or a few members of the coalition in such a way that other members perceive no threat to themselves. In such a case it is possible that the allies, in the spirit of mutual commitment, may come to one another's assistance even though there is no direct danger to themselves. However, in some cases, they may fall back on their own self-interest and leave the threatened ally to shift for itself. In short, in such a case the alliance entails an uneven distribution of liabilities, which may be disruptive of cohesion.

5. The relationship suggested by this hypothesis does not necessarily operate in one direction alone, for there may be some reverse effects. Not only may international conflict be treated as a cause of alliance cohesion, but that cohesion may itself contribute to intensified international conflict. In this case the increased unity of alliances may tend to enhance the polarity and rigidity in the international system, thereby

increasing the degree of interalliance conflict. This hypothesis is sum-marized by Kaplan: "While integration among the national actors within a bloc increases, the disintegrative processes operate between the supranational blocs."[17] Indeed, some authors have carried this hypothesis so far as to indicate that alliances are themselves among the major causes of war,[18] especially since they "inevitably intensify an atmosphere of distrust."[19] On the other hand, a loosening of the alliance systems may itself contribute to the increased plurality of the inter-national system, thereby reducing and cutting across an otherwise abrupt cleavage.

A second hypothesis to be tested in this study relates the degree of cohesion in the communist system as the dependent variable to the nature of the international system as the independent variable. This hypothesis focuses on the effects on coorientation among alliance members of changes in the polarity of the international system over time. It states:

Hypothesis 2: The more bipolar the international system and the more dominant international cleavages reinforce one another along bipolar lines, the greater the attitudinal consensus among the members of both alliances.

In some ways this hypothesis may appear to be true by definition in the sense that one characteristic of declining bipolarity is the reduced cohesion of the component alliances. But there are other factors which accompany the loosening of bipolarity, such as an increase in inter-system interactions or an increased role for mediating or nonaligned actors; these changes have occurred over the past twenty years in the international system, and this hypothesis suggests that such changes over time should be accompanied by a declining coorientation among allies in both systems during this postwar period. In some ways the findings may be interpreted as serving as indicators of the extent to which bipolarity in the international system has declined in all its relevant aspects in the postwar period as a function of other changes in intersystem interactions.

Essentially this hypothesis assumes that a tight bipolar system splits the international system into two competing blocs with a chasm across which there is little interaction, so that virtually all friendly relations are confined to the internal relations within each coalition. As K. J. Holsti suggests: "In the polar . . . system, alliances tend to be closely-knit structures in which the smaller alliance partners do not easily remove themselves from the bloc."[20]

This hypothesis further implies that interactions in a bipolar system will be almost completely confined to one's own alliance. Kaplan writes that "In the tight bipolar system communications within the blocs increase and communications between the blocs decrease."[21] Therefore, insofar as interactions may contribute to integration, the restriction of interaction patterns to intrasystem exchanges may have an integrative effect on the alliances.

Conversely, this hypothesis suggests that, as bipolarity breaks down in the international system, as characterized by an increased role in international politics for mediating actors and by an increase in intersystem interaction, then alliance cohesion is likely to decline. In such a case, secondary allies may desert the alliance and attempt to establish improved relations with members of the other bloc to increase their negotiating power against their major ally.[22] This general tendency for intrasystem interaction to decline as intersystem interactions increase in a less bipolar international system was further confirmed by Brody in his simulation study of the effects of nuclear proliferation. He found that the tendency to interact predominantly along bipolar lines, which was found in the relatively bipolar system existing prior to the spread of nuclear weapons, did not persist afterwards. On the contrary, Brody reports that in the period after nuclear proliferation took place, "There may be as much interaction (cohesion) between the blocs as within the blocs—the marked preference for communicating within the blocs, which existed prior to nuclear diffusion, is no longer evident."[23]

In summary, these two hypotheses suggest that there is a relationship between the structure and interactions within the international system and the degree of cohesion within the component coalitions. Specifically, they suggest that more intense conflict between coalitions and a more bipolar structure for the international system will both tend to contribute to increased cohesion within the international coalition.

III. MODELS FOR THE MEASUREMENT OF COHESION AND CONFLICT

Given these hypotheses, it is necessary next to establish some empirical indicators which may enable us to measure the relevant variables in these hypotheses. The independent variable in hypothesis 1 is the degree of conflict between the two international coalitions. This will be indicated by the perceptions of the decision-makers in each country of the hostility of the opposing coalition, as measured through the techniques of content analysis to be described in the next section. In hypothesis 2, the independent variable is the degree of bipolarity in the international system. In this project we will measure this variable only roughly by assuming that polarity in the international system has declined throughout the postwar period. The system has clearly changed from a fairly tight to a progressively looser bipolar system, due largely to the increased role played by the nonaligned bloc and to the increased communications between subordinate members of each bloc. Thus we have taken as our indicator for declining bipolarity in the postwar period simply the passage of time.

The problems involved in the measurement of the dependent variable for both hypotheses, cohesion within an international coalition, are somewhat more complex. For this project we have selected a model for the measurement of cohesion based upon the symmetry of perceptual responses by coalition members to common external stimuli. This model postulates that greater attitudinal consensus in response to the same objects during a given event will be indicative of increased cohesion.[24] In selecting this type of a model we have employed an indirect research strategy. We have chosen to define cohesion in attitudinal rather than behavioral terms because of the responsiveness of the decision-makers' attitudes to immediate events. Inasmuch as cohesion clearly includes both behavioral and attitudinal components, this limits the breadth of our indicator in a manner which cannot be avoided but which must be taken into account. Therefore, we have elected to measure cohesion using as an indicator the degree of coorientation by decision-makers in their attitudes toward an external actor which is perceived by all members of the coalition. This strategy is based on the assumption that the actions of one nation toward others largely depend on how the decision-makers in that nation perceive other actors in their external environment. In other words, the decision-makers' "definition of the situation" determines how they behave toward other members of their coalition.[25]

This model which we have employed as an indicator of cohesion is derived from Newcomb's A-B-X model, a simple model of interpersonal communication.[26] The model consists of two actors, A and B, who are interdependent and hence have simultaneous orientations toward an external object, X. The relations between the three parts of this model constitute a system which is characterized by a balance of forces. This balancing mechanism always creates " 'strains' toward preferred states of equilibrium."[27] Based on this postulate, the model assumes that the coorientation or consensus between A and B can be measured on the basis of the similarity of their perceptions of X. Since we have treated coorientation as a major attitudinal component of cohesion, we may use this measure as a rough indicator of the degree of cohesion in an international political coalition.

Thus the A-B-X model suggests that coorientation between A and B with respect to X will exist in a situation in which A and B have similar orientations toward X. Newcomb observes that, while any system may be at rest at any given time, a system is characterized not by an absence but by a balance of forces. Also a change in any part of the system may lead to a change in other parts. Thus, within the system there are always pressures toward the creation of balance in the relations among the three components of the model. Bonds which connect the three points of the A-B-X triangle may carry either a positive or a negative charge. The relations among the three points are balanced only when the number of negative bonds connecting them is even or zero. If both

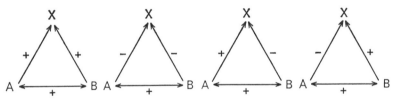

FIGURE 1. The Above A–B–X Triangles Constitute the Four Possible Balanced Configurations of the Model. Any Other Configuration Is Imbalanced and Creates a Strain Toward Balance.

A and B have a symmetrical orientation (either positive or negative) toward X, then, in order for the system to be in balance, the relationship between A and B must be positive; if their orientations differ, that is, if one has a positive attitude and the other is negative, the relationship tends to be negative. These four possible balanced configurations are diagramed in Figure 1. With any other combination the system is in a state of imbalance, with pressures being exerted to restore balance. Therefore, insofar as one can assume that an A-B-X system is balanced, one may be able to infer the relationship between A and B from their coorientation toward X (the similarity between A-X and B-X).

The crucial assumption upon which this inference rests is that the system is in balance, a sometimes uncertain assumption. Yet, if we accept Newcomb's statement that "the system tends towards balance," then we may be able to conclude that over time systems will attempt to reduce strain and restore equilibrium. Newcomb also suggests three variables which may enable one to predict the parameters of strain to restore equilibrium. First, the strength of attraction between persons (A and B) affects the amount of strain that nonconsensus about the object of reference (X) will produce. Second, the importance or salience of the object of reference affects the degree to which nonconsensus about the object will produce strain. Nonconsensus over an object of virtual indifference would thus produce little strain toward balance. Third, the joint relevance for both of the objects of reference affects the amount of strain that a symmetrical orientation will produce. Discrepancies in perceptions of an item which has no common impact on both parties will produce little or no strain.[28] Therefore, one may assume "strain toward symmetry" only in a system where the following three conditions are met:

1. The members of the system are highly salient to one another.
2. The object of reference is important to all members.
3. The object has joint relevance for all members.

In applying this model to international politics we have employed as an indicator of cohesion the degree of coorientation among allies toward salient external objects or events. The validity of this indicator can be explained partially in terms of international relations theory by what Deutsch calls "mutual relevance" and "responsiveness." Because symmetrical evaluations of significant external actors tend to enhance mutual responsiveness, they also tend to increase cohesion.[29] Thus coorientation by members of the communist system toward significant external actors like the United States would be likely to enhance cohesion among those nations. This is summarized in the following postulate, upon which our measurements of cohesion were based.

> *The greater the similarity of orientations toward a common external object by the decision-makers in all member nations of an international political coalition, the greater the cohesion of the coalition in relation to that object.*

Thus we attempted to determine the direction and intensity of A's and B's and all other coalition members' attitudes toward the same X along a positive-negative dimension. This enabled us to treat the relations between each pair of allies separately in terms of the basic A-B-X model. Such a configuration for a simple five-member coalition is diagramed in Figure 2. In such a coalition there are $N^2 - N/2$ (10 in this case) dyadic relationships connecting the member countries. Like Bavelas, we employed the notion of "distance" among nations in each configuration.[30] These distances were then measured in terms of differences in orientations toward X. Then, as Bavelas suggests, comparisons of interaction patterns in each period could be made on the basis of comparing the sum of internal differences defined as $\Sigma d_{x,y}$.[31] If the sum of internal differences were greater at a later period than at an earlier one, for example, we might conclude that cohesion within the system had declined between these two periods. Thus, this model provides a basis for comparing the degree of cohesion in one alliance in different points in time, for comparing the differences between any two or more pairs of allies within an alliance at any given period of time, and for comparing the degree of cohesion in different alliances at the same or different periods of time.

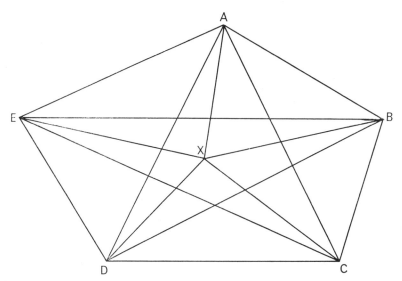

FIGURE 2. A Model of the Coorientation of Five Actors (*A, B, C, D,* and *E*) Toward an External Object (*X*). The Ten Relations Linking These Five Actors May Be Inferred from the Differences in Their Relations Toward *X*.

When applied to international political coalitions, several significant limitations to the A-B-X model must be made explicit. First, similar orientations at the time of a certain event can only be expected to facilitate cohesion with respect to *that* event. This model says nothing about the relationships among A, B, etc., toward other objects (e.g., Y and Z) at the same time or toward the same object X at the time of other events, although of course there may be some spillover effect. Second, there may be circumstances in which similar orientations do not indicate cohesion. For example, two nations may have similar orientations toward object X for entirely different reasons. Thus, similar orientations may exist in conditions where there is little cohesion; coorientation is neither a necessary nor a sufficient condition but merely a facilitative condition for cohesion. Third, these quantitative measures of attitudinal interactions must eventually be supplemented by an analysis of the processes of decision-making and their effect on the transformation of perceptions into overt behavior. Several social psychologists working with theories of cognitive balance have also reached the conclusion that these models must be supplemented by decision-makers' calculations of costs and gains in making policy decisions. For example, in their studies of cognitive balance, Rosenberg and Abelson found that:

> In resolving cognitive discrepancies ... subjects seek out not only the attainment of cognitive balance and consistency but they seek also to alter their beliefs and evaluations in ways that will maximize expected gain and minimize expected loss; when both forces converge so that they may be gratified through the same change or changes, a formally "balanced" outcome will be achieved; when these forces diverge, the typical outcome will not meet the requirements of a simple formal definition of cognitive balance.[32]

It is for this reason that this research might usefully be supplemented by a more thorough analysis of decision-makers' costs and gains with respect to their desired goals. For the present, however, we must acknowledge these limitations, and proceed to operationalize the relevant variables in the model so that they may be employed to test the hypotheses suggested above. In general, it must also be emphasized that the validity of these indicators as measures of the relevant political variables has not yet been fully established, so that one purpose of this research project may also be to examine their relevance for research on the communist system.

IV. COMPUTER CONTENT ANALYSIS
AS A TECHNIQUE FOR MEASURING COHESION
IN THE COMMUNIST SYSTEM:
THE RESEARCH DESIGN

One of the new research techniques which may have considerable value in the study of relations among the Communist Party states is computer content analysis. This provides an indirect research strategy through which we can measure the attitudes of national decision-makers without having to interview them directly. In order to test our hypotheses we have thus used computer content analysis to measure the degree of coorientation among decision-makers in the communist system in response to four events during the postwar period, two conflict periods and two of relative international détente. In addition, to test hypothesis 2, we have selected one period of each type from the first decade of the postwar period (before 1956) and one period of each type from the second decade (after 1960). Thus we have selected four events for this analysis:

1. June 25, 1950, the date of the outbreak of the Korean War.
2. July 17, 1955, the opening of the Geneva Summit Conference.
3. July 25, 1963, the signing of the Nuclear Test Ban Treaty.
4. February 7, 1965, the first day of regular American bombing missions over North Vietnam.

These four events thus provided two roughly comparable periods of conflict and two similar periods of détente early in the postwar years and in the decade of the 1960s. Both crisis events were wars in Asia, separated by fifteen years, and they involved conflicts between divided countries with the United States playing an active military role in both. The periods of détente include the 1955 Geneva Summit Conference and the 1963 Test Ban Treaty, perhaps the most significant attempts at East-West negotiation before and after the transition period mentioned above. Therefore, although we cannot necessarily attribute any differences between the first two and the last two events to time alone, we have attempted to select the most comparable events possible in a real historical situation. Although other factors may play a role in influencing changes from the earlier to the later sets of periods, time may certainly be considered to be an important factor.

A few such specific events were selected rather than routine state-

316

P. TERRENCE HOPMANNP. TERRENCE HOPMANN

ments such as May Day speeches or other regular speeches of that type for several reasons. First, there were not sufficient documents of speeches available in translation on any one such date from all communist countries. Second, such speeches seldom focus enough on one external actor to serve as an object (X) to obtain stable measures of coorientation in the A-B-X model. Third, the periods selected clearly distinguish between conflict and détente, a necessary distinction for testing hypothesis 1, yet one which would often be ambiguous in more routine statements. The overall generality of the findings from these four periods to all periods of high and low tension in which the communist system was involved, however, can only be determined by further studies.

In this project we have analyzed the response to these four events, of eleven Communist Party states, including the Soviet Union, the Chinese People's Republic, Albania, East Germany, Poland, Czechoslovakia, Hungary, Rumania, Bulgaria, North Korea, and North Vietnam. Yugoslavia was not considered to be a member of the communist system even though it had been a Communist Party state throughout the entire period. However, ever since Yugoslavia was expelled from the Cominform in 1948, she has not really been an integrated part of the system; in particular she has not really been a member of either of the major multilateral organizations of the communist system in Eastern Europe, the Warsaw Pact or the Council of Economic Mutual Assistance. Cuba was also excluded from this list inasmuch as it was not a member of the communist system prior to January 1, 1959; the inclusion of Cuba in the latter two periods only would destroy the basis for comparison of the four periods. A similar problem remained for one country which was included, namely North Vietnam, which did not formally become a communist country until 1954, when Vietnam was divided by the Geneva agreements. For the 1950 period we have included a document monitored from the official radio of the Viet Minh under the command of Ho Chi Minh, and this should be taken into account in evaluating the results reported later. Finally, Outer Mongolia was excluded due to the failure to obtain any documents stating their response to three of the four events listed above.

For these eleven countries documents were then selected representing the first response of their decision-makers to each of these four events, in which they made substantial reference to the role of their enemy, the

Western bloc. The selection of the first reaction makes the assumption that this response is the least likely to be distorted by intervening events. The forty-four documents selected for the communist system thus included commentaries made over government-controlled radio stations following each of these events. Even though all of these statements may not have been authored directly by decision-makers, the state ownership of the radio stations in Communist Party states provides considerable assurance that these broadcasts reflect the basic attitudes of major decision-makers. It is, of course, clear that the selection of only one document for each nation in each time period represented a fairly small sample, but a larger sample was precluded due to limited resources. However, as Berelson writes: "For most purposes, analysis of a small, carefully chosen sample of the relevant content will produce just as valid results as the analysis of a great deal more—and with the expenditure of much less time and effort."[33]

One further problem is that computer content analysis presently requires that all documents be rendered into English, inasmuch as the dictionary for the content analysis program is in English. This means that some distortion can enter as a result of translation. For these communist countries we attempted to minimize this distortion by taking all documents from one translated source, so that translations were assumed to be fairly consistent. Since we were interested primarily in making comparisons among documents rather than in obtaining absolute values for any single document, this procedure hopefully minimized the extent to which differences among documents could have been caused by different translations.

These documents, selected by the above-mentioned procedures, were then subjected to computer content analysis. Content analysis has been defined jointly by Holsti and Stone as "any research technique for making inferences by systematically and objectively identifying specified characteristics of messages."[34] The content analysis procedures which we employed made use of a computer to permit rapid processing of data, and it processed the documents on the basis of a program which is an adaptation of the General Inquirer[35] for the analysis of political documents. This version of the General Inquirer, written in Pl/1 for use on an IBM 360/67, makes it possible to measure the coorientation of the decision-makers in the communist system in response to the role of their perceived enemy in these four events. The attitudes of the communist decision-makers toward the enemy, both the United States alone and the entire Western bloc, were measured on the three dimensions of Osgood's semantic differential.[36] This procedure measures attitudes on the basis of frequency of use times intensity of the attitude, with intensity based on scores ranging on a seven-point scale from -3 to $+3$ on three dimensions:

1. Evaluative: positive . . . . . negative
2. Potency: strong . . . . weak
3. Activity: active . . . . passive

By using the Bavelas formula for distance among actors discussed above, we may measure the distances between any two communist countries on the basis of the differences in their perceptions of the object X on these three dimensions. Thus, a content analysis procedure employing scales based on the semantic differential is directly applicable to the research questions raised by the model which we have employed as our indicator of cohesion in international coalitions.

The documents selected for analysis were coded by the procedure described by Holsti.[37] The coding procedure focuses not on the meaning of the documents but on the functions of the word in each theme. It distinguishes between agents of action, the action itself, and the targets of action, and thus provides both perceptions of attitude objects in their role as agents and as targets, and it also provides perceptions of the actions linking agents and targets. Since this procedure is based purely on the structure of each theme and is unrelated to the content or "meaning" of the documents, opportunities for the coders' bias to enter in at this stage are strictly limited. The attitude attributed to any given theme is assigned by the computer program on the basis of a dictionary in which all words are coded independently with respect to their position on the semantic differential. Therefore, all words in the dictionary were coded in advance on a seven point scale for all three dimensions. "The dictionary thus reflects the proposition that when decision-makers perceive themselves, other nations, events—or any stimulus—the most relevant discriminations are made in a space defined by these three factors."[38] The dictionary thus provided a common yardstick against which all themes could be compared. This made it possible to determine the differences in the aggregate perceptions held by decision-makers in each of the eleven communist countries in response to each of these significant international events.

In order to obtain quantitative measures for the differences between each country's perceptions of the enemy, we have obtained for each of these three dimensions a plus score (positive, strong, and active), a minus score (negative, weak, and passive), and an average score, which is the sum of the plus and minus scores divided by the frequency—all of which are found in Table 1. As an example of how the "average score" is computed, if in one period country A perceived X with a total

TABLE 1

COMMUNIST SYSTEM PERCEPTIONS OF THE WEST AND THE UNITED STATES ON THE EVALUATIVE DIMENSION: (WEST) PLUS SCORE/MINUS SCORE: AVERAGE SCORE; (UNITED STATES) PLUS SCORE/MINUS SCORE: AVERAGE SCORE

	1950	1955	1963	1965
Soviet Union	10/49:–1.34	9/10:–0.08	40/43:–0.07	10/105:–1.73
	10/49:–1.34	3/4:0.17	19/25:–0.26	10/105:–1.73
Communist China	33/188:–1.52	97/144:–0.37	37/77:–0.73	3/147:–2.36
	26/172:–1.60	42/78:–0.58	24/69:–1.00	3/147:–2.36
Albania	7/48:–1.58	14/27:–0.52	37/194:–1.48	6/139:–2.22
	7/48:–1.58	2/15:–1.63	24/193:–1.71	6/139:–2.22
East Germany	14/91:–1.60	25/35:–0.31	51/42:0.21	28/190:–1.74
	8/97:–1.85	21/29:–0.32	11/23:–0.80	11/171:–2.05
Poland	22/72:–1.09	54/32:0.46	11/10:0.11	18/161:–1.64
	22/72:–1.09	54/32:0.46	3/8:–1.00	18/161:–1.64
Hungary	8.83:–1.79	18/15:0.13	3/30:–1.42	23/69:–1.02
	5/83:–2.00	6/5:0.13	1/15:–1.56	23/69:–1.02
Rumania	50/256:–1.60	10/21:–0.65	33/25:0.28	25/192:–1.62
	38/181:–1.49	9/21:–0.75	2/8:–1.00	25/190:–1.62
Bulgaria	8/48:–1.67	14/10:0.31	6/11:–0.63	12/97:–1.70
	8/41:–1.57	9/7:0.22	3/11:–1.14	11/40:–1.32
Czechoslovakia	22/76:–1.20	15/19:–0.24	27/39:–0.35	5/99:–1.84
	14/40:–1.24	14/19:–0.31	5/13:–0.89	5/99:–1.84
North Korea	11/87:–1.85	44/32:0.29	85/312:–1.30	17/341:–2.33
	11/75:–1.73	17/27:–0.45	60/303:–1.52	17/341:–2.33
North Vietnam	29/69:–0.91	50/17:0.63	36/309:–1.84	7/189:–2.22
	29/62:–0.80	15/7:0.44	29/269:–1.89	7/189:–2.22

score of 4 positive on the evaluative dimension with a frequency of 2, and a score of 16 negative with a frequency of 8, the "average score" in each direction is 2. These are then weighted by relative frequency. Since 80 percent of the score was negative, the −2 average is multiplied by .8 producing a −1.6; then +2 is multiplied by .2, producing .4; these are then summed to produce an "average score" of −1.2. Next we constructed an index of relative hostility, found in Table 2, which is based on the average of the mean negative, strong, and active scores. Thus the hostility index too may range from +3.00 (greatest perceived hostility) to −3.00 (least hostility).

Finally, we calculated the difference between the "average scores" of every pair of nations in the communist system for each period as an

TABLE 2

HOSTILITY INDEX

(a) COMMUNIST PERCEPTIONS OF WESTERN HOSTILITY

Year	Evaluative	Potency	Activity	Average Hostility
1950	−1.74	1.53	1.55	1.52
1955	−0.03	1.44	0.82	0.76
1963	−0.66	1.62	0.98	1.09
1965	−2.68	1.68	1.78	2.05

(b) COMMUNIST PERCEPTIONS OF THE UNITED STATES' HOSTILITY

Year	Evaluative	Potency	Activity	Average Hostility
1950	−1.48	1.73	1.50	1.57
1955	−0.24	1.36	0.74	0.71
1963	−1.16	1.59	1.01	1.25
1965	−1.85	1.69	1.80	1.78

TABLE 3

COMPARISON OF COORIENTATION AMONG COMMUNIST NATIONS IN
FOUR POSTWAR PERIODS

	Responses to the West	Responses to the U.S.
Total Rank Order for Each Year (closest to farthest apart):		
1950	4540	5023
1955	6133	7126
1963	8246	6199
1965	5391	5962
Total for High-Tension Periods (1950 and 1965)	10673	10985
Total for Low-Tension Periods (1955 and 1963)	14379	13325
Mann-Whitney U-Test for Significance of Difference Between Two Sets of Periods:		
$U=$	3826	4880
$z=$	−4.7113	−2.4785
Significance of Difference Between High- and Low-Tension Periods, One-Tailed Test: p	< .001	< .01
Total for Early Periods (1950 and 1955)	10673	12149
Total for Late Periods (1963 and 1965)	13637	12161
Mann-Whitney U-Test for Significance of Difference Between Two Sets of Periods:		
$U=$	4568	6044
$z=$	−3.1394	−0.0127
Significance of Difference Between Early and Late Periods, One-Tailed Test: p	< .001	> .10 (not significant)

index of coorientation. These pairs were then rank-ordered from closest
to farthest apart. Then lastly the periods to be compared were separated,

as done in Table 3. To test hypothesis 1 the high-tension and the low-tension periods were separated, whereas to test hypothesis 2 the early periods and the late periods were separated. The significance of the difference between the two sets of periods was then calculated on the basis of a Mann-Whitney U-test, which indicated whether the difference in the sum of the rank orders was significant in the predicted direction. Although this analysis was performed for all three dimensions of the semantic differential separately, we placed the greatest confidence in the results for the evaluative dimension for three reasons: (1) The positive-negative dimension was most relevant to the Newcomb A-B-X model, since the bonds connecting the three points were defined in terms of this dimension. (2) Osgood found that the evaluative dimension accounted for approximately twice as much variance in human cognition as each of the other two dimensions. (3) Inter-judge reliability for our dictionary was higher for the evaluative dimension than for the other two.

In short, the content analysis results provided us with data on the perceptions by every member of the communist system in each time period of numerous external objects (X's), especially their enemies, the United States and the entire Western bloc. By calculating the differences between each country's perceptions of these X's in each period, we could develop an index of coorientation necessary to test the hypotheses suggested earlier. The average differences among Communist Party states in all four time periods on all three dimensions are summarized in Table 4.

Before proceeding to an analysis of the quantitative results, it is necessary to make explicit several limitations and qualifications to our methodology and research design.

First, the content analysis dictionary assumes that the same word has approximately the same meaning, in terms of Osgood's three dimensions, in different countries. To the extent that this assumption is invalid, some important differences among countries may be overlooked.

Second, the content analysis dictionary is not fully equipped to deal with words having multiple meanings in different contexts, so that word taggings often reflect some "average" or most common meaning. But the meaning attributed to most words is assumed to be relatively constant regardless of context. Again, insofar as this assumption does not hold, distortion may ensue.

TABLE 4

MEAN DIFFERENCE AMONG "AVERAGE SCORES" (COORIENTATION)
FOR ALL MEMBERS OF THE COMMUNIST SYSTEM ON THREE
DIMENSIONS IN PERCEPTIONS OF THE ENEMY

(a) PERCEPTIONS OF THE WEST

	Evaluative	Potency	Activity
1950	0.35	0.69	0.26
1955	0.51	0.39	0.44
1963	0.90	0.37	0.46
1965	0.45	0.16	0.33
Average Low-Tension Periods	0.71	0.38	0.45
Average High-Tension Periods	0.40	0.43	0.30
Average Early Periods	0.43	0.53	0.35
Average Late Periods	0.68	0.28	0.39

(b) PERCEPTIONS OF THE UNITED STATES

	Evaluative	Potency	Activity
1950	0.40	0.50	0.32
1955	0.70	0.35	0.48
1963	0.54	0.46	0.53
1965	0.51	0.16	0.31
Average Low-Tension Periods	0.62	0.41	0.51
Average High-Tension Periods	0.46	0.33	0.32
Average Early Periods	0.55	0.43	0.40
Average Late Periods	0.53	0.31	0.41

Third, the content analysis procedures assume that explicit statements of decision-makers in some way reflect their attitudes. It is often
suggested that national leaders may attempt to distort their statements
for purposes of suppressing information or to deceive their audience,
and that computer content analysis may not be sensitive to this fact.
Robert Jervis has charged:

> ... a country's statements of perception cannot be taken at face value
> either by other states or by scholars.
>
> The fact that statements may be designed to give false impressions
> makes especially questionable the attempts to apply the Stanford
> techniques and model to recent history where the scholar can use only
> public documents.[39]

This may often be true, but this problem is hardly confined to computer content analysis, as any kind of textual analysis such as that
undertaken by the traditional diplomatic historian may be subject to
the same kind of distortion. Furthermore, we assume that where a
nation's leader makes a statement which does not accurately reflect his

private attitudes, then he does so for a reason, and this reason may be directly relevant to our investigation. For example, if the leader of an Eastern European country issued a statement almost identical to that of Soviet leaders, it makes little difference if his private attitudes were different; this is still representative of his desire, whether voluntarily or as a result of coercion, to maintain some degree of unity with the Soviet Union. Thus, in this case, it is the overt verbal behavior rather than the private attitude which is most relevant to the testing of our hypotheses. Certainly it cannot be denied that computer content analysis results, like all forms of textual analysis, cannot be treated completely independent of the behavioral and logical situation which forms their context. It must be clearly understood that the content analysis instrument measures primarily manifest and not latent content of messages. But the fact that it does not measure what decision-makers are "really" thinking does not invalidate its validity for testing many hypotheses about relations within the communist system.

Fourth, the content analysis measures employed in this project are primarily measures of attitudes as expressed in verbal communications; they give no direct indication of overt, nonverbal behavior. This general problem of the relationship between verbally expressed attitudes and overt nonverbal behavior is most serious in this project with respect to the problem of drawing any inferences about cohesive behavior from measures of attitudinal coorientation. It is for this reason that our data must be interpreted cautiously and in the light of their behavioral and situational contexts.

With these limitations in mind then we may proceed to examine the results which were obtained when these procedures were applied to analyze the responses of eleven Communist Party states to two events each of international conflict and of relative détente in the postwar period.

V. THE RELATIONSHIP BETWEEN SYSTEMIC FACTORS AT THE INTERNATIONAL LEVEL AND COHESION IN THE COMMUNIST SYSTEM: THE QUANTITATIVE RESULTS

The first hypothesis concerns the relationship between the degree of conflict between the Western bloc and the communist system and the degree of communist bloc cohesion in response. Stated in general terms it reads:

Hypothesis 1: The greater the intersystem conflict, the greater the intrasystem cohesion.

If this hypothesis is valid we would expect to find in our content analysis results more similar evaluations of the United States and of the West by the eleven Communist Party states in the two periods of conflict (1950 and 1965) than in the periods of reduced tensions (1955 and 1963). This hypothesis was generally confirmed by these data. Looking first at their perceptions of the Western bloc on the evaluative dimension, Table 3 indicates that the total of the ranks was 14,379 for the low-tension periods and greater than the ranks for the high-tension periods, which reached only 9931. This indicated that the differences were ranked higher for low-tension periods because the distances among the eleven nations were greater on the average. This produced a Mann-Whitney U-score of 3826, which, assuming a normal distribution, falls at a z-score of -4.7113, far into the predicted tail of the distribution.[40] Thus the differences among these eleven communist countries were significantly greater (at better than the .001 level of significance, using a one-tailed test) during periods of détente than during periods of conflict. During times of high tension and greater external threat there was a substantially greater degree of coorientation among the communist nations than during times when the external threat was not so great. On the potency dimension the difference between the crisis and noncrisis periods was not significant beyond the .10 level of significance, but the difference which did exist was in the predicted direction. On the activity dimension again the difference was significant beyond the .001 level in the predicted direction.

Turning to perceptions by the communist bloc of the United States alone, similar results were obtained. On the evaluative dimension the coorientation during crisis periods was significantly greater than during noncrisis periods beyond the .01 level. On the potency dimension the difference was significant beyond the .05 level, and on the activity dimension the significance level reached .001. Thus, in their perceptions of their enemies, both of the United States and of the Western bloc, the communist countries showed a greater degree of coorientation during these two periods of crisis than during the two periods of détente, a difference which was statistically significant in five of six cases, including the evaluative dimensions in both instances when the United States and the West were the object of perception. Insofar as these measures are valid indicators of cohesion, we may conclude that they tend to confirm the hypothesis that, during periods of greater intersystem conflict, cohesion within the communist system tended to increase in comparison with periods of détente.

In order to explicate these findings somewhat more fully, we may examine in greater detail the communist system's perceptions of the United States and the West on the evaluative dimension.

In the first of the four periods, the outbreak of the Korean War in 1950, the communist countries perceived American actions as rather hostile, as is indicated in Table 2. These eleven countries on the average perceived the United States with a hostility score of 1.57, and on the evaluative dimension alone the average perceptions were predominantly negative, with the U.S. being perceived as -1.48. The Soviet Union perceived the United States with a score on the hostility index of 1.55, about average for the communist system, whereas Communist China perceived the U.S. as slightly more hostile than their Soviet allies, rating it with a score of 1.70. In short, the communist countries clearly perceived a substantial threat from their Western enemies as a result of the outbreak of the Korean War.

These data also tend to indicate that, in response to this external threat, there was a substantial degree of coorientation in the perceptions by members of the communist system of the United States. The average distance among all 55 pairs for the eleven nations in terms of "average scores" came to .40. As indicated in Table 4, these differences are relatively slight, being the lowest for the four periods contained in this study.

This is what we would have expected to find in 1950, when traditional scholarship tends to suggest that the communist system was still tightly centered around the Soviet Union. Under Stalin the unity of the communist system was maintained through the centralized power of the Soviet Union, which enforced what Brzezinski has described as ideological and institutional uniformity.[41] It is hardly surprising, therefore, that these data indicate that there was substantial unity of attitudes among these eleven communist nations in response to American involvement in Korea. The range among them varied from "average scores" of −0.80 to −1.85, only about one point out of seven possible between the extremes. Furthermore, the nation possessing the most positive attitudes toward the United States was North Vietnam, or in the case of 1950 actually the radio of the Viet Minh under Ho Chi Minh. Since this preceded the division of Vietnam under the terms of the Geneva agreement of 1954, the full integration of the Vietnamese communists into the communist system, and the full-scale development of the North Vietnamese conflict with the United States, this most divergent case in 1950 was not surprising. If this one case is excluded, then the nation perceiving the United States as next most positive was Poland, with an "average score" of −1.09, a range of only 0.76 between it and the most negative perceptions, a relatively small difference between even the most extreme cases. Thus, in this period at least ten of the eleven countries were fairly closely clustered around the Soviet Union, which was just about in the center of the most extreme cases, with an "average score" of −1.34. Also, Chinese perceptions of the United States, which averaged to −1.60, differed from their Soviet allies by only 0.26 points, less than the average for all 55 dyads. Albanian perceptions were an almost identical score of −1.58. Thus, in 1950 none of the conflicts which were to develop in later periods were indicated by our data, and the entire communist system demonstrated a substantial degree of coorientation.

By 1955 and the Geneva Summit Conference the communist countries clearly tended to perceive a reduced level of international tension, as indicated by the hostility index in Table 2. During this period on the average the communist countries perceived the West with a hostility score of 0.76 and the United States with a score of 0.71, substantially below the level of 1950. Indeed, they clearly perceived enemy hostility to be less in this period than at any other time included in our study. Perhaps even more striking was the fact that on the evaluative dimension alone, the United States was perceived on the average as only −0.03. At this time the Soviet Union perceived the United States on the hostility index with a quite low score of 0.43, whereas Communist China continued to perceive it as substantially more hostile, scoring 1.24, and Albania clearly perceived the Americans with the greatest hostility, namely a score of 1.52. Thus, on the average communist countries perceived their enemies as less threatening at this time than they had in 1950, although a few countries remained more rigid and continued to perceive substantial hostility. Our data further indicated that in this period of reduced East-West tension in 1955, the degree of coorientation among the communist nations had also begun to break down. In other words, a change in the independent variable, namely a reduction of intersystem conflict, was accompanied by a decrease of the dependent variable of bloc coorientation. Thus, as our major hypothesis predicted, reduced East-West tension was accompanied by growing dissensus within the communist system.

During the two years after the death of Stalin a greater degree of institutional and ideological diversity appeared in the communist system.[42] This diversity was clearly evident in the response of the eleven Communist Party states in the period of relative international détente during the summer of 1955. In terms of perceptions of the United States on the evaluative dimension, the average distance between all pairs of nations was 0.70 compared to 0.40 in 1950, indicating a substantial decline in coorientation by 1955.

In 1955 perceptions of the United States were naturally somewhat more positive than in 1950. In fact five of the eleven countries, the Soviet Union, Poland, Hungary, Bulgaria, and North Vietnam perceived it with positive "average scores." At this time, however, both China and Albania were among the most negative in their attitudes toward the American role at Geneva. In fact, Albania, with an "average score" of −1.63, was clearly the most negative member of the communist system, and the Albanians perceived the United States in even more negative terms than in 1950, when the score was −1.58. Sino-Soviet differences increased also to 0.75, greater than the average distance for all 55 dyads, and Albania differed from its Soviet allies by a score of 1.80. This divergence, especially on the part of Albania, which followed an even more extreme version of the Chinese line, is particularly interesting considering that most traditional specialists on the communist system have not found any significant indications of the Sino-Soviet conflict and especially of the Albanian-Chinese alignment prior to at least 1956. Whether the apparent indication of this deviation in response to the Geneva Summit Conference was a peculiarity of the data or whether it was significantly indicative of future events cannot be determined adequately. This finding, however, would appear to justify further investigation of the response of these two countries to the Geneva Summit Conference of 1955.

Not only were the average differences greater between all pairs of the communist system in 1955 than in 1950, but also the margin between the extremes was substantially greater. In 1955 the most positive perceptions of the American protagonists were held by Poland with a score of +0.46 and the most negative was Albania's −1.63, a range of 2.09 compared to 1.05 in 1950. Thus, in 1955 the coorientation of the Communist system's evaluative response to American actions at the Geneva Summit Conference declined substantially compared to their responses to American actions in Korea in 1950. This may be largely accounted for by China's and Albania's deviation in terms of their perceptions of the United States, which continued to be intensely negative at the same time that the Soviet Union and most of the Eastern European bloc, as well as North Vietnam, adjusted their perceptions to relatively more positive evaluations of the American role in the détente of 1955.

During the time intervening between 1955 and 1963 a major transition began to appear, both in the nature of East-West relations and in relations within the communist system. In 1956 Khrushchev delivered his de-Stalinization speech to the 20th Congress of the CPSU. At this time he questioned both the absolute validity of the Soviet revolution as the sole model for communist worldwide revolution, and he admitted the possibility of "different roads to socialism." Furthermore, he attacked the Stalinist "cult of personality" and thereby brought into question the absolute authority of the Soviet leader. As Lowenthal has written:

> Yet, in fact, the simultaneous admission of Stalin's "Great Power chauvinism" and of his disregard for "Socialist legality" aroused among Communists everywhere profound doubt about the "leading role of the Soviet Union," and searching questions about the inherent dangers of its system of government.[43]

However, the interpretation by many Communist Party states of the doctrine of "different roads to socialism" was quite different from that intended by the Soviet leaders. This doctrine had a good deal of appeal to many Communist leaders, like Imre Nagy of Hungary, who were critical of Soviet orthodoxy. Thus, ironically perhaps, one result of the increased liberalization was the outbreak of the Hungarian revolution in October 1956.

Soviet suppression of these uprisings in Hungary and also in Poland appeared superficially to indicate the Soviet intention to unify by force the communist system in an effort to retain at least some degree of

Soviet hegemony in Eastern Europe. Still a further irony, however, was the fact that this provided an additional incentive for the disintegration of the unity of the communist system. In the years immediately after 1956 Khrushchev attempted to replace the previous system of centralized discipline which Moscow exercised over the world Communist Party by an ideological union of countries which were formally independent, but which he hoped would continue to revolve around the Soviet Union as the ideological center of the system. The belief that this ideological authority of the CPSU could maintain effective political unity proved to be illusory, however, and by 1958 conflicts within the communist system, especially between the Soviet Union and China, clearly began to emerge beneath the appearance of ideological unity. The result was a series of ideological challenges to Moscow's leading role and its ideological authority originating from other Communist countries as well as from China.[44] Over the next five years the conflict expanded rapidly and became more explicit. At the same time political controls over the Eastern European satellites were gradually loosened, and many of the Warsaw Pact nations found room to maneuver both within the system and in relations with the West. Some, like Poland, attained some degree of internal liberalization, and others, like Rumania, were able to play the Soviet and Chinese interests against one another to achieve some independence in their foreign and economic policies. Through a variety of means most Communist nations managed to achieve some increased degree of independence.

By 1963 and the signing of the Test Ban Treaty—the third period analyzed in this study—the Sino-Soviet conflict reached the point of open schism. On July 31, 1963, the Chinese issued a statement denouncing the Test Ban Treaty as a fraud and accusing the Soviet Union of capitulation to United States' imperialism. Part of the text of that statement read as follows:

> But now the Soviet government has made a 180-degree about face, discarded the correct stand they once persisted in and accepted this reproduction of the U.S.–British draft treaty, willingly allowing U.S. imperialism to gain military superiority. Thus the interests of the Soviet people have been sold out, the interests of the people of the countries in the socialist camp, including the people of China, have been sold out, and the interests of all peace-loving people of the world have been sold out.
>
> The indisputable facts prove that the policy pursued by the Soviet government is one of allying with the forces of war to oppose the forces

of peace, allying with imperialism to oppose Socialism, allying with the
United States to oppose China, and allying with the reactionaries of all
countries to oppose the people of the world.[45]

The Chinese apparently perceived the Test Ban Treaty as directed in
part against themselves, especially against their own efforts to enhance
international power and prestige through obtaining nuclear weapons.
They further perceived that it represented an attempt by the United
States and the Soviet Union to agree tacitly to maintain hegemony over
their respective coalitions and thus to retain their joint world dominance
through their nuclear superiority. Thus, in the absence of an external
threat to pull in the opposite direction, the treaty undoubtedly contributed substantially to the further deterioration of Sino-Soviet relations.

During the 1963 period the Communist Party states tended to perceive the United States and the West as being more hostile than in 1955,
but still the average level of hostility was substantially lower than in
either of the two periods of intense conflict. On the average, the eleven
Communist Party states perceived the United States with a score of
1.25 on the hostility scale, greater than the 0.71 in 1955 but still less
than the 1.57 in 1950. Similarly, they perceived the West at 1.09 on the
hostility index, compared to 1.52 in 1950 and 0.76 in 1955. In their
perceptions of the United States, the Soviets continued to perceive a
relatively low level of hostility, at 0.83, but again China and Albania
rated the Americans as being substantially more threatening during
this period than did the Soviets, with almost identical scores on the
hostility index of 1.44 and 1.49, respectively. In short, the period of the
Test Ban Treaty on the average was one of relatively low perceived
hostility originating from the West, so that no conflict situation existed
to enforce greater unity among the disputing communist nations.

Indeed, one of the major sources of dispute between them was over
the issue of the extent to which the United States was a serious threat,
about which our data confirmed they had somewhat different perceptions. This was a particularly strong topic of disagreement between
the Soviet Union and China. In their perceptions of the United States,
the Soviet Union perceived their enemy with an "average score" of
−0.26, while China perceived them as −1.00. Thus the two parties
differed in their attitudes by 0.74, amounts about equal to those found
in 1955.

However, this substantial difference in attitudes was not confined
solely to this single dyad, but throughout the Communist system

coorientation was well below the 1950 level. In perceptions of the United States the average difference among all pairs of nations came to 0.54, and for the West as a whole the differences were an even more striking 0.90, clearly greater than the 0.51 in 1955 and the 0.35 average in 1950. Thus all of these data point to at least an equal and perhaps even greater decline in attitudinal coorientation in 1963 compared with both of the two preceding periods analyzed in this study. This decline in 1963 compared to 1955 occurred even though the average level of perceived détente was not as great as in the former period. Therefore, the level of conflict may not be the sole explanatory factor, a question which we will consider shortly in relation to hypothesis 2.

Also, in looking just at perceptions of the West we find that the most positive perceptions were held by Rumania, with an "average score" of +0.28. The most negative attitudes were held by North Vietnam with a score of −1.84, producing a range of 2.02 for this period. Other nations holding the most negative attitudes toward the West included in order, Albania, Hungary, North Korea, and China. Thus, with the somewhat curious exception of Hungary, by 1963 we can see in these data at least some indications of the formation of a subcoalition within the communist system, including the Asian party states plus Albania, all four falling at the most negative end of the spectrum in terms of their attitudes toward their perceived enemies. Thus by 1963 the communist system demonstrated substantial diversity in its response to the role of the West and the United States in the Test Ban Treaty, and this diversity was most clearly manifested in indications of the division of the bloc into two subcoalitions, one of the Eastern European countries around the Soviet Union and another of the Asian party states plus Albania around Communist China. This new division thus had become rather clear by this time, and it substantially changed the nature of intrasystem relations within the communist system.

American bombings of North Vietnam in February 1965 brought a temporary end to the divergent attitudes which appeared in the previous two periods analyzed in this study. Observers in numerous communist countries noted that American attacks on a "fraternal socialist state" had seriously endangered the détente in East-West relations which had been developing ever since the successful resolution of the Cuban missile crisis in 1962. The result was that the hostility index rose to the highest point for any of the four periods in this study. Communist bloc perceptions of the West on the average produced a score of 2.05; these were based largely on negative perceptions on the evaluative dimension which reached −2.68 for the West and −1.85 for the United States only. Presumably the extreme hostility perceived as originating from the West is based largely on highly negative perceptions of America's Asian allies in this event, especially South Vietnam.

In terms of attitudes of the members of the Communist system toward the United States, this increased hostility was also accompanied by a substantial increase in coorientation. The average difference among the eleven countries in "average scores" was 0.50, farther apart than the 0.40 figure for 1950, but still the second closest together of all periods. At this time the least negative perceptions of the United States were held by Hungary with a score of −1.02, and this made Hungary clearly the most distant from its allies of all members of the communist system. In their reaction the Hungarians still held out hope that there would be an exchange of visits between the Soviet leaders and President Johnson, although they observed that Johnson had severely damaged the chances for such a meeting by attacking one of the Soviet Union's allies at the same time.[46] The most negative perceptions of the United States were held by the Chinese People's Republic, with a score of −2.36, followed closely in order by North Korea (−2.33), North Vietnam (−2.22), and Albania (−2.22). Thus, as in 1963, these four countries tended to be grouped together at the most negative end of the spectrum in terms of their perceptions of the Americans, providing further evidence of the formation of a primarily Asian subcoalition. including also Albania.

The distance between the Soviet Union and China in this period was 0.63, slightly greater than the average distance for all 55 dyads of 0.51. Still the two nations' attitudes toward the United States were closer together than at any time since 1950 when the average difference was only 0.26; by 1955 the difference had widened to 0.75, and it remained an almost identical 0.74 between their "average scores" in 1963. Thus even the long standing Sino-Soviet conflict may have been affected somewhat, even if only temporarily, by these conflict events. Indeed, these data tend to indicate that the degree of coorientation among all eleven Communist Party states increased substantially in response to American bombings of North Vietnam in comparison to the previous two periods of relatively relaxed intersystem interactions.

This high degree of coorientation in response to the Vietnam crisis may be somewhat surprising in the light of the development of the

Sino-Soviet conflict in the years immediately before. Of course, it is obvious that the growth of polycentrism has not followed a simple linear progression over the years. In fact, this study has indicated that it has varied partly in response to changes in the overall international environment, such as the degree of external threat. Thus the Vietnam conflict may have brought at least a temporary easing of the conflict. It is important to emphasize, however, that our data for the 1965 period do not prove that the Sino-Soviet conflict was repaired over the issue of Vietnam; subsequent events simply are not consistent with such a conclusion. What these data do mean is simply that, in terms of attitudes toward the perceived enemy, in this case the United States and the entire Western bloc, the eleven communist nations included in this study exhibited a high degree of consensus in response to this crisis event. However, as mentioned before, unity of perception does not necessarily lead to unity of action, especially since it is possible for nations to hold the same attitude toward an external actor for somewhat different reasons. Subsequent Soviet and Chinese competition to aid North Vietnam and to gain political influence in Hanoi may indicate that their mutual antagonism toward the West in February 1965 was based largely on their efforts to gain the favor of the North Vietnamese rather than serving as a sign of cohesion between themselves.

In general, therefore, these data tend to suggest that the communist system has exhibited greater consensus in relation to its enemies during times of intense conflict than during times of lesser conflict and relative détente. The second hypothesis relates cohesion in the communist system to another variable in the international system, namely its structure. It states:

Hypothesis 2: The more bipolar the international system and the more the dominant international cleavages reinforce one another along bipolar lines, the greater the attitudinal consensus among the members of both alliances.

In testing this hypothesis we may assume that the bipolarity of the international system has decreased over recent years, and that the tight bipolar system has evolved at least into a loose bipolar system with some evidence of a potential multipolarity. Thus we may postulate that the international system was less bipolar in the latter two time periods than in the first two, and thereby use the time dimension as a rough indicator of changing bipolarity. By so doing we could confirm this hypothesis if there was less attitudinal coorientation in the 1963 and 1965 periods than in 1950 and 1955, controlling of course for the level of conflict.

Looking only at the evaluative dimension we found that, when the entire Western system was the object of perception, this hypothesis was clearly confirmed. In Table 3 the sum of the rank orders was 10,673 for the early periods and a higher 13,637 for the later ones, indicating the extent to which the dyads were farther apart and thus given higher rank-ordered positions in the two periods of 1963 and 1965. This difference produced a Mann-Whitney U-score of U $= 4568$, which has a z-score of -3.1394, significant beyond the .001 level. In this case the mean distance between "average scores" in the high-tension periods was even greater in 1965—0.45—than in 1950—0.33; similarly, the differences in the low-tension periods were greater in 1963 when they reached 0.90 than in 1955 when they were only 0.53.

Looking at perceptions by the communist nations of the United States, this finding was not supported, however. In this case the sum of the rank-ordered dyads for the early periods equaled 12,149, and for the later periods it reached an almost identical 12,161; this resulted in a score of U $= 6044$, and in a z-score of -0.0127. Obviously this does not begin to approach even the .10 level of significance. A question then remains concerning why this hypothesis was confirmed when the Western bloc as a whole was the object of perception and not for the United States alone. One plausible explanation, although it is largely speculative, is that when the communist nations perceived the United States they continued to perceive the world in essentially bipolar terms, with the United States being the enemy superpower. When the entire Western system was the attitude object, however, at least some of the Communist Party states were probably sensitive to the changes in the foreign policy behavior of at least some of the Western nations in recent years, especially France, a part of the general phenomenon of declining bipolarity. Thus it is quite conceivable that the tendency of some communist countries to adapt their perceptions to accord with these changes in the Western systems, while others did not adapt, may account in part for some of the divergences in their perceptions of the West in the later periods. Since these differences were probably based largely on different perceptions of the nature of the relations among the different components of the Western system, it is unlikely that they would carry over to their perceptions of one component alone, namely the United States.

In brief there seems to be at least substantial evidence to support the hypothesis that attitudinal coorientation had declined among the communist nations in recent years following the breakdown of the tight bipolar international system in contrast to the earlier periods when the international system was essentially bipolar. Since this hypothesis did not hold up in communist responses to the other polar superpower, the United States, we must at least maintain some doubt about the generality of this finding.

VI. CONCLUSION

In summarizing the quantitative results, we have reached several major conclusions.

First, hypothesis 1 was generally confirmed. During periods of greater conflict the Communist Party states exhibited significantly greater coorientation than during periods of lower conflict when the common external enemy, the United States and its allies in the Western bloc, were the object of perceptions. In general we may consider this finding confirmed only in the attitudinal responses to the enemy, and we cannot infer from this anything about the relations among the communist countries in response to other events or actors. But in response to those actors which were the source of external threat, that threat clearly had an integrative effect on the attitudinal orientations of the members of the communist system.

Second, hypothesis 2 was only partially confirmed. This hypothesis contended that, as the bipolarity of the international system broke down (as it has during the postwar period), the degree of coorientation within the communist system would decline also. When the Western bloc's role in these four events was the object of perception, the differences on the evaluative dimension of the semantic differential among all 55 dyads linking the eleven communist countries together were greater in the later periods after bipolarity had broken down than in the earlier periods of the relatively tight bipolar system. When the United States was the attitude object, however, there was virtually no

difference between the first two periods and the last two. It was specu-
lated that this might be explained by the fact that the impact of declining
bipolarity was not as significant for the Communist Party states'
responses to the United States alone as it was for the entire Western
bloc, where the impact of these changes away from bipolarity was
perceived by at least some members of the communist system. Thus, in
response to those objects for which the decline of bipolarity was relevant, it appeared that the coorientation of the communist system
declined in the years after the dissolution of the tight bipolar system,
so this hypothesis was confirmed in a limited manner only.

Finally, it appeared that the quantitative findings obtained in this
project were generally consistent with the observations of substantive
specialists on relations within the communist system. In many ways
this project simply supplemented and reinforced a good deal of that
literature. But it also attempted to do several things which were not
possible when using more traditional research techniques. In particular,
there are several advantages to the development of specific hypotheses,
to the creation of a general model which suggests interrelations among
variables of theoretical concern, and to the application of a systematic,
empirical research methodology to analyze these relationships. This
enabled us to begin to explain some of the changes which have taken
place in the communist system in a systematic manner. By isolating
several relevant variables, it made it possible to identify a few ways in
which the nature of interactions within the international system have
an impact on the internal cohesion of the communist system. In addition, by formulating hypotheses, using a general model for measurement, and using a general research technique, this approach enhances
the comparability of findings. Thus we are currently comparing the
findings obtained from this study of the communist system with the
responses of the NATO nations to the same events, using parallel
procedures in every respect.[47] This may make it possible to explore
more systematically the generality of the findings obtained in this study.
By so doing, this entire procedure may enable us not only to explain
better those factors which affect the changing internal relations of the
communist system but to understand more about the dynamic processes
of international politics which may effect the cohesion of all international political coalitions. In this manner we may be able to begin
developing better empirically grounded, middle-range theories of a
general nature about cohesion in international political coalitions.

Notes

1. Georg Simmel, *Conflict* (New York: Free Press, 1955), pp. 92–3.
2. Lewis Coser, *The Functions of Social Conflict* (New York: Free Press, 1956), p. 88.
3. *Ibid.*, p. 38.
4. *Ibid.*, p. 95.
5. *Ibid.*, p. 90.
6. *Ibid.*, pp. 103–4.
7. *Ibid.*, pp. 148–9.
8. *Ibid.*, p. 147.
9. *Ibid.*, pp. 92–3.
10. George Liska, *Nations in Alliance* (Baltimore: Johns Hopkins, 1962), p. 13.
11. *Ibid.*, pp. 98–9.
12. Jan F. Triska and David Finley, "Soviet–American Relations: A Multiple Symmetry Model," *Journal of Conflict Resolution*, IX (1965), 38–9.
13. Karl Kaiser, "The Interaction of Regional Subsystems," *World Politics*, XXI (1968), 98–9.
14. Morton Kaplan, *System and Process in International Politics* (New York: Wiley, 1957), p. 45.
15. Herbert Dinerstein, "The Transformation of Alliance Systems," *American Political Science Review*, LIX (1965), 597.
16. Arnold Wolfers, *Discord and Collaboration: Essays on International Politics* (Baltimore: Johns Hopkins, 1962), p. 29.
17. Kaplan, *op. cit.*, p. 145.
18. M. M. Ball and H. B. Killough, *International Relations* (New York: Ronald, 1956), p. 176.
19. R. L. Buell, *International Relations* (New York: Holt, 1925), p. 483.
20. K. J. Holsti, *International Politics: A Framework for Analysis* (Englewood Cliffs: Prentice, 1967), p. 110.
21. Kaplan, *op. cit.*, p. 120.
22. Dinerstein, *op. cit.*, p. 597.
23. Richard A. Brody, "Some Systemic Effects of the Spread of Nuclear Weapons Technology: A Study Through Simulation of a Multi-Nuclear Future," *Journal of Conflict Resolution*, VII (1963), 735–6.
24. This model was selected over several alternatives. First, an integration model like that employed in Karl Deutsch, *Political Community at the International Level* (New York: Random, 1954) and "Communications Theory and Political Integration," in Philip E. Jacob and James V. Toscano (eds.), *The Integration of Political Communities* (Philadelphia: Lippincott, 1964), and Bruce M. Russett, *Community and Contention: Britain and America in the Twentieth Century* (Cambridge: M.I.T. Press, 1963), was not sufficient to handle the immediate responses of national decision-makers to specific events. Second, a sociometric model was not employed because it measures cohesion on the basis of direct attraction of nations to one another, and documents reflecting decision-makers' direct attitudes toward one another were not publicly available. For a further elaboration of the reasons for rejecting these two approaches see P. Terrence Hopmann, "International Conflict and Cohesion in the Communist System," *International Studies Quarterly*, XI (1967), 216–18.
25. Richard C. Snyder, H. W. Bruck, and Burton Sapin, *Foreign Policy Decision Making* (New York: Free Press, 1962), pp. 65–6.
26. A forerunner of Newcomb's A-B-X model may be found in Fritz Heider, "Attitudes and Cognitive Organization," *Journal of Psychology*, XXI (1964), 107–12, and Fritz Heider, *The Psychology of Interpersonal Relations* (New York: Wiley, 1958). The primary explications of Newcomb's model may be found in T. M. Newcomb, "An Approach to the Study of Communicative Acts," in E. F. Borgatta

and R. F. Bales (eds.), *Small Groups* (New York: Knopf, 1955); T. M. Newcomb, "Communicative Behavior," in Roland Young (ed.), *Approaches to the Study of Politics* (Evanston: Northwestern U.P., 1958); and T. M. Newcomb, "The Study of Consensus," in Robert K. Merton, Leonard Broom, and Leonard S. Cottrell (eds.), *Sociology Today: Problems and Prospects*, Vol. 2 (New York: Harper, 1965). Further useful elaborations of the model are found in Robert B. Zajonc, "The Concepts of Balance, Congruity, and Dissonance," *Public Opinion Quarterly*, XXIV (1960), 280–96; its extension in consistency theory in Charles E. Osgood, "Cognitive Dynamics in the Conduct of Human Affairs," *Public Opinion Quarterly*, XXIV (1960), 341–65; and its extension in graph-theoretical terms in Dorwin Cartwright and Frank Harary, "Structural Balance: A Generalization of Heider's Theory," in Dorwin Cartwright and Alvin Zander (eds.), *Group Dynamics* (New York: Harper, 1956).

27. Newcomb, "The Study of Communicative Acts," *op. cit.*, p. 152.
28. Newcomb, "The Study of Consensus," *op. cit.*, p. 283.
29. Deutsch, "Communications Theory and Political Integration," *op. cit.*, pp. 66–70.
30. Alex Bavelas, "Communications Patterns in Task-Oriented Groups," in Cartwright and Zander, *op. cit.*, p. 671.
31. *Ibid.*, p. 672.
32. Milton J. Rosenberg and Robert F. Abelson, "An Analysis of Cognitive Balancing," in Carl I. Hovland and Milton J. Rosenberg (eds.), *Attitude Organization and Change* (New Haven: Yale U.P., 1960), p. 145.
33. Bernard Berelson, *Content Analysis in Communications Research* (New York: Free Press, 1952), p. 174.
34. Ole R. Holsti with Robert C. North and Joanne K. Loomba, "Content Analysis," in Gardner Lindsey and Elliot Aronson (eds.), *The Handbook of Social Psychology*, Vol. 2 (Reading: Addison, 1968), p. 601, and Philip J. Stone, Dexter C. Dunphy, Marshall S. Smith, and Daniel M. Ogilvie, *The General Inquirer: A Computer Approach to Content Analysis* (Cambridge: M.I.T. Press, 1966), p. 5.
35. Stone *et al.*, *ibid.*, *passim*.
36. See Charles Osgood, George J. Suci, and Percy H. Tannenbaum, *The Measurement of Meaning* (Urbana: U. of Illinois P., 1959), esp. Chaps. 1–3.
37. Ole R. Holsti, "An Adaptation of the 'General Inquirer' for the Systematic Analysis of Political Documents," *Behavioral Science*, IX (1964), 384–6.
38. *Ibid.*, p. 383.
39. Robert Jervis, "The Costs of the Scientific Study of Politics: An Examination of the Stanford Content Analysis Studies," *International Studies Quarterly*, IV (1967), 380.
40. For the statistical procedures used here see Sidney Siegal, *Nonparametric Statistics for the Behavioral Sciences* (New York: McGraw, 1956), pp. 116–27.
41. Zbigniew K. Brzezinski, *The Soviet Bloc: Unity and Conflict* (New York: Praeger, 1961), esp. Chap. 6.
42. *Ibid.*, esp. Chap. 8.
43. Richard Lowenthal, *World Communism: The Disintegration of a Secular Faith* (New York: Oxford U.P., 1964), p. 45.
44. *Ibid.*, p. 256.
45. Chinese Statement on the Test Ban Treaty, July 31, 1963, reprinted in William E. Griffith, *The Sino-Soviet Rift* (Cambridge: M.I.T. Press, 1964), p. 327.
46. Radio Budapest, February 8, 1965.
47. Ole R. Holsti, P. Terrence Hopmann, and John D. Sullivan, *International Alliances: Unity and Disintegration* (Homewood: Dorsey, forthcoming).

13

Soviet Relations with the Developing States: An Application of Correlation Analysis

DAN C. HELDMAN

There has been much discussion in recent years concerning the directions which should be taken by students of Soviet affairs and of the communist system, discussions which parallel those in many of the social sciences generally and political science specifically. The implication of the recent *Slavic Review* symposium, "Comparative Politics and

The assistance of Professor Alan M. Shinn (University of Texas, Austin) in certain questions of methodology and of Mr. Richard Shorter in matters of computer programming is gratefully acknowledged. Of those who offered suggestions on development and conclusions, those of Professor Roderick Bell (University of Texas, Austin) were particularly helpful. Final responsibility in these areas is, of course, mine.

Notes to this Selection begin on page 361.

Communist Systems," is that the field of Soviet studies lags as far behind political science in the application of theoretical and behavioral techniques as political science is supposed to lag behind the rest of the social sciences.[1] In this respect, Triska and Finley's groundbreaking study of Soviet foreign policy (which must be considered a major contribution toward ending the deficiency) begins by noting that the early unicausal questions have been replaced by more sophisticated multivariate ones, but that the latter are still largely divorced from appropriate empirical evidence; the authors of that work address themselves to the "how" and "why" of Soviet international behavior, based on relatively well-established answers to the historical "what" of such activity.[2]

Obviously (as the present collection of articles testifies) this effort must be encouraged, but it must not be forgotten that the purpose of all these techniques is to generate hypotheses about political phenomena and to reject those formulations which are not supported by the available empirical data within accepted limits of statistical significance. Finally, limited access to so-called "hard" (reliable) data concerning the Soviet Union, the great variety of assumptions required by certain techniques, and the concomitant crudeness of some measures used require the explicit understanding that what is attempted here is tentative and exploratory. With this in mind, we turn to a discussion of Soviet behavior toward the developing countries in an effort to understand that behavior with the use of correlation analysis and related techniques.

The background of Soviet relations with the "Third World" of developing countries in Africa, Asia, and Latin America has been fairly well presented. While it is by no means complete, nevertheless it is sufficient for a beginning.[3] From Stalin's "two camp" to Khrushchev's "three camp" view of the world, the developing countries have moved from being of only peripheral interest to being perhaps the single most important area of East-West contention. This shift in perspective became abundantly clear around the end of the 1950s and coincided roughly with the wave of African national independence movements which made the Soviet leadership painfully aware of their immediate incapacity to take advantage of events potentially embarrassing to the West. One result of this sharp increase in Soviet attention toward African affairs was a renewed interest in the problem of non-Soviet economic and political development—"renewed" because Marxism in its pre-1917 phase was basically a unicausal theory of development which, however, took a back seat to Lenin's activist politics following the Bolshevik assumption of power.

These two related events taken together—the emergence to national status of many former colonial areas and evidence of new Soviet interest in these areas—indicate that the period from the mid-fifties to the early sixties is a particularly propitious one in which to investigate Soviet international behavior.

Both Triska and Finley[4] and Dallin[5] assert that Soviet foreign policy incorporates distinctions between maximum and minimum goals, as do most other areas of policy-making. This continuum should not be confused with the distinction between strategy and tactics such as is employed by Beim in his study of Soviet foreign aid:[6] goals represent objectives to be pursued while strategies and tactics describe the pursuit. Goals may be maximum or minimum depending upon the priorities assigned to them by the decision-makers on a variety of political, ideological, or social bases. Priorities are thus the result of desires and perceptions about the probability of goal attainment. On the other hand, behavior is described as strategic or tactical depending upon whether its relevance to a goal (either maximum or minimum) is long range and indirect or immediate and direct.

For example, Dallin and Triska and Finley note that at one end of the goal continuum may be found incorporation and integration of the developing states into the Soviet political system (maximum) while, at the other end, encouragement of a "positive neutralist" stance by which influence in these areas is denied to the West (minimum). Beim, however, lists four precise ways in which foreign aid can lead to influence—promotion of goodwill, creation of a condition of dependency, establishment of military advantage, and cultivation of ideological allies—calling the first purely tactical, the next two either tactical or strategic, and the last purely strategic.[7] But influence for what purpose? Obviously, either of the two different goals described above as well as any intermediate ones may be pursued by any of the means Beim proposes. The point is that Soviet behavior with respect to the emerging nations during the late fifties and early sixties can be characterized by the priority given to more minimal goals, which does not, in and of itself, signify any overriding emphasis on purely tactical maneuvers.

To investigate such goal-directed behavior is the purpose of this essay; specifically, it attempts to construct input-output models of

Soviet-African (developing nation) interaction. Beim utilizes one such model following his conception of foreign aid as a three-player, non-zero-sum game (see Figure 1).[8] A variety of complexities can and should

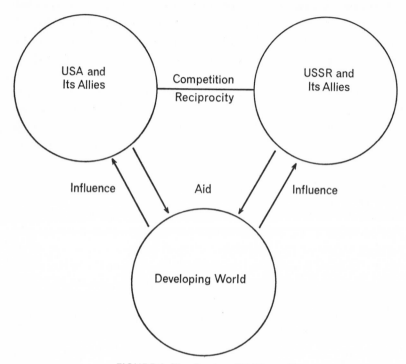

FIGURE 1. The Foreign Aid "Game."

be introduced into the above model, particularly in the U.S.S.R./ developing-world leg which is most relevant here. For example, what inputs to the Soviet decision-making mechanism are likely to produce aid? Is the granting of economic aid the only medium for obtaining influence? These are only a few questions raised by such a scheme and point to the occasional necessity of isolating some portion of a larger conception so as to inspect more closely the possibilities of interaction and the emergence of previously unsuspected variables. Foreign aid is, after all, only one sort of bilateral relationship among nations and it, like other sorts of international activity, has a domestic as well as a foreign component. To pursue these and related questions, we utilize data assembled for this article and described below.

Figure 2 represents a more complex input-output model in which

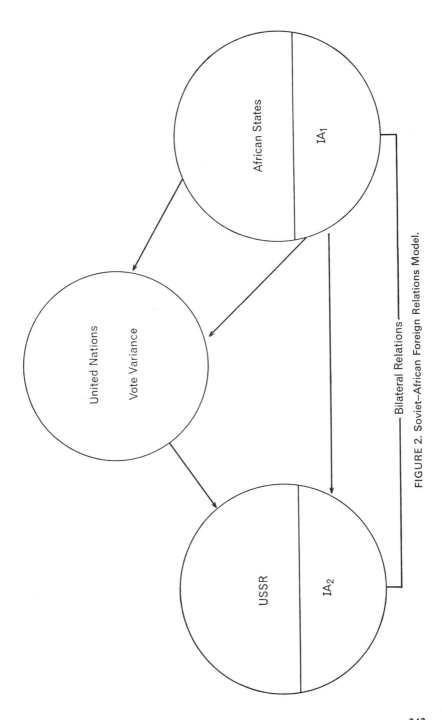

FIGURE 2. Soviet–African Foreign Relations Model.

343

Soviet influence is translated into favorable African votes in the United
Nations; Soviet aid is expanded into a dimensional measure of bilateral
relations; and this latter measure is associated in turn both to UN
voting and to Soviet perceptions (IA_2) of certain phenomena internal
to the African states (IA_1). As has been implied, we are concerned here
with African countries solely rather than with the gamut of developing
states. The twenty-five chosen[9] comprise both old and new, large and
small, former British and former French possessions, culturally diverse
and the culturally homogeneous. African countries generally suffer less
the analytic "disability" of being proximate to a rich and powerful
state (as does Latin America) or of sharing a common racial heritage
with such a state (as do the Asian countries with the Chinese People's
Republic). Finally, they constitute the area first to receive attention
from the Soviet Union in the late fifties. The nature of the other
variables, especially UN voting, required some further limitations on
which African states should be included. Inspection of UN records
revealed the not surprising fact that the roll of African states increased
gradually from three in 1946, to eight in 1957, to nine in 1960. At the
889th–895th plenary meetings, however, sixteen new African states
were admitted, raising the total to twenty-five, a number which remained fairly constant through the 1121st plenary meeting. Accordingly,
these twenty-five states constitute the sample.

A measure of UN vote variation[10] was constructed for the set of
countries by comparing the formal vote of each with the vote
of the Soviet Union on a series of related issues drawing from data
collected by Hovet.[11] There are basically five formal voting positions
which a country may adopt in the UN—yes, no, abstain, present but
not voting, absent—labeled respectively Y, N, A, NV, and O. Each of
these positions relative to any other has some measure of meaning in
the context of a particular issue and set of countries. This is to say,
when one country votes yes, a vote of no by another represents a stance
farther removed than if that second country had voted abstain: rever-
sion of the yes and no votes, of course, would yield the same conclusion
which points to the advantage of measuring the differences between
votes rather than the votes themselves.

It is posited, therefore, that UN vote categories can be ranged along
a scale which has *yes* and *no* at opposite ends with the three other
categories together occupying a median position as shown in Figure 3.
It should be added that there may indeed be either important and poli-

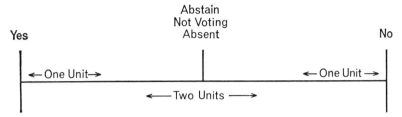

FIGURE 3. United Nations Vote Categories.

tical or accidental and trivial differences among these three median
vote types. On the one hand, an African representative may just happen
not to be present at a particular time (thus registering *O*), though this
becomes less likely for important issues. On the other hand, "not
voting" seems to imply less inclination to participate in the proceedings
than does "abstain." Nevertheless, we assume that such differences are
slight compared with the differences among the three main segments of
Figure 3:[12] we have assigned an arithmetic variation equal to one unit
between the median position and both extremes resulting in a variation
of two units between yes and no. The amount of variation between the
votes of any two countries can thereby be calculated for any one issue
and the individual variations summed over a series of issues. The end
products of this operation are shown in Table 1: the summation (VV_1)
is over ninety-five issues beginning with a procedural question on the
Congo crisis (November 9, 1960) and ending with a resolution on
Southern Rhodesia (June 28, 1962).[13]

It should be added, in further description of this measure, that only
plenary roll call votes were included, while votes on "separable paragraphs" were excluded, and that the implications of any vote analysis
are limited by two considerations of unknown significance. First, UN
diplomatic representatives are occasionally given open instructions so
that some votes may not directly reflect their government's explicit
policy; and, second, a vote may be cast in a particular context (e.g.,
trade-off) which would have been different in the absence of that
context. It would seem, however, that both of these considerations are
reduced in significance by choosing issues which are relevant and
important to the countries involved: again, as before, we are led to
concentrate therefore on African questions. The contention that UN
voting may not adequately indicate a pro-Soviet stance was tested by
calculating another measure of vote variation over the same issues, but

TABLE 1

VOTE VARIATION TABULATIONS (MULTILATERAL VARIABLE)

African States	VV_1 Variation from U.S.S.R.	VV_2 Variation from U.S.
Cameroon	84	64
Central African Republic	71	71
Chad	68	68
Congo (Brazzaville)	70	66
Congo (Leopoldville)	72	70
Dahomey	78	64
Ethiopia	35	93
Gabon	72	68
Ghana	21	103
Guinea	14	118
Ivory Coast	81	57
Liberia	52	76
Libya	39	97
Madagascar	73	65
Mali	21	113
Morocco	21	113
Niger	73	62
Nigeria	45	78
Senegal	70	62
Somalia	46	82
Sudan	34	98
Togo	47	87
Tunisia	48	80
United Arab Republic (Egypt)	22	114
Upper Volta	72	79

$$\bar{X} = 53.16 \qquad \bar{X} = 81.92$$

this time from the positions of the United States (VV_2, Table 1). The correlation between these two, as shown in Table 4, was extremely high and negative. The necessary implication is that African votes on these issues are as close to the Soviet Union as they are far from the United States. (The one objection that cannot be answered is that it might be the United States which is "anti-African" and not Africa which is "pro-Soviet.")

The next major variable used in this model is a dimensional measure of bilateral association, essentially a sum of the types of bilateral relations an African country has with the Soviet Union. The various types can be grouped under such headings (dimensions) as trade, diplomatic, economic, cultural, and military. There are, moreover, two additional types limited to the Soviet Union—agreements for permission to place a Tass newsgathering and dissemination agency and for sponsorship of a Soviet Friendship Society in the object country. The best and most effective use of these dimensions to measure bilateral association is, of course, to inquire into the content of each, to quantify trade in terms of percent of GNP or even in terms of dollar values exchanged, economy in terms of grants and loans extended, or military in terms of the value of military hardware sent by the Soviet Union. It must be equally obvious, however, that no effort at quantification could sufficiently describe the "value" of cultural exchanges or agreements on Tass agencies or Friendship Societies. Furthermore, even where the data are available, can such quantification distinguish between an aid agreement which calls for repayment of a $42 million credit over twelve years (Ghana, 1960), and one which charges $2\frac{1}{2}\%$ interest on $35 million (Guinea, 1959), or a straight $2.8 million gift (U.A.R., 1956)?[14] Can any scale of values differentiate between grants for specific projects and those with purposes unspecified or between those which call for repayment in cash and those to be repaid in goods? At the present time, at least, the answer must be that they cannot be so quantified and that we must consider them as dimensions of bilateral association only.

But even with this very real limitation it is possible to do more than simply note the kinds of agreements concluded between the Soviet Union and the African countries in our sample. Common sense suggests that at least some of these dimensions—perhaps all—are related to others such that, taken together, they all measure one thing, e.g., association. It is, for example, highly likely that cultural agreements would not be concluded with a country with which one does not have some sort of diplomatic arrangement nor grant military assistance to a country likely to use it in ways inimical to one's interests. It was with these assumptions that a Guttman scaling technique was employed. Used extensively in analyzing responses to attitude surveys, a perfect Guttman scale strongly supports the assumption of an ordinal (i.e., rank-order) scale on the part of items which evidence cumulative properties. Variables are ranked according to increasing quantities of whatever it is that all of the variables are supposed to possess in common, in this case "bilateral association." Consider, for example, the simple case of a series of four questions, each of which has only two possible responses—yes or no:

1. Are you less than four feet tall?
2. Are you less than five feet tall?
3. Are you less than six feet tall?
4. Are you less than seven feet tall?

Presumably, all but a very few would answer no to the first question, fewer to the second, still fewer to the third, and almost none to the fourth. Further, once having answered yes to any of the questions, the respondent would be obliged to answer similarly all of those following. In this case the questions are already ranked and on a very obvious basis (the property of "height" is known to be "rankable"). It is not always this easy nor are perfect scales ever obtained in practice. The results of this technique applied to our dimensions of bilateral relations are shown in Table 2. Associated with the Guttman scale are two

TABLE 2

SCALOGRAM ANALYSIS OF BILATERAL ASSOCIATION VARIABLE

	T	D	E	C	Ta	Fs	M	Sum
Central African Republic								0
Chad								0
Congo (Brazzaville)								0
Gabon								0
Liberia								0
Ivory Coast	x							1
Madagascar						x		1
Upper Volta						x		1
Cameroon	x		x	x				3
Congo (Leopoldville)	x	x				x		3
Libya	x	x			x			3
Morocco	x	x					x	3
Niger	x	—	x					3
Nigeria	x	x		x				3
Dahomey	x	—	x	x				3
Senegal	x	x	x	x				4
Ethiopia	x	x	x	x	x			5
Somalia	x	x	x	x	x			5
Togo	x	x	x	—	x	x		5
Tunisia	x	x	x	—	x	x		5
Sudan	x	x	x	x	x	x		6
Ghana	x	x	x	x	x	x	x	7
Guinea	x	x	x	x	x	x	x	7
Mali	x	x	x	x	x	x	x	7
U.A.R. (Egypt)	x	x	x	x	x	x	x	7

T: Trade D: Diplomatic E: Economic C: Cultural Ta: Tass Fs: Friendship Society M: Military

Number of responses: 175 Number of "error" terms: 13 CR = .92571 MMR = .61714

Computer program BMD05S (BIOMED), 1965 version, UCLA.

coordinate tests of significance (or "fit"), the coefficient of reproducibility (CR) and the minimal marginal reproducibility (MMR).[15] While there are no rigorous parameters for either of these tests, a CR greater than .9 and a CR-MMR greater than .2 is generally considered to describe a sufficiently significant Guttman scale.[16] As shown by the CR of .92571 and CR-MMR of .30857, these conditions have been met and attention is called to the BMD05S program readout in which the dimensions are scaled in a manner which produces the minimum number of error terms. The resulting scalogram clearly indicates that African states which have, say, military agreements with the Soviet Union are quite likely to have agreements in all other bilateral dimensions: the implication is that the concluding of such an agreement represents the culmination of an increasingly "close" relationship. Alternatively, it is possible to theorize that what is being described here is the political nature of the dimensions which increase as we move from trade (T) to military (M). Significantly, the scalogram is in accord with our commonsense notions about international behavior: trade and diplomatic agreements are widespread and involve considerations which are more generalized and less political than those types at the other end. We have no reason for supposing on the basis of this technique that the intervals between types are anything other than equal: in other words there is no evidence for or against assuming that the amount of change in either bilateral association or political nature between T and D is different from the amount of change between Fs and M.

The third and fourth major variables used here are two independently determined but related estimates of the level of activity of communist- or socialist-oriented groups within the African countries. Students of international relations have found it useful to dichotomize influences on national foreign policies (e.g., voting in international organizations or initiation of various bilateral relations) into foreign (external) and domestic (internal) categories.[17] They point to the existence of groups of various sorts within polities which seek to alter, influence, change, or otherwise to ensure a foreign policy compatible with the interests they articulate. Implicit therein is a crude though workable concept of power: domestic groups have power (capacity to ensure favorable policy decisions) to the extent that they are able, by acting in certain ways and/or by having certain resources at their disposal, to have these questions decided with results at least partly consonant with their interests. Furthermore, a domestic group will have the requisite resources for influencing government policy if it is articulate, if it actively participates in government, and if it controls some important segment of the social system (see Figure 4).

Students, labor, intellectuals, technicians, local government, and others may all at one time or another be needed by policy-makers to lend support to their policies. If these segments are, indeed, recognized and coordinated groups (e.g., labor unions), then they gain in influence,

350

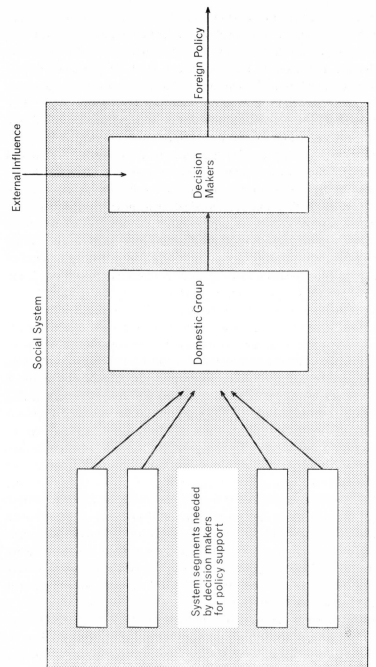

FIGURE 4. Foreign Policy and the Power of Domestic Groups.

and it follows that the more segments of society which are bound together in a group, the more influential that group will be. It also follows that if we are to look at foreign policy outputs such as the two variables described previously, then we would do well to take into account the domestic facet. To do so, it is necessary to construct an ordinal scale measuring increasing amounts of control a domestic group has over segments of the social system when that group's demands are related to the specific policy outputs in which we are interested. Since we are concerned with such outputs related to the Soviet Union, it is natural that we should turn to communist- or socialist-oriented groups.

Again, as before, we are forced by circumstances to choose second-best indicators. As Taborsky points out,[18] Communist Parties are few and small in Africa and, more importantly, all but one (in Lesotho) are illegal or suppressed and hence their size and activities are circumscribed severely. But there are a number of more visible and active "worker's national-democratic and left-wing socialist parties" whose orientation toward the Soviet Union parallels that of the underground Communist Party, especially in questions of foreign policy between East and West. Constructing the ordinal scale is thus a two-step procedure: first, identify a group's orientation; second, determine its control over relevant segments of the social system. It is known, for example, that the Union des Populations du Cameroun, a radical offshoot of the defunct leftist Rassemblement Démocratique Africain (RDA), adhered formally to the 1961 Moscow Declaration of 81 Communist Parties and that it was allied with the Confédération Générale Camerounaise du Travail, a trade union affiliated with the Soviet-led World Federation of Trade Unions; or that the Democratic Party of Guinea and the Union Soudanaise of Mali, both also debris from the RDA fragmentation, sent representatives to congresses of the CPSU and the French CP, and are considered "comradely" and "fraternal." Other criteria used were the public pronouncements of leaders and other party elites or their contributions to Soviet political and academic journals.[19] No attempt was made to compare relative orientation (e.g., to determine that the PAI of Chad is less communist-oriented than, say, the PAI of Senegal).

Having fixed the orientation of various African domestic groups, a necessarily subjective determination was made of each group's position within the social system according to the following ordered scale:

0. No clearly recognizable communist- or socialist-oriented groups exist.
1. Such groups exist, are articulate (publicly visible), but are inactive.
2. Such groups exist, engage in public activities (strikes, demonstrations), and control some segment of the social system.
3. The group (political party) represents a major portion of, if not the, ruling elite.

The results of this determination are shown in Table 3 and reflect generally historical data collected on such trade unions as the CGKT of Cameroon, Lagos Nigerian Trade Union Congress,[20] Union Générale des Travailleurs de l'Afrique Noire of Guinea, the All-

TABLE 3

ACTIVITY LEVEL OF COMMUNIST-ORIENTED DOMESTIC GROUPS*

African Country	IA_1 Level	Soviet Perception of IA_1 (IA_2)
Cameroon	2	3
Central African Republic	0	1
Chad	1	2
Congo (Brazzaville)	0	1
Congo (Leopoldville)	2	2
Dahomey	2	4
Ethiopia	1	3
Gabon	2	3
Ghana	3	5
Guinea	3	5
Ivory Coast	1	1
Liberia	0	3
Libya	1	3
Madagascar	2	4
Mali	3	5
Morocco	2	4
Niger	1	2
Nigeria	2	2
Senegal	2	2
Somalia	2	3
Sudan	2	3
Togo	1	2
Tunisia	2	4
U.A.R. (Egypt)	2	4
Upper Volta	1	1

* IA_1: Internal activity level of communist-oriented groups based on Figure 4.
IA_2: Internal activity level of communist-oriented groups based on Soviet sources.

African Trade Union Federation; student-intellectual groups such as the Jeunesse du Rassemblement Démocratique Africain of Guinea, the Nigerian Youth Congress, Mouvement Gabonaise d'Action Populaire of Gabon, and "the Nucleus" of Ghana; and numerous others.[21] It is recognized that the above methods for determining the level of internal

activity are highly judgmental, but, for reasons already discussed, more appropriate measures are either unavailable or unreliable.

As a check, however, on their accuracy and also to test for possible distortions in Soviet perceptions of this internal activity (which we are theorizing is part of the Soviet policy input), a second and independently arrived-at measure of the same phenomenon (IA_2) was drawn from Soviet literature on the developing countries. Specifically, a five-point ordinal scale ranging from "progressive" to "reactionary" (in Soviet terminology) was constructed paralleling one mentioned by Dallin as having been used by Soviet commentators in 1960–62.[22] Placement on this scale was accomplished according to Soviet descriptions as found in various scholarly works and journals[23] and as made implicit in the "greetings" sent to countries, peoples, and parties around the world by *Pravda* on special occasions such as May Day each year. This placement is also shown in Table 3 and, as can be seen in Table 4,

TABLE 4

INTERCORRELATION MATRIX

	IA_1 (1)	IA_2 (2)	VV_1 (3)	VV_2	BA (4)
IA_1 (1)	1.0000	.7508	−.4594*	.4668*	.7007
IA_2 (2)		1.0000	−.6604	.6517	.6524
VV_1 (3)			1.0000	−.9589	−.7486
VV_2				1.0000	.7228
BA (4)					1.0000

the correlation obtained between the two separate measures is significant at the .001 level. The conclusion seems inescapable that Soviet perceptions of the nature of these twenty-five African countries are positively related to the level of activity of communist-oriented internal groups. To reiterate, therefore, although IA_1 and IA_2 are highly correlated (56 percent of the variation in one can be explained by variation in the other), it is the former which is a domestic input for African policy-making and the latter which is a foreign (external) input for Soviet policy-making.

We have hypothesized that these three variables—voting in the UN, dimensions of bilateral relations, and internal activity of communist-oriented groups (or perceptions thereof)—should all be connected such that low vote variation is associated with high internal activity and close bilateral relations. The intercorrelations among the variables are shown in Table 4. Because Pearsonian correlations (r) are symmetrical, the matrix is also symmetrical about the diagonal and, therefore, any more than half a matrix would be redundant (a correlation of a variable against itself is 1.0000). The statistical significance of each correlation was checked and it was found that all but two (marked by an asterisk in Table 4) were significant at the .001 level or higher; those with asterisks were, however, still significant at acceptable levels (.05).[24] In addition, tests for nonlinearity were computed, the result of each being negative.[25]

All too frequently, the investigator who has constructed his variables and obtained his correlations goes no further than this. To be sure, much has already been said, sufficient for some purposes perhaps, but more can be done if one is prepared to explore the fringes of his methodology and to recognize that what he is doing is not yet settled and sure. There is no doubt that correlation and regression coefficients are useful. From them can be determined the direction of a relationship (the slope of the least squares line, b, positive or negative), the amount of the relationship (r^2), and even predictive statements about the dependent variable according to the linear regression equation ($Y = a + bX$). But does this *explain* the relationship or aid our understanding of the mechanism and/or processes which connect any two variables? In other words, do we have causal knowledge?

As Bunge has pointed out, "the causal principle fell into disrepute during the first half of our century" under the impact of a growing predilection for empiricism and the tremendous growth in statistics as an operational, experimental tool.[26] Blalock argues in a most persuasive way that there are actually two languages, one for theory and one for operating empirically, and that there appears to be no logical way to bridge the gap. Nevertheless, Blalock continues, causal thinking, which is solely on the theoretical level, need not therefore be abandoned and causal laws can be developed which have implications at least indirectly testable.[27] To do this, it is necessary to make several simplifying assumptions which are themselves untestable. Even so, the best that can be hoped for is to reject some of the alternative models on the basis of the empirical evidence without being able to demonstrate the ultimate and unqualified correctness of any of the remaining ones. The social scientist, who must face these limitations perhaps more resolutely than the nonsocial scientist, should not become discouraged by this. All methodologies, regardless of their nature, require the making of assumptions—it is only that statistics requires they be made more explicit than usual, which tends to make us more aware of uncomfortable limitations. Further, the rejection of alternative explanations is the stuff of which all attempts to understand are made.

Some of the more basic simplifying assumptions include system isolation, linearity, additive properties, and the randomness of measurement error. By system isolation, we mean that a set of variables has been postulated and that all other variables are either trivial to the relationships being described or that their effect on the system is felt equally by all components (error terms are uncorrelated). Models are always in some sense an abstraction from and hence a distortion of reality. Thus, some phenomena are included in the explanation, while others are excluded on the assumption that further inclusion would not substantially add to our understanding. It remains possible to object to this, but to leave the model open is to allow the introduction of new properties or variables such that no causal law could ever be negated.[28] The point is that we can never prove that a system is isolated, but must *assume* it is if we are to make causal inferences. The assumption that the model follows an additive and linear pattern is for convenience only. Nonadditive (e.g., multiplicative) and curvilinear relationships certainly exist, but they involve complexities beyond the scope of this paper. We also assume that measurement errors (which are always presumed to exist to some extent or another) are random and constant such that their effect is taken into account by the regression equation constant (a). The point is important enough to repeat that all of the above assumptions are not testable—they may or may not be true— and they form the weakest point in making specific causal inferences. Finally, making such inferences is not the same thing as predicting. Mathematically, the regression equation is symmetrical, i.e., it makes little difference which variable is considered dependent and which independent; the formula $Y = a + bX$ could just as easily be written $X = Y/b - a/b$. Given a positive correlation, say, between amount of rainfall and crop yields, either variable could be predicted from the other for past years. We know, however, that the causal relationship is asymmetrical, that crop yields do not produce rainfall. The distinction is that correlation and regression coefficients describe the scope and amount of association but not its nature; it is the latter which undergirds the notion of causality.

We have used the terms "correlation" and "regression" coefficient.

Without going into an involved discussion of each one, its properties and implications, we follow Blalock in asserting that it is the regression coefficients "which give us the laws of science" and it is to these that we ought to turn in making causal inferences. In testing causal models, however, we are justified in using the correlation coefficient when we expect the relationship between two variables to disappear.[29] Since it will be necessary for our purposes to use the regression coefficients to test nondisappearing relationships, they are given in Table 5.[30]

TABLE 5

REGRESSION COEFFICIENTS*

	IA_1 (X_1)	IA_2 (X_2)	VV_1 (X_3)	BA (X_4)
IA_1 (X_1)		1.1000	−11.8556	1.9889
IA_2 (X_2)	.5124		−11.6335	1.2640
VV_1 (X_3)	−.0178	.0375		−.0823
BA (X_4)	.2468	.3367	−6.8058	

* By conventional notation, b_{13} is read as the regression of variable 1 (IA_1) on variable 3 (VV_1).

In Figure 5 we have listed nearly all of the possible causal models which can exist given our three variables as an isolated system. The set of models for Soviet input-output is exactly the same as for African input-output except that we have replaced IA_1 with IA_2. By "causal model" we mean a graphic representation of cause utilizing arrows to indicate direction, i.e., "$A \rightarrow B$" should be read as "A causes B" or "change in A produces change in B." For theoretical reasons we reject models 1 and a, and any similar model showing X_1 or X_2 as a dependent variable. They are undoubtedly dependent on something ($IA_1 \rightarrow IA_2$, for example), but that dependence is on variables outside the postulated system. We can find no convincing reason for supposing that the internal activity level of communist oriented groups depends upon either bilateral relations or votes in the UN. Furthermore, we reject models 2 and b and any similar model showing reciprocal (mutual) causation for reasons which are both convenient and necessary—convenient because the equations for such causal situations are quite complex and beyond the scope of this paper, necessary because reciprocal causation generally implies a time sequence with feedback (change in X produces change in Y which then produces a new change in X) and the data used in this study were not collected with respect to time sequences.

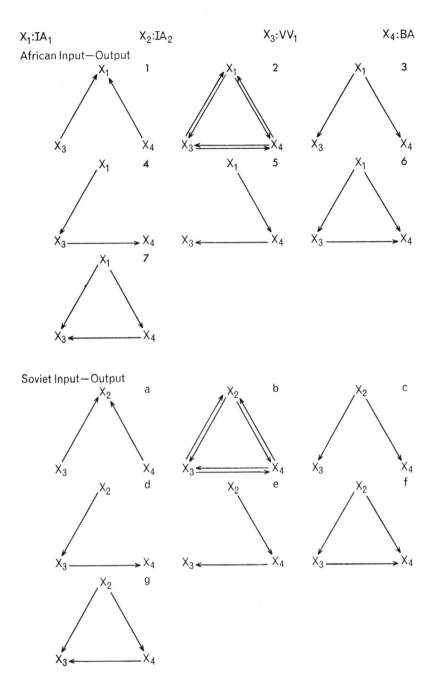

FIGURE 5. Three-Variable Causal Models.

357

Models 3, 4, 5, c, d, and e can be tested using the correlation coefficients since each implies that an experimentally obtained correlation will disappear (within the limits of measurement error) if the effect of the appropriate variable is controlled. In other words, to take model 5 as an example, what is being said is that the correlation between variables 1 and 3 ($r_{13} = -.4594$) is spurious, that X_1 is only an *indirect* (intervening) cause of X_3 through X_4. If, therefore, the effect of X_4 should be controlled by means of a partial correlation coefficient ($r_{13.4}$), then that partial should equal or nearly equal zero. This becomes the predicting equation for model 5 and, if it is met, then the model cannot be rejected; similarly (with appropriate notational changes) for models 3, 4, c, d, and e. The predicting equations for each are shown in Table 6

TABLE 6

PREDICTING EQUATIONS FOR DISAPPEARING CORRELATIONS

Model	Predictions	Actual r_{xy}	Expected $r_{xz}r_{yz}$	Difference $r_{xy}-r_{xz}r_{yz}$
3	$r_{34.1} = 0$ or $r_{34} = r_{31}r_{41}$	$-.7486$	$-.3219$	$-.4276$
4	$r_{14.3} = 0$ or $r_{14} = r_{13}r_{43}$	$.7007$	$.3439$	$.3568$
5	$r_{13.4} = 0$ or $r_{13} = r_{14}r_{34}$	$-.4595$	$-.5245$	$.0651$
c	$r_{34.2} = 0$ or $r_{34} = r_{32}r_{42}$	$-.7486$	$-.4308$	$-.3178$
d	$r_{24.3} = 0$ or $r_{24} = r_{23}r_{43}$	$.6524$	$.4944$	$.1580$
e	$r_{23.4} = 0$ or $r_{23} = r_{24}r_{34}$	$-.6604$	$-.4884$	$-.1720$

along with the computed results. Note that, in general form, $r_{xy.y} = 0$ as a predictor is the same as $r_{xy} = r_{xz}r_{yz}$, a fact which can be readily deduced from the standard operational formula for a three-variable partial correlation. As with the significance tests associated with the Guttman scale, we have no rigid standard by which to reject models for the failure of their intercorrelations to behave as predicted. By inspection, though, models 3, 4, and c produce differences between actual and expected values of r which are nearly significant in themselves. For these models, therefore, we conclude that controlling for the appropriate variable does not produce the anticipated results and that they should be rejected. Models d and e produced differences which conceivably might be but probably are not within the limits of measurement error and are thus also rejected, but with somewhat less assurance. The difference of .0651 for model 5 is quite small relative to the others; we conclude that, but for measurement errors, the model 5 partial correlation has been reduced to zero and it is not rejected.

The remaining models not indicated in Table 6 are 6, 7, *f*, and *g*, all of which carry different implications than the preceding models. In these four models we predict that no correlations should disappear controlling for any one of the three variables. In these cases, then, the behavior of correlation coefficients is not adequate for testing purposes, and we must turn to the regression coefficients or slopes of each relationship. With respect to these, what we are saying is similar to the previous situation except that now we predict that the slope of the direct causal link should be reduced (not eliminated) if we control for the intervening variable. In other words, taking model 7 as an example, X_3 is caused by X_1 both directly and indirectly, and any correlation obtained experimentally between the two is partly the result of this direct relationship and partly spurious, i.e., the result of indirect cause through X_4. If this is so, then controlling for X_4 ($b_{13.4}$) should produce a slope which is more horizontal (disregarding negative or positive direction) than before. The predicting equations drawn from this line of reasoning are shown in Table 7. Since we are concerned not with

TABLE 7

PREDICTING EQUATIONS FOR NONDISAPPEARING SLOPES*

Model	Predictions	Actual b_{xy}	Expected $b_{xy \cdot z}$
6	$b_{14 \cdot 3} < b_{14}$	1.9889	2.3033
7	$b_{13 \cdot 4} < b_{13}$	−11.8556	3.8202
f	$b_{24 \cdot 3} < b_{24}$	1.2640	.6970
g	$b_{23 \cdot 4} < b_{23}$	−11.6335	−6.8902

* Positive and negative are here taken as slope directions and not as arithmetic signs. A slope of 2.5 is thus more horizontal than a slope of −5.0.

differences but with inequalities, the "Difference" column has been dropped. As before, by inspection, we see that the inequality prediction is upheld in models 7, *f*, and *g*.

With what are we left? Models 5 and 7 of African input-output and models *f* and *g* of Soviet input-output could not be rejected for either theoretical or statistical reasons. As for the first, both African models could be argued persuasively. Communist-oriented groups have more power with respect to decisions to conclude bilateral agreements with the Soviet Union than they have with respect to decisions on the UN voting policies of their country. This seems supported by the association

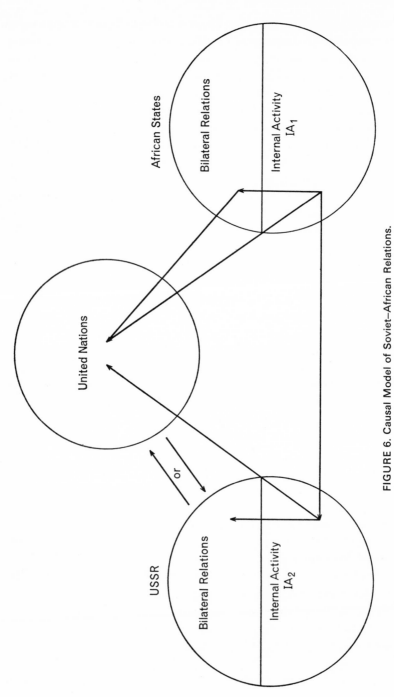

FIGURE 6. Causal Model of Soviet–African Relations.

360

between IA_1 and IA_2 in which IA_2 is a factor in Soviet decisions also to conclude such agreements. Finally, African decisions on UN voting have both an external and an internal dimension. The conclusion is that model 5 probably describes the power of communist-oriented groups, while model 7 describes the sources of influence on African decision-makers with respect to their UN voting policies. As for Soviet input-output, the picture is not so readily interpretable. Neither models f nor g could be rejected, and the major difference between them is the direction of the causal link between $X_3(VV_1)$ and $X_4(BA)$. Soviet perceptions of the progressive-reactionary nature of African countries are a direct cause of both Soviet voting policy and the closeness of bilateral associations. The question is whether either (and if so, which) of the links is also partially indirect. We conclude that the difference is too fine for us to distinguish here. We note also in this respect that, according to Table 4, IA_2 "explains" (r^2) as much of VV_1 as it does of BA.

We are now in a position to close the study by reinspecting Figure 2, the general input-output model, and by making appropriate emendations according to the above findings (see Figure 6). The result is a model which only superficially resembles Figure 2. In effect, we have combined the unrejected causal models with the earlier postulated connection between our measure of "internal activity" and our Dallin's measure of Soviet perceptions (IA_2). Thus, a set of causal relationships is shown among three variables and between two political entities—one, the Soviet Union and the other, a group of twenty-five African states.

Consonant with our conclusion regarding the interchangeability of models f and g, we have included both causal links not rejected between UN voting behavior and Soviet decisions on bilateral relations. We must also reassert that doing so does not imply reciprocal causation. Ability to reject more than one causal model should not be the basis for concluding that the "real" situation is somehow a combination of all unrejected models. We merely note that one or the other link exists but that empirical testing has not been able to distinguish between them.

Notes

1. See John A. Armstrong, "Introductory Remarks," *Slavic Review*, XXVI (1967),

1–2; Robert S. Sharlet, "Systematic Political Science and Communist Systems," *ibid.*, 22–6.

2. Jan F. Triska and David O. Finley, *Soviet Foreign Policy* (New York: Macmillan, 1968), pp. xiii, xvi.

3. See particularly Zbigniew Brzezinski (ed.), *Africa and the Communist World* (Stanford: Stanford U.P., 1963). Though dated, its documentation is extensive. Such relations are also perceptively analyzed in Kurt London (ed.), *New Nations in a Divided World* (New York: Praeger, 1964).

4. Triska and Finley, *op. cit.*, pp. 254–6.

5. Alexander Dallin, "Soviet Union: Political Activity," in Brzezinski, *op. cit.*, pp. 12–13.

6. David Beim, "The Communist Bloc and the Foreign Aid Game," *Western Political Quarterly*, XVII (1964), 784–99.

7. Dallin, *op. cit.*; Triska and Finley, *op. cit.*, pp. 254–5; Beim, *op. cit.*, pp. 785–8.

8. *Ibid.*, p. 786.

9. See Table 1.

10. "Variation" is a term adopted for convenience only. It should not be confused with the statistical concept of variance.

11. Thomas Hovet, Jr., *Africa in the United Nations* (Evanston: Northwestern U.P., 1963), pp. 232–326.

12. The likelihood of a "not present" vote is reduced by the choice of issues, i.e., those which, at least on the surface, should be seen as important by the African members, namely, African questions. See esp. Appendix C in Hovet, *ibid.*, pp. 262–326.

13. *Ibid.*, pp. 314–26. In Hovet's numerical listing, issues 629, 632–7, 646–56, 660–91, 696–701, 707–10, 713, 716–18, 720, 724–5, 735–9, 747–9, 757, 762–4, 769–73, 779–89.

14. Maurice David Simon, "Communist System Interaction with the Developing States, 1954–1962: A Preliminary Analysis," Research Paper No. 10 of the *Stanford Studies of the Communist System* (Jan. 1966), Appendix Table 4.

15. The coefficient of reproducibility measures the actual error terms (shown in Table 2 as underlined x's and blank spaces) by which the experiment scale differs from a perfect scale, while the minimal marginal reproducibility measures the number of errors which would exist if the variables are unrelated in a cumulative pattern, i.e., by chance. See Louis Guttman, "Relation of Scalogram Analysis to Other Techniques," in Samuel A. Stouffer *et al.*, *Measurement and Prediction* (Princeton: Princeton U.P., 1950), pp. 172–212; and Matilda White Riley, *Sociological Research: A Case Approach*, Vol. 1 (New York: Harcourt, 1963), pp. 469–99.

16. Guttman, *op. cit.*

17. For example, James N. Rosenau, "Pre-theories and Theories of Foreign Policy," in R. Barry Farrell (ed.), *Approaches to Comparative and International Politics* (Evanston: Northwestern U.P., 1966), pp. 27–92; and Rosenau, *National Leadership and Foreign Policy; A Case Study in the Mobilization of Public Support* (Princeton: Princeton U.P., 1963).

18. Edward Taborsky, "The Communist Parties of the 'Third World' in Soviet Strategy," *Orbis*, XI (1967), 128–48.

19. Explanations and justifications, as in Leopold Sedar Senghor, *On African Socialism*, translated by Mercer Cook (New York: Praeger, 1964), are not uncommon.

20. This should not be confused with the Trade Union Congress of Nigeria, which was affiliated with the Western-oriented International Confederation of Trade Unions (ICFTU).

21. All of these groups and activities are based on observations for the years 1959–62, inclusive; much has changed since then, but that is another study.

22. Unfortunately, Dallin neglected to mention his source for this scale. His description of its categories was taken as valid and meaningful, however, and its

content was broadened to include all of the countries used here. Dallin, *op. cit.*, p. 14.

23. Examples, Akademiia nauk SSR, Institut Afriki, *Afrika*, (Moscow, 1961); V. P. Nikhamin, *Mezhdunarodnye problemy sovremennoi Afriki* (Moscow, 1960); *Narody Azii i Afriki* (Moscow, 1960–63); I. I. Potekhin, *Afrika smotrit v budushchee* (Moscow, 1960); *Aziia i Afrika segodnia* (Moscow, 1961–63); and *World Marxist Review* (Moscow, 1960–63).

24. Degrees of freedom were 1 and 23. A standard "Distribution of F" table was used from H. M. Blalock, *Social Statistics* (New York: McGraw, 1960), pp. 453–5.

25. *Ibid.*, pp. 311–17.

26. Mario Bunge, "Causality, Chance, and Law," *American Scientist*, XLIX (1961), p. 432.

27. Hubert M. Blalock, *Causal Inference in Nonexperimental Research* (Chapel Hill: U. of North Carolina P., 1961), p. 6.

28. *Ibid.*, pp. 11–14.

29. *Ibid.*, p. 51. $b_{xy} = \Sigma xy/\Sigma y^2$; $r_{xy} = \Sigma xy/(\Sigma x^2)(\Sigma y^2)$, so $r_{xy} = 0$ if $b_{xy} = 0$.

30. Regression coefficients (b) are not symmetrical, i.e., $b_{12} \neq b_{21}$ so, unlike the correlation matrix, the regression matrix is not symmetrical about its diagonal. The relationship between regression and correlations coefficients is given by $b_{xy}b_{yx} = r^2$. See the note to Table 5.

Index